Ideology, Faith, and Family Planning in Latin America

A POPULATION COUNCIL BOOK

Ideology, Faith, and Family Planning in Latin America

Studies in Public and Private Opinion on Fertility Control

by J. Mayone Stycos

WITH THE ASSISTANCE OF: *S. Betsy Cohen, Edgar H. Elam, Evelyn L. Hand, Robert B. Hartford, Elizabeth L. Johnson, Barent F. Landstreet, Jr., Axel I. Mundigo, Alan B. Simmons, and Sergio S. Sismondo*

McGRAW-HILL BOOK COMPANY
New York   St. Louis   San Francisco   Düsseldorf   London   Sydney
Toronto   Mexico   Panama   Kuala Lumpur   Montreal   New Delhi
Rio de Janeiro   Singapore

This book was set in Times Roman by York Graphic Services.
It was printed on permanent paper and bound by The Maple
Press Company. The designer was Christine Aulicino. The
figures were drawn by Robert Aulicino. The editors were
Herbert Waentig, Nancy Tressel, and Judy Duguid. Frank
Matonti and Alice Cohen supervised the production.

Library of Congress Catalog Card Number: 79-161848

123456789   MAMM   7987654321

07-062297-3

To my students

*We were aware of the population danger, but . . .
we took refuge in working harder to further our
development and our political aims. Why were
we so blind?*

Lord Caradon, 1967

*How many times did we tremble in fear of
offering an easy concession to public opinion, or
one badly received by today's society.*

Paul VI, 1968

Really, this is something you cannot plan.

Fidel Castro, 1968

Preface

This is a book written with the assistance of, and to a large extent by, my students. It is an outgrowth of two summer projects in Colombia, in which I accompanied a small group of students from the International Population Program. We designed and carried out a variety of research projects dealing with population problems, some of which are reported in this volume. While most of the papers have been heavily edited, they are essentially original contributions of the students, in terms of field work, analysis, and report writing. Two of the contributions were written by undergraduates.

Some of the information presented here has been published previously. Chapter 1 appeared in R. N. Farmer, J. D. Long, and G. J. Stolnitz (eds.), *World Population—The View Ahead* (Bloomington: Bureau of Business Records, Indiana University, 1968) and Chapter 2 appeared in F. T. Brayer (ed.), *World Population and U.S. Government Policy and Programs* (Washington: Georgetown University Press, 1968); part of the Introduction to Part 2 and part of the Introduction to Part 3 appeared in *Studies in Family Planning,* March 1970, no. 51 (Population Council), and are included in a longer paper prepared for a National Academy of Science study on population, sponsored by the U.S. Agency for International Development; Chapter 4 appeared as "Opposition to Family Planning in Latin America: Conservative Nationalism," *Demography,* vol. 5, no. 2, 1968.

Both the University of Los Andes Economic Development Center (CEDE) and the Colombian Association of Medical Schools (ASCOFAME) were generous with office space, time, and assistance in making the contacts necessary for the research. Among the many individuals outside these institutions who were of assistance, we would like especially to thank the staff at Instituto Materno Infantil (Dr. Hernando Amaya León, Srta. Emma Ortiz Castillo, and Srta. Graciela Velosa Solano); Enrique Perez, now a research associate with CEDE; Dr. Mario Jaramillo; and Jorge Eliécer Ruiz.

At Cornell, Mrs. Lee Matson and the office team at the International Population Program deserve special appreciation for valiant efforts and high-quality performance on a taxing manuscript.

In presenting such a volume of materials on opinions, much of it in the form of detailed verbatim quotations, we have had two broad objectives. The first is to lead the reader to appreciate the complexity of the fertility control issue in Latin America; the great emotion it generates among elites for political, religious, ideological, and moral reasons; and the growing concern about it among the general mass of the population. The second is to throw both light and warning lights on the family planning programs currently underway in Latin America, programs which are usually financed from abroad and often neatly tucked away in the maternal and child health divisions of the Ministries of Health. We hope that our analysis may shed some light on why the population problem receives such a low priority in Latin America.

Finally, we hope that these materials will make some contribution to the social history of Latin America. Two decades ago Kingsley Davis could write, "South America is the dark continent sociologically speaking. Its social organization is more obscure to us than that of African natives." With a qualification or two, these words could be written (and hereby are) with equal truth today.

J. MAYONE STYCOS   *Ithaca, N. Y.*
August 1970

Contents

xi

PART 3
PRIVATE OPINIONS OF THE PUBLIC

PART 4
THE FUTURE OF FAMILY PLANNING

Ideology, Faith, and Family Planning in Latin America

PART 1

The Context of Public Opinion Formation

CHAPTER 1

Backgrounds
to Ideology

The deliberate restriction of birth, by means of either postconception or preconception controls, is an aspect of human culture which appears to be common to all societies. What vary are the conditions under which birth control is legitimately employed, the pervasiveness of its utilization throughout society, and the efficiency of its utilization.

In the past decade, there have been extraordinary developments in all these spheres. The pious prayers for "cheap, safe, and effective contraceptives," intoned almost ritualistically at every planned parenthood meeting prior to the 1960s, have been answered. The use of contraceptives, once viewed as more appropriate for houses of prostitution than for houses of decent people, is now espoused by champions of everything from human rights and responsible parenthood to economic development and social modernization. Indeed, that controlled fertility is here to stay in the developed countries, for members of all religions, is a thesis which should no longer merit serious debate. That it will also be characteristic of the peoples of the underdeveloped nations is also not in question. The questions are only, How long will it take, and can the "natural" process of its adoption be accelerated by deliberate efforts on the part of the state?

A decade ago the population debate centered around resources and population growth, with the optimists insisting that resources and technology would keep well ahead of population. Such optimists are fewer in number today, and the debate is now centered around the question of *how* or *how soon* widespread birth control practices will be effected in the underdeveloped areas. The optimists regard the ideological, technological, and organizational explosions in family planning as at least matching the population explosion—and soon overtaking it. They believe that just as contemporary mortality levels can be achieved by modern medical science with a minimum of social and economic change, so can modern fertility levels be achieved with minimal changes. Opponents of this view feel either that birth control *will* not really take hold until broad socioeconomic changes occur in underdeveloped areas or that it *should* not be encouraged until such changes occur. A brief historical review should clarify these differences.

Under the conditions of high mortality characteristic of most of man's history, sheer replacement of the population (plus a margin of safety for catastrophes) requires high fertility. Accordingly, we would not expect a successful society to show a high incidence of birth control practices prior to the achievement of modern mortality levels. On the other hand, the reduction of mortality would appear to be a necessary but not sufficient cause for widespread fertility reduction. In Europe the gradual reductions in mortality which occurred in the last two centuries were a consequence of such broad social changes as the agricultural, industrial, and scientific revolutions and the improvement of socioeconomic conditions. These general forces directly affected not only mortality but fertility, probably by altering the perceptions of costs and benefits of children. Although the transition from high to low levels of fertility lagged considerably behind mortality declines and often took as long as 150 years, it is noteworthy that they were generally achieved without modern birth control technology, without systematic publicity on family planning, and in the face of opposition from church and state.

In the underdeveloped areas today, declines in mortality are not normally the product of broad social changes, but are much more efficiently being effected by the application of medical technology. That high fertility has in fact persisted for decades in many Latin American countries with rapidly declining mortality lends some empirical evidence to the argument that basic socioeconomic changes are necessary preconditions for fertility decline.

More optimistic experts, however, view the contemporary situation as ripe for rapid declines in fertility prior to modernization. They can point to (1) recent breakthroughs in contraceptive technology; (2) the legitimation of birth control by churches and states; (3) improved methods of disseminating information; and (4) the desire for small families even on the part of poorly educated populations around the world.

TECHNOLOGY

There is little doubt that modern methods of contraception represent a major advance in technology. If pills, intrauterine devices, and sterilization had been available to European women over the past two centuries, it might be assumed that the decline in fertility would have been much faster. On the other hand, it is probable that the decline of European and American birth rates was more attributable to male than to female contraception, namely by means of coitus interruptus and the condom. The new contraceptives are almost exclusively for females, as were the methods unsuccessfully promoted by planned parenthood groups in the first half of this century.

There is no doubt that modern female methods require far less motivation than was ever the case with classical technology. The IUD in contrast with the diaphragm, for example, requires only one decision every year or two, is not associated with the sexual act, and, since it is inserted by physicians, shares both the glamour and the medical neutrality of an innoculation. In these respects it has all the advantages of sterilization, without the disadvantages of irreversibility and possible postoperative complications. Just as Puerto Rican women responded enthusiastically to sterilization prior to the development of IUDs, so can many women in other regions be expected to respond to IUDs. It is not likely, however, that modern methods alone will be adequate to bring fertility down rapidly in the underdeveloped areas. Quite aside from the question of the number of women for whom such methods are not advisable (because of side effects, medical contraindications, expulsions, etc.), there is the problem of a possibly sizable "hard core" of women who cannot be influenced, or who cannot be influenced early enough.[1]

COMMUNICATION

In earlier days, information on birth control was spread almost entirely by word of mouth, often surreptitiously. This was the case not only because illiteracy existed, but because birth control was not a permissible subject for the printed page. There is some evidence, however, that on the few occasions when literature on birth control was widely read, it was not without effect. Thus, when British sales of Knowlton's *Fruits of Philosophy* jumped from about 1,000 per year to over 100,000 per year in the years immediately following the Bradlaugh-Besant trial in 1877, we cannot help but wonder whether the long-term decline in British fertility, which began in 1876, was not accelerated by the huge increase in public information.[2] And one cannot help but wonder whether, in nonpuritanical and highly literate postwar Japan, the more precipitous decline in birth rates was not in part due to the greater dissemination of printed information via newspapers and women's magazines.

In more than half of the Latin American countries today literacy exceeds 50 percent of the adult population and the potential for the printed page is greater than in England of the 1870s. Moreover, as we shall see, there is no doubt that those who read newspapers today are learning far more about fertility control than readers of newspapers in any previous point in history. Further, and in the light of the current legitimation of family planning, mass media never before available for such purposes are at the disposal of family planning programers. A good example is provided by the media treatment of a three-day visit by a Mexican priest to Costa Rica in 1967. Father Orozco, who named overpopulation as the number one world problem and who maintained that the right to limit births is absolute and unconditional, received no less than $3\frac{1}{2}$ hours of national TV time, recorded three 15-minute radio programs, and received 609 inches of newspaper publicity.[3]

In Eastern countries everything from puppet shows to popular songs are utilized as educational media. In a family planning program in East Pakistan, "Publicity and information were disseminated by a singing team . . . recruited from local artists who performed in towns, villages, and bazaars . . . the troup composed songs in the local medium, some in a question and answer format [emphasizing] the economic and family health aspects of family planning."[4]

LEGITIMATION

While the Eastern religions have never been a major stumbling block to family planning, the Christian churches have traditionally bitterly opposed it. The consequences for fertility, however, have not been particularly striking. All the Catholic countries of Europe have low levels of fertility, and in the United States and Latin America both the ideal family size and contraceptive practice of Catholics are surprisingly close to that of non-Catholics.

Nevertheless, that many Protestant churches have declared themselves in favor of family planning, and that many individual Catholic churchmen have become permissive about it, makes the situation in Christian underdeveloped nations, even after *Humanae Vitae,* much more propitious for family planning than was ever the case in the past. Probably the major impact of the more liberal views characteristic of this decade will be in drawing public attention to the problem, in allowing free discussion, and in softening governments' attitudes toward national policies.

While Rome's new hard line on family planning may slow the pace of government programs in some Catholic nations, it may also crystallize public opinion and mobilize pro-family planning groups in a way not possible without opposition. In the past the battle was so one-sided that it was suicidal to elicit church opposition. At the present time, some countries, particularly in Latin America, *need* to make birth control a public issue in order to make the matter salient through the mass media and to arouse courageous public-spirited citizens to take political and social action.

The greatest shifts in the legitimacy of family planning, however, are being made more by states than by churches. Up until the last decade, the only nations in the world with any experience in attempting to influence fertility were those European nations which tried, and continue to try, to *increase* it. Comparable in importance to the revolution in contraceptive technology is the growing trend for nations to formulate explicit policies for the reduction of fertility. Perhaps the most remarkable document of the century was published on Human Rights Day, December 10, 1966. The heads of twelve national states, subsequently joined by others, declared their belief that "the population problem must be recognized as a principal element in long-range national planning," that "the opportunity to decide the number and spacing of children is a basic human right," and that "family planning . . . frees man to attain his individual dignity and reach his full potential."[5] Signed by the leaders of nations as diverse as Ghana, the Netherlands, the United Arab Republic, Morocco, and Colombia, the statement was a clear indication that the worldwide legitimation of birth control is not far off. In the same century, what sent Margaret Sanger to jail is extolled as a basic human right by leaders of the world.

While words do not necessarily mean action, they can certainly hasten it. An increasing number of nations are adopting national programs specifically designed to curtail human fertility. Whether or not they can succeed depends in part on the demand for the services they supply. What do we know about this demand?

POPULAR DEMAND FOR FAMILY PLANNING

Over the past decade an unusually large number of studies of attitudes toward family size and contraception have been conducted around the world. Uniformly they have disclosed that women would prefer a moderate number of children, but know little about birth control and would like to learn. Such studies have utilized public-opinion polling techniques, and typically employ such questions as "Do you want any more children?" and "If you could live your life over, how many children would you like to have?" It is usually found that women regard as ideal about a quarter fewer children than they in fact have by the end of their childbearing period. The responses to such questions have led to great optimism on the part of family planners concerning the probable outcome of contraceptive programs. Critics of these studies feel that such questions often fail to tap the true attitudes of people, who may be much more indifferent to the question of family size than their responses to simple queries indicate. In the absence of public discussion of the question prior to the 1960s and in the light of general ignorance about the "controllability" of human fertility, it is not surprising that women's attitudes are not intense, not crystallized, and not unswerving. But at the same time there is little doubt that there is, as we shall see, at least a latent preference for a moderate family size rather than for a large one.

There are three things which might be done with such a latent preference: (1) we may leave it as it is and make the technology so easy that birth control practice could be precipitated without further increases in motivation (for example, if there were a temporary sterilizing pill which could be taken annually, accompanied by an effective system of distribution, I believe that most of the women in the world would take it after having three or four children); (2) we may wait for the latent preference to become activated "naturally" as a product of social and economic changes which will alter aspiration levels; (3) by means of direct education it may be reinforced, crystallized, and intensified to the extent that the individual will act.

The "great debate" today is between the latter two alternatives. In the scientific world, the hypothesis that the demographic transition can be achieved by means of direct educational techniques is exemplified by Bogue: "Most [traditional demographic theories] are based on correlations between fertility and other variables that are incapable of being manipulated rapidly. . . . Family planning research . . . begins with the assumption that by the discovery of new principles we may be able to devise programs that can accomplish the desired results more quickly than would be possible if we waited for the solution along the lines of increased literacy—rising urbanization, improved levels of living, increased contact with technological-cultural change." [6] We should note that Bogue is not only propounding a theory of social change, but an *ideology*. It is not surprising that it collides with at least one other combined theory of social change and action ideology—Marxism.

IDEOLOGICAL CONFLICT

Throughout most modernizing countries, and especially in Latin America, we can distinguish at least three major ideological types— the conservative, the social reformist, and the revolutionary. The conservative puts the status quo first and revolution last, with social change occupying a reluctant second place. The reformer puts social change first and the status quo last, with revolution occupying a second place. The revolutionary puts revolution first and social change last. He prefers the status quo to social change because the latter might stem the revolution, while the former, the more intolerable it becomes, can only precipitate it. [7]

Increasingly, economists are of the opinion that population control can accelerate economic development by such means as decreasing the dependency ratio, reducing the cost of social services, decreasing unemployment, and raising per capita product. In addition to spreading the benefits of economic development less thin, there should be positive generation of economic development as a result of increased savings for investments in capital-producing enterprises. Finally, by alleviating food shortages and other pressures attributable to population increase (e.g., rural overcrowding and urban migration) social tensions might be eased. It should be noted that the gains from population control can occur without any basic changes in the economic and social structure, e.g., without any radical change in the distribution of wealth, ownership of the means of production, etc. Strictly rationally, population control should be of the highest priority to conservatives; of importance, but secondary importance, to social reformists; and an anathema to revolutionaries.

As usual, the revolutionaries have reacted most consistently and have resisted population control as another palliative of the social reformist ilk which will ease the pressures leading to revolution, diverting attention from the true source of society's ills—the capitalist economic system. As we shall see, some Communist spokesmen have recently softened the traditional Marxian hostility to Malthusian theory to the extent of admitting that population growth can impede economic progress and that birth control can alleviate population growth. They feel that birth control, however, will be and *should be* a natural response to the necessary revolutionary changes in society. That Communist nations have some of the most efficient birth control programs in the world while condemning population control is proof that they are not opposed to birth control per se, but only to the *ideology* of population control and to its proposed sequence in the development of societies.

The conservatives, who should be most enthusiastic about birth control, are split because of conflicting ideologies and credos. In Latin America they tend to be the more traditional and orthodox Catholics who may have moral objections to family planning, and they are also from the business world which sees more consumers and a cheap labor supply as the very fuel of industry.

In point of fact, birth control is making greatest headway among the liberals or social reformers who are gradually becoming convinced that it can speed the economic development they desire without jeopardizing any of the social reforms they espouse. Of equal or even greater importance, they see birth control as a social measure, as a means of reducing abortion and illegitimacy, and as a way of increasing human freedom and control over man's nature. Since they tend to be nominal Catholics or leftist activist Catholics, moral-religious considerations are not of paramount importance. Their main preoccupation about family planning is with respect to its suspiciously enthusiastic promotion by the United States. The more they are convinced, by President Johnson and others, that $5 invested in birth control is worth $100 invested in economic development, the more concerned they are that the bargain-loving United States will choose the $5 investment. In addition, unaware that the conservatives are confused on the issue, they are afraid that both American and local conservatives will substitute Lippes loops for agrarian reform.

In sum, not only is there academic debate over whether or not direct education and services can bring down birth rates, but there are definite ideological differences concerning the desirability, sequence, and overall place of birth control in the strategy of development. Given the present trajectory of technological and communications advances in birth control programs, such ideological obstacles may loom larger in the future, even affecting the vitality of family planning programs among the countries where these are initiated.

North American ideology is also crucial, for the United States dollar is already strongly determining the nature of family planning programs of many countries. Currently identified with an aggressively favorable policy toward family planning, the United States until recently was the world's most militant bastion of Christian prudery. While the American government's family planning policies flowered suddenly in the mid-1960s, the roots are so shallow that they deserve a closer look.

NOTES

1. The hypothesis should be entertained that it would be cheaper and more effective to reach their husbands, and to reach them with male contraceptive methods— new and better ones when they are developed, but in the meantime, the classical male methods. It is entirely possible that after the first enthusiastic group of higher-parity, older, and better-educated women have been reached, the second-round efforts might profitably be directed at males, who are more likely to see the salutary economic consequences of early spacing than are their wives. Clearly there is an important area here for research, involving both technological and sociological considerations.

2. Parker G. Marden, "The Bradlaugh-Besant Trial: A Case Study in Declining Fertility," unpublished M.A. thesis, Brown University, Providence, R.I., 1964.

3. *Planifamilia* (Costa Rica), February 1967. Another Latin American example is the thirteen-episode soap-opera series on problems of excessive family size produced by the Population Reference Bureau and currently being broadcast by at least twenty Central American radio stations. "When the imminent arrival of a seventh child into an already crowded household becomes known, the topic of abortion is raised and counsel is sought from a social worker who advises that the mother seek further advice from a doctor and a priest. The dialogues bring to light sound medical thinking on the topic of abortion and responsible parenthood, as well as liberal Catholic counsel." Alvaro García-Peña, "National and International Informational Programs on Population Problems," PASB Conference on Population Dynamics, February 1967. (Mimeographed.)

4. Harvey M. Choldin, *Studies in Family Planning,* no. 13, August 1966, pp. 8–9. A similar musical effort has been initiated in Kenya, where ". . . one of the leading pop groups in Africa, the Equator Sound, has a new number called 'Maisha Mema' which tells of the benefits of birth control. 'It is a cautionary tale of the unplanned family contrasted with the good life of the planned family,' explained their manager, Charles Worrod." *The Observer* (London), Aug. 11, 1968.

5. "Declaration on Population by the World Leaders," cited in *Victor Fund for the International Planned Parenthood Federation,* no. 8, Spring 1968, p. 18.

6. Donald J. Bogue, "Family Planning Research: An Outline of the Field," in Bernard Berelson (ed.), *Family Planning and Population Programs* (Chicago: University of Chicago Press, 1966), p. 274.

7. See Albert O. Hirschman, *Journeys Toward Progress* (New York: The Twentieth Century Fund, 1963), pp. 276–297.

CHAPTER 2

The United States and Family Planning

For a nation which sometimes had trouble getting its priorities straight, the United States has recently shown admirable clarity in focusing on the significance of the population problem. As early as August 1965, Lyndon Johnson put the problem in a new and startling perspective when he announced, "Second only to the search for peace, it is humanity's greatest challenge." While most proponents of population reacted ecstatically, a few refused to accept even a second billing for population problems. Thus, Raymond Ewell told the National Academy of Science's Agricultural Research Institute that the food-population problem "will in a few years dwarf and overshadow such political problems in Vietnam, Cuba, the Congo, Cyprus, Kashmir, Berlin, and others."[1] Seemingly convinced, President Johnson subsequently announced that "Man's *greatest* problem is the fearful race between food and population." [Italics added.] Even though he reassigned it "next to the pursuit of peace. . . ." in his 1967 State of the Union message, one could only conclude from these and twenty-nine other Johnsonian statements on population that the biggest problems on the mind of the President of the United States were peace and population.

The President could not be accused of being a man far ahead of his public, and other Washington influentials emitted powerful echoes to the Presidential credoes. Thus, in October 1966, the United States Senate was told by Joseph Tydings that "There can no longer be any doubt . . . that this Congress was determined to defuse the population bomb. The population clock ticks every hour of every day. There is not a moment to lose in dealing with what President Johnson has called the most profound challenge to the future of the world."[2]

Senator Fulbright told his colleagues that "population growth is the greatest single obstacle to economic growth in much of the underdeveloped world";[3] and after twenty-eight public hearings on the population problem, Senator Gruening likened the givers of testimony to the "pioneers [who signed] the Declaration of Independence, and those who ratified the Constitution of the United States."[4]

But heroism of the word was singularly unmatched by heroism of the deed. As President Johnson was telling the nation that "The time for rhetoric has clearly passed, the time for concerted action is here and we must get on with the job," AID's top man in population was having difficulty getting his letters typed. In 1965, AID expended on the world's number two problem an amount equivalent to the cost of seven M-60 tanks; in 1966, the cost of seven attack helicopters; and in 1967, somewhat more than the cost of a B-52 bomber. Even in 1968, a year of potential budgetary triumph for population activity, AID was allocated for its worldwide program in population considerably less than India had budgeted for its national program.

Money which failed to materialize for foreign programs was rapidly matched by money which failed to materialize for domestic programs. Senator Tydings could complain in 1967 that "the promise of significantly increased funds for domestic family planning programs has proved illusory . . . even the limited family planning services offered in antipoverty programs are struggling to remain at present funding levels. The prospects that the OEO would expand the services and institute new services . . . which appeared likely a year ago . . . have now virtually vanished . . . the executive branch has completely let us down."[5]

In the Department of Health, Education, and Welfare, although the Secretary established family planning as one of "six priority areas," a consultants' report written for the Department late in 1967 could state that "none of the DHEW Regional Officers or operating agencies presently places high priority on family planning . . . the actions of the 90th Congress made clear it is considerably ahead of most DHEW officials in recognizing the need for greatly expanded Federal assistance in the delivery of family-planning services. In our view, the Department must respond with prompt and vigorous action, not merely on the level of policy, but on the more meaningful level of allocation of resources."[6] What accounted for so great a discrepancy between talk and action that even seasoned Washingtonians began to note it? To account for the phenomenon, more historical background is necessary.

Americans have always enjoyed the luxury of being the most planless nation in the world. That private property is sacred and inviolate, that waste is fun, and that that government is best which governs least are aspects of the American credo of individual freedom which have enabled us to plunder our natural resources, keep both beauty and function at a minimum in our cities, effect gross inefficiencies in political administration, pay enormous sums for pedestrian education, perpetuate a bizarre system of medical services, etc.—and still be "better off" than any nation. The apparent success of planlessness further intensified the hostility toward planning, especially of the comprehensive social and economic kind. So sensitive to the very word was the United States Congress, that as late as World War II, in terminating Roosevelt's National Resources Planning Board, it ". . . solemnly abjured all future Congresses from using the word 'planning' in the name of any future similar federal agency."[7] Member nations of the Alliance for Progress accustomed to United States insistence on national planning boards and the rationalization of intra-Ministerial goals and procedures might be surprised at the fact that it was only in the mid-1960s that the United States President "issued his now famous directive to federal departments and agencies, directing them that they install program planning and budgeting systems involving the definition of long-range goals and objectives, consideration and evaluation of alternative means of attaining objectives, and analysis and evaluation of performance."[8]

There has been, however, a minor but increasingly important goal to national planning in the United States—it is our own insistence to our less affluent brothers that *planning* is *necessary* and that *planning* is *good*. These principles, which appear so self-evident to Americans when looking at foreign countries, are embarrassingly absent from our own way of life. Since it would violate our democratic principles to answer the foreigners' innocent query about American planning by replying honestly that "we're too rich to need it," we have shown an increasing willingness to consider planning in the United States. Indeed, if underdeveloped nations did not exist, surely American liberal intellectuals would have invented them, to compel careful local introspection about the merits of planning. With respect to population problems, the impact has been excruciating.

Not only has the United States never had a population policy, but for most of its history it has had an ethos favoring population growth. America achieved spectacular additions to its labor force in the nineteenth century virtually without cost. Europe was the manpower factory which bore the costs of producing, rearing, and educating men and women to the point where they could be shipped totally assembled and duty-free to America's burgeoning industries. America's seemingly boundless resources, its vast territories, the expanding world markets, the bargain-rate European labor force, and industry's quest for an ever-increasing number of consumers led to the equation of a growing population with a healthy population.

So deeply ingrained was pronatalist thinking in this country that the first serious social-psychological studies of fertility were initiated in the 1930s, and not as a response to the threat of overpopulation, but as a response to the threat of population *decline*. That the United States rate of population growth might be slowed by deliberate national action has, prior to the mid-1960s, never been a matter for serious consideration among United States policy makers.

If a pronatalist, or at best laissez-faire, attitude has been characteristic at the macrodemographic level, at the level of the family the deliberate restriction of fertility has always been practiced but not preached. Foreign Catholics have always marveled at the efficiency and power of the church-militant in the United States, but the puritanical strains of Protestantism have perhaps been equally influential in the suppression of contraceptive information in this country. While it has always been sinful to utilize contraceptive devices in most states of the Union, as late as 1965 it was both sinful and criminal in the state of Massachusetts. (A tribute to American regional diversity was the fact that what one could go to jail for possessing in Massachusetts was being dispensed free by the state of South Carolina. Another interesting way of looking at it is that the only significant group denied birth control in the North has been the Negroes, while in the South they are the only significant group which gets it free.)

It is true that while Margaret Sanger was being jailed and vilified, the American birth rate continued unperturbedly to decline, but the public reaction to family planning in the United States has varied between disgust and silent resignation to a necessary evil. At best it was viewed as so delicate and risky that it was a matter of "individual conscience." As such, it was a matter so totally private, so sacred (or profane), that no external agents, and certainly not the state, should have anything to do with it. As late as 1958, when the Draper Committee on the Foreign Aid Program recommended to President Eisenhower that the United States "increase its assistance to local programs relating to maternal and child welfare" and "assist these countries . . . on request, in the formulation of their plans designed to deal with the problems of population growth," the President reacted with the astonishment and indignation of a man surprised in his bedroom by an internal revenue agent. "I cannot imagine anything more emphatically a subject that is not a proper political or governmental activity," he stormed. "This Government will not . . . as long as I am here, have a positive doctrine in its program that has to do with birth control. That's not our business."

In short, the United States, which has always been reluctant to plan anything, has been especially loath to promote planning within a sacred private institution by means sometimes considered obscene, immoral, or criminal. What has caused the abrupt shift from this position? In addition to a change in popular values and in the thinking (if not the teaching) of the Catholic Church there has been an accelerating acceptance of at least three principles: (1) that population increase in the underdeveloped areas is impeding their modernization and dissipating the effects of United States economic aid, (2) that it is now technologically feasible to lower national birth rates, and (3) that what we do unto others we must do unto ourselves. None of these beliefs was seriously entertained a decade ago in high government circles.

ECONOMIC AID

While the economic development of most of the non-European nations has been disappointingly slow, the evolution of their expectations for possessing the good things of this life has been alarmingly rapid. For example, in Latin America the gains attributable to the Alliance for Progress, while substantial in an absolute sense, fall so far short of the Latin nations' needs and expectations that pressures have built up rapidly to "do something." One obvious answer is more external capital, but with a war abroad and rumblings of economic discontent at home, the United States is in no position materially to increase economic aid. This has led to renewed respect and attention to our foreign-aid dollar. Since it must be stretched, there is not only a greater concern for long-range planning but also a search for new ways of maximizing our developmental investments. This search soon came to rest on a demographic diagnosis and a medical prescription. First, Washington became aware that population increase was consuming much of potential economic and social gains of development, and then began to see that population control investments might have high positive returns. The first phase has been pressed hard by Gen. William Draper, who frequently states unequivocally that "unless and until the population explosion now erupting in Asia, Africa, and Latin America is brought under control, our entire economic aid program is doomed to failure."[9] As early as June 1965 Senator Clark advised the United States Senate to promote family planning for the underdeveloped countries, ". . . thus preventing American aid from being poured down a rat-hole."[10] Moreover, the world agricultural setbacks in the mid-1960s and the increasing awareness that the United States grain surpluses were rapidly disappearing have produced a return to Malthusian pessimism among many of the Capitol's agricultural experts. According to the new poetry of the War on Hunger, "the stork is outrunning the plow."

The major economic apologist for direct attack on the population problem has been Stephen Enke, who flatly told the 1965 World Population Conference that "1 percent of total developmental budgets spent reducing births could be as effective in raising output per head as the other 99 percent altogether." Elsewhere he calculated "the value of permanently preventing a birth in a typical Afro-Asian country is about $250," while the actual cost of doing so is only about one dollar a year per participant.[11] This hardheaded approach to "man's greatest challenge" swayed some of the hardest heads in Washington. President Johnson, for example, broke the news to a startled United Nations audience in June 1965 by saying, "Let us act on the fact, that less than five dollars invested in population control is worth a hundred dollars invested in economic growth." While Johnson's experienced budgetary hand had upped the cost ratio substantially, one thing was clearly nailed down: Family planning was the bargain of the Development Decade.

TECHNOLOGY

Before the sixties, even those few developmental economists who saw a relation between population growth and economic modernization went little farther than to worry about it, since they believed that population growth rates could never be manipulated in the under-developed areas. Aside from the question of religious taboos, birth control technology was so crude that very high motivation was required to practice it effectively. Without a "technological breakthrough," it was felt it was easier to adjust the economy to the population than to adjust the population to fit the economic situation. The development of the oral progesterones and the intrauterine devices, their acceptance by lower-class populations in pilot projects, and the willingness of a number of governments to allocate significant budgets to their dissemination have caused many of the economists to take a second look at the "controllability" of demographic variables. (Interestingly enough, the basic research in reproductive physiology necessary for rapid technological development in contraception is as recent in the United States as are our applied programs of family planning. A succinct indication of the state of our knowledge was given late in 1967 by a distinguished medical researcher at a high-level conference of population experts: "Nobody," he said, "can yet tell me how the IUD works.")

WHAT WE DO UNTO OTHERS

For decades in the United States, small organized groups of courageous women have been insisting that the health and social welfare of the woman depend on the ability rationally to regulate the number and timing of her births. Such arguments received the degree of respect and attention normally accorded to small organized groups of courageous women in the United States. At the same time, however, a handful of less vociferous but more influential men of affairs began to be concerned about the economic and political implications of world population growth, in particular, about the growth of the underdeveloped areas. Their fears included starvation, unrest, war, and communism. While the means sought by both groups were identical, both the ends desired and the *modi operandi* were entirely different. Not only were there few men among the family planners and few women among the population planners, but their average personalities and methods of working were very different. The women were more concerned with American than with foreign problems, and they wanted to antagonize and do public battle both with the church and with puritanism. They opened clinics, distributed leaflets, defied laws, and went to jail. The men located the problem beyond American shores and desired scientific study of the problem and discreet programs of public information. They established philanthropic foundations, sponsored international meetings of scholars, set up news bureaus, and endowed chairs. While the two groups avoided each other as much as possible, when thrown together at an occasional conference, they regarded each other with the combined suspicion and hope of exploitation found only at a social function of ivy league boys and towny girls.

The successes of the men were evidenced by the creation of such agencies and organizations as the Demographic Division of the United Nations, the Population Reference Bureau, and the Population Council. Before long, considerable numbers of foreigners were trained in the U.S. as demographers, to such an extent that American demographers often complained that the foundations were virtually anti-American in their prejudices. New competence in demography, combined with a new orientation toward rational social and economic planning, forced upon many developing nations the significance of their newly derived census statistics. While Eisenhower was still insisting that family planning was a private affair, several Asian countries were pressuring the international agencies for technical and financial assistance, and only the assurance of being turned down kept them from requesting aid from the United States.

Meanwhile, the family planners had achieved the important objective of making family planning a more serious public issue which could be openly discussed and debated, but their legal and clinical gains were painfully slow in coming. In Arkansas, Delaware, Idaho,

Montana, Oregon, and Wisconsin only physicians or pharmacists may sell contraceptives, while Arizona, Missouri, Pennsylvania, and other states have laws restricting the advertising, display, or promotion of birth control devices.[12] In 1970, a nation which prescribed birth control for so many other nations was still forbidding the importation to its shores of any contraceptive drug or article, according to the Tariff Act of 1930.

While Americans are accustomed to lagging laws, they are not accustomed to lagging services. Yet, even today, America's greatest cities are only beginning to introduce family planning programs with public funds. "It was only eight years ago," Dr. Hans Lehfeld noted recently, "that the first municipal birth control clinic was opened in New York City. Many other American cities still have no such clinics at all." [13] A recent analysis of family planning services in New York, New Jersey, Pennsylvania, and Delaware led to the conclusion that outside of New York City, "only about 11 percent of the target population are being served." [14] In 1965, the year in which AID issued its first instruction on population problems to all its missions, less than 5 percent of all United States short-term general hospitals reported the availability of family planning services, and about three-quarters of all local health departments in the United States offered no family planning services. In that year, probably no more than 300,000 United States women received family planning assistance through hospitals or local health agencies, and an additional 200,000 medically indigent women received assistance from Planned Parenthood agencies. While perhaps a half million are receiving some form of public assistance on family planning, "it is estimated that as a minimum, five million fertile medically indigent women in the United States are unable to afford contraceptive services." [15]

The middle class, of course, has continued to receive contraceptive assistance from private physicians, unaware of the short change they are receiving from a profession hardly better educated about contraception than their patients. According to a recent study, of seventy-eight non-Catholic medical schools, seven include no materials on family planning in their curricula and seventeen others offer no clinical observation and practice. Of the schools which offer any instruction at all, half devote no more than *two hours* during the four years of medical school.[16] Nurses probably get even less. "Very little basic knowledge was given to us as students," [17] complained Nurse

Elizabeth Edmands of Johns Hopkins School of Hygiene and Public Health recently, leaving open the question of whether the nurses *ever* learn about family planning. As for the doctors, one can only hope that after leaving the medical school they read about family planning, since they apparently fail to talk about it. When a national survey of physicians was asked, "How frequently does the subject of contraception control come up for discussion when you are with other doctors?" only 2 percent said "often," and three-quarters said "rarely" or "never." Perhaps it is a blessing that half of them admitted they never introduce the topic of family planning to their patients, even "in situations in which it is appropriate." [18]

In the face of this massive conspiracy about birds, bees, and IUDs, it is another tribute to the native cunning of the American people that they have been able to keep the national birth rate within reasonable limits; but it gives our exhortations on national family programs a certain hollow ring abroad. We can only conclude on the moral side as one honest physician concluded recently on the technical side: "As an assisting nation," said the War on Hunger's deputy administrator ruefully, "our position on the technical side of population work is all too similar to that of the developing countries." [19]

But if the home front was a shambles on birth control facilities, ideologically and organizationally there has been a consolidation of forces of some importance, and the distinction between the family planners and the population controllers has faded markedly. During the summer of 1967, while the head of the Planned Parenthood Federation of America was in Asia advising the Thais and Indonesians on their population problems, the head of the Ford Foundation's population division was in Washington advising on the domestic family planning program. Around the time that the Population Council added a division on technical assistance, Planned Parenthood added a division on research, and if the Population Council still employs a few women, it is clear that the masculine takeover of Planned Parenthood is nearing completion. As the men began talking to the women, even their conference formats changed. Almost as if a concordat had been signed, all demographic conferences now end with a section on family planning, and all family planning conferences open with a section on demography. Thus, the needs on the world front have forced upon us an awareness of the shabby condition of our own house.

By the end of the 1960s it began to look as though the United States was taking population seriously. AID allocations for population and family planning moved from 35 million dollars in 1968 to 75 million in 1970, while domestic spending increased from 43 to 70 million. For 1971, 47 million has been allocated for domestic family planning services, 24 million for Office of Economic Opportunity projects, and 28 million for population research. The Tydings Family Planning and Population Act, adopted by the U.S. Senate on July 14, 1970, calls both for nearly a billion dollars for research and services over a five-year period and for the establishment of a national center for population and family planning. In one major address, President Nixon surpassed in quantity the total Johnsonian verbal output on population, and no fewer than fifty-one bills on population were presented to the first and second sessions of the Ninety-first Congress. A dramatic illustration of the accelerated pace of population developments in the United States was that Senator Tydings could simultaneously introduce one family planning bill with a budget of 89 million dollars for 1971 and another to repeal the Tariff Act prohibition against the importation of contraceptives!

These then are the shallow roots of family planning in the United States. When we are so ill prepared at home, what are the dangers involved in our exportation of population control? We turn to Latin America, a region slowly awakening to the population problem, as an example of the hazards ahead.

NOTES

1. Raymond Ewell, "Population Outlook in Developing Countries," Oct. 10, 1966. Cited in *People in Crisis* (pamphlet), Population Crisis Committee, Washington, n.d., p. 20.

2. *Congressional Record,* vol. 112, 184, Oct. 25, 1966.

3. *Congressional Record,* vol. 113, 41, Mar. 14, 1967.

4. Senate speech, May 3, 1967.

5. *Congressional Record,* vol. 113, 54, Apr. 12, 1967.

6. O. Harkavy, F. S. Jaffe, and S. M. Wishik, *Implementing DHEW Policy on Family Planning and Population,* September 1967. (Mimeographed.)

7. H. Fagin, "The Evolving Philosophy of Urban Planning," in L. F. Schnore and H. Fagin (eds.), *Urban Research and Policy Planning* (Beverly Hills, Calif.: Sage Publications, 1967), p. 311.

8. L. C. Fitch, "Social Planning in the Urban Cosmos," in *ibid.,* p. 332.

9. *Foreign Aid for Family Planning* (pamphlet), Population Crisis Committee, Washington, 1967 p. 17.

10. Senate speech, June 14, 1965.

11. Stephen Enke, "Economic Growth through Birth Control," *Challenge,* May/ June 1967, p. 41.

12. Roy Weinberg, *Laws Governing Family Planning* (New York: Oceana Publications, 1968). Cited in A. D. Sollins and R. L. Belsky, "Commercial Productions and Distribution of Contraceptives," *Reports on Population/Family Planning,* no. 4, June 1970.

13. *Family Planning and Mental Health* (pamphlet), Population Crisis Committee and National Institute of Mental Health, Washington, January 1966, p. 21.

14. Frederick S. Jaffe, "The United States: A Strategy for Implementing Family Planning Services," *Studies in Family Planning,* no. 17, February 1967.

15. G. W. Perkin and D. Radel, *Current Status of Family Planning Programs in the United States,* Population Program, Ford Foundation, 1966.

16. *Ibid.*

17. *Family Planning and Mental Health,* p. 17.

18. M. J. Cornish, F. A. Ruderman, and S. S. Spivack, *Doctors and Family Planning* (New York: National Committee on Maternal Health, Inc., 1963), pp. 67–68. "Love-ins" or no, the children of the middle class seem no more enlightened than their parents. Dr. Joseph English, chief psychiatrist of the Peace Corps, recently mused in apparent wonder that "we thought we could assume with this population that comes from the middle class and good colleges that they would know something about family planning. The remarkable thing was to hear from our medical consultants, psychiatrists, and health educators around the country, how totally naive a remarkable percentage of this population was about basic things." *Family Planning and Mental Health,* p. 24.

19. Malcolm Merrill, "Current Activities," in Franklin T. Brayer (ed.), *World Population and U.S. Government Policy and Program* (Washington: Georgetown University Press, 1968), p. 15.

CHAPTER 3

Latin America
and Family Planning

There is nothing new about Latin America's economic and social problems. They have their roots in colonial exploitation, feudal agricultural systems, rigid social stratification, and domination by a few industries, a few crops, and a few people. What is new is a growing hope that these roots can be either pulled up altogether or recultivated by modern means in order to produce a more salubrious product. The revolutionaries favor the root-pulling, while the liberals, the moderate left, and the ideologists of the Alliance for Progress place their faith in the applications of modern technology and administration.

Over and above the old problems and new hopes for change, however, there has been added in recent decades a biological phenomenon which exacerbates virtually all the social and economic problems and renders their solution still more complex and costly—the acceleration of natural increase. In the light of birth rates (for most countries) which are among the world's highest, the mortality declines to modern levels in the past few decades have produced unparalleled rates of natural increase for much of Latin America.

At the turn of this century all Latin America was populated by about 63 million persons, a figure well under the present population of Brazil. At current rates of increase, Latin America would multiply ten times by the end of this century, and rival the current population of China. Indeed, "the increase in the population of Latin America during the last half of this century may equal the total increase in population of man during all the millennia from his origin until 1650."[1] A Pan-American Assembly held in Colombia in 1965 concluded that "Most Latin American nations . . . have rates of population growth which are high, both in terms of their growth of national product, and in comparison with the demographic growth of nations in other areas or eras . . . the population of the region will double in about 25 years, but the number and severity of the problems will increase by an even higher factor."[2]

Until recently the population problem seemed totally insoluble. International migration sufficient to absorb an appreciable share of the natural increase is no longer possible on a crowded planet with hardened political boundaries, and slowing down the declines in mortality is both unethical and unfeasible. As for the possibilities for spontaneous declines in the birth rates, the industrialization and education generally believed to produce such declines are not only slow in coming but retarded in part precisely because of the rapid population growth. The early fertility declines in Argentina and Uruguay were not followed by other nations (with the possible exceptions of Chile and Cuba) and can perhaps be attributed to the unique influence in these two countries of European migration. Clearly, anyone counting on "modernization" to reduce Latin America's fertility would have to have an unusual degree of optimism, patience, and faith.

The only method remaining, then, for reducing birth rates is population control—programs created by the state or other agencies and directed at reducing fertility, probably by facilitating the use of birth control on the part of sexually associating couples. But any student of history, by combining the fact of North America's bitter experience with Catholic militancy on the birth control issue with the fact of the political power of the church in Latin America, could readily dismiss population control in Latin America as politically and ideologically unfeasible.

There were also more direct indications of its unfeasibility. The attempts at instituting public facilities for birth control in Puerto Rico showed how the church in a Latin culture, even if it lost a struggle, could totally devitalize its opponents.[3] Further, efforts to mobilize private family planning organizations in Latin America were almost totally without success. In 1955 the first regional Western Hemisphere Conference of the International Planned Parenthood Federation was held in San Juan, Puerto Rico. It was picketed by indignant Puerto Ricans, and the quantity and quality of participants from the Latin American nations were little short of pathetic. Subsequent conferences were held in Jamaica in the late 1950s to the accompaniment of wall scribblings saying "Birth control is to kill the Negro," and any genuine Latin American courageous enough to attend was virtually lionized. By 1960 there was not a single family planning organization to be found among the twenty Latin American republics, other than one in Mexico with an essentially North American management; and the mass media contained little information on population or family planning. Whether viewed at best as irrelevant or at worst as scandalous, the effect was the same—the problem was ignored. But Latin Americans have always baffled North Americans, and their behavior in the area of family planning is no exception.

THE AWAKENING OF THE PUBLIC CONSCIENCE

By the mid-1960s the topics of population and family planning were much in evidence for the literate Latin American. In 1965 the Cornell International Population Program hired an international clipping service to provide us with all clips on the topics of population and family planning appearing in the Latin American press. The volume was surprising. In 1965, 6,125 clips were cataloged, a figure which rose to 8,400 in 1966 and to nearly 15,000 in 1967. That the volume grew by 144 percent in two years may in part be attributed to the increasing experience of the scanners in locating population topics, but it is also doubtless an indication of the growing attention to the problem on the part of the urban elites.

In terms of sheer volume, Mexico dominates the scene with nearly a quarter of all the clippings (Table 1). The next country in rank, Colombia, is represented by only a third of the Mexican volume. However, the volume figures cannot be interpreted as a comparative measure of national attention to the problem in any other than the most general sense, since they are affected by the number of newspapers as much as they are by the clippings per newspaper. A better

Clippings on Population and Family Planning Received from
Latin American Newspapers

	1967 Clippings, Percent	Percent Increase in Total Volume, 1965–1967
Argentina–Uruguay	8.5	105
Brazil	8.0	185
Chile	7.5	309
Colombia	9.4	199
Mexico	25.5	190
Peru	5.3	11
Venezuela	7.9	140
Latin Caribbean	5.5	202
British Caribbean	4.9	37
Central America	11.8	182
Others	5.4	111
Total	99.7	144
Number (14,930)		

measure is the absolute volume of clippings from the major newspaper in each nation (Table 2). In each case we have selected a leading
daily from the capital city which showed the largest number of clippings in 1967. The figures shown have been corrected for under-
reporting.[4] Again, the volume is surprising. *El Universal* in Venezuela
averaged *more than one item per day,* and nine of the countries had
at least one every two days. In 1967 it would have been hard for
a newspaper reader in the Latin American capitals to avoid the topic
of population—unless he happened to live in Montevideo.

These overall figures do not tell us the extent to which *local*
population questions are being considered. In 1965, only 44 percent
of the clippings originated in the nation which printed the story, and
less than a third dealt with local population questions. But by 1967,
the proportion of local origin had risen to 49 percent and the proportion with local content to 41 percent. The proportion with reference to *other* Latin American countries, moreover, rose from 26 to
31 percent. Between 1965 and 1966, in only two of nineteen countries
did the percent of locally originated articles decline, and in twelve

TABLE 2

Number of Clippings on Population and Family Planning for
Newspaper with Largest Number of Clips for 1967

	Clips Received	Adjusted Number	Newspaper
Argentina	120	129	La Razon
Bolivia	35	140	Presencia
Brazil	177	192	Journal do Brasil
Chile	186	214	El Mercurio
Colombia	234	244	El Tiempo
Ecuador	182	200	El Comercio
Paraguay	68	76	La Tribuna
Peru	99	187	El Comercio
Uruguay	17	29	El Dia
Venezuela	341	371	El Universal
Mexico	200	225	Excelsior
El Salvador	143	147	La Prensa Grafica
Guatemala	139	170	Imparcial
Honduras	46	88	El Dia
Nicaragua	62	76	La Prensa
Panama	136	143	La Estrella de Panama
Dominican Republic	194	234	El Caribe
Puerto Rico	150	273	El Mundo
Jamaica	165	172	Gleaner
Trinidad	137	147	Guardian

it increased by 5 or more percentage points.[5] Between 1966 and 1967, the rise was even more dramatic. In only two countries (El Salvador and Uruguay) was there a decline in the percentage of local clippings, and in another two the changes were less than 3 percentage points in either direction. In eight countries the increase was between 4 and 9 percentage points, and in eight others it was 10 percentage points or more. Since total volume was more than doubling at the same time, it is clear that national population problems were increasingly becoming news in the Latin American countries. Further, there was a marked increase in the proportion of locally originated articles which were *news* items, as opposed to opinion (features, editorials, cartoons, etc.). In 1965, two-thirds of local articles were opinion, but by 1967 the proportion had shrunk to 44, another indication that by 1967 local population problems had become news.

In terms of content, two-thirds of the 1967 clippings of local origin mentioned population growth, size, or density, as compared with only 54 percent of the others. On the other hand, two-thirds of the foreign-originated articles mentioned birth control as opposed to 54 percent of the local articles. Interestingly, foreign articles (34 percent) were much more likely to include mention of the Catholic Church than were local articles (19 percent). In terms of the main topics of the articles, we see from Table 3 that the local articles showed more concern with demographic and economic aspects of the problem, somewhat less with family planning and the pill, and much less with the church.

Whereas 60 percent of the foreign articles on birth control took no position, this was true of only half of the local articles, which tended to be somewhat more unfavorable to birth control than were foreign articles. Nevertheless, the ratio of favorable to unfavorable local articles was 2 to 1 (as opposed to 3 to 1 for the foreign articles).

In addition to publicity of a general character, testimonials to the importance of the population problem were made by some of the most prestigeful figures in the hemisphere. The ice was broken by Alberto Lleras Camargo (ex-President of Colombia), who spoke

TABLE 3

Main Topics of Newspaper Clippings, by
Origin of Article, 1967, in Percent *

	Local	Foreign
Family planning	45	51
Economics	23	18
Population data	27	21
Church	10	29
Food and agriculture	18	18
Housing, urbanization	7	2
Abortion	4	5
Pill	7	11
Health–Medical	7	5

*Percentages total more than 100 since up to two main topics
were coded for each article.

publicly in favor of family planning on his own territory in 1965. He was soon followed by heads of state who took even greater political risks:

The President of Chile: "The population explosion is a problem that cannot be evaded. It is necessary not only to study it, but to work out solutions and face up to it with courage. This is a problem affecting not just each family and each country, but all humanity."[6]

The President of Costa Rica: "In these times and all over the world, there is a clear awareness that humanity cannot remain indifferent to the extremely serious problem of demographic increase . . . the encyclical of Pope Paul VI establishes the bases for state action in family planning."[7]

The President of Colombia: "We cannot fail to adopt very soon a demographic policy because the problem becomes more serious every day. . . . The State not only has the right but the obligation to place within the reach of parents the information necessary for the rational planning of their family size."[8]

THE BIRTH OF FAMILY PLANNING ORGANIZATIONS

By the mid-1960s, family planning services began to appear in the Western Hemisphere. In contrast to the three earlier Western Hemisphere conferences, IPPF's 1964 Conference saw delegates from seventeen Latin American nations, and the delegates tended to be high-quality physicians and government officials. More important, private family planning associations offering contraceptive services began functioning early in the 1960s, and by the end of the decade, only Cuba, Bolivia, Nicaragua, and Haiti were without one (Table 4).

TABLE 4

Year of Formation of Private Family Planning Associations in
Latin American Countries

1961–1962	Chile, Guatemala, Honduras, Puerto Rico, Uruguay (Barbados, Jamaica, Trinidad)
1965–1966	Argentina, Brazil, Colombia, Costa Rica, Dominican Republic, Ecuador, El Salvador, Mexico, Panama
1967	Peru, Venezuela, Paraguay

SOURCE: *Family Planning in Five Continents* (pamphlet), International Planned Parenthood Federation, March 1968.

While their budgets are small in relation to their needs, the associations are not operating on a shoestring. In 1968 the International Planned Parenthood Federation budgeted 2.7 million dollars for Western Hemisphere countries other than the United States, representing over 40 percent of the total world budget of IPPF. About two-thirds of the disbursements went to South American, just over a fifth to Central American, and 15 percent to Caribbean countries. The disbursement per 10,000 population averaged just under $500 in the Caribbean as a whole, as compared with under $200 in Central America and just over $100 in South America.

While IPPF provides the principal support for the private associations, other organizations, such as the Population Council, the Ford Foundation, and the U.S. Agency for International Development, provide funds for universities and for government programs. As an example, the U.S. Agency for International Development's annual inputs for population studies and family planning programs in Latin America increased from just under 1 million dollars per year in 1965 and 1966 to nearly 8 million dollars in 1968. In the latter year, Latin American dollar obligations for these purposes accounted for over a quarter of the world total. (In 1965 and 1967, Latin American allocations represented the majority of the regional allocations.) Thirteen Latin American republics received, directly or through other agencies, over $100,000 each from AID in 1968, with Chile, Ecuador, the Dominican Republic, and Peru receiving $7,500,000. Among those who have never requested such aid are the important countries of Argentina, Uruguay, Mexico, and Brazil.[9]

By the end of the decade, fifteen countries, including Cuba, had programs sponsored by *national governments,* a development totally unforseen a decade earlier. In addition, the Organization of American States has organized a population program and set up an inter-American advisory committee on population, the Pan American Health Organization receives requests for technical and financial assistance on family planning, and the Pan American Federation of Medical Schools has a population division which sponsors teaching and research programs on population problems.

But once we recover from our astonishment at the remarkable signs of Latin America's coming to grips with its population problem, we must raise the inevitable next question—will it work? In terms of the magnitude of national population problems, current family planning programs are more symbolic than substantive. They represent the establishment of an important principle, but their case loads are in most instances insignificant and almost exclusively urban in character. Furthermore, the expressions of the statesmen we have presented probably represent a minority opinion. Again, while it is remarkable that they exist at all, the sentiments they reflect, as we shall see, are neither widespread nor of great intensity among Latin American leadership classes.

Successful family planning programs require a substantial degree of commitment on the part of the strategic groups of the leader class, and something ranging between acquiescence and enthusiasm on the part of the public to be served. Our thesis is that the public is in a more favorable state of readiness than the leaders.

NOTES

1. Harold F. Dorn, "World Population Growth," in P. M. Hauser (ed.), *The Population Dilemma,* (New York: Prentice-Hall, Inc., 1963), p. 21.

2. *Final Report,* First Pan-American Assembly on Population, Aug, 11–14, 1965.

3. J. Mayone Stycos, *Human Fertility in Latin America* (Ithaca, N.Y.: Cornell University Press, 1968), chap. 7.

4. Because of problems with the mails, or with a particular newspaper, it is frequently the case that the clipping service fails to receive certain issues. In the case of the newspapers in Table 2, the percentage of issues not received during 1967 ranged from 25 percent in Bolivia to 97 percent in El Salvador. Raw figures have been prorated to derive an expected total for the year.

5. Cuba, Haiti, and English-speaking islands are excluded. Puerto Rico is included.

6. Eduardo Frei Montalva, "Welcoming Address to the 8th International Planned Parenthood Federation," Santiago, Chile, April 1967. Cited in *Victor Fund Report,* no. 6, Summer 1967.

7. April 1 address of Dr. José Joaquin Trejos Fernández. Cited in *Planifamilia* (Costa Rica), April 1967.

8. Carlos Lleras Restrepo, "Un Programa de Transformación Nacional," speech at the Coliseo Cubierto de Bogotá, Nov. 27, 1965; and speech at the inauguration of the Panamerican Conference on the Teaching of Demography in Schools of Medicine, *Boletín FEPEFAM* (Bogotá), July 1968.

9. *Population Program Assistance,* U.S. Agency for International Development, September 1968. See also "Planned Parenthood in Latin America," Planned Parenthood Federation of America brochure, n.d., C. 1967. Between 1967 and 1970 the Population Council made over 6 million dollars in grants to Latin America (private report, July 1970).

PART 2

Public and Private Opinion of Elites

INTRODUCTION

§ THE SIGNIFICANCE OF PUBLIC AND PRIVATE OPINION

We assume that national contraceptive service programs are not only desirable for philosophical and medical reasons but can be of great, if not major, importance in effecting declines in national fertility levels. This is not to say that such reductions cannot occur "spontaneously," or will not "eventually" occur without such programs. It means that given the existing levels of income and education in most Latin American countries, "eventual" declines are too far off to be acceptable. The only feasible short-run solution is birth control programs stimulated by the institution in Latin America with sufficient resources to do the task—government. The first step is to convince governments to introduce programs, but whether or not such programs succeed depends upon the receptivity of the target groups and the degree of adaptation of the programs to this receptivity. If the public receptivity is intense, the programs can be inconspicuous and innocuous and still be successful; but if public receptivity is less than intense, the programs will have to be imaginative, large, and expensive. The latter, in turn, requires deep commitment on the part of national leaders. As we see it then, there is a problem of commitment and appropriate action both at the level of elites and at the level of the public.

The importance of assessing both elite and public opinions should therefore be clear, and indeed provides the rationale for the content and organization of this book, Part 2 of which is devoted to studies

37

of the elite, Part 3 to studies of the public. An additional organizing principle has been the delineation of private and public opinions, a conceptual distinction closely linked to the research methods we have employed. The distinction is primarily of significance at the level of the elite, whose public opinions (i.e., an opinion expressed in public) may not only be different from but of greater significance than their private opinions. Investigators have often made the error of applying to elites the same technique of polling private opinions that have been used with the general mass of the population, when the *public* opinion of the elites may have been of more importance, both in terms of impact on the general society and in terms of predicting behavior of the elite. We devote a great deal of attention to describing elite opinions as expressed in the mass media—newspapers and books—and have described their private opinions by reporting the results of polls and private interviews. In the case of the general public, we report the results of two classical KAP studies (surveys of contraceptive knowledge, attitudes and practices), but have virtually no information on the public opinions of the masses, other than a brief report in Chapter 16 of "inquiring photographer" type interviews reported in the Latin American press. The various techniques, including those in cell four which we did not employ, are summarized below:

Opinion Research Methods

	Private opinions	*Public opinions*
Elite	Focused interviews	Newspaper content analysis
General public	KAP interviews	Group interviews Participant observation

§ THE PRIVATE OPINION OF ELITES

A wide variety of surveys has shown that knowledge and use of birth control are directly proportional to education and social class in Latin America (see Chapter 9, for example), but surveys based on probability samples rarely have a sufficient number of "elite" respondents to permit separate analysis of this class. In 1964 and 1965, however, surveys sponsored by the United States Information Agency (USIA) in a number of Latin American cities were apparently so designed as to ensure an analyzable number of upper-status cases. In the earlier survey, in three out of four cities there was no difference between respondents with university educations and those with primary school educations in responding to the question: "Would you approve or disapprove of helping people learn how to limit the number of children if they wish?" In Buenos Aires, Caracas, and Rio de Janeiro, the proportion of the population with no more than elementary school educations which approved was 59, 70, and 66 percent, while for those with more than secondary school education, the corresponding figures were 60, 69, and 62 percent.[1] This gives us our first clue that the upper classes may not especially preach what they practice, while the lower classes may not be practicing what they preach. In this instance there was no difference between educational levels, but in the following year the USIA carried out another survey series utilizing a more stringent question and a categorization by social class rather than by education. That the "upper class" are elites in at least a statistical sense is indicated by the fact that they represent only a small proportion of the total sample in four of the five cities (Table 5).

TABLE 5

Approval of a National Birth Control Program, by
Socioeconomic Class, Five Latin American Cities,
1965 *

"All things considered, how would you feel about a birth control program to encourage people [in your country] to have fewer children—would you approve or disapprove of such a program?"

Country	Percent Who Approve		Number in Base		Percent "Upper" of All Cases†
	Upper Class	Lower Class	Upper	Lower	
Buenos Aires	37	61	46	209	9
Caracas	48	76	37	303	7
Mexico City	60	72	35	284	7
Rio de Janeiro ‡	63	69	119	254	24
Santiago	70	78	40	301	8

*USIA Attachment 2, Policy Program Directive, no. 10–67. (Mimeographed.)
†"Middle class" cases have not been presented here, but tend to fall between the other two categories in degree of approval, though much closer to the lower class.
‡"No answers" in Rio de Janeiro ranged from 12 percent of the upper class to 20 percent of the lower, and therefore have been removed from the bases before calculating. In other cities, since the percentage of "no answer" does not exceed 8 percent for any class category, the "no answers" have been left in the bases.

In all cases, but to a substantial degree in the first three cities, the lower-class respondents are more favorable to the notion of a national program than are the upper-class respondents.

In a number of countries special surveys of elite groups have revealed a high degree of conservatism concerning the implications of population growth and programs to contain it. In Honduras a 1969 study of 300 elites (100 lawyers, 100 industrialists, and 100 government officials) found half of them to be against "a national family planning program to lower the rate of population growth" and only a quarter to agree with the World Bank statement, "the major obstacle to economic and social progress in developing countries is rapid population growth."[2]

In Bolivia, 97 men and women from law, government, the military, journalism, education, and the clergy were interviewed from a list of 140 "agreed-on national leaders." Some representative findings are summarized below:

75 percent believe current national population growth to be slow or static.

56 percent desire national population growth to be rapid in the next decade.

74 percent believe world population growth to be a serious matter.

73 percent would favor a national family program.[3]

In Medellín, Colombia, a survey of 170 educators, politicians, industrialists, journalists, and female leaders found that while from 66 to 100 percent of each of these groups had used birth control, from a third to a half thought physicians should not prescribe contraceptives.[4] This occurred in a nation where close to nine out of every ten physicians believed as early as 1966 that "it is the physician's duty to prescribe family planning to medical cases that require them, despite the position of the Catholic Church."[5]

A survey of 1,100 male and female adults in Lima, Peru, included a special group of 100 opinion leaders. Selected comparisons between the leaders and the general population are given in Table 6.[6]

In the first set of questions the leaders are clearly more conservative than the followers, but the reverse is true in the second set, a fact which leads us to conclude that the former sample, heavily weighted with uneducated respondents, has a greater tendency to agree with any statement (a kind of "yes set") than do the opinion leaders. At least, however, it seems likely that the leaders and followers are not

TABLE 6

Opinions on Population and Family Planning, Lima, 1966

Percent Who Agree That:	General Sample	Opinion Leaders
Rapid population increase slows national progress	65	51
Steps should be taken to regulate births in Peru	79	63
To control the number of children is to contribute to the well-being of the family	91	79
The state should teach people to limit the number of children	81	75
The state should reward large families	72	46
Each new child arrives with his own loaf of bread*	42	34
The Catholic woman should not use contraceptives	54	45
Many children are needed to assure one's old age	35	12
Number of cases	(1,000)	(100)

*A rough English equivalent might read: Nature ensures that each child produces as well as consumes.

far apart on the basic issues. That half the elite believe the state should reward large families and half believe that population growth does not slow Peruvian progress shows a substantial conservative inclination with respect to population growth and fertility, despite a relatively liberal orientation toward birth control.

In Mexico, a sample of 240 national leaders in political, religious, and professional occupations was found to be quite conservative on the question of population growth.[7] When asked the loaded question, "What means should be taken in view of the population growth, for the good of Mexico?" only 42 percent were willing to volunteer that the growth should be limited. Not only did over a quarter say "no means," but 28 percent said that population growth should be *stimulated*. Indeed, less than half believed Mexico's population was growing very rapidly, and a clear majority (58 percent) believed that the nation's population growth was increasing its economic potential. Further, four in every five felt the ideal number of children to be five or more, and only four out of ten regarded the pills as acceptable. Twenty percent felt that control of pregnancy was *never* acceptable. On the few items where comparisons with a more general survey were possible, leaders were more in favor of families of five or more than were nonleaders, but more liberal on the acceptability of birth control. (The high proportion of "don't knows" among the general population on questions concerning specific contraceptives, however, should be considered in interpreting the latter finding.)

In Guatemala, a sample of 114 national leaders proved to have a relatively liberal view of the population problem and family planning, with 86 percent declaring themselves in favor of a national family planning program for Guatemala and three quarters in favor of birth control information for single people. Even so, no more than two-thirds believed that a slower national population growth was desirable, despite the fact that 95 percent characterize this growth as "rapid." The leaders seemed less liberal when it came to their explanations for the population growth, with 17 percent attributing it to "promiscuity, irresponsibility, and lack of recreation" and 95 percent agreeing that "irresponsible parenthood is a factor in the rapid population growth." [8]

In sum, the available evidence from Latin American studies of leadership groups indicates that (1) large proportions are unconvinced that a population problem exists in their country; indeed, many believe that rapid population growth is needed; (2) most favor family planning programs, as opposed to population control programs, but even here substantial minorities are against such programs; (3) there is some evidence that the upper classes are more conservative than the lower.

§ PUBLIC OPINION

There is no doubt that the upper classes practice family planning much more than the lower and that their fertility is much lower. We have also noted that their private opinions tend to favor family planning but not population control. What they say in public, however, is a matter of much greater importance than what they say and do in private. In this context elites may be defined as those who feel strongly enough about population and family planning to speak *publicly* on it, and whose prestige is great enough to merit publication of their views by newspapers or magazines.

Table 7 schematizes the nature and source of elitist opinion on family planning and population control, with special reference to groups in the Western Hemisphere. It must first be pointed out that

TABLE 7

Major Elitist Public Arguments in the Western Hemisphere for
and against Family Planning and Population Control,
by Political Position

	Left	Center	Right
Family planning			
In favor	"Individual human right"	"Anti-abortion" "Family health and welfare"	"Responsible parenthood"
	New Left Old Left	Physicians Social workers	Young clergy
Opposed	"Populationism"	0	"Hedonism, promiscuity"
	Black militants		Old clergy
Population control			
In favor	0	"Economic development"	"Political-economic stability" "Welfare costs"
		Economic planners	Politicians
Opposed	"Anti-imperialism" "Revolutionism"	"Coercion"	"Nationalism" "Abundant labor supply" "Populationism"
	Castroites Peking Communists	Liberal intellectuals	Military Big business

aside from the zeros, there is no attempt to indicate relative frequencies in the cells. In fact, the scales are probably tipped in the favorable direction toward family planning and possibly narrowly so toward population control, though North-South differences would be especially striking here. Leftist opposition to family planning and centrist opposition to population control are especially small categories.

While we have exemplified each category by a group which tends to maintain such a position, there is no suggestion that all members of the group believe or proclaim it or that there are not other groups who do so. Further, as we have seen from our national poll data, since attitude toward family planning does not predict attitude toward population control, any group should properly be classified twice in the table. For example, Castroites tend to favor family planning and oppose population control, while many economists favor population control and are uninterested in family planning programs.

While crude, the scheme provides a springboard for a number of generalizations: (1) The opposition to family planning in this hemisphere is concentrated among the far right and left. Indeed, on the one hand the Black Muslims and the older hierarchy of the Catholic Church constitute the major organized opposition in the hemisphere, the former for reasons of "populationism" (the equation of numbers and group power), the latter for fear of increasing hedonism and weakening the family as the basic social unit. (2) Opposition to population control on the other hand is found at all points of the political spectrum, though for different reasons. The revolutionaries see such programs as imperialistic schemes to weaken the likelihood of drastic social and economic change, while the rightists see them as imperialistic schemes to emasculate the Third World. (3) Approval of family planning naturally refers to its salutary effects on the individual or family. The leftists see it as enhancing individual (especially female) freedom, the centrists as improving family health and welfare, and the rightists as a means of increasing the discipline, responsibility, and stability of the lower classes—the other side of the promiscuity-hedonism coin. (4) Among those favorable to population control, the center sees it as a means of enhancing or accelerating economic development or as another general public health measure. The right favors it as a way of improving the lot of underdeveloped peoples without excessive disturbance of the distribution of power, and as a way of reducing the growing costs of social welfare programs.

In the following chapters we will elaborate the public positions of various major groups—nationalists, churchmen, and Marxists—as well as devote some attention to such key professions as medicine and the social sciences. Private opinions will be assessed by case studies of two groups in Colombia—priests and university professors.

NOTES

1. *Some Attitudes in Less Developed Areas toward Population Control,* United States Information Agency, 1964. (Mimeographed.) In the case of Mexico City, two-thirds of the better educated were favorable as opposed to only half of the poorly educated.

2. Axel Mundigo, "Elites, Poverty and Population," Ph.D. dissertation, Cornell University, Ithaca, N.Y., in progress.

3. *Leaders' Opinions on Population Problems and the Family,* Center for Social and Economic Development, La Paz, n.d., c. 1969.

4. Mario Jaramillo, "Report on the Evaluation of the Experimental Program of Medellin," *Regulation of Fertility* (Bogotá: Tercer Mundo, 1968), vol. 2.

5. Hernán Mendoza-Hoyos, "The Colombian Program for Public Education, Personnel Training and Evaluation," *Demography,* vol. 5, no. 2, 1968, p. 833.

6. Carlos A. Uriarte, "Study on Attitudes toward the Size of the Family," *Studies of Population and Development,* Lima, Peru, vol. 2, no. 2, 1968.

7. Luis Leñero Otero, *Research on the Family in Mexico* (Mexico D.F.: Instituto Mexicana de Estudios Sociales, 1968), chap. 10.

8. *Encuesta de Opinión y Actitudes de Líderes Nacionales sobre el Problema Demográfico y la Regulacion de la Natalidad en Guatemala* (paper), Instituto Centroamericano de Población y Familia, Guatemala, 1970.

CHAPTER 4

Nationalists

We have selected the published work of three men to illustrate the nationalist way of thinking. The writers represent three important professions (law, medicine, and journalism), three countries (Peru, Colombia, and El Salvador), and three different but typical types of situations. In Peru, a nation just beginning to examine its population problem, we deal with reactions to its first population conference. In Colombia, a nation which has both articulated a broad policy and introduced a pilot program, we get reactions to concrete national efforts to deal with the population problem. In El Salvador, we deal with more diffuse reactions to what is viewed as a vast racist plot on the part of the white Western world.

PERU: FELIX CRUZAT ALEGRE

In December of 1965, for the first time in its history Peru held a national conference on population. The fact that such a conference could be held at all in Peru was considered an achievement; and the conference papers—technical, antiseptic, dull, and noncontroversial—confirmed the impression that this was only a very early step in Peru's coming to grips with its population problem. Indeed, President Fernando Belaunde Terry's reaction to the conference was to turn, perhaps in desperation, to the Incas ". . . I can only give homage," he said in his closing address, "to those who in remote times wanted to confront the population explosion to the point of evolving a system of government which by means of statistics and geographic study could assure every citizen his right to sustenance."[1]

But if the papers were academic, the conference conclusions, which bore no apparent relation to them, were not. E.g., the second of fourteen conclusions stated that "the advantages of a larger population in Peru are only hypothetical."[2] So astonishing was this conclusion to one of the participants that it prompted him to publish a monograph in 1968 entitled *Birth Control or Neo-Fascism?*

A Lima lawyer and teacher, Felix Cruzat Alegre, states his wish in the book's prologue that the work have a "nationalist and especially humanist basis," currents which are not insignificant among Latin American intellectuals. His humanistic bent is evident from literary and religious allusions, the polemic style, and the unscientific character of his observations on society. While the book leaves his politics in doubt, his nationalism, apart from an explicit ode to it in the concluding chapter, is evident from the incessant excoriation of the United States, of which the following is a pertinent example: "While the U.S. writes 'danger of cancer' on (its own) cigarettes, . . . in Peru where someone dies every eight hours of cancer, they conduct big campaigns to increase cigarette smoking. Could this be by any chance a means of population control?"[3]

While he never answers this challenging question, he does answer a number of others. Indeed, his basic thesis is introduced by means of a challenging assertion—that to speak of "population control of the developing nations, virtually depopulated and with immense riches in their soils, sub-soils, seas, rivers, lakes, etc. is absurd at best, since their poverty is not caused by overpopulation, because this does not exist, but by archaic socio-economic structures."[4] Everything stems from this basic premise—the obvious absurdity of Peru's having a population problem. Like many of his fellow Latin American intellectuals, not all of them humanists, he defines population problems exclusively in terms of national population density and equates potentially exploitable natural resources with current wealth. Peru's strikingly low population densities and strikingly large abundance of potentially exploitable natural resources would compel any thinking man to wonder why the "nations interested in imposing population control in the under-developed nations and not in their own, are the super-populated and super-industrialized Europeans, at the head of which is the United States."[5] Obviously such nations are not so foolish as to have failed to observe the same low population density in Latin America as the author has observed. Their advocacy of population control, therefore, must be concealing *"hidden interests,"* as Cruzat entitles his second chapter. What would these be?

Essentially there are two. The first is the North American desire to keep the underdeveloped countries weak and underdeveloped. Population control accomplishes this by several direct and indirect means. In blasting the conclusions of the 1965 Peruvian conference ("sponsored and financed by the Ford Foundation, the Rockefeller Foundation and the Millis Bank [sic]"), Cruzat tells us that population growth and social change are virtually equivalents: "There is not the slightest doubt that these gentlemen want to assure that Peru will never have structural changes, and that everything remains *static and stationary* while other countries *grow and progress.*"[6] [Italics added.] "The Americans know" that population growth could create both internal markets and a new outlook threatening the imperialists: "The Americans know that in 20 or 30 years they will have 400–500 million living in 7.8 million square kilometers and that Iberoamerica with 23 million square kilometers . . . and 200 million people could grow to match it in population, which would cause the yankis the loss of raw material deposits and markets . . . as well as cheap labor, because . . . by then Latin America would have awakened."[7] Ultimately, the plan calls for a once vigorous and youthful nation enfeebled by senescence and sterility: "Finally, the desired objective would be achieved, millions of sterilized women, . . . an absence of young people and a population of old people who could not promote the nation's development, and, naturally, the stagnation or retrogression of Peru."[8]

But this is only the first part of an ingenious plot. The striking feature of Cruzat's theory is its reliance on population density not only for Latin America but for the industrialized societies. Since he sees the former as underpopulated and the latter as overpopulated, he draws the ultimate conclusion: "In the light of this situation [of population stagnation in Peru] there would be no alternative to importing people from the over-populated countries, which is precisely what they are after. . . ."[9]

COLOMBIA: HERNÁN VERGARA

The most sophisticated of our three nationalists, Dr. Hernán Vergara, is a psychiatrist and professor of psychology in Colombia. Although his reading in the area of family planning has been confined to local sources and to the 1965–1966 hearings of Senator Greuning's subcommittee on foreign aid, he is far better informed than either of our other examples. This is because Colombia has produced more literature on family planning than any other Latin American nation, because the Greuning hearings in fact contained a great deal of expert testimony, and because Dr. Vergara reads with great care.

In the introduction to a 1968 monograph entitled *The Layo Complex: Antecedents and Questions Concerning Demographic Policy*,[10] he denies having a pronationalist bias, disclaims interest in particular contraceptives (which he leaves to the church to decide), and states his purpose as "defending authentic and honest information so that married couples rather than the State or its lackeys can determine the responsibility of each family." Indeed, almost immediately he contrasts Margaret Sanger favorably to Malthus and to the Ford and Rockefeller foundations (because of the former's concern for family welfare rather than national economic welfare), and expresses concern over society's rapid transition from prohibition of contraception not only to tolerance of it but "for the first time in the history of western civilization . . . to State *contraceptive policy.*"

Noting the U.S. government's interest in giving aid for population control, he raises a pair of questions often heard in Latin America: "What moved President Johnson to take this step, and why is Latin America its principal object?"[11] A partial answer is not long in coming: "The U.S. has sent to our countries its contraceptive brigades for the same reason that imperial Rome sent its legions into those nations in its sphere of influence . . . at the request of certain leaders of these nations."[12] Vergara thus identifies his dual fears of contraceptive coercion from without and contraceptive coercion from within the nation. Ex-President Lleras Camargo, because of his testimony to the Greuning committee and his statements to the Pan-American Assembly, is established as the principal "quisling,"[13] with Dr. Herman Mendoza and the Colombian Association of Medical Schools identified as the detailed architects of treachery.

The willingness of the distinguished nationals to be used in such a manner is never entirely explained, though the alleged anti-Catholicism of certain liberal party members, and the "true necessity in these countries . . . to earn dollars" provide part of the answer. His principal explicit charge against the national groups is deception—they claim to be scientific when they are political, they claim to be local when they are in essence foreign, they claim to be educational when they are service organizations, and they claim to be working with the church when they are anticlerical. The first two points merit further elaboration.

An interesting and crucial aspect of Vergara's argument concerns the role of scientific research. He maintains that the population problem "has not originated in studies done in Colombia" and that it "is not a problem discovered by men of science." [14] These asseverations are especially striking in the light of the fact that the Colombian movement has from its inception been sponsored by the Colombian Association of Medical Schools, an organization which has insisted on its almost exclusive interest in research and education on family planning.[15] Vergara argues that the association has consistently misused science for its own ends. He claims that the names of such disciplines as demography and sociology are used to account for actions "which have their true origin in political considerations." Whereas the family planners have argued that demographic data prove the need for population control, Vergara argues that the demographic statistics are so poor that they cannot prove anything. He speaks of "doctors turned demographers [*habiltados*]" and cites Lleras Camargo, "the trustee of the Rockefeller Foundation," as suggesting the establishment of Colombian demographic centers "to apply to our own national circumstances . . . such information as we are receiving from private agencies all over the world and especially from the U.S." [16]

When Dr. Mendoza states that it has been established as a fact that family planning prevents abortions, Vergara charges that Mendoza has been subject to biased foreign literature "with no adherence to the requirements of a truly scientific literature" [17] and cites his own foreign authorities (taken from the Greuning hearings) to demonstrate the contrary. He names and indicts the foreign advisers used by the association and in a special appendix exposes their use of psychological principles to manipulate public opinion.

This brings us to one of his most basic fears—that the philosophy, motivation, and strategy for the movement is essentially *alien.* Borrowing a phrase from Lleras Camargo describing Colombia as a nation "racially mixed and tropical," he says that "the least that could be required for a demographic policy would be that it be structured by experts who are racially mixed, tropical, and accustomed to the Catholic environment." [18] Instead, he finds "quislings" structuring it. The explanation for this peculiar kind of imperialism is worthy of a psychiatrist: it is the product of a conflict between North America's "great passion for democracy" and "the felt need for the white, non-Catholic privileged sectors of the highly developed temperate zone to slow down—or end, who knows—the procreation of racially mixed, tropical and Catholic Latin Americans." [19] This conflict is resolved by what Vergara terms "the etiquette of democracy, the invasion of the Latin American continent at the request of the most outstanding spokesman of Latin America." [20]

Underlying the anger and the revulsion at the deception and treachery of one's compatriots who sell out to the enemy lies perhaps the greatest fear of all—the fear of extinction by a clever and powerful foe. Perhaps this is the meaning of the book's title, which refers to a treacherous and lecherous Greek who tried to murder his child, but who was fated to die by the hand of that very son.

EL SALVADOR: ALTAMIRANO REVISITED

The years have dulled the sharpness of neither pencil nor tongue of Latin America's most articulate pronatalist, Napoleon Viera Altamirano. In our earlier exegesis of his editorials appearing in El Salvador's *Diario de Hoy* between 1962 and 1964, we described his mystique concerning Latin America's population growth and his charges of racial genocide leveled against North American family planners.[21]

Since these editorials of the early 1960s, when a fight against birth control in Latin America could only be described as quixotic, much has happened. The U.S. and various international agencies have declared themselves in favor of family planning technical assistance; governments, even in Central America, have instituted family planning programs; and well-financed private programs have emerged in virtually every Latin American nation, including an especially vigorous one in El Salvador. In response, Altamirano has not slowed down the velocity of his fire. In a thirty-three-month period beginning in mid-1965, no less than fifty-one of his editorials on population have come to our attention. Scarcely a month goes by without at least one editorial, and in several months there have been one or more per week.

The substance of these editorials has changed in only subtle ways. Slightly shaken (it provoked three consecutive editorials) by Lleras Camargo's flat advocacy of birth control in mid-1965, he reminded Colombia's ex-President that the continent could easily host two or three billion inhabitants and warned him that even serious problems would not warrant "converting the American mother's womb into a slaughter-house or latrine." [22]

Altamirano's identification of population growth and nationalism continues to be a dominant theme. A heady mix of Juan Bautista Alberdi's demographic slogan with one of Altamirano's favorite biological metaphors produces the following: "To populate still means to civilize, the only difference being that [in this century] the population still needed to civilize America should emerge vigorous and pulsating from the womb of [Latin] American mothers." [23] So vital a force is population growth that its antonym (birth control) is death's synonym: "When we achieve the demographic density of the great European powers, we shall see if the threat of poverty allows no alternative to suicide." [24]

Little wonder that Altamirano can refer to Lleras's position as one of "extreme pessimism" when his own approaches ethereal optimism:

> The sea is yielding herself to us like a virgin land that once offered herself as a path to unknown territories and fabulous resources. Technology makes of every inch of land a source of riches. Where a tree cannot grow, something else is produced for man. The craggy mountain peak becomes a site to store the water or snow which produces the electricity which in the hands of man will make bread fall from heaven . . . yielding sustenance for all.[25]

Five years ago such optimism was typical of the Latin American intellectual and even, to a lesser extent, of the international agencies. In the past few years, however, Altamirano has had to deal with a growing number of agencies such as "the FAO, the UNICEF, and even the UNESCO and the OAS, entering the movement under the supreme command of the U.N., spreading the crass error that our population growth is falling behind the increase in food production." [26] His charges against the international organizations soon became more specific, and the new year of 1967 was ushered in with an editorial entitled "Both UNESCO and the FAO in the Racist Plot." It should not be thought, however, that the plot is restricted to the European and North American organizations typically the target of Altamirano's ire. In condemning demography as a new profession created "to manipulate statistics to prove that the whirlpool of population growth requires birth control," he jabs quickly at the Economic Commission of Latin America (ECLA).[27] In other editorials he adds the Inter-American Committee on the Alliance for Progress (CIAP),[28] the Pan American Health Organization, and the Latin American Center of Demography (CELADE), which he terms a "Genocidal Center."[29]

Indeed, there are few institutions or classes of people which are exempt from attack. In one editorial he attacks "leader classes, academicians, thinkers and statesmen";[30] and when one hundred Nobel Prize winners called attention to the population problem, the scientists were likened to "monstrous mathematical animals . . . the same scientists who gave us the dreadful arms for nuclear war." [31]

Even the church cannot remain entirely without suspicion. In a critical editorial devoted to the September 1965 statement of Cardinal Suenens, Altamirano warns darkly that "today there are ideological currents deliberately aimed at destroying the spiritual power of the Church." [32] Soon he is hinting more darkly still at infiltration: "The great fallacious and deceiving argument that demographic growth lags behind economic growth has already been accepted by the Alliance for Progress and *some sectors of the Church,* as desired by the non-Catholic racists." [33] [Italics added.] In disparaging the argument that slowing population growth will improve income distributions, he contemptuously attributes it to "CEPAL, Moscow, Washington, *Rome,* Peking, and Havana." [34] [Italics added.] The changes in the church are so incomprehensible they can only be attributed to evil forces. He admits he witnessed "with stupefaction" how a South American Cardinal during the last ecumenical council "referred with disrespect and blasphemy to the dogma of the Virgin Mary," and announces forthrightly the source of "the enemies without and the traitors within": it is no less than a Communist conspiracy. ". . . the Marxist circles, assured that the Church would fall, little by little, into their hands, . . . tried to carry the socialist ideology

to the encyclicals, pressuring for all possible agrarian reforms . . .
their conspiracy against clerical celibacy. . . . In Colombia Camilo
Torres soon appeared . . . then to join the criminal communist
gangs." [35]

The reader may have noted a not infrequent reference to a "racist
plot," a plot which lies at the heart of Altamirano's crusade, "a vast
racist communist and imperialistic conspiracy . . . to socialize, depopulate and de-Catholicize us." The latter phrase is frequently used
in the editorials and provides a useful point of departure for explica-
tion of his position. Let us consider each of its three terms.

§ SOCIALISM

The Marxist infiltration of the church is one small piece of a much
grander design. Altamirano sees a "multi-continental, world-wide"
effort to "take-over." He sees the UN "plagued with agents of international leftism" [36] and the FAO "falling into the hands of activists
of the socialist left." [37] Naturally, hemispheric institutions have been
included. The Alliance for Progress, he feels, has felt the "lethal leftist
influence" from its inception and has been moving farther and farther
toward destroying freedom in Latin America.[38] The Economic Commission for Latin America is clearly under the influence of socialist
economists.

§ DEPOPULATION

The effort to depopulate Latin America is a part of the socialist
conspiracy. The link is on occasion explicitly established.

> Not only was it necessary to check demographic growth by birth control,
> but structural reforms were imposed in order to guarantee a better distribu-
> tion of wealth making possible a true social justice. In other words the
> constructive work which the FAO could do was converted into a socialist
> and Malthusian promotion.[39]

Or again:

> . . . the leftists not only are trying to check our social development,
> socializing and regimenting us prematurely, but also holding back our
> population growth.[40]

At the same time, however, and sometimes in the same editorial,
Altamirano can attribute the plot or its financing to "industrial

interests of a certain medical kind."[41] Equally unusual for a socialist plot is its success "thanks to the resources made available as much by the U.S. government as by the contraceptive firms"[42] or to financing "by racists from the United States and Nordic Europe."[43]

At any rate, there is no doubt that the United States is directly implicated, though it is not singled out for attack as often as in earlier years. Outside of its financial backing, it is usually grouped with other Nordics, Europeans, or "many people" who feel that there are too many "negros, indians, mulatos, and mestizos," and are attempting to prevent "the Central-American man from taking firm possession of his land."[44]

§ DECATHOLIZATION AND THE FERTILITY MYSTIQUE

If the Latin man is the ultimate target of this foreign attack, the Latin woman is the medium. Altamirano's view of woman is in the tradition of conservative Catholicism notable in an encyclical of Pope Paul. Altamirano refers to "the blessed womb of the Central American woman" from which "millions more beings will come to fill the cities."[45] To stop such prolificity would be to stop nature, so that birth control assumes "proportions of genocide in the very maternal cloister of our America."[46] In attacking those who would substitute birth control for abortion, he shows his revulsion for sins of the flesh: "Why should the poor woman have to be taught to sin without conceiving."[47] The sexual freedom it might bring the woman would be intolerable, as "The mother becomes sterile at will."[48] He sees American women "colored, mestizo, indian, mulato, etc." being used in Brazil as "guinea pigs to try out the best methods to check the growth of these peoples";[49] and 40,000 Colombian women "submitting for over two years, to a process of sterilization with chemical contraceptives . . . financed by North American firms and possibly with the approval of Alliance functionaries."[50] The fertility mystique and fears of socialism blend nicely in his phrase "regimentation of the womb." His concern over depopulation and his fertility mystique are also blended in the affirmation "a people's will to grow is as authentic as its wish to live, because it is the will to power, a will stemming from the very wellspring of life."[51]

Increasingly, one gets the impression that Altamirano is beleaguered by the growing shift of public opinion away from his nineteenth century view of capitalism, Catholicism, and motherhood.

"Not a single month passes," he complained recently, "without a conference being held in some South or Central American capital, which under the pretext of christianizing the family, poses the population problem;" [52] and as early as 1965 he noted that "Hardly a week passes without some newspaper, magazine, radio or T.V. program inundating us with alarmist messages on the danger of population growth." [53]

Are there any signs of change? Perhaps the tiniest of cracks appear in two editorials. In one, he admits that "if the present rate of increase in the underdeveloped countries continues, humanity would be approaching the limits of subsistance," but goes on to say the present problem is *depopulation.*[54] More recently he even admits the right of parents to choose their own kind of family (even one composed of children "deformed by thalidomide") and of the state to decide "if the nation should cease to grow or even decline," but of course he goes on to say the opposite course would be both appropriate and noble.[55]

On the whole, however, the major changes seem to be an increasing defensiveness and a toning down of the earlier lusty accusations of national castration and womb defiling. More accurately, the changes have been less with Altamirano than with the world around him, leaving the sound of his voice increasingly hollow. Although the modern world may in fact be engulfing Altamirano, one sees the philosophy of this would-be superego of Latin America sinking slowly into the culture's collective unconscious—becoming a part of age-old repressed horrors, bits of which occasionally appear in dreams.

NOTES

1. *I—Seminario Nacional de Población y Desarollo* (Lima: Centro de Estudios de Población y Desarollo, 1966), p. xxxiii.

2. *Ibid.,* p. 367.

3. Feliz V. Cruzat Alegre, *Control de la Natalidad o Neo-Fascismo?* (Lima: Talleres Gráficos, 1967), p. 40.

4. *Ibid.,* p. 15.

5. *Ibid.,* p. 29.

6. *Ibid.,* p. 35.

7. *Ibid.,* p. 30.

8. *Ibid.,* p. 36.

9. *Ibid.,* p. 36.

10. Hernán Vergara, *El Complejo de Layo* (Bogotá: Tercer Mundo, 1968).

11. *Ibid.,* p. 18.

12. *Ibid.,* p. 20.

13. Frequent citations from J. M. Stycos ("a Northamerican personality as involved as anyone could be in the strategy of this assault on a continent") are used to verify the key nature of Lleras's role.

14. Vergara, *op. cit.,* p. 97.

15. That there is some substance to this claim is indicated by the association's recent publication of two large volumes of original research, a productivity record much larger than any comparable organization in the Western Hemisphere.

16. Vergara, *op. cit.,* p. 100.

17. *Ibid.,* p. 75.

18. *Ibid.,* p. 100.

19. *Ibid.,* p. 102.

20. *Ibid.,* p. 103.

21. See "Latin American Intellectuals and the Population Problem," in J. M. Stycos, *Human Fertility in Latin America* (Ithaca, N.Y.: Cornell University Press, 1968). While most of the editorials cited here are unsigned, we have, for reasons of style and their editorial position, attributed them to Altamirano. All references refer to *El Diario de Hoy,* whose circulation is 56,000 daily and 80,000 on Sunday.

22. "También Lleras Camargo contra la madre y el niño," Aug. 9, 10, 1965.

23. "La campaña mundial a favor de la natalidad," Sept. 23, 1965.

24. "Asamblea adversa control de natalidad," Nov. 15, 1965.

25. "La explosión demográfica y la conspiración racista," Jan. 13, 1966.

26. "La campaña racista del control de la natalidad," Feb. 23, 1966.

27. "La campaña mundial a favor de la natalidad," Sept. 17, 1965.

28. "También nos será impuesto el control de natalidad," Feb. 11, 1968.

29. "Reunión en Puerto España para activar el control de la natalidad," Nov. 11, 1967.

30. "El seminario anti-cristiano en Tegucigalpa," June 13, 1966.

31. "Cién bárbaros Nobel ante su Santidad," July 16, 1965.

32. "El daltonismo axiológico del Cardinal Suenens," Oct. 12, 1965.

33. "Las falacias económicas de los racistas," Sept. 9, 1967.

34. *Ibid.*

35. "Piden supresión de leyes contra el aborto," Sept. 11, 1967.

36. "Como la UNESCO, tambien la FAO en el complot racista," June 16, 1967.

37. "La FAO al servicio de la conspiración racista," Apr. 11, 1967.

38. "La campaña racista del control de la natalidad," Feb. 23, 1966.

39. "El pretexto del hambre en la conspiración racista," Apr. 14, 1967.
40. "¿Contra el hambre o contra el hombre?" Mar. 28, 1965.
41. "Reunion en Puerto Espagña," Nov. 11, 1967.
42. "Gobierno adversa control de natalidad," Dec. 2, 1967.
43. "Genocidio malthusiano de mujeres en Brasil," July 13, 1967.
44. "Gobierno adversa control de natalidad," Dec. 2, 1965.
45. "La santa misión de uñir pueblos," Sept. 15, 1966.
46. "Genocidio malthusiano de mujeres en Brasil," July 13, 1967.
47. *Ibid.*
48. "Cien bárbaros Nobel ante su Santidad," July 16, 1965.
49. "Genocidio malthusiano de mujeres en Brasil," July 13, 1967.
50. "Esterilizan a 40 mil mujeres Colombianas," Feb. 21, 1967.
51. "El deber de poblar y el derecho de dejar nacer," Feb. 11, 1968.
52. "Para el año dos mil todos viviremos en las ciudades," Sept. 12, 1967.
53. "Gobierno adversa control de natalidad," Dec. 2, 1965.
54. "La campaña racista del control de la natalidad," Feb. 23, 1966.
55. "El deber de poblar y el derecho de dejar nacer," Feb. 11, 1968.

CHAPTER 5

Nationalism— A Broader View

The cases we have presented are somewhat extreme examples of points of view which are by no means untypical in Latin America, a region composed of both large and small nations in a huge continent. The continent is so poor in capital and technology, it is little wonder that Latin Americans have often looked to their human capital as a source of power and prestige. "Population is a factor of power," writes a Venezuelan newspaper, "not only from the economic but especially from the geopolitical point of view."[1] The notion of a large and densely settled population is closely identified with the concept of the ideal state: "Three million square kilometers with 20 million people are a landscape, a country; but a hundred million people in the same area are a Nation."[2]

In a continent with many small states, each state becomes especially concerned about his neighbor's power and population, not only because the two are seen as related, but because each may lead to a need for *Lebensraum*. Thus the Caracas Chamber of Commerce, in maintaining that there is neither "overpopulation nor demographic explosion in Venezuela," noted uneasily that "we are a nation bordering a Colombia twice our size and a Brazil immense in population."[3]

One of the clearest instances of the population-power concept is provided by the island of Hispaniola, where Haitians and Dominicans live side by side in mutual fear. In May of 1968 the Dominican National Frontier Council, concerned with defense and development of the territories bordering on Haiti, declared itself opposed to family planning. "We should not control our fertility," announced its president, Carlos Sánchez y Sánchez, "when we have neighbors with a larger population who do precisely the contrary." [4] Sánchez was immediately answered by a Dominican priest, Dr. Priamo Tejeda, who maintained that depriving people of family planning information because of the needs for frontier population would constitute coercion on the part of the state;[5] and by Dr. Orestes Cucurullo, head of the Family Planning Association, who argued that while Haiti's population would double in thirty-one years, the Dominican Republic's would double in twenty.[6] In reply, Sánchez expanded his arguments. He cited the writings of Haitian intellectuals to prove their intention to solve Haiti's population problem by territorial expansion. "Our gravest danger," he said, "is in pacific invasion; . . . from a numerous and desperate population to one which is less densely settled." He forecasted Haiti's five millions of people increasing to forty million in a hundred years and asks what could hold back "that black sea which advances in a direction opposite to the path of the sun." The consequences of birth control would be "suicide, or resort to inhuman and uncivilized measures, or war." What about the Dominican population? "Since we have two-thirds more territory than Haiti," he maintains, "we have a right to have two-thirds more population than they." [7]

Hopefully Sánchez was reassured by data provided a week later by demographer Hernando Pérez Montás, who pointed out that in only a decade or two the Dominican population would equal Haiti's, that Haiti's rate of growth was much slower than the Dominican Republic's, and that "with or without family planning, the Dominican population would grow to 10 or 12 millions in about 33 years." [8]

While Sánchez was digesting the futuristic information, the Frontier Council's secretary, Dr. Gustavo Turull, resorted to historical documentation. "From the seventeenth century," he announced grandly but vaguely, "economists have held that a nation's wealth is in proportion to its population density." [9] Another member of the Council, in a television presentation, announced that "what we need on the frontier is people, more people, and overpopulation." [10] As of September 1968, Sánchez was still making headlines by referring to the danger of "biological conquest" by the Haitians and the necessity of "creating a biological conscience in the frontier zone, increasing the population in order to serve as a barrier to the Haitian exodus." [11] In case there were any doubts, Sánchez disassociated his views from "the theological question." "Our opinion," he said, "is from the nationalistic point of view." [12]

BUSINESS AND LABOR

Another source of pronatalist fervor is the world of big business, which often sees people as the very fuel of industry—its consumers on the one hand and the source of cheap labor on the other. At its eleventh Plenary Meeting in Mexico City in 1966, the Inter-American Council for Commerce and Production concluded coolly that "Population increase must be accepted as a legitimate and welcome price for improvement in sanitary and living conditions." [13] Other spokesmen for business have been less subtle. "If we adopt birth control what would happen," asks a Chilean "to industries making sheet glass or socks if the market became saturated and there was nobody more to sell to?" [14] "A developing country," says the vice-president of Peru's Society of Industries, "needs more and more labor supply (*brazos*). . . . an economic policy must be adopted which will permit the private sector to create the industries in which Peruvians can find productive and well-compensated employment." [15] "If birth control is used," according to a Dominican, "potential consumers will be reduced, slowing industrial development." [16] "Radical opposition to any birth control policies" has been proclaimed by the Venezuelan Federation of Chambers of Commerce. In its place they recommended "producing more, fighting for optimum productivity, laboring tirelessly for the expansion of consumption." [17] "Only the lower class reproduces," writes a Brazilian. "Office workers are perhaps not aware that these men are offering a great contribution to the nation—two Brazilians per couple per year, one in January and one in December." (While the reproductive burden on the proletariat might be thought to be lessened by birth control, the writer believes this would be even more burdensome. "I believe it to be immoral," he continues, "to advise a creature of that species to practice birth control . . . to men who do nothing more than work and sleep. They are like the lilies of the field and the birds of the heavens . . . they are born, grow, and reproduce, having faith that God will give them clothing in conformity with the cold." [18])

While it might be expected that organized labor take a dim view of this lilies and birds view of their existence, they have shown little appreciation of the relation of family planning to their own well-being. Compared with the trade union movement in other parts of the world, most Latin American unions have been, in fact, quite conservative. The Christian labor movements, indeed, have taken positions as militantly pronatalist as big business. Thus, the Central Unica de Trabajadores (CUT) of Chile "irrevocably rejected birth control programs designed to retard the transformation of Latin American social and economic structures. . . . Unexploited natural resources abound in Latin America and population density is low." [19] The Costa Rican Federation of Christian Rural Workers recently announced that "our workers should not seek the solution to their economic and social problems in birth control, but in organizing themselves for better salaries and living conditions. . . . as the "party" of the poor, we will not permit sterilization of the wombs of our women." [20] The executive secretary of the Latin American Trade Union Confederation told the 1967 OAS population conference that "for us there is not a single Latin American too many; on the contrary, many millions more are needed. And this should not be viewed as a lyrical expression. . . ." [21]

If business interests in Latin America have in fact been pronatalist, this is a characteristic often conveniently overlooked by its opponents, who find it embarrassing to agree with capitalists on *anything*. As a consequence, a few ingenious reasons have been developed to account for an alleged capitalistic *antinatalism*. A good example is provided by the Peruvian APRISTA leader and University Rector, Luis Alberto Sánchez, who maintains that the "individuals most interested in birth control are the large landowners and proprietors, and the most backward capitalists." [22] He argues that the relentless demands for consumption on the part of growing populations would compel the capitalist to share his wealth rather than increase it, thus motivating him to promote family planning so "that the number of consumers not be increased . . . sharing the wealth [and] . . . breaking the monopolies." [23]

(The notion that the capitalists are reluctant to share their wealth with the poor is not limited to the left, and was most effectively utilized in Paul VI's United Nations message suggesting that the wealthy nations increase the food at life's table rather than reduce the number of guests.)

Another direct link to capitalism is seen through the contraceptive industry. In a twelve-page postencyclical special captioned "The Pill," Peru's *Crónica* carried a picture of an imposing oil-well derrick. The caption beneath reads "The pill yields more than the profits of Standard Oil." [24] As if this was not power enough, Peruvian Archbishop Luis Bambaren subsequently charged that "powerful producers of contraceptives have infiltrated the ranks of the church. . . . even priests have fallen, converted into their unwitting agents." [25] Finally, not only do the underdeveloped countries become the new huge market place for pills, but they are subjected to the indignity of "being converted into the laboratories of the favored nations." [26]

DENSITY AND OPTIMISM

Most Latin American intellectuals regard Malthusian pessimism as alien and incomprehensible. Far from fearing that population growth may outstrip resources, they see their natural resources as unexploited because of a scarcity of people; or at the very least they can see no cause for alarm. The relation of density to feelings of optimism can be observed in such statements as:

· Mexico can sustain a population three or four times its present size.[27]
· Peru can easily house 100 million inhabitants.[28]
· If all the populations of Latin America and Africa would go and live in Argentina, demographic density would still be below that of India today.[29]
· England and Belgium would fit perfectly within the territory of Peru.[30]
· We need not be concerned since Guatemala continues to be an under-populated people.[31]
· The Dominican Republic can absorb perfectly more than ten million more people than we now have.[32]

The notion that Latin America can support such population increases stems not only from a comparison of its population density with that of Europe and Asia, but from a boundless optimism in the huge potential of Latin America's natural resources—an optimism based more on nationalism than on a realistic appraisal of the immediate exploitability of these resources. As expressed by a Colombian journalist, "We live on an immense papaya, on top of a gigantic *arepa*. . . . the land we inhabit is pure food. . . . food for a million times more people than we have now."[33]

The great nationalist mystique, most clearly seen in the case of Brazil, is one of a vast population cultivating and exploiting vast areas of uninhabited land and vast quantities of natural resources. The *falta de bracos* theme and the efforts to promote a *marcha para oeste* all had parallels in the United States during earlier periods. The essential differences lie in the shrinking of the world markets, the relative absence of capital and skills in contemporary Latin America, and the phenomenal rates of population increase due to *natural* increase rather than to migration. But the failure of many Latins to recognize the economic and social costs of rapid population growth stems from more than nationalism—it has been due to an absence of reliable statistics on the one hand and the failure of relevant professionals to attend to this problem on the other.

THE SOCIAL SCIENTISTS

We have discussed elsewhere the inadequacies of census and vital statistics in Latin America.[34] But even organizations deeply involved in the analysis of economic and social statistics, such as the Economic Commission of Latin America, have been so concerned with grinding other axes, such as the Common Market, that they have chosen to play down population growth as a problem. Each lobby group, whether advocating land reform, infrastructure development, community development, or free trade, has tried simultaneously to play down population and play up its particular approach.

"If all the coffee, cacao, sugar, bananas, and other crops that can be produced by the Latin American farmer could be sold," writes the agricultural expert, "rapid population increase would represent an additional factor of progress."[35] "It's often a deception to seek the causes of rural poverty in the population explosion," writes the sociologist. "The mal-adaptation of agrarian structures constitutes the most decisive factor in emigration to the cities. . . ."[36] "If it only could be utilized," writes the economist, "the high rate of increase of the young labor force could result in a rapid transformation of the economy." [37] "We must not succumb to 'demographic fatalism,'" writes an expert on banking, "since the interaction of technology and social institutional changes will bring about an increase in the productivity of capital sufficient to overcome the initial population pressures." [38]

The more conservative and nationalistic social scientists, moreover, are concerned about the moral and cultural implications of population control. A good inventory of their fears is given in a publication of the Jesuit-related Research and Social Action Center of Bogotá:

Progressive aging of the population; disturbance of the economic and demographic equilibrium; traumas due to the brusque change of norms; decrease in the number of deliberately large families; contagious devaluation of paternity and maternity; secret hostility against life; serious errors over the meaning of marriage, love and sex; development of individual and collective egotism; constant evasion of the spirit of sacrifice, initiative and responsibility; abdication of the educational duties of parents.[39]

If these are the social consequences, the economic advantages of family planning would have to be rather imposing to offset them. But while each of the social science professions has been lobbying for its particular point of view, *there have been virtually no demographers* to lobby for the importance of population variables,[40] and the planning boards which emerged as a result of the Alliance for Progress failed to hire the few that exist. As a result, many planners are still ignoring the implication of population growth. "Our country," announces Peru's Planning Institute director, "doesn't need birth control since it is rich enough to face the growth in numbers by means of marshalling all its sources of natural resources." [41] "Planners have been reluctant to recommend [population] goals," writes an analyst of the Caribbean situation. "They have been content to cite the likely resources to be required by various rates of population increase." [42] Commenting more broadly on the state of Latin American planning, Luis Escobar of the World Bank states, "It is not easy for social scientists and policy makers in the United States and Europe to understand the difficulties which their Latin American counterparts face in recognizing the existence of a demographic problem. . . ." [43]

On the whole it is probably safe to say that planners have been closely associated with a position attributed to the socialists by the Yugoslavian demographer, Vogelnik: "You capitalists," he said in the United Nations Population Commission, ". . . want to plan the population in order to adapt it to the defects of the economy; we, on the contrary, wish to adapt the economy to the population."[44] But perhaps the planner's state of mind was most faithfully analyzed by a former Prime Minister of Jamaica, who said: "I have been a Socialist all my life, but I think birth control is best left to private enterprise."[45]

THE MEDICAL PROFESSION

If the planners have not fully faced the issue, what about the doctors? The history of the birth control movement in the United States and England shows that the doctors were always cool to, if not downright opposed to, the dispersion of family planning beyond their private practices. The medical profession has always been socially, ethically, and economically conservative, and in the days of family planning's infancy, the subject was ethically questionable, socially dubious, and economically impracticable. In Latin America there is no shortage of physicians who would fit such descriptions. Certainly up until the early 1960s the characteristic attitude was that birth control was not a medical problem, since the physician's task was to save lives, not prevent them. "Should we then," writes Dr. Abraam Sonis, "invest in maternal and child services to reduce death rates, and simultaneously invest in a campaign to prevent more children from being born? To write with one hand and erase with the other, to dissipate our efforts by working toward contradictory ends?"[46] Physicians, too, have given freely their "medical opinions" on the dangers of contraception, ranging from such statements as "Women who take contraceptive pills undergo psychosis in almost 90 percent of the cases,"[47] to the allegation that by practicing birth control we may be "limiting the possibility of variation, that is to say evolution, thus checking progress toward a superior Man."[48] In Brazil, the Medical Association of Guanabara declared that oral contraception was contrary to "the normal function of the hypofisis and the ovaries, altering the sexual physiology of the female and the pharacological bases of human therapy, producing serious and frequent complications such as multiple births and monsters, liver damage, pulmonary embolism, coronary thrombosis, and cancer of the uterus. The IUD causes . . . repeated abortions, perforations of the uterus and tubal complications . . . with grave danger to life."[49]

While physicians regarded birth control as within their professional province, they did not regard the *population problem* as a health problem. Thus, while they freely prescribed contraceptives for the *convenience* of their middle class patients, they never conceived of a public contraceptive program as pertinent to national problems of health. Moreover, if the economists were not convinced that birth control was related to economic development, the physicians could hardly be expected to foster medical programs toward *that* end. Thus, Peru's Minister of Health, a day after signing an agreement for a large national family planning program within his Ministry, could cheerfully announce that "birth control was not justified in Peru given its [low] density. . . . on the contrary a larger population was necessary to exploit the nation's great riches." [50] In addition, while physicians could accept the popularity of contraception among the middle class, they saw no demand for services on the part of the lower class and viewed the fact of their prolificity as proof of their desire for large families. This combination of doubts and beliefs on the part of the medical profession was succinctly expressed by Chile's Minister of Health: ". . . the seemingly specific remedy of restriction of the birth rate would have little importance as an instrument of development. . . . I have plainly expressed our doubts. Doubts as to the advantage . . . of a policy of reduction of the population growth in connection with raising the per-capita income; doubts as to the efficacy of the instrument of family planning to secure a reduction of the birth rate." [51]

Thus, while the economists were busy saying that birth control was not related to economic development, the physicians were busily adding that it was not related to health either. Only when they began to see it as a medical and social problem did they begin to change. The change occurred largely because of the increasing evidence that induced abortion, clearly a medical problem, was becoming of epidemic proportions—an incidence not only taxing hospital facilities but demonstrating a demand on the part of the lower classes for fertility control. [52]

In the early 1960s studies by Chilean public health physicians showed that four out of every ten admissions to Santiago's emergency services were abortion complications, that one out of every four women in the reproductive age group admitted an induced abortion, and that two out of every five maternal deaths were due to abortion. [53]

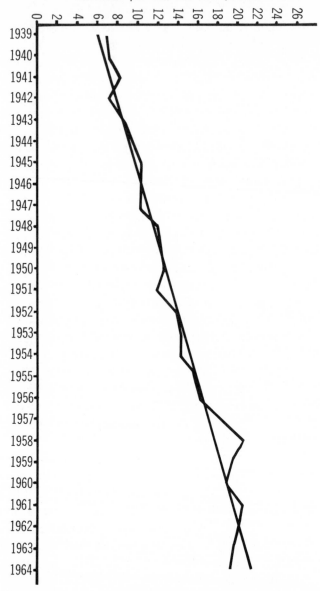

FIGURE 1.

Abortions per 100 patients attended in the Concepcion
Palacios Maternity Hospital, Caracas, Venezuela,
1939–1964. Source: L. A. Angulo-Arvelo, *Esquemas de
Demografia Medica* (Caracas: Universidad de Venezuela,
1968), p. 157.

68

Figure 1, from Venezuelan studies, is typical of the kind of data which began to be assembled for Latin American countries, demonstrating convincingly that birth control was indeed a health problem. Distinguished physicians, such as University del Valle's dean of medicine, could begin to insist that women "are earnestly looking to our profession for help. It is not a Catholic problem or a moral problem, or a political problem, *it is a health problem. Our people are asking the doctors for an answer.*" [54] [Italics added.] Once they could see human suffering, the physicians, unlike the economists, also recognized the cure and began to be impatient with the economic debates. Thus, Dr. Velásquez complained that "during the first five or six meetings of our group the specialists in other fields (planners, economists, and experts in urban development) were the ones who shrank from facing the need to study the problem. All the recommendations we heard were of an economic nature, and it was assumed that the rate of population growth would fall in line . . . perhaps by some miracle. . . ." [55]

So comfortable are the physicians with their new medical rationale, that they have dusted off and transformed their older folklore that birth control programs should not or cannot work. Now they often seem to be saying that birth control should not be used for any other reason than to prevent abortion, and that if it is used for abortion, it will not influence the birth rate.

In Chile, the following recorded message is intoned to potential family planning patients: "This instruction is given with the single aim of your never resorting to criminal abortion to limit your family." [56] If family planning is thus a lesser of two evils for the individual, its consequences at a national level could be even more pernicious if the sanctity of a high birth rate is generally accepted. Dr. Viel refers to "medical groups which base and justify their action on the fight against abortion, making clear that they will not affect the birth rate, since contraceptives will not influence the number of live births but only those pregnancies which would have terminated in abortion." [57] Chilean health authorities have been careful to point out that "inducing families to reduce their size is not a function of this information," [58] and the Minister of Health announced to a bewildered meeting of the International Planned Parenthood Federation that his extensive family planning program was "oriented solely to preventing and combatting criminal abortion" and that "raising the standard of living of the poor and educating the ignorant would produce lower birth rates without a program of contraception." The programmatic implications of such an ideology were made clear by the Minister: ". . . it is addressed to these groups exposed to the risk [of abortions], priority therefore being accorded to women attending for abortions, and to women who already have several children." [59]

NORTH AMERICAN MOTIVES AND POPULATION CONTROL

Given the failure on the part of the social scientists and the medical profession to perceive a population problem, the average intellectual or policy maker cannot be expected to be enthusiastic about programs of population control. "It is difficult to conceive how anyone in his right mind," writes an incredulous Peruvian to the editor of *La Prensa*, "could advocate birth control in a country like ours with immense areas without a single inhabitant." [60] Equally exasperated, Brazil's Cardinal Jaime de Barros Camara recently publicly praised an article in the Brazilian medical journal *General Pathology*, which termed the "pretense of a population explosion" as a "lie" and as "international blackmail." [61]

If there is no population problem and if national programs of family planning are not in Latin America's best interest, then why is the United States so vigorously advocating them?

• They want to prevent Latin America from becoming, because of its population, a power within the next 15 years. [62]
• What do the demographers and statisticians of the West fear? . . . By year 2000 if the Third World aligns itself with Communism, there will be over 5 billion inhabitants of Communist countries, and 1 billion, 200 million inhabitants of Capitalist countries. [63]
• The country to the North is in fear and panic at the demographic expansion of the nations in its economic sphere, since it realizes that they will some day seek their liberation on a basis of their human capital. [64]

Such extremist goals would clearly require extremist means. While Cruzat-Alegre saw the Americans killing off the Latins by their cigarettes, others see equally ingenious methods:

• To achieve their ends it is not enough to kill with napalm and missiles, but also with pills. [65]
• In order to win the war against poverty they will kill the poor. . . . educa-

tion for health has practically disappeared in rural areas. . . . deaths will increase and births decrease.[66]

Relatively few intellectuals, however, attribute such gross goals or such crude methods to the United States, a nation usually accorded more respect for the deviousness of its foreign policy. One more popular explanation imputes a kind of North American desperation at the failure of the Alliance for Progress. "Kennedy was assassinated," writes a Mexican journalist, "and all his good intentions were stalled. Then the Americans saw an easy way out—preventing the birth of more hungry people!"[67] This is probably the most frequently heard explanation among Latin American moderates and liberals, who see the North American's heavy commitments in space and in Vietnam compelling them to shop for $5 bargains in foreign aid.

As one moves farther to the left, the explanations gradually become more sinister, and North American efforts are viewed as a way of slowing down or stopping completely the tendencies for social reform or revolution; in short, a way of shoring up the status quo. To many Latin Americans, social justice is of equal or greater importance than economic progress. Thus land reform and redistribution of wealth are not only means to economic development, but are *social ends* which could be bypassed by the "panacea" of birth control. "The Malthusian approach to the demographic problem," says one commentator, "may adversely affect the solution of major problems of the region, including land reform, the improvement of export returns, and the full utilization of national resources. . . . If birth control should be presented as though it were a valid alternative to the badly needed structural reforms, [it could cause] irreparable harm to the movement for improving rural structure in Latin America."[68] Another form of this thesis argues that *population pressure itself* is necessary to effect the desired social reform. To remove the population pressure would also be tantamount therefore to preserving the status quo. Of the two evils, most Latins today would prefer the population pressure. Thus, Ambassador Tomić tells us that "the most efficient individual agent for modernization in Latin America is demographic pressure. . . . what would be the effect of reducing the pressure that demographic growth is exerting on semi-feudal and oligarchical structures of so many nations. . . . there is a real risk . . . in choosing as an alternative for Latin America the reduction of natality and the weakening of the pressure upon obsolete and inefficient social structures."[69]

CONCLUSIONS

Latin Americans of the left and right do not have a great deal in common, but fear and distrust of the United States is a not-uncommon theme anywhere in the political spectrum. In the absence of analyses of the causes and consequences of its rapid population growth, in the face of its vast uninhabited areas, and in the light of its general suspiciousness of United States motives, it is little wonder that much of Latin America is somewhat alarmed at North America's sudden interest in population planning and that the intensity of such feelings seem proportionate to the degree of nationalism. Under such circumstances, tact, patience, and careful study are necessary, along with the comforting realization that our greatest gift to Latin Americans may well be in the crystallization and maintenance of their nationalism.

NOTES

1. *Ultimas Noticias* (Caracas), May 12, 1967.
2. "La Argentina desde afuera," *El Mundo,* Dec. 30, 1962. Cited in Abraam Sonis's *Salud, Medicina y Desarrollo Económico-Social.*
3. *El Universal* (Caracas), Sept. 22, 1967.
4. *El Caribe* (Santo Domingo), May 24, 1968.
5. *Ibid.,* June 11, 1968.
6. *Ibid.,* June 12, 1968.
7. *Ibid.,* June 15, 1968.
8. *Ibid.,* June 25, 1968.
9. *Ibid.,* July 4, 1968.
10. *Ibid.,* July 6, 1968.
11. *Ibid.,* Sept. 6, 1968.
12. *Ibid.,* Aug. 2, 1968.
13. *How Low Income Countries Can Advance Their Own Growth,* Committee for Economic Development, New York, 1966.
14. Dr. Manuel Sanhueza, cited in *Crónica* (Concepción, Chile), Apr. 19, 1967.
15. Ing. Eduardo Dibós Chapuis, cited in *El Comercio* (Lima), Sept. 5, 1968.
16. Dr. Carlos Cornielle, cited in *El Caribe* (Santo Domingo), June 21, 1968.
17. *El Universal* (Caracas), Sept. 22, 1967.
18. Domingos Gusmâo de Lima, in *O Povo* (Fortaleza), Dec. 30, 1967. Cited in Herman Daly, "Economic Development and the Population Question in Northeast Brazil," *Revista Brasileira de Economia,* in press.

19. *Visión,* June 19, 1970.
20. *La Nación* (San José), Aug. 11, 1968.
21. Miguel Cardozo, *Los Trabajadores Latinoamericanos y la Política de Población,* Caracas, September 1967. (Mimeographed.)
22. L. A. Sánchez, "Urban Growth and the Latin American Heritage," in G. H. Beyer (ed.), *The Urban Explosion in Latin America* (Ithaca, N.Y.: Cornell University Press, 1967), p. 2.
23. *El Correo* (Lima), Oct. 11, 1967.
24. *La Crónica* (Lima), Aug. 16, 1968.
25. *La República* (Bogotá), Sept. 27, 1968.
26. Armand Mattelart, *El Reto Espiritual de la Explosión Demográfica* (Santiago: Editorial del Pacífico, 1965), p. 48.
27. G. P. Serrano, Mexico's ex-Secretary of Communications, *Diario de Centro América* (Guatemala City), July 30, 1968.
28. Presidents of Peru's Christian Family Movement. Cited in *La Crónica* (Lima), Aug. 16, 1968.
29. Radomiro Tomić, *Family Planning, Economic Development, Respect for the Human Person,* paper presented at Cornell University, November 1967. (Mimeographed.)
30. Editorial in *El Comercio* of Lima. Cited in *Presencia* (La Paz), Sept. 1, 1968.
31. *Diario de Centro América* (Guatemala City), July 30, 1968.
32. *El Caribe* (Santo Domingo), June 21, 1968.
33. *La Patria* (Manizales, Colombia), Aug. 18, 1965.
34. J. Mayone Stycos, *Human Fertility in Latin America* (Ithaca, N.Y.: Cornell University Press, 1968), pp. 33–38.
35. Remy and Freire, "Population Policy and Agricultural Development in Latin America," *Working Document for OAS Preparatory Seminar on Population and Development,* Jan. 31, 1967. (Mimeographed.)
36. Mattelart, *op. cit.,* p. 64.
37. "La Situación Demográfica en América Latina," *Boletín Económico de América Latina,* vol. VI, no. 2, October 1961. Cited in Sonis, *op. cit.,* p. 97.
38. Victor Urquidi, "Population Growth and Economic Development in Latin America," in *Proceedings of the 1965 World Population Conference* (New York: United Nations, 1967), vol. IV, p. 38.
39. *La Revolución Demográfica,* CIAS. (Bogotá: Tercer Mundo, 1966), p. 13.
40. Stycos, *op. cit.,* pp. 33–38.
41. Carlos Pestana, in *La Crónica* (Lima), Aug. 16, 1968.
42. Kent Earnhardt, *Politics and Population in the Caribbean,* in press.
43. Luis Escobar Cerda, "After Caracas: Problems and Perspectives," *Population Bulletin,* vol. XXIV, no. 1, February 1968.
44. Cited in Benjamín Viel, *La Explosión Demográfica* (Santiago: Universidad de Chile, 1966), p. 114.
45. Cited by Lord Caradon "Planned Parenthood . . . a Duty and a Human Right,"

in *Proceedings of the Eighth International Conference of the International Planned Parenthood Federation* (Hertford, England: Stephen Austin and Sons, 1967), p. 12.

46. Sonis, *op. cit.,* p. 91.

47. Dr. Luis Solis Salazar, cited in *La Crónica* (Lima), Aug. 1, 1968.

48. Dr. Alfredo Planchard, research chief of Venezuela's National Institute of Nutrition, cited in *Páginas* (Caracas), May 9, 1967.

49. *O Globo* (Rio de Janeiro), Mar. 9, 1968.

50. Cited in *El Universo* (Guayaquil), Aug. 3, 1968.

51. R. Valdivieso, "Opening Address," in *Proceedings of the Eighth International Conference of the International Planned Parenthood Federation,* p. 5.

52. The communication of such information among the medical community, the mobilization and precipitation of medical opinion, and the creation of organizational outlets for this concern were largely effected by the work of private organizations such as the International Planned Parenthood Federation and the Population Council.

53. See J. Mayone Stycos and Jorge Arias (eds.), *Population Dilemma in Latin America* (Washington: Potomac Books, 1966), pp. 237–240.

54. Gabriel Velásquez Palau, remarks cited in *Working Document Prepared by Secretariat,* appendix II, Organization of American States, August 1967. (Mimeographed.)

55. *Ibid.*

56. Reported by Thomas Sanders, "Family Planning in Chile: The Public Program," *American Universities Fieldstaff Reports,* vol. XIV, no. 4, December 1967.

57. Viel, *op. cit.,* p. 231.

58. Dr. José Ugarte Avendaño, *Posicion del Ministerio de Salud Pública frente a los Problemas de Población y Familia,* Apr. 21, 1966. (Mimeographed.)

59. Valdivieso, *op. cit.,* p. 3.

60. *La Prensa* (Lima), Apr. 24, 1967.

61. *O Globo* (Rio de Janeiro), Mar. 9, 1968.

62. Andres Nercau, Latin American Conference of Christian Labor Unions. Cited in *Ultimas Noticias* (Caracas), May 12, 1967.

63. *Novedades* (Managua), July 13, 1967.

64. Armando Tovar, president of the Peruvian Christian Family Movement. Cited in *El Commercio* (Lima), Feb. 8, 1968.

65. *Claridades* (Mexico, D.F.), May 13, 1967.

66. Mario Guzman, *Ultimas Noticias* (Caracas), Aug. 19, 1967.

67. Ulises Victoria, cited in *El Porvenir* (Monterrey), Apr. 4, 1967.

68. R. T. Freire, *op. cit.*

69. Tomić, *op. cit.*

CHAPTER 6

Churchmen

Prior to the 1960s, there was no militancy on the part of the Latin American hierarchy concerning family planning; indeed there was nothing resembling public church opinion on the subject. On the one hand the church had plenty of other things to worry about, such as illegitimacy, anticlericalism, a scarcity of priests, and poor attendance at church. On the other hand, the mass of the population knew little about birth control and less about its relevance to Catholicism. As an example, a 1967 survey of lower-class women in Santiago, Chile, disclosed that 54 percent did not know the church had a position on birth control and an additional 10 percent thought the church favored it.[1] In short, birth control was simply not an issue, and the church was hardly going to raise it.

Elsewhere in the hemisphere, church leaders were more articulate, but always in response to a public challenge. Early efforts in Puerto Rico to launch a federally supported birth control program were blocked by effective political pressures in Washington, and subsequent efforts by the insular government led to the formation of a Catholic political party and a bitter campaign based largely on the issue of family planning.[2] On the mainland, as late as 1959, the U.S. bishops used language which in Latin America is more characteristic

75

of the nationalist extremists. In an official statement they referred to the population explosion as a "terror technique phrase . . . a smoke screen behind which a moral evil may be foisted on the public." They referred to "hysterical terrorism and bland misrepresentation of data" and charged that to speak of a population explosion in the United States was "the sheerest kind of nonsense." [3] Surely there are cultural differences in degree of militancy between the Latin priest and his Irish-American counterpart, but the essential difference is this: *In North America the birth control issue was raised by non-Catholics and at a time when the church stand on birth control was clearly and unequivocally negative. In Latin America the issue was raised by Catholics and at a time when the church position had become unclear and ambiguous.* In the latter instance the period of church indecision was of sufficient length and permissiveness to allow public opinion to be wakened, never more to sleep.

PUBLIC OPINION

No soundings of public or private opinions prior to the 1960s with respect to family planning were taken in Latin America, other than in Puerto Rico. Our impression is that prior to the 1960s the mass media contained little information on population or family planning; that in the early 1960s it began to carry a good deal of information on the population problem, especially concerning non-Latin parts of the world; and that around the middle 1960s there was a marked increase in information on the population problem, on family planning, and on contraceptive techniques.

In 1965, when the Cornell International Population Program began to collect newspaper articles on population appearing in the Latin American press, we were astonished both at the absolute volume and at the increase over time. As an example, in 1965 we collected no less than 1,300 clippings on population and family planning from Mexico alone, a number which rose to 3,800 for the year 1967. The latter figure can be expressed as ten clippings for every day of the year, in the various newspapers of Mexico.

The church was in no small way responsible for these clippings. Indirectly, by announcing that the topic was under discussion at the Vatican, it opened the doors for discussion everywhere. What had been unequivocally wrong and therefore beyond discussion now might even be right, and was certainly worthy of discussion and debate. New contraceptive methods such as the oral progesterones, moreover, lent themselves much more easily to public discussion than had douches, diaphragms, condoms, and coitus interruptus. Further, the new methods seemed more "scientific." They worked in complex and mysterious ways, and the moral implications were not as clear to Catholics as had been the case with classical contraception. This gave ample opportunity for medical journalism, complete with photographs of white rats, white coats, white plastic, and white pills.

Most of all, however, the church itself was news. *Over a third of the nearly 15,000 clippings we received for 1965 and 1966 mentioned the Catholic Church,* ranging from 24 percent in Jamaica to 48 percent in Bolivia. No small part of these articles concerned an "impending decision" on the part of the Vatican, giving the whole issue a kind of cliff-hanging suspense which intensified its salience and whetted readers' appetites for more information on family planning. To better convey a sense of a drama which lasted for several years, we have chosen a period of a year and a half toward the beginning of the controversy and have selected representative headlines from the newspapers of Colombia, March 1965 to August 1966. While the headlines are unique, the stories are all UPI or AP releases which found their way into most of the newspapers of other nations. The headlines are listed in chronological order.[4]

PAUL VI MEETS WITH BIRTH CONTROL
   COMMISSION   *Vespertino*
CHURCH READY TO DECIDE ON BIRTH CONTROL
   Espectador
POPE URGES BIRTH CONTROL COMMISSION   *Pais*
PAUL VI TO REVISE TRADITIONAL BIRTH CONTROL
   CONCEPTS   *Espectador*
BIRTH CONTROL COMMISSION DIVIDED   *Tiempo*
DOCUMENT RELATED TO RESPONSIBLE
   PROCREATION UNDER REVISION   *Espectador*
PAUL VI SOON TO DECIDE BIRTH CONTROL
   QUESTION   *Patria*
POPE ANNOUNCED YESTERDAY DECISION SOON ON
   BIRTH CONTROL   *Espectador*
VATICAN AGAINST NEOMALTHUSIANISM   *Pais*

POPE TO MAKE BIRTH CONTROL DECLARATION
Occidente
PONTIFICAL BIRTH CONTROL COMMISSION
STYMIED   *Occidente*
COUNCIL CONDEMNS BIRTH CONTROL   *Diario*
CHURCH REJECTS BIRTH CONTROL   *Pais*
FINAL VOTE ON BIRTH CONTROL DECEMBER 4
Tiempo
POPE OPPOSES BIRTH CONTROL   *Tiempo*
POPE OPPOSES CONTRACEPTION   *Tiempo*
WILL BE DOCTRINAL CHANGE ON NATALITY
Occidente
TOMORROW DECISIVE VOTE ON BIRTH CONTROL
Tiempo
POPE REORGANIZED BIRTH CONTROL STUDY
COMMISSION   *Correo*
CHURCH MAINTAINS MATRIMONY AND NATALITY
DOCTRINE   *Siglo*
BELIEVE THERE WILL BE NO CHANGE IN CHURCH'S
POSITION   *Diario del Caribe*
BIRTH CONTROL COMMISSION MEETS IN VATICAN
Diario del Caribe
BIRTH CONTROL STUDY COMMISSION IN FINAL
STAGE   *Patria*
POPE WILL DECLARE HIMSELF ON BIRTH CONTROL
AT END OF MONTH   *Occidente*
POPE WILL SPEAK SOON ON BIRTH CONTROL
República
PROBABLE CHANGE IN CHURCH'S BIRTH CONTROL
ATTITUDE   *Diario*
BIRTH CONTROL COMMISSION INITIATES "FINAL
STUDY"   *Espectador*
LIMITED USE OF "PILL" RECOMMENDS PAPAL
COMMISSION   *Espectador*
NO OFFICIAL ANNOUNCEMENT ON
CONTRACEPTION   *Occidente*
POPE MEETS CONCERNING THE "PILL"   *Pais*
THIS WEEK PONTIFICAL REPORT ON
CONTRACEPTION TO BE RELEASED
Diario del Caribe

POPE REQUESTS CLARIFICATION OF BIRTH CONTROL
REPORT   *Pais*
POPE STUDYING BIRTH CONTROL DECISION
Occidente
PAUL VI MAY AUTHORIZE CONTRACEPTIVE PILL
Diario del Caribe
POPE MAY AUTHORIZE PILL TO CONTROL FEMININE
CYCLE   *Espectador*
NO ONE KNOWS PAPAL DECISION ON NATALITY
Occidente
CHURCH'S BIRTH CONTROL POSITION WILL NOT
CHANGE   *Patria*
POSSIBLE CHANGE IN BIRTH CONTROL   *Espectador*
PAUL VI AWAITS DIVINE INSPIRATION FOR
DECISION   *Occidente*

During the long period of Vatican vacillation, churchmen in Latin America could no longer afford to be entirely aloof to the problem. Church liberals, seeing a morally revolutionary and socially liberal issue on which they were backed by their parishioners, began to use it as part of the platform for church reform. Even conservatives could not ignore it, since they were dealing with an aroused public which expected concrete answers from its confessors. The urban population which reads the newspapers comprises disproportionally the population which attends mass, goes to confession, and contributes financially to the church. (In each of eight major Latin American cities, e.g., women who have completed primary school attend mass substantially more regularly than those who have not.[5]) Both within the privacy of the confessional and in more public situations, this concerned, articulate public kept asking a blunt, unambiguous question of its church, "May I use the pill *now*?" While history does not record the private answers, some of the public ones have been preserved. We have organized them into broad categories of liberal and conservative.

THE LIBERALS

The liberal clergy are those who wish both to see the church take a more active role in social problems and to reform Latin American social structures in order to effect a more equalitarian distribution of worldly goods and services. These priests tend to be young, in touch with their parishioners, and deeply concerned about the grinding poverty in Latin America. While some liberals (Don Helder Camara of Brazil is a good example) see the need for social reforms as so urgent that they refuse to be distracted by something called the "population problem," most of the liberals favor family planning and had hoped and expected a more liberal ruling from the Vatican. However, their primary rationale has rarely been the population problem in broad economic or demographic terms, but is more likely to have been related to problems of the family, especially at a level of enhancing social harmony within the family. In *A Regulação dos Nascimentos,* Father Calderon Beltrão cites Richard Fagley, "spokesman of the World Council of Churches," when he wishes to illustrate the "macrosociological" point of view and adds that any policy of population restriction is condemned; but in demonstrating the "social necessity for birth control" he explains that the "problem is not *primarily* of demographic-economic nature, but psychological, microsociological. . . ."[6]

Writing for a volume on the *Population Dilemma in Latin America,* Father Gustavo Pérez of Colombia never mentions population. Instead he stresses "the drama of millions of well-intentioned couples who find great difficulties in reconciling, within the framework of existing directives, the different ends of marriage, education of children, and mutual love. In innumerable cases, these difficulties are leading to conflict, perversion of conscience, abandonment of the Church, and a loss of harmony between the spouses."[7] When six Latin American priests attending the 1967 world conference of International Planned Parenthood discussed the role of the state in family planning, they noted that it had a *supplementary role* to play. Even here its ends were to assist the *family:* "The state has the obligation to formulate policies in matters of population, particularly in a continent in which the most dispossessed groups are unable, have no incentive or are prevented from adopting a responsible attitude toward procreation."[8]

With some of the clergy this kind of talk could be viewed as political—the rhetoric which they believe would have maximum impact on their peers. However, not only are the *private* opinions of liberal priests generally consistent with the "microdemographic" point of view, but public statements of other authorities make the division between micro and macro a decisive one.

A good example is provided by the Jesuit director of Colombia's Centro de Investigación y Acción Social. With an M.A. in economics from Columbia University and a doctorate in economics from the University of Paris, he can hardly have ignored the economic implications of population growth. Yet he looks at population control as follows:

> The implicit idea in the present neomalthusian strategy, financed from the United States, is the tacit recognition of the failure of the Alliance for Progress, and the abandonment of efforts for a real policy of socio-cultural change in Latin America. They are continually giving the impression that the Alliance . . . has failed and they want to replace it with contraceptives.[9]

Is Father Gonzalez an opponent of family planning? Not at all. He explains how the problem should be divided into its micro and macro elements:

> The reasoning of the pronatalists often is: "How can there be a reason for birth control in a country without over-population?" . . . they forget that the problem of birth control does not necessarily originate in population problems. On their part the neomalthusians state: "The existence of a population explosion in our country justifies family planning; and the State even has the right to impose birth control in the nation." . . . ignoring the question of whether other kinds of reasons justify it morally from the personal or family point of view.[10]

The most liberal and authoritative statement issued in Latin America originated with the bishops of Chile. As a group the most liberal hierarchy in Latin America, the Chilean bishops not only recognize the duality of familial and societal ends, but perceive a tight interdependence of the personal and social. They note that the perspective of Vatican II was not "exclusively familial but also referred to the demographic problem at a societal level. This interdependence between the levels . . . is also seen when marriage is studied not only in its isolated and individual expression but in its total relation to humanity. . . ."[11] This interdependence justifies the role of the state in what appears to be the most intimate and personal function of the family. In a crucial sentence drawing its spirit from *Populorum Progressio,* the bishops state:

> Church doctrine is aware that procreation belongs to the most private world of the human being . . . but this does not imply a negation of the civil authority, responsible for the common good, in a matter so vital to the Community.[12]

In short, the bishops are saying that if the sum of intimate personal acts is affecting national welfare, then it is the responsibility of the state to do something about these acts. They have, however, two major concerns. The first is that the state not exceed its powers. They oppose "psychological pressure and methods of persuasion" and maintain that "the intimate details of personal, conjugal and family life should not be subject to the authority of State functionaries." [13] The second is that "simplistic" approaches be avoided. While the former concern is clear as far as it goes (and they carry it no farther), the simplistic argument requires further elaboration.

Latin Americans are understandably dubious about new and enthusiastic North American approaches to the solution of their problems. They have heard a few before and have seen the dollars come one year and vanish the next for projects which seemed of the highest priority. Even worse, they have seen dollars channeled away from projects they like to those they consider to be North American fads. While some of these fears may have touched the bishops, we believe that they are referring to a different matter. They see human reproduction and its consequences for society as an extremely complex problem demanding complex solutions. Indeed, even in order "to judge a couple's procreative behavior" not only economic considerations but "social, cultural, religious, political, medical, juridical and genetic" factors must be taken into account;[14] and in order to study the problem of procreation, "different disciplines" are needed "to achieve a global focus on the problem, in all its dimensions." Worst of all, they fear an approach which would have a complex problem solved by gadgetry. In their words, "The social aspect of the demographic explosion cannot be reduced to simple economic or medical dimensions." [15]

Behind these innocuous sounding generalities lie deeper sentiments, such as those expressed by the liberal editor of Chile's Jesuit review *Mensaje,* who rejected the "cold nordic rationalism" of the Planned Parenthood approach. As an example, he cited a paragraph from *Time:* "With its percentage of failures higher than the pill, says Dr. Alan Guttmacher, the IUD is not good enough for the reader's wife, but is really adequate for a program in underdeveloped countries." [16]

The bishops' suggestions have been carried out and indeed have been much influenced by a Chilean-based Catholic organization known as the Latin American Center for Family and Population (CELAP), whose parent organization is the Center for Latin American Economic and Social Development. Founded in 1965 by Father Roger Vekemans, it works toward moving both the hierarchies and the Catholic populations of Latin America toward acceptance of family planning within a broad context of responsible parenthood, and it sponsors research, conferences, and publications in a number of countries. In order to do this it "enlisted a team of sociologists, anthropologists, psychologists, demographers, economists, doctors, social workers, legal experts, and ethical philosophers." [17] (Elsewhere architects are added to the list.) Often CELAP's publications sound as if they were in fact written by such a conglomerate, but their pedantic and obfuscatory character is also attributable to an attempt to cast family planning in the larger mold of the parent organization, which is devoted to "cultural mutation" and the elimination of "marginality."

In justifying its expansive approach, CELAP continually denigrates simpler or more direct approaches. "It is not enough to see demographic growth from the 'technicist' angle of demography, nor from mere economic or health perspectives. . . ." [18] Occasionally CELAP's writers bite the hand that feeds them. Thus, Dr. Manuel Borgoño Vial commented that "foreign aid, especially from the United States, is easy to get [for family planning] and more difficult to obtain for public health programs of a higher priority. . . . we regard it as indispensable that these problems be viewed in their multidisciplinary context, rather than having the 'veterinarian' approach of *birth control.*" [19] The "veterinarian" concept is a favorite one of Father Vekemans and has captured the imaginations of many Latin public officials, who see the plastic "serpentina" as the personification of the Anglo-Saxon approach to Latin culture.

So involved are the CELAP staff in these broader social changes that they sometimes seem to be saying that everything must change before anything changes. Thus one writer posits ". . . the necessity of profound social, economic, cultural and political changes as necessary conditions for the final solution of the fertility problem" and insists on ". . . an examination of the Latin American reality at every level in order to locate the phenomenon of the demographic explosion . . . within the many faceted problem of global development." [20]

Another influential church radical who rejects family planning is Ivan Illich, Director of the Intercultural Center of Documentation in Cuernevaca, Mexico. Illich argues that birth control will never be accepted by Latin America's masses, since "having fewer children does not represent a significant bettering of the level of life" for the poor.[21] Moreover, the poor recognize that efforts to improve birth control are an evasion and reject it. Behind such allegations about the psychology of the poor lies Illich's deep resentment toward both North and Latin American paternalistic efforts to convert the poor to middle-class values. Thus, he describes the IUD as "the North American serpent which solicits the tropical Eve to taste the apple of abundance." Like many radicals, Illich is not really against birth control; he is really against its manipulation by ruling classes in the long-run disinterest of the poor.

THE CONSERVATIVES

Chile provides an exception to the general conservatism of the Latin American hierarchy, a conservatism nowhere more apparent than in Colombia, where the hierarchy has recently been faced with both an active, government-approved family planning program and the fact that some of its younger liberal priests were working with it.

Within Colombia, Antioquia is generally considered to be the most religiously conservative department, and it was here as early as 1965 that the bishops began to meet the new challenge with vigor. In September of that year Bishop Botero of Medellín released a pastoral letter in response to "indiscriminate propaganda on birth control." In view of the time and place it was not especially conservative. Although it forbade any drugs or devices which "directly frustrate the physiological phenomenon of generation," it gave various pros and cons about the pill, concluding that it could be used in cases of "double effect." Interestingly enough the bishop found it necessary to say that only physicians should prescribe them: "in no case may priests recommend them."[22]

Later in the month, however, a more energetic and nationalistically toned group statement was issued by the bishops of Antioquia. They joined over 300 departmental physicians in protesting the campaign in favor of birth control, which they regarded as a "serious crime against God, society, and country." They congratulated the 300 physicians for "protecting the sacred interests of God and country," suggested that the new contraceptives "may cause abortion," and reminded their parishioners that "those who procure an abortion . . . incur excommunication."[23]

Around this time, other bishops were issuing vague and moderate statements approving of family planning for "legitimate ends with legitimate means" and reminding their parishioners that Rome would soon be giving the final word.[24] But as the family planning program gained momentum, the hierarchy became increasingly uneasy, both about their parishioners and their priests. In late 1966, Bishop Botero issued a statement "at the request of many priests and laymen." He repeated that immoral methods could not be used and that the Pope would have the last word.[25] Early in 1967 the bishop of Barranquilla found it necessary to state that "no priest is authorized to give talks on family planning in the name of the Catholic Church."[26]

In January of 1967 the Catholic periodical *El Catolicismo* initiated a strong attack on the birth control program, which tripped off a Senate debate and further action on the part of the bishops. The weekly had only recently been purged of liberals and had become the leading outlet for conservative Catholic opinions. By this time church conservatives and some of the political conservatives had joined forces, and the attack was spearheaded by Dr. Hernán Vergara, author of *El Complejo de Layo*.

Although *Catolicismo* insisted that its policies were independent of the church hierarchy, the subsequent pattern of events shows a high degree of consistency. In March, only shortly after the newspaper campaign, Cardinal Luis Concha Cordoba issued a pastoral letter, the severity of which had previously been characteristic only of Antioquian pronouncements. He not only denied that the national birth control program was proceeding with the approval of the church, but indirectly rebuked the priests who had been unofficially cooperating with it. Most importantly, he made a statement about contraception which makes *Humanae Vitae* seem bland by comparison: "Every contraceptive method which tends directly to impede generation—pills, drugs, or mechanical instruments—is illicit and those who use them commit mortal sin."[27]

To the liberal Colombian clergy the unusually inflexible message on the assumed eve of a papal pronouncement seemed imprudent, and a number of priests neglected to read the pastoral to their parishioners. By now, however, the Conservative wing was feeling stronger, and whether by design or in response to the now intense public pressures, in July 1967 the bishops of Colombia issued a long and conservative statement entitled "Responsible Parenthood and Family Planning Programs."

An important characteristic of this document is its belittling of the macrodemographic point of view: "Birth control in itself does not bring about economic development, as some publicity campaigns would have the naive believe; at most it diminishes certain difficulties of development, and may create new ones. . . ." At the level of the family and individual, moreover, the effects are not salutary: "Reduction of births is not accompanied by a physical, intellectual, or moral improvement of the population. [In countries where it is practiced] the proportion of illegitimate children has not diminished. Nor do abortions necessarily diminish and at times have increased."

The bishops explicitly attack the family planning programs of the Colombian Association of Medical Schools, and in the international sphere they speak rather obliquely of "a new form of Colonialism." They "profoundly deplore" that North American foundations, "by means of large financial resources, have promoted birth control programs without due respect for the values of our culture. . . ." Most importantly, where the Chilean bishops had invoked the concept of the "common good" to justify the state's action in family planning, the Colombian bishops invoke it to condemn the state's activities:

> The State will never have the right to promote or approve campaigns leading to a deterioration of the public morality, which is a part of the common good. . . . State functionaries must be vigilant, since public funds cannot be used to the detriment of the common good.[28]

Apparently heartened, a few months later, the bishops of Antioquia made an even stronger statement. They refer to birth control propaganda as having "declared war on children, representing them as enemies of economic development" and charge that birth control damages "the Church, the Fatherland, Society, and the Family." But the nub of the conservative argument comes at last. Where the Chilean bishops clearly saw procreation as a matter so "vital to the community" that the use of civil authority was appropriate, the Antioquian bishops wish to see this area as the exclusive province of the individual—and the church. In saying that responsible paternity requires a "conscience sufficiently informed of moral principles established by Divine Law, whose proclamation and interpretation corresponds exclusively to the Church," they stake out an *exclusive* claim to informing the individual conscience. In case any doubts were left, the bishops dispelled them with the following sentence:

No government, no medical association, and no person can usurp for itself what God entrusted exclusively to the Church.[29]

NOTES

1. Cited by T. G. Sanders, "Family Planning in Chile, Part II. The Catholic Position," *American Universities Fieldstaff,* vol. XV, no. 1.

2. J. Mayone Stycos, "The Bishops, Politics, and Birth Control," in *Human Fertility in Latin America* (Ithaca, N.Y.: Cornell University Press, 1968).

3. *Explosion or Backfire* (release), National Catholic Welfare Conference, Nov. 26, 1959.

4. Headlines assembled by Anthony Marino for term paper, "Family Planning and the Medical Profession in Colombia," January 1968.

5. Stycos, "Contraception and Catholicism in Latin America," in *op. cit.*

6. Pedro Calderon Beltrão, *A Regulacão dos Nascimentos* (Rio de Janeiro: Editora Globo, 1963), p. 39.

7. Gustavo Pérez Ramírez, "The Catholic Church and Family Planning" in J. M. Stycos and J. Arias (eds.), *Population Dilemma in Latin America* (Washington,: Potomac Books, 1966), pp. 211–212.

8. *New York Times,* Apr. 14, 1967.

9. Miguel Angel Gonzalez, "La Controversia Demográfica," in *La Revolución Demográfica,* CIAS (Bogotá: Tercer Mundo, 1966), p. 222.

10. *Ibid.,* p. 224.

11. "Declaración del Episcopado Chileno sobre la planificación de la familia," *Revista Mensaje* (Santiago), June 1967, p. 256.

12. *Ibid.,* p. 259.

13. *Ibid.,* p. 259.

14. *Ibid.,* p. 258.

15. *Ibid.,* p. 257.

16. Reported by Abraham Santibáñez, "Entre La Maldición y el Desafio," *Ercilla* (Santiago), May 27, 1967.

17. *Reportaje DESAL* (Santiago), October 1967.

18. *Reportaje DESAL* (Santiago), April 1967.

19. M. Borgoño Vial, *Crecimiento Demográfica y Salud Pública,* CELAP, October 1965, pp. 6–7. (Mimeographed.)

20. Ismael Silva Fuenzalida, *El Condicionamiento Cultural de la Fecundidad en América Latina: Conceptos y Líneas de Estrategia en la Limitación de los Nacimientos,* CELAP, September 1965, pp. 26, 69. (Mimeographed.)

21. The discussion is drawn from Thomas G. Sanders, "Opposition to Family Planning in Latin America: The Non-Marxist Left," *American Universities Fieldstaff Reports,* vol. XVII, no. 5, March 1970. Citations are from Ivan Illich, "Birth Control et Conscience Politique," *Espirit,* vol. XXXVII, pp. 1056–1069.

22. *El Correo* (Medellín), Sept. 6, 1965.

23. *El Espectador* (Bogotá), Sept. 29, 1965.

24. Two months previously, the archbishop of Cali, Mon. Uribe Urdaneta, commented favorably on the Pan-American Population Assembly held in Cali, because it did not propose "illicit methods." *El Occidente* (Cali), July 7, 1965. A few months later the archbishopric of Bogotá noted that the question was still open for the church and denied knowledge of a birth control campaign. *El Siglo* (Bogotá), Dec. 9, 1965.

25. *El Correo* (Medellín), July 4, 1966.

26. *La República* (Bogotá), May 17, 1967.

27. *El Espectador* (Bogotá), Mar. 12, 1967.

28. *El Siglo* (Bogotá), July 30, 1967.

29. *El Tiempo* (Bogotá), Jan. 28, 1968.

CHAPTER 7

Marxists

Prepared by **Barent Landstreet, Jr.**

Since the time of Malthus, a concern with "population problems" has been much more closely associated with the political right than with the left. Within the left, Marxist writers in particular have, until recently, devoted comparatively little attention to the subject of population. During the 1960s, however, as preoccupation with the world's rate of population growth has become increasingly widespread, Marxists have more and more been drawn into the general discussion. During this period, remarkable changes in attitude have occurred in some sectors of Marxist opinion concerning the relationship between population growth and social welfare.

In this chapter, our primary focus is on the development of Cuban and Soviet attitudes toward population during the last decade. We have felt it desirable to place the Cuban attitudes in comparative perspective by tracing in some detail recent changes in Soviet attitudes toward problems of rapid population growth in underdeveloped countries. The choice of Soviet materials for contrast was dictated by several considerations. First, the Cuban-Soviet comparison gives an idea of the current diversity of Marxist opinion in this area. Second, Soviet writers have recently directed considerable attention to the demographic situation of the underdeveloped countries;

Chinese writers, on the other hand, have written voluminously on their own country's population problems, but virtually not at all on those of other countries. Third, the post-1965 changes in Soviet attitudes have probably already influenced intellectual opinion in Third World countries, and may be expected to have even more influence in the future.

Throughout, it should be borne in mind that there can be no simple equation of "Marxist" population theory with theories held by writers in the Soviet Union, in Cuba, or even in all the Communist countries taken collectively. The former includes the latter, but there is also the work of Marxian writers in non-Communist countries to be considered. Sydney Coontz's *Population Theories and the Economic Interpretation*[1] is probably the most significant recent English-language publication in this vein. It is a literature which we have not drawn upon in this chapter, however.

Finally, in order to facilitate the understanding of Cuban and Soviet positions, we have prefaced the main body of this chapter with a brief resumé of the original views of Marx and Engels on population.[2]

THE MARXIST POSITION

Much of what Marx and Engels wrote on the subject of population was in reaction to Malthusian theory and its political implications. Malthus's "principle of population"—that population growth tends to outstrip increases in the means of subsistence, thus preventing any major improvements in the living levels of the lower classes—had a profound impact on economic thinking during the first half of the nineteenth century and was still widely accepted as accurate during the time Marx was writing. Underlying Malthusianism was a view of society with political consequences which Malthus himself made quite explicit. He contended that the "great error" of the socialists was that of "attributing almost all the vices and misery that are seen in civil society to human institutions," which in reality are "mere feathers that float on the surface" of an eternal demographic dilemma.[3]

That the principal and most permanent cause of poverty has little or no *direct* relation to forms of government, or the unequal division of property;

and that, as the rich do not in reality possess the *power* of finding employment and maintenance for the poor, the poor cannot, in the nature of things,
possess the *right* to demand them; are important truths flowing from the
principle of population, which, when properly explained, would by no means
be above the most ordinary comprehensions.[4] [Italics in the original.]

Marx recognized that if the principle of population were a "law
of nature," as Malthus believed, then "socialism cannot abolish
poverty, *which has its basis in nature,* but can only *generalize* it,
distribute it simultaneously over the whole surface of society!"[5]
[Italics in the original.] One line of attack which Marx and Engels
took against Malthus was that of stressing the potentialities of agricultural technology and science in general, "the progress of which
is just as limitless and at least as rapid as that of population."[6] Engels
pointed out that even with the present technology, "only one-third
of the earth can be described as cultivated, and . . . the productivity
of this third could be increased sixfold and more merely by applying
the improvements which are already known."[7]

A second line of attack was based on the idea that Malthus had
identified a genuine problem, but that he had incorrectly diagnosed
it: Malthus was "right, in his way, in asserting that there are always
more people on hand than can be maintained from the available
means of subsistence."[8] Where he had erred, they argued, was in
mistaking the *means of employment* for the *means of subsistence.* The
fact that a great proportion of the European population lived in
poverty did not prove that there were insufficient resources to permit
the poor to live comfortably, but only that capitalism could not
provide them. There was, then, fundamentally, not a "population
problem," but a problem of economic organization. Engels believed
incidentally, that Communist social organization would be conducive
to lower fertility, although he left open the "abstract possibility" that
even under Communism numbers might eventually have to be limited.[9]

In addition to criticizing Malthusian theory, Marx attempted to
formulate a theory which would *replace* it, a theory that would
account for the facts of apparent "overpopulation" in advanced
capitalist countries. It is a theory which applies only to capitalism,
for "every special historic mode of production [Communism, capitalism, feudalism, etc.] has its own special laws of population,

historically valid within its limits alone." [10] (Actually, Marx never elaborated the population "laws" of the other periods.) Under capitalism, the argument runs, industrialists attempt to accumulate as much capital as possible, but competition forces them to invest more heavily in machines than in labor. Thus capital is divided into a *constant* component (the means of production) and a *variable* component (the sum total of wages), and the accumulation process is characterized by a progressive decline of variable capital relative to constant capital. But it is the variable component alone which determines the demand for labor, so that "the labouring population therefore produces, along with the accumulation of capital produced by it, the means by which itself is made relatively superfluous, is turned into a relative surplus-population; and it does this to an always increasing extent." [11] In this manner is formed the "industrial reserve army" of unemployed, underemployed, and irregularly employed workers, whose existence is functionally necessary to capitalism, since employers must be able to expand and contract the size of their work force according to the state of the market. The size of the industrial reserve army in the short run depends on the state of the business cycle, but in the long run it must increase progressively until capitalism is replaced by socialism. In capsule form, then, what the Malthusians called "overpopulation" was actually "relative surplus labor," a growing mass of impoverished, technologically displaced workers, produced by a necessary process of "automation" within the system of capitalist economic organization.

In conclusion, we may simply note briefly a few of the major criticisms which have been brought against this theory. [12] The growth of the industrial reserve army has been kept much lower than Marx apparently expected, partly due to the development of the tertiary (service) sector of the economy, and partly by the pressure of organized labor for job security, a shorter work week, and reduced working hours. As for the unemployed workers themselves, various programs of social welfare and unemployment benefits have generally kept them from sinking to the level of absolute impoverishment. Furthermore, there is no apparent recognition of the possibility that workers, by restricting the number of their children, could deprive the industrialists of a good proportion of their future reserve army of labor, forcing a rise in wages in the process. It could be argued that this actually occurred, for example, in England, with the long decline in the birth rate, which seems to have started shortly after Marx's *Kapïtal* was published in 1867.

POPULATION THEORIES AND POLICIES IN THE SOVIET UNION

By the time of the Russian Revolution, very little had been written on the subject of population in the future socialist society. Marx, as we have seen, developed no "law of population" for socialism, although Engels[13] mentioned the "abstract possibility" that problems of population growth might occur in a socialist society. He did not feel compelled to comment further on the matter, except to point out that a socialist society would be able to regulate population more easily than a capitalist one, if the need should arise.

Of Lenin's few writings on the subject of population, the most relevant for our purposes is an article entitled "The Working Class and Neomalthusianism," written in 1913. In it, he condemns "social neomalthusianism," which he characterizes as producing a petty bourgeois mentality, in which parents, in a mood of despair, try to limit the number of their children in order to keep them from suffering class oppression. Socialist parties and the working class must oppose this theory. Nevertheless:

It goes without saying that this does not by any means prevent us from demanding the unconditional annulment of all laws against abortions or against the distribution of medical literature on contraceptive measures, etc. Such laws are nothing but the hypocrisy of the ruling classes. These laws do not heal the ulcers of capitalism, they merely turn them into malignant ulcers that are especially painful for the oppressed masses. Freedom for medical propaganda and the protection of the elementary democratic rights of citizens, men and women, are one thing. The social theory of neo-malthusianism is quite another.[14]

In 1920, Lenin's principle that individual families should decide how many children they will have was put into practice by the Soviet government when it legalized abortions.[15] Under Tsarist law, abortions—being equated with murder—were illegal, but rather frequently resorted to, since the use of contraception was not very common. Being illegal, they were generally performed under unhygienic conditions and resulted in high mortality. With the new decree in 1920, abortions were granted free of charge in state hospitals, and the abortion rate began to rise steadily. Moscow, which probably had the highest rates in the country, reported an increase from 19 abortions per 100 live births in 1921 to 270 per 100 live births in 1934. Soviet authorities were becoming increasingly disturbed by the high incidence of abortions, and in 1936 abortions were made illegal except under strict medical indications. In the same year, the first major program of family allowances was adopted. Eight years later, in 1944, an expanded pronatalist program was put into effect to make up for population losses suffered during the war. Total losses are difficult to estimate, but if we include all war-related deaths, the lowered birth rate, and emigration, the losses were perhaps between 35 and 45 million persons. The 1944 program expanded the family allowance system, instituted a "bachelor's tax," increased maternity leave for working mothers, and provided for the awarding of medals to mothers with especially large families. Meanwhile, the incidence of (illegal) abortions was increasing again, and in 1955 the government issued a decree reverting to the older policy of providing free abortions in state hospitals, upon the request of the mother. (A similar abortion policy is followed in most Eastern European socialist countries.) The official statistics have not been published in the Soviet Union, but a recent estimate puts the rate at at least one abortion for every live birth.[16] (That this is not necessarily an exaggerated estimate is indicated by the fact that Hungary, which does publish official abortion figures, in 1964 reported 140 abortions per 100 live births.) Efforts have been underway to reduce the number of abortions by dispensing contraceptive devices and information.

Despite the availability of abortions and the recent efforts to promote contraception, current *policy*—insofar as one can speak of an explicit population "policy" at all—seems to be mildly pronatalist. (It will be remembered that the Soviet Union is not a densely populated country and that its rate of population growth is only half that of, say, Latin America.) Various Soviet officials have spoken of a three-child family ideal, and the desire seems to be to maintain the current growth rate of approximately 1.5 percent per year. Those who have suggested a present or future need to influence the rate of population growth, either in a positive or negative direction, have generally justified it in terms of future labor force demands. Actually, systematic theoretical discussions of population questions under socialism have been relatively infrequent in the Soviet Union. Explanations of population patterns in the socialist countries are not usually given in terms of a single "law of population under socialism"; while the existence of specific laws governing each type of society has not been denied, it is stressed that "the concrete forms of these laws are dependent upon a complicated complex of socio-economic, cultural-historical, and other factors." [17] Such phenomena as class differences in fertility, rising or falling birth rates, and the like have frequently been interpreted as "holdovers" from presocialist characteristics or as the result of various policies (such as wage differentials) necessary during the transition from socialism to Communism.

It is in the area of opinions about population problems in the developing countries, however, that we find some striking recent theoretical developments. During the Stalin period, opinions of Soviet economists and demographers seem to have been quite homogeneous, and usually took the form of condemning any theories or policies having "neo-Malthusian" overtones. An apparent "population problem" could only have an economic solution. Mr. Rabichko, Soviet delegate to the United Nations Population Commission, stated the position very succinctly in 1947: "We consider any proposition formulated by this commission in favour of limiting marriages or births in wedlock as barbarous. Overpopulation is only a fruit of capitalism; an adequate social regime can meet any increase of population. It is the economy which should be adapted to the population, and not vice versa." [18] Soviet condemnations of theories that rapid population growth or overpopulation could present serious difficulties for national development and international order reached a crescendo in the early 1950s. The following quotation is typical of that period: "Malthusian propaganda has been heard from false scientists . . . ; from writers . . . ; from ministers, politicians, diplomats, etc. . . . Masquerading as scientists and philanthropists, these lackeys of American monopolies openly advocate cannibalism and try to justify the demoniacal plans for the mass extermination of peoples." [19]

After Stalin's death in 1953, there was a general moderating of the tone of criticism against those who wrote about population problems and their possible solutions, but Soviet representatives to the United Nations continued to oppose that organization's involvement in any efforts to assist in family planning matters. Recently, however, the traditional views on population problems have been challenged within the Soviet Union itself. A public dialogue between exponents of the old and new views has been underway since November 1965, and may have been stimulated in part by participation in the World Population Conference sponsored by the United Nations, held in Belgrade, Yugoslavia, between August 30 and September 10, 1965. Before considering the issues raised in the current debate, we may note some of the positions taken by Soviet representatives to the Belgrade conference.

Several Soviet experts, K. Malin and N. M. Zhavaronkov among them, gave papers stressing the benefits that might come from a full application of scientific knowledge to agricultural production. It was projected that if solar energy could be more efficiently utilized and plant growing in the oceans became practicable, the earth could support a population of "three to four million million people." [20] Among those who dealt with the question of high fertility rates, there was general agreement that since they were primarily caused by socioeconomic factors, it would be necessary to change those factors in order to lower the rates to any appreciable extent. V. E. Ovsienko, in a paper on the "Influence of Social and Economic Factors on Demographic Characteristics," [21] formulated a "general law in the development of human society that the pace of economic development is more rapid than that of population growth." He repeated the idea that it is "the economy and the level of production which must be brought into line with population size," not vice versa, and that in any case, "a reduction in the birth rate cannot by itself promote an increase in production." Fertility will inevitably decline as a result of progress in industrialization, urbanization, and education, and there is no need to make any special efforts in this regard now.

One representative, Y. G. Mashbitz, dealt with the specific problem of population growth and food production in Latin America. [22] After asserting that "the high rates of natural population growth [in most Latin American countries] aggravate their social and economic problems and their food supply difficulties," he went on to analyze the structure of land tenure, declining per capita agricultural output, and other problems. Curiously, the possibility that a reduction of the population growth rate might ameliorate the situation is never considered. Mashbitz merely states the obvious, that "it has been proved beyond doubt that even at the present level of science and technology the natural conditions in Latin America are such that the region's entire demand for food and agricultural raw materials could be fully met." Population growth and per capita food production and consumption statistics are brought in apparently only to show how serious the situation is; a "demographic solution" is simply ignored.

The closest any of the Soviet representatives came to endorsing birth control as a means to facilitate economic development was in a paper given by Y. N. Guzevaty.[23] Referring to the countries recently liberated from colonialism (i.e., excluding Latin America), he described a "transitional period" typically characterized by rapid population growth, which can aggravate capital shortages. But population limitation makes sense only in the context of structural reforms: "The wider the scale of economic and cultural development the more progressive the development of demographic processes towards stabilization of reproduction of the population, and consequently, the more feasible the possibility to accelerate them, if necessary, by means of birth control." Guzevaty was later to expand this view greatly in an article published in 1966, which we shall consider shortly.

Less than three months after the conference, an open dialogue on the subject of population and economic development was begun, centered mainly in the intellectual newspaper *Literaturnaya gazeta.*[24] The articles which formed the core of this dialogue began to appear approximately once a month and were predominantly oriented towards challenging traditional Soviet views on population and development, although several articles defended the older theses. It is quite possible that the issues discussed and arguments presented at the conference, which was attended by many representatives from the developing countries, had an impact upon the Soviet representatives. Dmitry Valentey, an important Soviet demographer, and author of one of the first articles, stated that although there were neo-Malthusian ideas hidden in many of the papers presented at the conference, "among the participants there was not even one who openly declared his adherence to the Malthusian theory."[25] While this statement itself is undoubtedly true, the *way* the matter is stated indicates a change of attitude from the kind of vituperation characteristic of the early 1950s, when the terms "Malthusian" and "neo-

Malthusian" were used indiscriminately as smear words to avoid discussing the issues involved (as some Soviet demographers now admit).

The articles expressing the new approach to population have not been limited to the *Literaturnaya gazeta* exchange, so we have selected several of the most relevant for our purposes, from various sources, to present here in some detail. The first, entitled "Scientific Calculation or Reliance on Spontaneity?", appeared in *Literaturnaya gazeta* on June 11, 1966, and was written by E. Arab-Ogly, a demographer who is section chief in the Laboratory for Population Problems in the Department of Economics, University of Moscow. He criticizes Soviet demographers and economists who have maintained that only urbanization and industrialization can bring about a decline in birth rates and that increased food production can take care of any future increases of population. While rejecting the neo-Malthusian idea that population problems are the primary concern, he states that they are real, and in many developing countries policies must be implemented to cope with them:

> The striving to establish conditions worthy of man on earth as soon as possible for everyone without exception, and the intention merely to "feed" the maximum number of people possible are by no means the same thing. The former is a slogan of humanism and the goal of Communism; the latter is an echo of feudal morality, when the rulers prided themselves on which one had the most subjects.
>
> The capital investment which any society can afford every year is not arbitrary; the amount is limited by annual accumulations. Every accumulation is a deduction from current consumption. Depending upon how they are earmarked, these capital investments can in turn be directed toward either increasing the national per capita income of the present population (economic investments) or providing the annual population increase with the standard of living already achieved (demographic investments). Society must choose whether it prefers doubling the prosperity of a constant population, say every twenty years, or doubling the population while maintaining the same standard of living in approximately the same period. One and the same pudding cannot be eaten twice under two different names.
>
> Of course in real life one cannot exclude as unpurposeful either economic or demographic investments. Reduction of population increase would in due course result in extremely negative economic and social consequences for all of society. That is why in every specific case there exists some kind of *optimal combination of these investments* depending upon the already achieved standard of living of the population, its age structure, growth rate, etc. . . .

People may now already begin to fight successfully for the prevention of world wars, for the elimination of hunger and illiteracy and for the deliberate regulation of demographic processes in behalf of the future of mankind.[26]

The second article is by Y. Guzevaty, senior research worker in the Institute of World Economics and International Relations, U.S.S.R. Academy of Science. Although he also contributed to the exchange in *Literaturnaya gazeta,* the article abstracted here appeared in *International Affairs,* an intellectual journal published in Moscow for foreign distribution. Entitled "Population Problems in Developing Countries," [27] it deals with the causes and effects of rapid population growth, examines the specific population problems and programs of several developing countries, and elaborates on the distinction between neo-Malthusian and Marxist approaches to population problems. The following abstract omits the sections dealing with specific countries.

Guzevaty focuses his attention on the "population explosion" in the emerging nations of Asia and Africa, which has been caused by rapidly declining mortality rates (due especially to public health measures), in conjunction with backward social structures which sanctify large family norms. The rate of population growth of these countries is expected to increase, not decline, in the near future. The decline in fertility in the industrialized nations was due to the disintegration of the patriarchal system, the emergence of new opportunities for young people through increased education, the social emancipation of women, and the increased demand for cultural and material values. These conditions, by and large, do not exist in the Afro-Asian countries, and hence we can expect no substantial decline in fertility. Abstractly, rapid population growth should be a social good, but given the concrete circumstances of these countries, this social good is turned into its antithesis. The following problems ensue from the population explosion: (1) Given backward technology and the lack of capital, there is a "redundance" of manpower. (2) The main economic areas suffer an irrational increase in density, and resettlement programs in underpopulated areas are prohibitively expensive. (3) Rural-urban migration leads to an unhealthy urbanization in the context of housing shortages and low demand for labor. (4) The food supply is strained, and in many regions population growth is outstripping agricultural production. (5) The capital shortage is aggravated by the necessity to provide for the annual population increase; an increasingly high percentage of the national income must be spent merely to maintain the former living standard, not to speak of raising it. It becomes ever more difficult to provide the growing population with articles of primary necessity, as well as schools, hospitals, and other services. (6) The "dependency burden" worsens; that is, there are increasingly more dependent children relative to the number of productive adults in the population as a whole. (7) Lastly, due to all the aforementioned factors, which aggravate the problems of development, the potentiality for national independence is seriously weakened. Forced to turn to the imperialist countries for aid, the nation opens the door to control by foreign capital, and in the process internal reactionary forces are strengthened.

The solution to problems of national development requires, of course, a progressive government, a planned economy, and a cultural revolution which breaks down archaic social structures and transforms the previous feudal mentality. But the population explosion frustrates development, and economic success *"cannot be achieved unless population factors are taken into account and efforts are made to influence them."* Although *"radical social and economic transformations are the chief and indispensable requisites for solving the population problems, . . . they will not necessarily solve those problems immediately."* [Italics in the original.] National family planning programs are needed. The main difference between the Marxist and Malthusian approaches is that Marxists insist that birth control programs cannot be effective unless accompanied by profound socioeconomic transformations.

Almost two years after the *Literaturnaya gazeta* population debate had begun, Boris Urlanis, one of the best-known Soviet demographers, delivered an authoritative paper on "Marxism and Birth Control" to the International Union for the Scientific Study of Population.[28] Much of the presentation was dedicated to showing that Marxists are and always have been opposed to neo-Malthusianism as a doctrine that preaches the *primacy* of population problems and attempts to disorient workers from the class struggle, but that they do not deny the existence of population problems. Given the long-term decline in the U.S.S.R.'s birth rate (18 per 1,000 in 1966), that country is beginning to be faced with the problem of encouraging more births. But the situation is just the opposite in the developing countries, says Urlanis: birth rates must be brought down. "Each man is a consumer for the duration of his natural life, and for the duration of his economically active life he is a producer." In the case of many developing countries, "consumption exceeds the amounts they have produced," and rapid population growth becomes a "millstone around their necks." Almost as if to indicate that the Soviet debate over population problems had already been resolved, Urlanis states:

> Soviet demographers believe that together with an economic solution there must also be a demographic solution, that is to say a lowering of birth rates by means of an effective demographic policy. The aim of such a policy must be to spread planned families, and this implies the use of birth control by the population. . . .
> Natural fertility, i.e. rates determined solely by physiological fecundity, should be regarded as an atavism, an inheritance of the past, a remnant of colonialism.

It is interesting to note that, in spite of the above reference to ex-colonial countries, Urlanis specifically includes Latin America in his analysis. Some other Soviet writers have restricted the recommendation of birth control to countries with "progressive" governments, which would exclude almost all Latin America from their analysis, but Urlanis does not take that position:

> Marxists believe that although the limitation of family size among the working class has become widespread in capitalist countries, this in no way affects the intensity of the class struggle on the part of the proletariat.

Later on we will contrast this attitude with current Cuban writings, which assign the "population explosion" a key role in the disintegration of the old order in Latin America.

The writings we have been examining reached something of a culmination in a second *International Affairs* article by Y. Guzevaty, published a year after the first one.[29] Here, Guzevaty takes for granted many of the economic problems of rapid population growth in the developing countries and goes on to discuss their implications for world politics. First, he traces the growing gap between industrial and nonindustrial nations squarely to the population explosion:

> The rapid population growth is forcing the young national states to spend more and more on keeping up with the old living standards.

That is why, despite the historic successes scored by national-liberation revolutions, the economic gap between the liberated less developed countries and the old industrialized states, far from narrowing down, is continuing to grow. This is leading to an instability in the world economy and in world politics which may have serious consequences.

Secondly, he elaborates on a point made in his previous article: the stagnation of development and the inability to achieve increasing rates of per capita food production leads to a politically unhealthy dependence on imports (whether gifts or purchases) from capitalist countries. Several cases are cited in which the U.S. used desperately needed food shipments as a lever to extract political concessions from India and the U.A.R. This dependence is increasingly "typical of the third world as a whole." Guzevaty warns, however, against seeing population growth as the main problem from which underdeveloped countries suffer: the only permanent solution lies in a sharp increase in national agricultural production, and the force which blocks that is still imperialism, as witnessed by the fact that the 25 billion dollars a year which the U.S. is spending on the war in Vietnam is "equivalent to the cost of organizing the production of artificial fertilizers in the quantities required by the developing countries."

Turning to deal with another political problem of population growth, Guzevaty condemns "the notorious living space theory" which has been adopted by the German, Italian, and Japanese fascists; the "West German revanchists and the Israeli expansionists"; and "the present leaders of the Chinese People's Republic." The latter country has made claims on the territory of nearly all its neighboring countries:

Mao Tse-tung tried to mask this line of undermining the foundations of international relations and provoking armed frontier incidents with demagogical arguments about "justice," which demands a redivision of territories because of the uneven distribution of the world population.

Finally, as a last surprise, Guzevaty turns to the question of optimum world population size, a problem which previously Soviet demographers had usually dismissed as irrelevant:

. . . it must be admitted that it would be shortsighted to ignore the problem of an optimum population of the world or to leave the whole problem in the lap of future generations. After all, the demographic factors which will operate in the next century are being shaped in our own day. Apparently, it is not the best solution to suggest cities on the bottom of the seas and oceans, underground cities and so forth. . . . The main task of man in the future Communist society is to make life on earth worth living.

The Soviet writings on population and development of the last few years which we have reviewed show an extraordinary degree of agreement with the analysis made by at least some Western writers on the same subject. In this respect it is necessary to distinguish, as the Soviet writers often have done in their recent articles, among various schools of thought which have in common only the fact that they advocate the increased use of birth control. Without attempting to exhaust all positions, we will briefly compare the current Soviet opinions with those of Western (mostly nonsocialist) writers on two issues: The question of what kinds of changes in social structure (if any) are needed to significantly reduce birth rates in the underdeveloped countries, and the question of what role reduced population growth rates might play in the economic development of the same societies.

1. The Soviet writers we have cited have, by and large, abandoned the argument that birth rates decline "automatically" with increased urbanization and industrialization. As a long-run generalization this is certainly sound, but in the short run there is much variation, and in some large cities in the underdeveloped countries fertility levels have actually risen. In any case, to view it as an automatic response is rather like saying that since the educational level of the population shows a clear tendency to rise with economic development, there is no need to waste money building schools. The effect of urbanization and industrialization on the birth rate has to be modified by some form of birth control methods, and it is precisely these methods which a national family planning program attempts to provide.

Most of the Soviet authors assert explicitly that change in the social structure of an underdeveloped country is essential in order to achieve any considerable drop in birth rates. To say the least, this had not been a dominant concern of Western writers on the subject of population, although there have been exceptions. Kingsley Davis, in a critique of current family planning programs,[30] stresses the scarcity of research on the social and economic determinants of fertility levels. He points out that most present population policies in the underdeveloped countries undertake to influence only a few of the determinants of population growth and that their impact may consequently prove to be slight. He proposes a series of measures affecting female roles in society, including greater rewarding of nonfamilial roles, the organization of social life around the work place rather than the home, expanding women's educational opportunities, and especially increasing female participation in the labor force. Davis notes that "approximately this policy is now followed in several Communist countries, and even the less developed of these currently have extremely low birth rates."

In terms of the scope of social changes that the Soviet writers deem necessary to effect considerable declines in birth rates, reference is usually made to accelerating components of what might be called the "modernization process": education, urbanization, industrialization, and a "cultural revolution" overturning the traditional value system. Some writers, such as A. Ia. Kvasha, actually posit the necessity of socialism: "'the demographic crisis' is capable of being resolved solely by a course of fundamental socio-economic changes—the course of socialism." [31] But their argument is based on the assumption that only through socialism can there be an effective "modernization" of the underdeveloped countries. It would seem that there is at least a latent agreement among Soviet and Western students of population that there is a range of social phenomena (norms, values, aspirations, occupational roles, urban-industrial patterns) which can vary independently of the fact of socialist or capitalist organization, and that it is these factors which are crucial in determining population growth rates. It is quite possible that, in the future, disagreements will be less over the specific determinants of fertility and more over political questions—especially the kinds of public policy which can most effectively influence these determinants.

On the Soviet side, then, it would appear that the main recent changes in attitude involve a recognition that "population problems" do exist, in the sense of being attributable at least in part to high fertility levels, whatever may be the determinants of those fertility levels. Furthermore, there is a recognition that while, in the long run, fertility levels are determined by broad socioeconomic forces, in the short run they can also be influenced by the activities of family planning programs (making contraceptives available and engaging in propaganda for their use).

2. As for the role that population limitation might play in the process of socioeconomic development, we have seen that none of the Soviet authors give it "primacy." By this they mean that population problems should not be seen as the "main" difficulty facing underdeveloped countries, the position which they characterize as "neo-Malthusian." Such a view is perhaps not dominant, even in the United States, but it is far from rare. Lauchlin Currie, a respected development economist, is one of the many who might be cited as typifying this position: "I regard the rate of growth in the population of the underdeveloped countries as the single most important obstacle to development and, hence, the single most important problem of the world. . . ."[32] Such a point of view seems also to have been implied in Lyndon Johnson's United Nations speech of June 25, 1965, in which he said: "Let us act on the fact that less than five dollars invested in population growth is worth a hundred dollars invested in economic growth." Many others take a more moderate position, not ranking population limitation as a "solution" above questions of social reorganization, political changes, etc. They see a reduction in birth rates as a factor which would facilitate economic growth, but by no means guarantee that it would take place. They point out, for example, the economically beneficial effects of a fertility decline in terms of investment opportunities and the relative proportion of economically active to inactive persons, but also indicate that general consumption levels might rise, thereby preventing the resources saved from being invested in the productive "infrastructure" of the economy.

The changes in Soviet attitudes which we have been examining from articles in the specialized and mass media have had their counterpart in changed voting patterns on population issues within United Nations councils and associated agencies. Against a history of opposing UN involvement in family planning matters, in May 1966, at a meeting of the World Health Organization in Geneva, the Soviet delegate supported a mild resolution permitting that organization to "advise members, upon request, in the development of activities in family planning." Subsequently, the Soviet Union has largely supported resolutions on population and family planning within WHO. In May 1968, for example, the U.S.S.R. not only approved a resolution on the health aspects of population but also proposed an amendment stressing that "family planning . . . plays a role in economic and social development." Other cases illustrating the new voting trend might be cited. For example, in June 1968 the U.S.S.R. supported a resolution in the UN's Economic and Social Council requesting the Secretary-General to

. . . give special attention to further developing those aspects of the work in population fields which are of direct benefit to developing countries, especially advice and technical assistance requested by Governments in population fields within the context of economic, social and health policies. . . .

although it "reserved its position" on a paragraph of the resolution calling directly for the financing of projects.[33]

Thus the years 1966–1968 saw the beginnings of a shift in behavior related to population issues corresponding to the change in attitudes which began somewhat earlier.

POPULATION THEORIES AND POLICIES IN CUBA†

Like recent work in the Soviet Union, much of the postrevolutionary Cuban writing on the subject of population has been concerned with the relations between population and underdevelopment internationally, especially with reference to Latin America. In fact, discounting purely statistical reports, there appears to have been considerably more written on the demographic situations of other Latin American countries than on Cuba herself. One particular focus of attention has been the inapplicability, in the Cuban view, of neo-Malthusian solutions to the plight of these countries, and the motives of the United States in promoting such solutions. Cuba herself does have a national policy of providing contraceptive means to all citizens who wish to use them, but the official explanation of this policy is in terms of maternal health and female emancipation, not the economic

† The preparation of this section, although primarily based on published Cuban materials (newspaper and journal articles, speeches, demographic statistical reports, etc.), was facilitated by interviews I had with several Cubans during a visit to the island in August 1968. Dr. Juan Pérez de la Riva, professor of demography at the University of Havana; Dr. Celestino Alvarez Lajonchere, head of instruction in gynecology and obstetrics at the University of Havana Medical School and head of the special group on gynecology and obstetrics in the Ministry of Public Health; and Dr. Francisco Rojas Ochoa, head of public health statistics in the Ministry of Public Health, generously took time to be interviewed from very busy schedules, and I would like to express my appreciation to them here.

benefits that might accrue from such a policy. In what follows, we shall first deal briefly with recent Cuban demographic trends, for information on them is much scarcer than in the case of the Soviet Union.[34] We shall then look at current Cuban policies and their rationale, and finally we shall examine the prevailing views on how population problems are related to the broader question of Latin American underdevelopment.

Compared with other Latin American countries, Cuba has had a relatively low birth rate, although it is high in comparison with fertility levels in the industrialized countries. Historically, Cuba was the third Latin American country, following Uruguay and Argentina, to begin the transition to low fertility. Although Cuba's birth rate was in the high 40s (per 1,000 population) in the first decade of this century, the country's fertility fell sharply during the second and third decades, before leveling off at somewhat over 30 during the 1930s and 1940s.[35] By the years 1955–1959, the birth rate had fallen below 30,[36] although the precise figure is difficult to establish with any certainty because of the poor quality of birth registration data. (The last Cuban census, that of 1953, put the birth rate at 29.6.)[37] Thus, at the time of the revolution, Cuba had the third lowest birth rate of all Latin American countries.

In contrast with most other Latin American countries, Cuba's birth rate declined more or less evenly with her death rate, the latter reaching the very low level of about 7 per 1,000 during the decade of the 1950s.[38] The symmetry of the declines in the two rates, which kept a distance of about 20 points from each other, gave Cuba an annual rate of natural increase that fluctuated around 2 percent from the beginning of the century through 1959.[39]

After the revolutionary victory in January 1959, the long decline in the birth rate was reversed. From a level of about 27, or perhaps a little higher, in 1958, the birth rate rose each year until it reached a maximum of about 37 in 1962. Small declines were registered in the three following years, with the rate standing at slightly less than 35 in 1965.[40] Subsequently, the decline accelerated, with the preliminary figures for 1967 indicating a crude birth rate of 29.2.[41]

It should be emphasized that the above figures are crude birth rates, and as such they are dependent on changes in the age structure of the population; e.g., if the heavy outmigration in the first few years after 1959 was selective of older persons, this would have had the effect of raising the crude birth rates even if the fertility behavior of Cuban women in the reproductive ages had remained unchanged. Lacking the necessary data on emigrants to determine whether this was so, we can only surmise that an increase of ten points in the crude birth rate (between 1958 and 1962) is too large to be explained away by compositional differences and that there was indeed a real rise in fertility during this period. Juan Pérez de la Riva, professor of geography and demography at the University of Havana, has offered some speculations about why this happened:

The demographic explosion after 1959 is explained by the new conditions created by the Revolution: the total disappearance of agricultural unemployment; new possibilities offered in the towns, especially to young people; the exodus from the rural areas; and, in general, an atmosphere of euphoria, optimism and unlimited confidence in the socialist future. All this was translated into a considerable lowering of the age at marriage and the almost total disappearance of family planning.[42]

Cuban marriage statistics are difficult to sort out, due to the large number of common-law unions, but a postrevolutionary increase in the rate of formation of new unions appears at least very plausible on the basis of available data.[43] Similarly, given the well-documented relationship (at least in the short run) between economic prosperity on the one hand and marriage and fertility rates on the other, the explanation offered by Pérez de la Riva seems satisfactory on a general level. The welfare of the majority of the Cuban population did rise dramatically in the first few years after the revolutionaries took power. Seers estimates that by 1962 total employment had expanded to a level approximately 33 percent higher than that of 1958.[44] Urban rents were cut in half, an agrarian reform was carried out, massive construction projects were begun, and food consumption rose appreciably. The real wages of workers rose by 25 to 30 percent during 1959 alone.[45] To extend the same line of reasoning, it is probably more than coincidental that the birth rate began to decline again after 1962, the year in which general food rationing was introduced.

The crude death rate appears to have changed very little since the revolution. Official Cuban figures, corrected for underregistration, show a death rate fluctuating around 7 per 1,000 population for the years 1960-1965.[46] This is not significantly different from the one given for the decade of the 1950s. Aside from the undetermined effects of changing age composition on this rate, several factors influencing it may be mentioned. On the negative side has been the fact that many physicians left Cuba during the years following the revolution. In addition, the emigrants in general have come disproportionately from the upper and middle social strata, those strata enjoying the best health conditions before the revolution (class differentials in mortality are wide in any underdeveloped country). On the positive side, the training of new physicians has been stepped up, and many new hospitals and clinics have been built (the number of hospital beds doubled between 1958 and 1964).[47] Medical facilities are also much less concentrated in the capital city than had previously been the case. It would appear, then, that these and other factors have combined to keep the crude death rate at about the pre-1959 level.

Although Cuba has low mortality, and fertility that is currently at a moderately high level, the actual rate of population growth since the revolution has been considerably depressed by emigration. It has been estimated that by the beginning of 1968 there were some 370,000 Cubans who had migrated to the United States since January 1959.[48] In addition, by 1966 there were approximately 46,000 emigrants living in Latin American countries and Spain.[49] The outmigration decreased considerably after the October 1962 missile crisis, when all flights from Cuba to the United States were suspended. After flights were resumed on December 1, 1965, an estimated 40,000 Cuban emigrés arrived in the United States (which is the destination of the majority of those leaving Cuba) in each of the following two years.[50] Thus, in spite of increased fertility, emigration had the effect of keeping the actual rate of population growth down to about 2.3 percent a year during the period from 1959 to 1965, a rate not significantly higher than in the 1953–1958 period. After 1965, the actual growth rate dropped rather sharply, due to the decline in fertility and the new rise in emigration. In 1966, the rate was 1.9 percent, and preliminary figures for 1967 show a rate of 1.6 percent.[51] According to these characteristics, Cuba's nearest demographic analog is Puerto Rico, which in 1965 had a similar death rate (7) and a somewhat lower birth rate (30) and whose population only increased by a rate of 1.9 percent a year from 1958 to 1966 due to heavy outmigration.

One of the obstacles to the thorough study of Cuba's demographic situation has been the shortage of trained demographers. I was informed that although a number of Cubans in government ministries and agencies are competent in handling population statistics, at the moment the country's only academic demographer is Juan Pérez de la Riva. He has taught two courses in general and urban demography at the University of Havana since 1962. There is no "department" of demography at the University, and there is no degree offered in the area, although a student can specialize in demography while majoring in another discipline (most commonly geography or economics). Additional training is gained through supervised research experience, from visiting experts (a professor from the Latin American Demographic Center gave a course in Cuba in 1967), and through foreign study (Chile and the U.S.S.R.). In the past there has been some resistance on the government and party levels, as there was during certain periods in the Soviet Union, to the idea of demography as an independent science, but these attitudes—which were probably never dominant—have been changing. The resistance, of course, comes from those who associate demographic science with the doctrines of Malthus or the neo-Malthusians and consider it a "bourgeois science." Among the indications that such an attitude is no longer common are the recent appearances of many demographic articles in the Communist Party newspaper *Granma* and the publication in 1967 of a book, *La Población Latinoamericana, Problemas y Perspectivas,* by the Latin American Solidarity Organization (OLAS).

It is difficult to gauge the extent of the interest of Cuban authorities in birth control during the first years after the revolution, but it is certain that the attention given to the subject increased noticeably from 1966 onwards.[52] Dr. Alan Guttmacher of the International Planned Parenthood Federation (IPPF) visited Cuba in 1966, where he lectured to doctors on contraceptive techniques, and Cuban observers attended the Eighth International IPPF Conference held in Santiago, Chile, during April 1967. In addition, Cubans have received training at the IPPF center in Chile, and the IPPF has provided "consultative and material assistance" on a limited scale to the Cuban birth control activities.[53]

Contraceptive devices, like all medical services, are available without charge from the Cuban public health service and are provided without regard to marital status. Cuba is divided into about

270 public health "areas," each of which has a general clinic (*policlinico*). (Regional hospitals serve patients needing more extensive treatment.) All the clinics are now staffed by gynecologists or physicians with some training in contraceptive techniques. Intrauterine devices (a variety of the Zipper ring, made by hand from nylon fishing line) are made in Cuba, and diaphragms are imported from Eastern Europe. Oral contraceptives are not available, partly because doubts exist about their safety and partly because, given Cuba's foreign exchange problems, they would be an unnecessary "luxury item." [54]

It would be incorrect, however, to speak of a birth control "campaign" in Cuba, or even of the existence of a national policy of actively promoting birth control. Certainly there has been nothing similar to the several campaigns that China, for example, has experienced. Aside from an occasional *Granma* article or television program which only gives information on the various contraceptive services available, there has been no concerted educational effort to popularize birth control or family planning: no billboards, pamphlets, signs in clinics, etc. In fact, physicians are instructed not to initiate the subject of contraception with a patient except following an abortion. In August 1968, there was still something of a "policy vacuum," and the Ministry of Public Health was not planning to accord birth control any higher priority in the absence of a clear directive from the government to do so. Opinions differed on whether such a directive would be forthcoming. Research is under way on the factors determining family size, as well as on the questions of whether Cuba needs to adopt any kind of population policy, either to increase or decrease the birth rate.

Few persons appear to be concerned about any negative economic consequences of Cuba's current rate of population growth; if anything, worries about a continued decline in the rate of growth seem more common. As the author of one *Granma* article put it, "The Revolutionary Government does not support birth control for economic reasons. We do not accept the capitalist premise that the population explosion is the cause of the people's misery." [55] The reasons commonly given for official Cuban support of birth control relate to medical considerations and to female emancipation.

On the medical side, there has been some concern over a possible increase in illegal abortions, after a generally successful crackdown in the first years of the revolution. The prerevolutionary law which permitted abortions only when carrying the child to term would "endanger the health or life of the woman" has not been changed, and the interpretation of this law has been left up to the directors of individual hospitals. This introduces an element of variability into Cuba's abortion policy, since some directors interpret the law broadly to include mental health, while others do not. The general result is that legal abortions are easier to obtain in Cuba than in any other Latin American country, but more restricted than in the Soviet Union and most East European countries. Public health authorities consider contraception to be much preferable to abortion. Dr. Celestino Alvarez Lajonchere, head of the "special group" in gynecology and obstetrics in the Ministry of Public Health, points out that by age thirty most Cuban women have attained their desired family size and face the need for some means of fertility control for the following fifteen to twenty years. If contraceptives are not made readily available, abortion is the only substitute for continued childbearing. He likens abortion to curative medicine, but indicates a strong preference for preventive medicine—contraception.[56]

Birth control also facilitates female emancipation, which both makes possible the tapping of an immense source of underutilized labor and provides psychic benefits for women themselves. Sonia Pérez Tobella, a *Granma* reporter, writes:

When children are very young, they require the greater part of their mother's time. This means that the mother must devote herself exclusively to routine domestic chores. Her participation in and contribution to society is therefore greatly limited.

In a nation where class differences have been eliminated, the woman, no longer an economic or socially dependent being, can develop her abilities and pursue the career of her choice. She can easily see that constant pregnancy, year in and year out, truly interferes with such activities. Contraceptives are therefore provided not so much as an economic measure, but rather as an effective means of freeing woman from the drudgery of household chores, releasing her for more productive service to society as a whole and freeing her talents for the benefit of all.[57]

Elena Díaz and Natasha Klein of the University of Havana school of Philosophy, in a paper delivered to the 1968 International Cultural Congress in Havana, also put birth control in the context of the liberation of women. To achieve this goal, it is not sufficient to eliminate capitalist relations of production from a society. Woman's fulfillment comes about through her being able to transcend "the small affective and domestic world to which she was limited, and engage in the creative and dynamic world which has been for men exclusively, sharing with him the task of transforming it." [58] But this is impossible without effectively redefining the roles of wife and mother; women must be freed, insofar as possible, from household tasks and the education of children. To this end, the state has taken it upon itself to provide public education for all children, enlarge a scholarship system so that students may study away from home without placing a financial burden on their parents, provide free meals in all elementary and secondary schools, establish free child care centers for working mothers, and ensure that the means of birth control are available to all women.[59]

The preceding are the main reasons given by Cuban writers for the provision of birth control means to the Cuban population today. Economic motives (except for the expansion of female labor force participation) are usually explicitly denied. Actually, very little appears to have been written on the question of the economic aspects of Cuba's population structure and growth. However, at least one writer, Prof. Juan Pérez de la Riva, has raised the question of the economic costs of Cuba's moderately rapid population growth and the possibility of future overpopulation in an article in the French demographic journal *Population*.[60] (As background, it should be mentioned that with 165 inhabitants per square mile, Cuba ranks fourth among Latin American countries in terms of density, although if we use a ratio of inhabitants per square mile of agriculturally utilizable land, Cuba drops to sixth place.[61]) At the beginning of his article, Professor Pérez de la Riva states that Cuba "already appears as a densely populated territory; and although one cannot speak of it as crowded, Cubans are wondering, for the first time, whether they are on the road to overpopulation." [62] No direct answer is given to this question, but at the end of the article the author broaches the important problem of capital formation under conditions of rapid population increase:

Yet if fertility trends continue, and once emigration has ended (which should happen soon), the island's population will exceed ten million in less than ten years, thus having doubled in less than thirty years. Cuba's soils are rich enough and well enough irrigated to support such an increase, but in order to maintain and especially to raise the standard of living, important capital investments will be necessary, which are difficult to find at the moment. Some think that fertility has reached its highest level, and will drop as quickly as it rose after the Revolution. That is possible, but by no means certain. It would be fruitless to attempt comparisons with Europe's evolution after the last world war.[63]

The above passage was written during the fall of 1966, before the new decline in Cuba's birth rate was apparent. When asked in 1968 whether his opinions on economic problems of population growth had changed, Pérez de la Riva replied that it was more a case of Cuba's demographic conditions having changed; he would now worry if the birth rate continued in its downward direction. He added that Cuba's problem in the future, far from one of overpopulation, might be one of assuring population replacement.

Judging from some recent informal comments, it would appear that Prime Minister Fidel Castro is not particularly worried about the rate of population growth in Cuba. In a speech on April 19, 1968, in the course of some remarks on the "population explosion" in Latin America, Castro made the following brief observation about Cuba:

> And, since children are going to keep on being born [in Latin America]— because I don't think they will pay much attention to Johnson and Company when they speak of birth control and family planning. . . . The whole thing is ridiculous. You know our countryside and our farmers; can you imagine what would happen if they came to them with such foolishness? They'd tell the planners to go to hell. Really, this is something you cannot plan.[64]

But this cannot be interpreted to mean that Castro is unaware of the difficulties entailed by the rapid growth of population. He recognizes the severity of the problem, but places his faith in revolution, with its consequent social and economic reorganization, rather than in population limitation. Shortly after making the above comment, he continued:

> This is one of the world's greatest problems—and one of the greatest problems to be faced by this continent in the coming decades and, in fact, even before, because the people are already suffering from unbearable poverty. There is no solution in sight. Those who are still alive live in overcrowded valleys.
>
> At the time of the Revolution the peasants had already settled in the mountains. Twenty or thirty years before, nobody would have gone to the

Sierra Maestra, and now they were practically on top of Turquino Peak. Give them a few more years and they would have wound up in Bartlett's Deep! . . .

The population kept growing, while the economy remained stagnant. The peasants were living on the tops of the mountains by the time we started our guerrilla warfare in that region. There was no solution to the problem. A little more time and the situation would have been unbearable. The population had doubled, while the number of sugar mills remained the same. . . .

It is impossible to emerge from underdevelopment under a capitalist system, with its feudal mode of land ownership and its contradiction between a bourgeois and oligarch minority and the people. The first thing we had to do was get rid of the latifundia and then deal with the problem posed by the tiny farmers. We had to develop new programs with the cooperation of the farmers, to find adequate solutions to all the farmers' problems that arose in connection with bringing the sugarcane fields closer to the mills, to plant what we needed where it was needed, to use heavy farm equipment and to increase productivity.[65]

It is evident that Castro considers *prerevolutionary* Cuba to have had a "population problem," as manifested by the imbalance between growing numbers and limited land and productivity, but a problem that was only solvable through a revolutionary restructuring of the economy. In *postrevolutionary* Cuba, he seems to take population growth as a given, as "something you cannot plan." His apparent laissez-faire population policy stands in curious contrast to the planned socialist economy. This contrast is even more puzzling in view of the fact that Castro is fully aware of another set of what can only be called "population problems" which affect capitalist and socialist countries alike. These have to do with (1) age structure and the "burden of dependency" and (2) investment levels necessary to offset the effects of population growth. On March 13, 1968 (one month before the speech from which we have just quoted), Castro gave a long statistic-laden speech announcing the initiation of a new "revolutionary offensive," which involved the nationalization of most remaining small businesses and a call to curtail consumption so as to maximize the resources available for productive investment. In the course of this speech, which described in detail many of the economic problems Cuba is currently trying to overcome, Castro gave extended attention to population problems, mainly as they apply internationally to underdeveloped countries. Here we will only quote from his remarks that apply specifically to Cuba:

A concrete example is Cuba, a country which began its economic development after the Revolution. The average rate at which the population of Cuba has been increasing during the past five years is 2.3% annually. This rate is three or four times as great as the population growth of the industrial countries when they began to industrialize. . . .

By 1970, according to present estimates, the population will reach a total of 8,349,000. . . . In all, there will be 3,255,000 persons under 15—that is, 39% of the total population of Cuba. Think how production will need to be increased, milk production, food production, the production of everything, for a population whose youth section is increasing.

With an annual rate of population growth of 2.3% and with almost 40% of the population made up of persons under 15 years of age, the effort that our people must make is considerable. Just to offset the population increase alone, no less than 12% of the available gross national product must be invested to compensate for such growth. And to assure a one percent rate of production growth, and double our income in 80 years we must use no less than 16% of the gross national product. And to develop the economy at a rate of no less than five percent of the gross per capita product annually, 30% of the available gross national product must be invested. And this effort must be primarily made by half the population, excluding children and persons over sixty.[66]

In spite of this analysis, which attributes certain difficulties squarely to demographic conditions (which are presumably not reducible to other conditions, in the sense that low per capita food production might be attributed to the failure to bring new land under cultivation or improve techniques, rather than to the growing number of people), Castro did not call for the adoption of policies that would slow the rate of growth of the population and alter its age structure. The difficulties arising from demographic factors are presented as the "context" in which the struggle for development must be waged, rather than as "variables" which can be altered. They are "something you cannot"—or for some unexplained reasons do not wish to—"plan."

We will now turn our attention to Cuban writings dealing with demographic aspects of Latin American development. Although the quantity of materials is not sufficient to make any firm statement (especially for the early years), in general there has occurred an increasing sophistication of the level of argument. Through 1966, the predominant concern seemed to be that of combatting the idea of Latin American "overpopulation," interpreted mainly in terms of density. From 1967 on, with the publication of the OLAS book, *La*

Población Latinoamericana, Problemas y Perspectivas, the terms of the debate begin to change in the direction of a more complicated view of the problems. The real change in newspaper (especially *Granma*) articles, however, is not noticeable until 1968. Interestingly, the same transition can be seen in Fidel Castro's speeches. In September 1966, for example, he referred to population as follows:

> There are some countries around which speak as though the solution lay in birth control. Only the capitalists, the exploiters, can say that, for no one who is aware of what man can achieve through technology and science can put a limit on the number of human beings there can be on the earth.[67]

By March 1968, in the "Revolutionary Offensive" speech we quoted earlier, Castro was dealing with demographic problems so complicated that it was later necessary to distribute explanatory materials to clarify what he had said.

One gets the impression that the frequent Cuban denial of the economic utility of fertility limitation—both for Cuba and other Latin American countries—is strongly conditioned by the prominent role played by American organizations (and more recently, the American government) in promoting birth control in Latin America. As early as November 1961, *Panorama Económico Latinoamericano* (a weekly Cuban economics review) published an article entitled "Too Many Latins?" which attempted to refute the "neo-Malthusian" views of the Planned Parenthood Federation of America and others who advocate population control.[68] The neo-Malthusian position is characterized simply as interpreting underdevelopment to be due to the pressure of increasing population on natural resources, agricultural production, and living space. On the ideological side, neo-Malthusianism is seen as a

> . . . weapon of imperialism to "justify" the underdevelopment of countries suffering from the super-exploitation of monopolies plundering their natural resources, deforming their economics and depriving them of capital by the familiar method of buying cheap and selling dear. This decapitalization, and the imperialist maintenance of feudal relations in agriculture, is the origin of underdevelopment, not the increase in population.[69]

As for the validity of the theory, special attention is given to the question of density, and much is made of the underdeveloped countries' relative underpopulation (in terms of inhabitants per unit of territory) as compared with Europe. Since density is interpreted as being central to the neo-Malthusian argument, the surprising observation is made that "If, as the neo-Malthusians hold, over-population engenders underdevelopment, then Europe should have a greater underdevelopment than Asia, which it obviously does not." [70] The concern with density, rather than rates of increase, shows up again in the following statement: "Underdevelopment means, among other things, lack of population, due largely to high mortality rates and especially the high infant mortality which underdevelopment brings with it." [71] With regard to the depletion of natural resources, the article says that jungle and polar regions have hardly been tapped, that marine resources are another potential source of supply, and that in any case many natural products are being replaced by synthetics. Similarly, no concern is expressed about the ability of agricultural production to keep ahead of population increases; UN statistics on recent gains in world per capita food production are cited. The conclusion is drawn that "The problem is not population increase (with all the neo-Malthusians' frightful predictions), but is basically a question of increasing production using modern techniques and of seeking a more rational distribution of what is produced." [72]

Another shorter piece, entitled "The 'Demographic Explosion' in Underdeveloped Countries," published in 1966 in the book *Tres Continentes,* focuses on the population problem exclusively in terms of density. The article begins by citing recent figures on world population growth and then goes on to ask:

But . . . where is the growth greatest? And is this growth considered in absolute or relative numbers?
The very concerned North American neo-Malthusians measure growth in percentages. There, certainly, the underdeveloped countries present "higher rates": 2.8%, 3.0%, 3.5%, etc., as opposed to only 0.6% to 1.7%. It is a fact, nevertheless, that relative numbers by themselves are misleading, for the countries that are "growing fastest" in percentages are, generally speaking, the most underpopulated ones. This is true, at least, considering the world by regions.
One area, Latin America, has a high growth rate: 2.6%, according to the last U.N. estimate. But, with respect to its *population density, which is what counts,* Latin America is the most underpopulated region of the world. [73] [Italics added.]

The article concludes by citing density statistics for several European countries (whose densities are much higher than Latin America's density as a whole), calculating hypothetical total world population figures based on the assumption of European densities, and asking whether the world could maintain such a large population. The conclusion is drawn that the imperialists have more to worry about in their own countries than in the underdeveloped areas.

Another *Granma* article shows the same tendency to transform the problem of rates of population growth into one of size and density:

> Concern over the rate of population increase is not justifiable. If according to estimates, in 33 years Latin America will have a population of around 600,000,000 inhabitants living in a total area of 20,500,000 square kilometers, this would mean a population density of less than 30 inhabitants per square kilometer, a moderate population density, barely half of Europe today. And, moreover, in a region with much richer natural resources.[74]

It is obvious that the preceding articles take the neo-Malthusian position in a rather simplistic form and even then do not provide very convincing refutation. Part of the difficulty lies in the use of regional or world statistics, rather than national ones; it is not very meaningful, for example, to speak of *Latin America's* low population density, when the range for individual countries varies from Bolivia's low of 9 inhabitants per square mile to Haiti's high of 415. Similarly, reference to trends in *world* agricultural production is misleading, since it is precisely the less-developed countries (and those with the highest rates of population increase) which are finding it most difficult to increase production. Thus, even on the authors' own terms (density, resources, and agricultural production) it would be possible to characterize certain individual Latin American countries—such as Haiti, El Salvador, and the Dominican Republic—as relatively overpopulated.

But the problem does not lie so much there as in the blurring of the distinction between population *size* (or density) and the *rate* at which the population is growing. Most of those who advocate population limitation in Latin America do not do so because they believe this area to be "overpopulated" in the sense that better productive techniques could not support many more people, but because they see the *rapidity* of population growth as engendering economic difficulties which could otherwise be avoided. Attention is focused in particular on two factors: investment and the burden of dependency.[75]

The first argument commonly runs as follows: The population of Latin America is presently increasing at about 3 percent a year. The capital output ratio (which expresses the number of units of capital that must be invested in order to produce an annual addition of one unit of output) is on the order of about 2.4.[76] If we apply these figures to an individual Latin American country, this means that 7.2 percent of its national income must be saved and invested just to keep the standard of living from falling (zero per capita economic growth). A per capita economic growth rate of 3 percent yearly could be achieved either by investing 14.4 percent of the national income if the population were increasing by 3 percent or by investing 7.2 percent of the national income if the population were stationary. Thus a rapidly expanding population means that capital which could otherwise be invested in the economic infrastructure of the country must be channeled instead into expenditures on consumption and services for the increased population.

The second common argument has to do with dependency, or the proportion of the population which is in the economically nonproductive years and hence "dependent" upon that proportion of suitable age to participate in the labor force. The main point here is that the higher the population growth rate is (excluding immigration), the larger the proportion of economically dependent children will be in the total population. Thus Uruguay, with an annual rate of population growth of 1.3 percent, has only 28 percent of its population between the ages of zero and fourteen years and has 64 percent between fifteen and sixty-four years. At the other extreme, Costa Rica, which is growing by 4 percent a year, has 48 percent of its population in the 0–14 years category and only 49 percent in the 15–64 years category. This results in the problem that the least-developed countries, which in Latin America are generally those with the highest rates of population growth, have the largest proportion of children dependent on the smallest proportion of economically productive adults. (It should be noted that the Latin American countries with slowly growing populations have relatively more persons in the older nonproductive years—65 and up—but the difference between these countries and the fastest growing countries is only a few percentage points.) This effect of rapid growth rates upon the age structure of a population is one of the main reasons why many demographers believe that a fertility control program would be beneficial to most Latin American countries. Such a program would not necessarily be in conflict with the desire for a larger population since no birth control program immediately imaginable would reduce the rate of population growth to zero; the desired size would simply take longer to arrive at. In addition, during about the first twenty years after the fertility reduction programs were instituted, the increase in numbers of persons entering labor-force age would be unaffected.

In July 1967, *Granma* published an article entitled "Is Population Growth Responsible for the Poverty of the People?"[77] which covers roughly the same ground as the 1961 *Panorama Economico Latinoamericano* article referred to earlier. After a brief exposition of the original Malthusian theory, it states that, in fact, "the population of Latin America . . . is increasing at a more rapid rate than the means of subsistence." The imperialists have seized on the Malthusian thesis (which has been enriched by the addition of "the A-bomb, bacteriological weapons and instruments of mass destruction" as checks to population growth) as the explanation of Latin America's plight: "They repeat that poverty is a result of the accelerated rise in population and stress that State-imposed birth control is the only solution to such poverty." After a discussion of infant mortality conditions in Latin America, the author comments ironically that from the neo-Malthusian point of view high infant mortality might be considered beneficial and that in combination with birth control it would assist in the solution of the region's economic problems.

But it is neither humanly nor economically correct to maintain such a thesis, as the problem does not lie there. The poverty which afflicts the people in aggravated form today is basically the same poverty which faced them in the 20's and 30's, when the population was considerably less, and the infant mortality rate was proportionately about the same.

What it does show is that hunger came before the population increase, and that this hunger is principally responsible for the high infant mortality rate. Therefore, birth control is no guarantee of political, economic or social improvement under the capitalist system. What will the people gain by reducing the population boom if they continue to live in the same subhuman conditions?[78]

This makes sense only if "neo-Malthusianism" is seen as attributing poverty to the single cause of rapid population growth, and that is a position more extreme than even Malthus himself ever took. In the light of our discussion of the effects of population growth rates on investment and age structure, the above argument obviously begs the central questions.

In 1967 there appeared a book which helped to alter the level of the discussion. *La Población Latinoamericana, Problemas y Perspectivas* was written by Professor Pérez de la Riva, but published anonymously by the Latin American Solidarity Organization. A sophisticated work, it is both a contribution to Latin American population studies and a polemic against neo-Malthusianism. Many topics are covered which, because of the limited aims of this chapter, will not be examined here: settlement patterns, immigration, urban problems, Latin American life expectancy and the economic value of the "lost years," population dynamics during the colonial period, etc. With regard to the issue of rapid population growth and development, we may abstract the structure of the book's argument as follows: Imperialism has led to Latin America's socioeconomic backwardness, which in turn has determined the demographic characteristics of high fertility and infant mortality, rapid population growth, an average life expectancy of twenty-four years less than that in the United States, etc. "Population growth in our day, and especially in Latin America, is a problem of social and economic development. Wishing to reduce the population because the economy is not growing is to put the cart before the horse, because we all know, and historical experience demonstrates, that when the economy grows the population will regulate the rhythm of its own growth." [79] But economic growth is frustrated by the Latin American oligarchies and imperialism—hence the necessity of revolution.

Pérez de la Riva does devote some attention to the question of simple density and population in relation to arable land and mineral resources, and dismisses the idea of overpopulation for most of the continent. "The novelty of the demographic phenomenon in the underdeveloped countries and in Latin America in particular is not precisely the size of the population but its progressively higher rate of growth, which enters into contradiction with the present underdevelopment." [80] Furthermore, there is no immediate prospect of a decline in birth rates, for "the accelerated urbanization process in Latin America does not appear to be associated with a new fertility

pattern, such as occurred in Europe in the second half of the nineteenth century."[81]

Because Latin America's population will grow to twice the size
of the United States' by the end of the century, an elaborate campaign has been launched "to traumatize the Latin American oligarchy into abandoning its religious prejudices and permitting Malthusian propaganda."[82] But while opposing this, revolutionaries must
not fall into an "irresponsible pro-natalism." Birth control is an
"individual matter for each couple." "We are not against demographic planning as such, but rather against those who, because of
their reactionary nature, are incapable of planning the economy and
assuring the well-being of the people; they have no right to attempt
to reduce the population, since by doing so they only seek to assure
the exploitation of the workers by the minorities allied with imperialism." One of the defining characteristics of neo-Malthusians is
their desire to "preserve the existing outworn socioeconomic structures, which in the case of Latin America means the maintenance
of a bourgeois latifundist regime which impedes development and
industrialization. The latifundists would, then, be the only benefi-
ciaries of the operation."[83]

Pérez de la Riva concedes the validity of the argument that rapid
population growth necessitates an exceedingly high level of national
investment in order to maintain an adequate growth in per capita
product. He also believes that most Latin American countries are
presently incapable of performing such a feat on a sustained basis.
The "revolutionary solution" to

. . . the challenge of population growth would be to raise production to the
point where the level of consumption would be propitious to a cultural
development which would slow down population growth by itself. . . .

[The imperialists] wish to stop population growth artificially, without
changing the rest. Let us be clear that by saying "artificially", we are not
referring to fertility as such, but rather to the socioeconomic situation. The
whole debate collapses when it is made clear that the industrialized countries
first raised the material and cultural level of the masses, and *later* reduced
fertility, whereas the imperialists propose that we *first* reduce fertility and
later raise the standard of living.[84]

This quite obviously is a "revolutionary" solution since, according
to the premises of Pérez de la Riva's argument, the Latin American
countries as presently constituted are incapable of following the first

alternative. But several difficulties remain. The first is that the "investment problem" in the face of rapid population growth is one which confronts capitalist and socialist countries alike, even though the latter may be more able to mobilize resources to solve the problem. This was made obvious in Fidel Castro's "Revolutionary Offensive" speech. The second difficulty lies in the analogy with European history, for it is clear that the demographic situation which characterizes Latin America today is qualitatively different from Europe's, in that Europe was never faced with rates of population growth as high as Latin America's present ones. This also was made explicit in Castro's speech:

> Can any underdeveloped country today repeat the history of [the industrialized] countries when they began their industrialization? If not, why not? What factors constitute the major obstacles? One factor is population increase. . . .
> So whereas the developed countries' population in the beginning of their development increased by 40% in 50 years—or could have increased by 40%—the countries that are now underdeveloped, any underdeveloped country that increases [sic] its population by 2.2%, will triple its entire population in 50 years and will need to invest no less than 12 percent of the gross product to compensate for the population increase.[85]

Thus, although he does not recommend fertility limitation ("Don't get scared; we're not promoting family planning or birth control"), Castro's own remarks are sufficient to make one doubt the wisdom of following the "revolutionary solution" of letting population growth slow down "naturally."

Pérez de la Riva also discusses the relationship of population age structure to economic development and again concedes that Latin America's present situation is unfavorable. But he presents a population projection of "over 700 million" for the year 2000, the age structure of which would be "ideal for economic development," and which would come about "if mortality control is widened, but excessive birth control is not practiced."[86]

	present,* %	year 2000, %
less than 15 years	43	23
15 to 64 years	52	68
65 years and over	5	9

*Year not specified

One can readily agree that the second age structure is ideal for economic development; what is puzzling is how it will come about without "excessive birth control" being practiced. Since the exact fertility and mortality assumptions upon which it is based are unfortunately not specified, we cannot judge the degree of realism of the second structure. It is certainly at variance with current United Nations projections for the year 2000, which bear a much closer resemblance to the present age structure than the second, and the only probable manner in which such a drop in the proportion of persons under fifteen years of age could come about would be through a rather drastic decline in fertility starting no later than the 1980s. And this is a development which is only likely to occur if the Latin American oligarchies are "traumatized" into adopting birth control programs in short order and on a large scale.

Given the admitted desirability of the second age structure and assuming the unlikelihood of its being reached even several decades from now without actively attempting to lower fertility levels through birth control, we may ask: Why not encourage such a policy? Part of the answer seems to lie in the *political* significance of rapid population growth. Although this avenue of thought is not taken up in Pérez de la Riva's book, it does appear in an article from the June 5, 1968, edition of *El Mundo,* a Havana daily newspaper. The article is apparently based on material from the OLAS book, for the same projected age structure for the year 2000 is used, based on "not practicing excessive birth control." One concern expressed about birth control campaigns is the possibility that physicians might insert intrauterine devices in many more women than they could subsequently provide adequate care for. But attention is also focused on the political consequences of Latin America's present young age structure:

This, in reality, will cause a collision between the present Latin American economic structures and the great mass of youths who will be in optimum condition for carrying out productive work, but who will find themselves stymied and without possibilities of obtaining it. If, in the present circumstances, the Latin American oligarchies and the imperialists are incapable of solving the problem of these great masses of men who desire to work but find it impossible to do so, one can imagine that in the future a solution will be entirely out of the question. These youths will consequently find it necessary to break the existing structures and replace them with new ones which will permit them to utilize their capacities.

We should point out that we do not predicate the breaking of the existing Latin American economic structures solely on this demographic phenomenon, but we do have to call attention to the fact that this factor is influencing to a great extent the sharpening of the crisis of these structures.[87]

The preceding is not the only indication that Cuban disinterest in, or opposition to, fertility limitation programs in Latin America stems in part from the belief that the population explosion will be a conditioning factor for the revolutionary explosion. Castro himself holds this view. In the April 28 speech cited earlier he said: "The population is going to keep on growing. And revolution is the inevitable result, as in an elementary mathematical equation." [88] And in his speech at the closing session of the Havana Cultural Congress on January 12, 1968, Castro spoke at some length on the same subject. After quoting a statement of Dean Rusk's linking the population explosion with the danger of nuclear war, Castro commented as follows:

The solutions put forth by imperialism are the quintessence of simplicity. Two-thirds of humanity is hungry; in order to rid themselves of hunger and misery, these people must make revolutions. Ah! But there must not be revolutions! Revolutions will be put down with blood and fire! There will be peace only if there are no revolutions. But, moreover, even if there are no revolutions, what will happen to that two-thirds of mankind that multiplies like rabbits? When they speak of the problems of population and birth, they are in no way moved by concepts related to the interests of the family or of society. No! Their premise is that humanity will die of hunger if it continues multiplying; and they advance this concept in these days, which are not the days of Malthus or of Methuselah! Just when science and technology are making incredible advances in all fields, they resort to technology to suppress revolutions and ask the help of science to prevent population growth. In short, the peoples are not to make revolutions, and women are not to give birth. This sums up the philosophy of imperialism. . . .
The imperialists know that without revolution there is no development, and they feel powerless in view of the reality that there is growth and development in the world, that the population is growing, and that—as a natural and inevitable phenomenon—revolutionary awareness is growing.[89]

These same themes of population growth, revolution, and development were elaborated upon in a recent lengthy *Granma* article by Julio García, entitled "Agrarian Revolution and Underdevelopment." [90] The article is an attempt to explain why Latin American development efforts are floundering, and, interestingly, population growth plays a key role in the explanation. Much of the analysis is similar to that made in portions of Castro's "Revolutionary Offensive" speech which we have not quoted. We have chosen to discuss García's article, rather than the other demographic portions of Castro's speech, because of its greater coherence and completeness as a theory. Reduced to essentials, the author's argument is as follows: The "classic" method of economic development, as exemplified by Western Europe, was based upon a long period during which agricultural productivity managed to keep ahead of the slowly growing population, permitting the agricultural surpluses to be used as resources for the initial industrial development. During this period, in addition, technical processes were simpler and required relatively smaller investments than today; wages were very low, and the untrammeled exploitation of labor—including women and children— was permitted; and since the technical skills required of workers were less, large public investments in education were unnecessary. For Latin America today, the "classic" way of development has become impossible. Workers cannot be exploited as they were previously; technology and equipment are much more complex and must be imported from aboard at a price which is constantly rising while the value of Latin America's exports undergo a relative decline; and large-scale investments in the eduction of the work force are necessary. The capital for industrialization must come basically from agricultural surpluses, because only in this sector is it possible to realize sufficient profits in a short time and with minimum investment. But Latin America's agricultural production is stagnating, partly due to the extreme maldistribution of land and the inefficient organization of the means of production, but also due to the unprecedented rate of population growth. This growth means that an increasing proportion of the population is made up of economically dependent persons, which exacerbates the investment problem. In the face of this situation, the first priority is an agrarian revolution which will reorganize production along more rational lines. This revolution must move towards socialism to obtain the benefits of central planning, put all arable land under cultivation, channel resources where they are necessary, and make possible the huge necessary investments in technology, equipment, and education. "Not to follow this road is to invite self-destruction. And rather than return to the famines of the Middle Ages, the people will, undoubtedly, make their revolution." [91]

The reference to "the famines of the Middle Ages" in García's article is striking, because this is the sort of warning of impending catastrophe which is so common in the writings of neo-Malthusians. It is all the more striking considering that one of the principal factors underlying this grim view of the future is precisely Latin America's spiraling population growth. This article which we have summarized constitutes the strongest *implicit* Cuban statement I have seen that a fertility reduction program in Latin America would be economically desirable, and perhaps even urgent. The economic utility of birth control (under the present Latin American social systems, at least) follows logically from García's arguments, for one cannot assert that rapid population growth contributes to the maintenance of underdevelopment and then deny that the elimination of this factor would facilitate development. Nevertheless, to say that population limitation would be "useful" is not necessarily to recommend it as a course of action, and in fact, García does not even mention it. Furthermore, he does not predict famines; he predicts revolution.

We are now in a position to see that there is one major question which is not dealt with seriously in the recent Cuban writings on population that we have been examining: To what extent—if any—would the slowing of population growth facilitate economic development under a *capitalist* system? It is clear that the Cubans consider the revolutionary socialist reorganization of society to be the most desirable goal; what is not clear is whether, short of that, a fertility reduction would be beneficial under the existing systems. The ambiguity on this issue is well illustrated by the following pair of statements made by Dr. Celestino Alvarez Lajonchere:

> Historical experience demonstrates that the rapid growth of population is not an obstacle to development, nor are the growth or reduction of population a guarantee of progress. . . . At any rate, rapid population growth makes the transformation of socioeconomic structures more imperative and urgent. . . .[92]

If the above is not to be taken as outrightly contradictory, the meaning must be that a socialist economy is capable of absorbing and putting to productive use increases in population which would create severe problems for a capitalist economy. There is probably a good deal of truth to this, and theories of "labor-intensive" versus "capital-intensive" forms of economic development center around this point. (Even many nonsocialist economists cede the superior ability of a socialist system to mobilize labor in an underdeveloped country.) Bypassing this issue, we are still left with the original question of what role fertility reduction would play in a Latin American country in which socialist revolution is not an immediate prospect. Only Pérez de la Riva seems to both grant partial validity to the economic arguments for fertility limitation and accept the operative feasibility of birth control programs in Latin America. But he simply states that under present conditions all the benefits would go to the ruling groups and does not discuss the matter further. Sonia Pérez Tobella denies that fertility limitation would help; however, she does not come to grips with the main economic arguments. Julio García's article implies that it would help, but does not say so explicitly. Fidel Castro, in the April 19 speech that we have quoted, avoids the issue by claiming that large-scale birth control programs have no chance of popular acceptance in the first place. And the recent *El Mundo* article speaks of the "impossibility of application of such projects in these countries."

But the issue cannot be avoided. Few serious persons believe the slowing of population growth to be a panacea for economic development; even if the age structure produced by slower rates of population growth is more suitable for making large-scale investments that will eventually result in a modern industrialized economy, this is no guarantee that such investments will be made. The lower rate of population growth and the consequently changed age structure should, however, *facilitate* these investments. In addition, given the relatively large proportion of persons who fall in the unemployed or underemployed categories in Latin America, there is no reason to fear a labor shortage, and the eventually slower increase in the number of workers might have a positive effect on wage levels. The food production problem would almost certainly be ameliorated, and the process of the fragmenting of land into smaller and smaller holdings could be slowed down. On the family level, moreover, all the benefits of birth control dealt with by Sonia Pérez Tobella and Dr. Alvarez Lajonchere would be operative: improved maternal health, lower infant mortality, fewer abortions, and a greater possibility of the woman's developing ability not related to household work.

All the above factors are far from adding up to a "revolution," of course, and the inevitable question is thus posed: What effect would a large-scale birth control program have on the future course of revolution in Latin America? Despite the obvious importance of this question, very little is to be found on the subject in the materials we have been examining. Fidel Castro in effect provided one reply when he said that in his opinion such programs did not have any chance of success to begin with. Somewhat more soberly, the recent *El Mundo* article which we quoted from states that revolutionary potentiality does not *depend* on rapid population growth, but that it is being influenced by it "to a great extent."

Having raised the question, I must disclaim any intention of attempting to answer it. An adequate answer would involve a detailed excursus into the sociology of revolutions. I would only warn against the immediate temptation to decide in a facile manner that such a program would necessarily lower the chances of revolution. As a corrective, one may reflect on the fact that the only socialist revolution in Latin America occurred in a country with the third lowest birth rate in the region.

In the meantime, a *Granma* editorialist has ably summed up the present Cuban position with grim humor:

> Theirs [the neo-Malthusians'] is not a true alternative but rather a subterfuge for avoiding the only solution: a change in the mode of production of man's material goods.
> And this must be effected soon. Some 10,000 children die daily of hunger throughout the world: one every $8\frac{1}{2}$ seconds, more than 400 an hour. In the next few seconds, the hunger born of imperialism will kill another child. In the next few seconds. . . .[93]

CONCLUSIONS

What remains today of the original Marxian positions on population? With regard to the analysis of underdeveloped countries, little use has been made—at least in the writings we have examined—of Marx's "law of population under capitalism." The existence of Latin America's "relative surplus population" is obviously less due to a relentless process of automation than to the general stagnation of the continent's economies. Additionally, however, Marx's formulation of the law was inadequate as a frame of reference for the study of population dynamics for the simple reason that it omitted specific consideration of the main demographic variables: fertility and mortality rates, migration, age structure, etc. Contemporary Cuban and Soviet writings seem to be more indebted to the general criticisms of Malthusian theory made principally by Engels, involving the refusal to regard the "principle of population" as an eternal biological-environmental dilemma, the insistence on population problems as being specific to certain kinds of social systems, and the stress on the potentialities of rationally utilized agricultural and industrial technology.

With regard to the growth of population under a socialist system, the original writings offer little guidance, either for theory or for policy. Even if Marx had formulated a law of population for socialism, it would have been based on the presupposition of a fully industrialized economy, and hence largely inapplicable to the conditions under which the Russians and Cubans began to construct socialism. The main thrust of Marx's and Engels' comments on this subject, it will be recalled, was that population growth would hardly present difficulties to a socialist society, although Engels left open the "abstract possibility" that numbers might eventually have to be limited. In effect, then, room was left for the adoption of policies suited to particular national needs. Thus it could occur that in 1963 when the Chinese government was deliberately attempting to reduce births through the popularization of contraceptives, abortion, and sterilization and did not consider that in so doing it was deviating from Marxism, the Soviet newspaper *Izvestia* attacked the Chinese efforts as "incompatible with the Marxist approach to these questions." According to the then-prevailing Soviet view, "Marxism teaches that among the chief task related to population problems are the growth of labor productivity and constant concern for raising the living standards of the people, *assuming a constant growth of the population*.[94] [Italics added.]

The original Marxian unconcern with population growth and its basic demographic components has led to a paradoxical situation: some of those countries which most strongly advocate comprehensive social and economic planning have dismissed the idea of population planning as either reactionary or as a matter which may have to be dealt with at some indefinite future time. Thus the Cubans have so far adopted no policies with the deliberate aim of influencing fertility levels (and hence the growth rate and age structure of the population), and it is left to nonsocialist students of population, such as Kingsley Davis, to point out that "What is rational in the light of a couple's situation may be totally irrational from the standpoint of society's welfare."[95] To be sure, in any concrete case it will be arguable in what direction population movements should be modified, but surely such questions as differential growth rates and age structures cannot be taken as matters of indifference from the point of view of economic development and general social welfare. The curiousness of this position is compounded even further when it is realized that a socialist government has a much broader range of policy options open to it to influence fertility levels than does a nonsocialist government. It has much more immediate control over the main socioeconomic factors (female labor force participation, educational requirements and opportunities, tax and income policy, etc.) which ultimately determine the birth rate. Actually, however, the Cuban position on this matter is now becoming somewhat unique among Communist countries. China has had policies of attempting to lower fertility intermittently since the mid-1950s. Rumania in 1966 drastically restricted the grounds for legal abortions, with the explicit aim of raising fertility. The Soviet Union has at various times taken steps to increase birth rates (through economic incentives and the restriction of abortions). Recently, the Soviet demographer Boris Urlanis called for a policy which would enable women to quit work and have more children, out of a concern that his country's birth rate is currently insufficient to adequately populate its territory.[96] And even in Cuba, as we have mentioned, research is underway to determine whether some population policy is needed.

Returning to Cuban and Soviet positions on the value of decreasing population growth in the underdeveloped countries, we must place the attitudes on this specific issue within the context of their foreign policy in general. Much of the debate over birth control and population growth fits into the mold of the classic "reform versus revolution" dilemma, which has plagued left-wing organizations for over a century. In essence, the dilemma consists in the fact that an organization whose long-range goal is revolution and a thorough restructuring of the society faces pressures to engage in struggles for short-run or "transitional" reforms (wage raises, for example), which will make life in the society as currently constituted more tolerable. Yet the accumulated impact of successful reforms can lead to a situation in which the organization has cut the ground out from under its long-range aim—revolution. (Or the organization becomes so adept at reformist tactics that the very aim of revolution becomes abandoned long before the reforms' effects frustrate it themselves.) Although the two approaches may not be ultimately incompatible, the history of leftist movements shows that it is exceedingly difficult to maximize both at the same time. The Cuban support for guerrilla warfare in Latin America places them unambiguously on the revolutionary side of the fence (in contrast with most Latin American Communist Parties), showing little interest in parliamentary methods and trade union activities. A whole series of possible reformist strategies is bypassed in order to better concentrate on the ultimate goal. This should clarify the meaning of Pérez de la Riva's comment: "The 'population explosion,' then, is a problem for imperialism, not for the revolutionaries." [97] And consequently, one's opinion of the Cuban position will be partly determined by his opinion of the possibility and desirability of revolution. For those who do not accept revolution as desirable or feasible, there is probably nothing in the Cuban writings that would dissuade them from supporting attempts to reduce Latin America's rate of population growth. Even Fidel Castro's many remarks contain no reference to advantages accruing from current growth rates, except for the facilitation of the revolution. (This is not to hold, of course, that one cannot logically support both revolution and policies to check population growth; it is simply that in practice the two positions do not tend to be found together.)

Soviet foreign policy, on the other hand, has been moving steadily away from a revolutionary position, especially with regard to Latin America. In contrast to the Cuban call to arms, according to current Soviet analyses socialist revolution is simply not on the agenda for most of Latin America; large trade credits have recently been extended even to the conservative dictatorships of Argentina and Brazil. These ideological differences between the Cuban and Soviet governments, which have become so prominent in the last several years, find their counterparts in demographic writings. Compare, for example, the political premises of the OLAS book on population with the closing statement of Y. G. Mashbitz's article on population growth and food supply: "Latin America, like all other regions of the world, can solve its vital problems only if there is peace, general and complete disarmament and effective international co-operation." [98]

The kinds of connections seen among birth control, fertility decline, social reform, and revolution are obviously relevant to the above considerations. The frequently heard assertion that "Communists oppose birth control because they believe that 'the worse things are, the better,'" simply obscures what have actually been complex and varying sets of perceptions and positions. We may summarize a few of the basic facts here: Lenin's position, as we have seen, was one in favor of birth control as a basic family right, but against attempts to lower national fertility based on neo-Malthusian convictions, including the effort to convince the oppressed that their plight was due to the size of their families. This position was arrived at despite his belief that birth control would make "the ulcers of capitalism" less "painful for the oppressed masses," and hence might lower the chances of revolution. If Urlanis's recent paper "Marxism and Birth Control" can be taken as representative, the new Soviet views attribute considerable importance to the socioeconomic problems of rapid population growth, but somehow "the limitation of family size among the working class . . . in no way affects the intensity of the class struggle." Cuban writers, until recently, have been at best ambivalent about tracing any major problems to even a partial source in rapid population growth. Of late, however, the status of the population variable has been upgraded, and it is now often described as a major causative factor in the impending Latin American revolution. Finally, it should be noted that since Lenin, Communists have almost uniformly supported the *abstract* right of individual couples to the means of birth control. Opposition or support (which obviously affects the practical exercise of the abstract right) for particular birth control programs has varied according to the sponsor of the program, its aims, the "target group," the relative "progressiveness" of the government of the country in question, etc. Even the Cubans do not seem to oppose programs having the simple aim of filling an existing demand for contraception, as long as no deliberate policy objective of reducing birth rates is involved.

Cuban and Soviet writers have shown varying degrees of willingness to differentiate among the types of rationales upon which support for birth control has been based by diverse organizations and individuals in North America and Western Europe. At worst, those who advocate population limitation in order to improve the prospects for economic growth in the underdeveloped countries and those who advocate it in order to stem the rate of decrease in the proportion of Caucasians in the world's population have been thrown indiscriminately into the category of "neo-Malthusians." The prevailing Cuban usage of the term is more similar in scope to the Soviet usage up through the early 1960s than to the current, more restricted, Soviet usage ("primary emphasis" upon birth control as a solution to development problems). Urlanis and Guzevaty, among others, have explicitly cautioned against confusing neo-Malthusianism with attempts to rationalize population growth. Over time, however, the term has been so abused that today it seems to have little more than rhetorical value. Because "neo-Malthusianism" has been used as a label for such diverse positions as being in favor of birth control, favoring demographic rather than economic solutions, seeing the root of social problems in biological-environmental rather than socioeconomic factors, as well as many other permutations on these themes, the attempt to find a "legitimate" meaning for the term is now probably a fruitless undertaking.

One feature of the socialist writings on population has been a concern with analyzing the motives of the foreign governments and organizations which are promoting birth control internationally. Lately this has focused almost exclusively on the United States, as private organizations and governmental agencies from this country have come to take the dominant role in these activities. Although recent Soviet writings show a decline in interest in this question, Cuban concern continues to be strong, sometimes dominating the discussion of birth control and population growth in newspaper articles. The most common interpretation places the American concern with the population growth rates of the underdeveloped countries in the context of an empire which is threatened by a combination of economic stagnation and revolutionary aspirations. Efforts to control population growth abroad, by private organizations (foundations, the Population Council, the Population Reference Bureau) or governmental agencies (the Agency for International Development), are seen as control mechanisms for the imperialist system. Regardless of the validity of this formulation, the problem is that it may easily lead to a sort of syllogism—since imperialism is pernicious and fertility reduction is used by the imperialists as an attempted control mechanism, fertility reduction is pernicious. This kind of implicit reasoning, avoided in the OLAS book but characteristic of some short articles, leads to a failure to examine adequately the substantive issues concerning the impact of population growth on social welfare. The problem is apparent when it is realized what range of policies and programs could be analyzed as control mechanisms of imperialism which would presumably demand opposition on those grounds alone: the effort by some North American and European businesses to pay higher wages than nationally owned firms; the construction of roads, schools and hospitals; anti-malaria campaigns; etc. This is not to imply that the reasons behind the current United States "birth control offensive" do not need careful study, nor is it to prejudge the specific issue of fertility reduction when viewed in this light, but only to suggest that an overpreoccupation with the *motives* of American organizations can potentially blind one to the practical issues involved in differing rates of population growth. There is no necessary paradox in the idea that revolutionaries and imperialists may have certain limited goals in common.

Nevertheless, an understanding of the nature of American population policy vis-à-vis the Third World countries—in both its governmental and private manifestations—is essential to an understanding of the development of Communist policies in the same area. It is hoped that future studies will be done examining American ideologies of population in a way similar to this treatment of Cuba and the Soviet Union. It will also be interesting to trace the development of opinions on the issue of the Latin American left wing outside of Cuba. The overall impression created currently is one of general confusion, which may be due in some part to the contradictory counsels issuing from Moscow and Havana. Whether or not the Latin American Communist parties follow the "demographic revisionist" lead of the Soviet writers Guzevaty, Urlanis, and others will be of particular interest. It would be ironic if the Communist Parties were to accept Cuban advice on this matter when they have accepted it on so little else.

Looking at the future, it seems relatively safe to predict that a Soviet reversal to the kind of population policies preceding the mid-1960s is unlikely. Barring a major change in the orientation of Soviet general foreign policy, it seems probable that in the years ahead even more emphasis will be placed on lowering the population growth rates of the underdeveloped countries. The current Cuban position, however, seems to be potentially less stable. This is due, first, to the attention given in recent Cuban writings (and in Fidel Castro's speeches) to the age structure and investment problems occasioned by rapid population growth. It is an easy step to conclude from current Cuban analyses that fertility control is desirable for Latin America after all, even if the Cubans themselves do not recommend it. A second source of change in the Cuban position could conceivably come if that country were to adopt an internal national policy of attempting to curtail population growth itself. This would obviously put a strain on the recommendation of unchecked population growth for other countries. While it is perhaps not probable that such an internal policy will be adopted, the content of Castro's "Revolutionary Offensive" speech suggests that it is still an open question.

In conclusion, we would like to note the relevance of the writings we have been examining to several important controversies among demographers (and students of development in general) today. It will be recalled that the original Marxian interpretation of "population problems" was that of the pressure of numbers upon the means of employment and production, rather than the means of subsistence. (Hence the necessity of social reorganization as a solution to these problems.) It is obvious that prerevolutionary Cuba—in spite of its only moderately high birth rate—could have been pointed to by many Western demographers as a country suffering from a "population problem." Evidence for this, aside from its density and growth rate, could have been drawn from unemployment statistics. From May 1956 to April 1957, the best year of the mid-1950s, *overt* unemployment fluctuated between 9 and 21 percent of the labor force.[99] Following the revolution, with the reorganization of the "means of employment" and the application of labor-intensive strategies to agriculture, the level of unemployment was drastically reduced. In addition, many observers have been predicting a mild agriculturally based "prosperity" in the near future, based on the increased infrastructural investments and mass mobilization of labor for intensive crop-planting of the last several years.[100]

The preceding is an indication that an economy reorganized along socialist lines can potentially provide productive employment for that substantial proportion of the labor force—unemployed and underemployed—which in the previous system might have been considered "excess population." At this level, it is a fact at least in keeping with the original Marxian idea of the specificity of population problems to certain kinds of social systems. But what of fertility levels and the age-structure and investment problems to which they give rise? Is Cuba likely to be the first Latin American country to attain a stable population? The issues involved in this sort of question have been discussed in recent articles by Judith Blake and Kingsley Davis. We have already had occasion to note some of the latter's ideas in the section dealing with the Soviet Union, and Blake follows similar lines of thought. She argues[101] that in order for the underdeveloped countries to drastically curtail their population growth, neither the "family planning" approach (propaganda for, and provision of, contraceptives) nor the "economic development" approach (expecting industrial development to bring about fertility declines by itself) will suffice, not even jointly. The first is limited by widespread large-family-size desires and the second by the problem that existing high rates of population growth stymie serious industrialization programs. Furthermore, economic development by itself may or may not reduce the utilities—economic *and social*—of having more than two children. In addition to policies which diminish for parents the economic utility of children, policies are needed which orient women away from strictly familial roles. If one of the principal reasons why women have many children is to fulfill well the socially prescribed role of "mother," then policies which encourage the adoption of alternative (nonfamilial) roles would attack directly one of the major components of reproductive motivation. Blake places particular emphasis on female labor force participation, a variable which has been shown to have a very strong negative association with fertility. (Note the recurrence of a concern with changes as in the "means of employment," though in a more restricted sense than previously.) This perspective would draw our attention not only to the steady expansion of female employment in Cuba, but also to the proliferation of adult educational opportunities and the growing participation of women in voluntary organizations. At the same time, of course, there are forces tending to lessen the "costs" of children, such as the abolition of rents (scheduled to be completed by 1970), the free child-care centers and schooling in general, etc. But the main thrust of current Cuban policies seems to be in the direction of creating an increasing number of extrafamilial or nonfamilial roles and the reorganization of social life increasingly away from the home, and

Blake's theory would lead us to expect this to have a profound impact upon childbearing patterns. These features of Cuban society are of course broadly similar to those of the Soviet Union and the countries of Eastern Europe, most of which have low birth rates, and in some of which there have been recent signs of concern that birth rates may be *too* low. (A growth rate of zero does not seem to have been taken as the immediate ideal in any socialist country yet.) In the light of this, it is more understandable why some Cubans consider that their long-run problem is less likely to be one of overpopulation than of maintenance of high-enough fertility to assure population replacement. It is to be hoped that the experiences of the socialist countries will force more theoretical attention to the issues raised by Blake and Davis and by contemporary Marxist students of population.

NOTES

1. Coontz (London: Routledge & Kegan Paul Ltd.), 1957.

2. Marx's and Engels' views on population and Malthusian theory are widely scattered throughout their writings. The best single source is a compilation assembled by Ronald L. Meek (ed.), *Marx and Engels on Malthus* (New York: International Publishers, 1954). In addition to bringing together twenty selections from the original writings, Meek provides a valuable introductory essay. Sidney Coontz's *Population Theories and the Economic Interpretation* (cited above) also provides a summary and discussion of the original Marxist position. In addition, see William Petersen's "Marx versus Malthus: The Symbols and the Men," in *The Politics of Population* (Garden City, N.Y.: Anchor Books, 1965), pp. 72–89.

3. "An Essay on the Principle of Population" (1st ed.), in T. R. Malthus, *On Population* (New York: Modern Library, Inc., 1960), p. 65.

4. "An Essay on the Principle of Population," in *ibid.* (New York: Modern Library, Inc., 7th ed., abridged), p. 591.

5. Karl Marx, *Critique of the Gotha Programme* (1875), in Meek, *op. cit.*, p. 107.

6. Frederick Engels, "The Myth of Overpopulation," *Outlines of a Critique of Political Economy* (1844), in Meek, *op. cit.*, p. 63.

7. *Ibid.*

8. Engels, "The Condition of the Working Class in England in 1844" (1845), in Meek, *op. cit.*, p. 74.

9. Engels, Letter to Kautsky of Feb. 1, 1881; and "The Myth of Overpopulation," in Meek, *op. cit.*, pp. 62, 109.

10. Marx, *Capital*, vol. I., chap. 25, in Meek, *op. cit.*, p. 88. It is in this chapter that Marx develops his general theory of surplus population.

11. *Ibid.*, p. 87.

12. D. E. C. Eversley, *Social Theories of Fertility and the Malthusian Debate* (London: Oxford University Press, 1959), pp. 265–269; and Petersen, *op. cit.,* pp. 80–89.

13. Letter to Kautsky of Feb. 1, 1881, p. 109.

14. In V. I. Lenin, *Collected Works* (Moscow: Foreign Languages Publishing House, 1963), vol. 19, p. 237.

15. The following account of policies affecting fertility in the Soviet Union is largely based on James W. Brackett, "Demographic Trends and Population Policy in the Soviet Union," in *Dimensions of Soviet Economic Power* (Washington: Government Printing Office, 1962), pp. 547–554; William Petersen, "The Evolution of Soviet Family Policy," in *op. cit.,* pp. 103–124; and David M. Heer, "Abortion, Contraception, and Population Policy in the Soviet Union," *Demography,* 1965, pp. 531–539.

16. Heer, *op. cit.,* p. 536.

17. B. Smulevich, "On the Laws of Population Growth," *Kommunist,* no. 12, 1958. Cited in Brackett, *op. cit.,* p. 546.

18. Cited in Sauvy, *op. cit.,* p. 248.

19. A. Y. Popov, *Sovremennoe Mal'tusianstvo—Chelovekonenavistnicheskaya ideologiia imperialistov* (Moscow: Gosudarstvennoe Izdatel 'stvo Politicheskoe Literatur, 1953), pp. 5–6. Cited in Petersen, "The Evolution of Soviet Family Policy," p. 115.

20. N. M. Zhavaronkov, "Chemistry and the Vital Resources of Mankind," in *Proceedings of the World Population Conference,* Belgrade, Yugoslavia, Aug. 30–Sept. 10, 1965 (New York: United Nations, 1966), vol. III, pp. 346–352. The population estimate is taken from a paper by K. Malin, "Food Resources of the Earth," *ibid.,* pp. 385–390.

21. V. E. Ovsienko, "Influence of Social and Economic Factors on Demographic Characteristics, in *ibid.,* vol. IV, pp. 87–93.

22. Y. G. Mashbitz, "Population Growth and the Food Problem in Latin America," in *ibid.,* vol. III, pp. 391–395.

23. Y. N. Guzevaty, "Modern Malthusianism and Problems of Social Development of Liberated Countries," in *ibid.,* vol. IV, pp. 130–131.

24. James W. Brackett describes this dialogue in some detail and gives quotations from the early articles in two papers: "The Evolution of Marxist Theories of Population," a paper prepared for the 1967 meeting of the Population Association of America, Cincinnati, Ohio, April 28–29, 1967; and "Population Policy and Demographic Trends in the Soviet Union," in *New Directions in the Soviet Economy* (Washington: Government Printing Office, 1966), pp. 599–604.

25. Untitled article in *Literaturnaya gazeta,* Nov. 23, 1965. Cited in Brackett, "Population Policy and Demographic Trends in the Soviet Union," p. 600.

26. From the English translation in *Atlas,* September 1966, pp. 24–26.

27. *International Affairs* (Moscow), September 1966, pp. 52–58.

28. Speech delivered to the Conference of the International Union for the Scientific Study of Population, Sydney, Australia, August 21–25, 1967. Urlanis is Senior Research Worker at the Institute of Economics, U.S.S.R. Academy of Science.

29. Y. Guzevaty, "Population and World Politics," *International Affairs* (Moscow), October 1967, pp. 59–64.

30. Kingsley Davis, "Population Policy: Will Current Programs Succeed?" *Science,* vol. 158, Nov. 10, 1967, pp. 730–739.

31. "Some Problems of the Demography of the Developing Countries of Asia and Africa," *Narody Azii i Afriki,* vol. 6, 1965, translated in *Soviet Sociology,* vol. IV, no. 4, Spring 1966, p. 10.

32. "Economics and Population," *Population Bulletin,* vol. XXIII, no. 2, April 1967, p. 36.

33. Based on material supplied by the Population Reference Bureau (Washington) and by Brackett, "The Evolution of Marxist Theories of Population."

34. The only general interpretative article on the subject of the postrevolutionary Cuban population that I have been able to find is Juan Pérez de la Riva, "La Population de Cuba et ses Problemes," *Population* (Paris), vol. 22, January–February 1967, pp. 99–110. Other materials that have been used in the preparation of this section include statistical documents published by Cuban and international organizations and short articles from Cuban newspapers, magazines, and journals.

35. O. Andrew Collver, *Birth Rates in Latin America: New Estimates of Historical Trends and Fluctuations* (Berkeley, Calif: Institute of International Studies, University of California, 1965), p. 27.

36. *Resumen de Estadísticas de Población, No. 2* (Havana: Junta Central de Planificación, Dirección Central de Estadística, September 1966), p. 23.

37. *Ibid.*

38. Carmen Miró, "The Population of Twentieth Century Latin America," in J. M. Stycos and Jorge Arias (eds.), *Population Dilemma in Latin America* (Washington: Potomac Books, 1966), p. 5.

39. See chart in Collver, *op. cit.,* p. 110.

40. *Resumen de Estadísticas de Población, No. 2. loc. cit.* The United Nations Economic Commission for Latin America (ECLA) has estimates for the years 1960–1965 which are virtually identical to those reported in *Resumen.* See the *Demographic Yearbook, 1966* (New York: United Nations, 1967), p. 208.

41. *Salud Pública en Cifras,* Havana, 1968, table one.

42. Pérez de la Riva, *op. cit.,* p. 102.

43. See the figures provided by Hector Hernández Pardo in "Weddings and the Revolution," *Granma Weekly Review* (English ed.), Havana, May 26, 1968, p. 7.

44. Dudley Seers (ed.), *Cuba: The Economic and Social Revolution* (Chapel Hill, N.C.: University of North Carolina Press, 1964), p. 39.

45. This estimate was made by the Cuban emigré economist Felipe Pazos (head of the National Bank of Cuba during 1959). Cited in Seers, *op. cit.,* p. 404.

46. *Resumen de Estadísticas de Población, No. 2, loc. cit.* ECLA makes a somewhat higher estimate for the crude death rate, 8–9 per 1,000 (*Demographic Yearbook, 1966,* p. 345). It should be noted that ECLA has not provided the *Demographic Yearbook* with corrected rates for the decade of the 1950s, so we cannot tell whether they believe the crude death rate had increased slightly since 1959.

47. *Profile of Cuba,* Havana, Ministry of Foreign Relations, Information Department, n.d., p. 192. The increase was from 21,780 beds in 1958 to 41,504 in 1964.

48. "Cuban Exiles Prove Asset to Economy," undated *Washington Post* newspaper article (appeared in early 1968).

49. "Adjustment of Status for Cuban Refugees," *Hearings before the House Committee on the Judiciary, Eighty-ninth Congress,* 1966, p. 15.

50. "Flow of Cubans to the U.S. Poses a Quota Problem," undated *Washington Post* newspaper article (appeared in early 1968). The *Resumen de Estadísticas de Población, No. 2,* p. 116, provides figures on "entry and exit of travellers" from 1955 to 1965 according to citizenship (Cubans/foreigners). Between 1959 and 1965, 493,923 Cubans are reported to have left and 271,000 to have arrived, giving a negative balance for the seven years of 222,912. (With regard to the "arrivals," it must be remembered that large numbers of Cubans were living outside of Cuba during the Batista regime, many of whom returned to the island after the revolution.) Unfortunately, these Cuban statistics do not differentiate between long-term outmigrants and Cubans leaving for only a limited period of time (tourism, education abroad, etc.).

51. *Salud Pública en Cifras,* table two. The 1953–1958 rate of population growth was slightly under 2.2 percent annually (*Resumen,* p. 9).

52. The rest of this section is based mainly on an examination of Cuban publications for materials relating to population and birth control. This search of the literature was less complete than would have been desirable, owing partly to the fact that the U.S. government places a limit on the amount of money that libraries can spend on the acquisition of Cuban publications, and library holdings are thus generally inadequate. Among the magazines and journals covered were the following (the period of years covered varies according to library holdings): *Panorama Económico Latinoamericano, Política Internacional, Cuba, Pensamiento Crítico,* and *Boletín de la Comisión Nacional de la Unesco.* The preceding contained only a few articles relevant to population or birth control. More fruitful was an examination of the *Granma Weekly Review,* which reprints articles appearing in the daily newspaper *Granma,* an official organ of the Central Committee of the Communist Party of Cuba. The period covered was from April 1967 to September 1968, during which time several lengthy theoretical articles on population and development, contraception, and neo-Malthusianism appeared, as well as shorter, factual items. During the Cultural Congress held in Havana in January 1968, two papers relevant to birth control and population were given by Cuban delegates. In addition, Castro touched on the subject of U.S. support of birth control programs in Latin America in at least three speeches in early 1968. Other sources will be cited below.

53. *Proceedings of the Eighth International Conference of the International Planned Parenthood Federation, Santiago, Chile, April 9–15, 1967,* December 1967, p. 183.

54. Part of this information can be found in "Birth Control Help for Cubans Rises," by Juan de Onis in the *New York Times* of Jan. 15, 1968.

55. Sonia Pérez Tobella, "On the Use of Contraceptives," *Granma Weekly Review* (English ed.), July 9, 1967.

56. Lajonchere, "Protecting the Health of the Mother within the Framework of

the Liberation of Women," paper delivered to the Havana Cultural Congress, Havana, January 1968. (Mimeographed.)

57. "On the Use of Contraceptives," *op. cit.*

58. Elena Díaz and Natasha Klein, "Women in Revolutionary Cuba," paper delivered to the Havana Cultural Congress, Havana, January 1968, p. 4. (Mimeographed.)

59. *Ibid.*

60. Pérez de la Riva, *op. cit.*

61. R. H. Fitzgibbon, "Political Implications of Population Growth in Latin America," *Sociological Review Monograph 11* (*Latin American Sociological Studies*), University of Keele, Staffordshire, England, February 1967, p. 30.

62. Pérez de la Riva, *op. cit.*

63. *Ibid.*, p. 110.

64. Speech by Fidel Castro at the ceremony commemorating the seventh anniversary of the defeat of Yankee imperialism at Playa Girón, Apr. 19, 1968. Text in *Granma Weekly Review* (English ed.), Apr. 28, 1968, p. 5.

65. *Ibid.*

66. Speech made on the eleventh anniversary of the events of Mar. 13, 1957, at the University of Havana. In *Fidel Castro* (Havana: Campamento 5 de Mayo, 1968), pp. 254–255.

67. Speech by Fidel Castro at the closing of the National Meeting of Monitors, Sept. 17, 1966, quoted in *La Población Latinoamericana, Problemas y Perspectivas* (Havana: Organización Latinoamericana de Solidaridad, 1967), p. 58.

68. "Too Many Latins?" reprinted in the book *Panorama Económico Latinoamericano* (English ed.) (Havana: Prensa Latina, 1964), pp. 318–325.

69. *Ibid.*, p. 322.

70. *Ibid.*

71. *Ibid.*, p. 323.

72. *Ibid.*, p. 325.

73. "La 'explosión demográfica' en los países subdesarrollados," in *Tres Continentes* (Havana: Prensa Latina, 1966), p. 696. The book is a political geography of Asia, Africa, and North and South America, published on the occasion of the Tricontinental Conference held in Havana in January 1966.

74. R. Pérez Pereira, "Population Explosion or Revolutionary Explosion?" *Granma Weekly Review* (English ed.), Dec. 3, 1967, p. 12.

75. These arguments can be found in various forms in innumerable books. For a brief and clear treatment, see Frank W. Notestein, "Some Economic Aspects of Population Change in the Developing Countries," in Stycos and Arias (eds.), *op. cit.*, pp. 86–100.

76. This capital output ratio is a weighted average for eleven Latin American countries, *circa* 1950–1960. See Wendell C. Gordon, *The Political Economy of Latin America* (New York: Columbia University Press, 1965), p. 226.

77. Sonia Pérez Tobella, "Is Population Growth Responsible for the Poverty of the People?" *Granma Weekly Review* (English ed.), July 2, 1967, p. 11.

78. *Ibid.*

79. *La Población Latinoamericana, Problemas y Perspectivas,* p. 3.

80. *Ibid.,* p. 57.

81. *Ibid.,* p. 53.

82. *Ibid.,* p. 12.

83. *Ibid.,* pp. 57–59.

84. *Ibid.,* p. 56.

85. Speech made on the eleventh anniversary of the events of Mar. 13, 1957 . . . , pp. 243–244, 249.

86. *La Población Latinoamericana, Problemas y Perspectivas,* p. 42.

87. "¿ Seremos 700 milliones de latinoamericanos en el año 2,000?" *El Mundo* (Havana), June 5, 1968. The article is taken from a work which I have not seen, *Investioaciones Demográficas sobre América Latina.*

88. Speech by Fidel Castro at the ceremony commemorating . . . , p. 5.

89. Speech by Fidel Castro at the closing session of the Havana Cultural Congress, Jan. 12, 1968. Spanish text in *El Mundo,* Jan. 14, 1968.

90. Julio García, "Agrarian Revolution and Underdevelopment," *Granma Weekly Review* (English ed.), May 26, 1968, p. 2.

91. *Ibid.*

92. Lajonchere, *op. cit.*

93. José A. Benítez, "In the Next Few Seconds," *Granma Weekly Review* (English ed.), Mar. 3, 1968, p. 12.

94. "*Izvestia* on Chinese Birth Control," *Current Digest of the Soviet Press,* vol. XV, no. 37, p. 15.

95. "Population Policy: Will Current Programs Succeed?" *op. cit.,* p. 737.

96. "Not Enough Births," *New York Times,* May 22, 1968.

97. *La Población Latinoamericana, Problemas y Perspectivas,* p. 58.

98. "Population Growth and the Food Problem in Latin America," *op. cit.,* p. 395.

99. Seers, *op. cit.,* p. 83.

100. Juan de Onis, "Castro Calls for Operation Bootstrap," *New York Times,* Feb. 11, 1968.

101. Judith Blake, "Demographic Science and the Redirection of Population Policy," *Journal of Chronic Diseases* (England), vol. 18, 1965, pp. 1181–1200.

CHAPTER 8

Case Studies
in Public Opinion Formation:
Colombia and Brazil

THE FLOWERING OF PUBLIC OPINION:
COLOMBIA AND BRAZIL

In the early half of the 1960s the tabooed topic of family planning came into public currency in much of the mass media of Latin America. The liberal reforms in the Catholic Church, the provisional returns of 1960 censuses of population, and the upsurge of world public attention to population problems stimulated the press of Latin America to feature population problems and birth control in editorials, features, and news stories. In so doing, a journalistic tiger was unleashed, for the population problem in Latin America contains some of the most sure-fire ingredients for prolonged public debate—sex, family morality, economic development, religion, and *Yanqui* imperialism, not to mention hormones, abortion, and medical gadgetry. Much of this publicity occurred at a time when newly formed family planning organizations would have preferred its absence, for they felt themselves too weak to withstand public attacks. On the other hand, such public attention could not only give technical information to the literate population, but give salience to an issue previously dormant. We have chosen two countries to illustrate

145

critical periods in the formation of public opinion through the newspaper medium—Colombia and Brazil.

§ COLOMBIA

During the early years of this decade, few influential Colombians recognized the possibility of a population problem in their nation. An outstanding exception was Liberal former President Alberto Lleras Camargo, who, from the vantage points of New York and Washington, began to issue statements in 1965 on the gravity of the population problem. As editor of *Visión* (an international weekly published in Spanish and Portuguese), he initiated provocative features and editorials on the topic. Toward the middle of 1965 astonished Colombians read that he had testified to a United States Senate Committee that the "Latin American demographic explosion is fostering misery, revolutionary pressures, hunger, and many other potentially disastrous problems staggering the imagination . . . we are even running out of cemeteries . . . the only solution is demographic control. . . . All legislation for population control would be beneficial." [1]

Among the medical profession, concern about the consequences of excess childbearing for nutrition, abortion, and family welfare was just coming to a head among a group of progressive physicians leading the Colombian Association of Medical Schools. Unlike many of their colleagues, members of this group were concerned about the role of medicine in the process of national development, were oriented toward public health and epidemiology, and were organizationally and politically sophisticated. A particularly active chapter of the association was located at the University del Valle in Cali, and when the American Assembly sought a site for a Pan-American conference on population, it quickly found one there, the conference being enthusiastically cosponsored by the University del Valle and the Colombian Association of Medical Schools.

On August 11, 1965, at the Pan-American Assembly on Population, Lleras Camargo gave a more explicit and controversial speech than ever, concluding as follows: ". . . for us, the human solution, the Christian solution, the economically and politically sound solution is birth control. And the sooner the better." [2] As we shall see, the conference was widely covered by the press, and accelerated public awareness of national population problems.

Not long thereafter, the Colombian Association of Medical Schools (ASCOFAME) established a population division with a full-time director and with financial assistance from North American foundations. The division sponsored conferences, stimulated and financed research on family planning, and, toward the end of 1966, announced that it had received counterpart funds to carry out, for the Ministry of Health, a training program in family planning for 1,200 physicians in the government service. This announcement produced a storm of controversy which propelled family planning into the political arena and made it a public issue. Let us follow the trends in public opinion over a crucial 2½-year period.

Newspaper Coverage 1965–1967
In the 29-month period between January 1, 1965, and May 31, 1967, a total of 1,293 clips on population problems and family planning were collected from Colombian newspapers, representing a monthly mean of 45, with a range from 12 to 213.[3] Seventy-three percent of these items were of Colombian origin, either news about Colombia or feature articles written by Colombians. As shown in Figure 2, the articles of foreign origin are not only in a minority, but show much less fluctuation than do local items, the only peaks of any consequence occurring during months of special attention to Papal Commission announcements (June 1966) and the International Planned Parenthood Conference in Chile (April 1967). The monthly average of about twelve items of foreign origin is unrelated to the volume of local clips and, because of the growth in number of local clips, the proportion of clippings of foreign origin declines over time.

While the first half of 1965 already showed considerable newspaper attention to the topics of population problems and family planning (over twenty-five clippings per month), most of the newspaper items of this period originated outside of Colombia. Moreover, more than four of every five clippings of local origin were editorials or features. In short, and entirely consistent with the situation at that time, there was simply little Colombian news to report.

In August, 1965, the curve skyrocketed to a total of two-hundred thirteen clippings—nine out of ten were of local origin, and two-thirds were news stories. As a result of the Pan-American Assembly on Population held at Cali, population suddenly became both big news and local news. In the two months following the conference

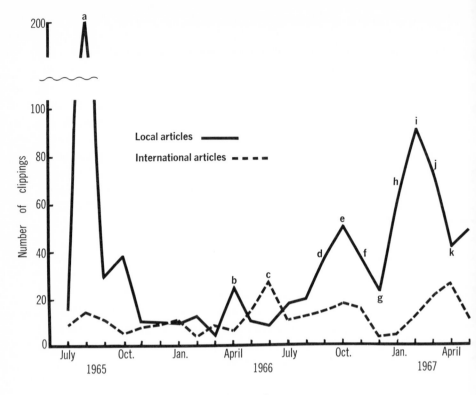

FIGURE 2.
Colombian newspaper articles on population and family planning, per month, 1965–1967.
(a) Pan-American Assembly Conference.
(b) Bishop of Cali attacks.
(c) Papal Commission.
(d) National Academy of Medicine *pro*, Cardinal Concha *con*.
(e) Population program established in ASCOFAME.
(f) Population Reference Bureau Office established.
(g) Lleras Restreppo signs world leaders' statement.
(h) *El Catolicismo* attacks.
(i) Senate debate.
(j) Cardinal and archbishop of Medellín attack.
(k) Provincial courses on family planning announced.

there is a precipitous decline to about forty clippings per month, tapering off to a low of just under twenty in the following six months. The ten-month period following the Cali conference shows little change in monthly averages from the half year preceding it, but a shift in quality has begun, evidenced by a marked increase in the number of local news stories. In the following year, beginning with July 1966, there is a more or less continual rise in total volume, with an average of over seventy-five clips per month in the first portion of 1967. From July 1966 on, the news becomes heavily local (seven to eight of every ten clips); a majority of the items are news rather than opinion, with local news stories reaching thirty-six per month in the first five months of this year.

Some notion of the extent to which the average newspaper reader of the capital city was exposed to news and opinion on population is provided by the fact that, between September 1965 and April 1967, *El Tiempo* averaged a story every $3\frac{1}{2}$ days, *El Espectador* every $4\frac{1}{2}$, and *El Siglo* every 6. (This does not include the unusually large number of clippings in August 1965.) The person who read both *El Tiempo* and *El Espectador* (and many residents of Bogotá do) was exposed to an average of an article every other day. In the first four months of 1967, he could have read an average of an article a day.

Political Orientation of Newspapers

The articles from August 1965 on were coded according to the political orientation of the newspaper. Just over half of the items appeared in Liberal newspapers, the balance in Conservative papers.[4] The first significant public event in the current population controversy occurred in August 1965, with the Cali conference and the news that Lleras Camargo, a Liberal, would address it. In the three weeks in August preceding the event the clipping agency reported thirty-three conference stories, nineteen in Conservative papers, fourteen in the Liberal press. While the Liberal newspapers gave the Lleras speech more front page attention, they were no more likely than Conservative papers to evaluate the conference beforehand (50 percent versus 42 percent, respectively), nor more likely to take a positive stand where they did evaluate. Immediately *after* the conference however, the battle lines had been drawn.

Virtually all comment in Liberal newspapers was favorable, all Communist comment unfavorable, with Conservative opinion evenly divided between favorable, unfavorable, and mixed. Subsequent to the conference, the newspapers continued in this vein. As seen in Table 9, two-thirds of the Liberal but only about one-third of the

TABLE 8

Attitude toward Population Problems or Family Planning,
August 1965 Editorials and Features
Following Cali Conference, by Political Orientation
of Newspaper, in Percent

	Conservative	Liberal	Communist
Clearly in favor*	32	82	0
Clearly opposed	32	4	100
Total number of editorials and features	(38)	(27)	(3)

*Each editorial was classified according to whether it was generally sympathetic or unsympathetic to family planning and the question of a population problem. Where the article recognized a population problem but was opposed to family planning as a solution, it was classified as "mixed."

Conservative editorials and features have been favorable to population or family planning.

The relationship is even more striking when we examine the editorial policy of individual newspapers. Table 10 shows the editorial tendencies of five dailies—the Liberal papers *El Tiempo* and *El Espectador,* the Conservative papers *El Siglo* and *Occidente,* and the Conservative but progovernment *La República.*

With respect to editorials, the two Liberal newspapers carried only one (mildly) unfavorable article and thirty-three favorable; Conservative *El Siglo* carried no favorable editorials; and the Con-

TABLE 9

Percent of Editorials and Features Favorable
to Population Problems—Family Planning

	Liberal Newspapers	Conservative Newspapers
Sept.–Dec. 1965	70	39
Jan.–Apr. 1966	93	37
May–Aug. 1966	69	47
Sept.–Dec. 1966	54	45
Jan.–Apr. 1967	65	29

TABLE 10

Editorials and Features of Five Colombian Newspapers,
August 1965–April 1967

Newspaper	Editorials		Features		Total
	Fav.	*Unfav.*	*Fav.*	*Unfav.*	
El Tiempo	20	1	20	10	51
El Espectador	13	0	10	9	32
El Siglo	0	7	7	10	24
Occidente	5	7	9	17	38
La República	0	1	8	10	19

servative but progovernment *La República* solved its editorial dilemma by ignoring the subject. Among the feature stories *El Tiempo* has two favorable stories to every unfavorable; *Occidente* shows a two-to-one *unfavorable* ratio, while the others are more equally divided, though all tipped in the direction of the newspaper's editorial policy.

The Period of Climax

The early months of 1967 witnessed one of the most powerful and concerted attacks on family planning which has ever been mustered in any nation, involving sustained journalistic efforts, a pastoral letter by the cardinal, and lengthy debates in the nation's senate.

In the three months January–March, close to ten times as many articles were published as in the first three months of the previous year. Since the news was generally unfavorable to family planning, the Conservative newspapers especially increased their news coverage. Comparing the four-month period prior and subsequent to January 1967, we find that while Liberal newspapers less than doubled the number of their news articles, the Conservative papers quadrupled theirs. For the first time since the Cali Conference, the number of articles in Conservative papers exceeds those in Liberal papers. Moreover, while the Conservative papers in previous periods characteristically editorialized more than the Liberals, the reverse situation is true in early 1967. The Conservatives barely increased the number of their editorials, while the Liberals increased theirs $2\frac{1}{2}$ times. Evidently the Liberal papers felt obliged to respond to the general attack, while the Conservatives were happily letting the facts speak for themselves.

The campaign was tripped off by a series of articles in the Catholic weekly, *El Catolicismo*. As we shall see (Chap. 9) the Liberal directors of this newspaper had recently been replaced by Conservative Catholics as part of the hierarchy's reaction to the threat of progressive reforms within the church. The new directorship chose family planning as their first major issue and trained their guns on the recent nationally announced training program in family planning for physicians.

El Catolicismo articles, as well as the Conservative attack in the Senate, stressed two related themes—American imperialism and psychological warfare. In the newspaper's opening editorial President Johnson was accused of wishing "to sterilize the underdeveloped nations," and is (mis)quoted as saying that "stopping the birth of a person from the undeveloped area costs $5.00, while developing him costs $95.00." Psychiatrist Hernán Vergara, author of *El Complejo de Layo,* charged that President Johnson's program was to upset established systems of religious beliefs, while another expert noted that some of the literature used "are literal translations of foreign material . . . gringoism . . . showing scant comprehension of the cultural traditions of the Colombian people." On the floor of the Senate, Diego Tovar Concha charged that the family planning campaign was a plan of capitalist countries to avoid population growth in underdeveloped countries, a form of "preventive genocide." Senator Tovar was joined by Conservative Senator Bayona Carrascal, who referred to family planning as "a fad of the blue-eyed blondes the Minister of Health consulted on his last visit to the United States." He termed the principal technique of family planning "the uterine corkscrew."[5]

Foreign advisors to the Colombian Association of Medical Schools came under heavy attack. *El Catolicismo* published a full-page reproduction from an ASCOFAME bulletin listing consultants from Chicago, Cornell, Princeton, the Ford Foundation, and the Population Council. Senator Tovar referred to "foreign planners of another culture, another race." A professor of law at the Jesuit Xavier University suggested that all foreign consultants be sent to South Vietnam "to help the warlike efforts of the U.S., instead of damaging the faith and morals of poor Colombian parents."

Closely tied to the argument of the "alienness" of the program was the notion of the diabolical, psychological manipulation of innocent women. A story in the *El Siglo,* citing "sources near the ecclesiastical hierarchy," reported that 40,000 rural and slum women were being sterilized in an "experiment conducted under the direction of professional men and North American physicians of the Ford Foundation." The women were reportedly enticed by means of "gifts of lipsticks and strings of artificial pearls."

This theme was also emphasized by Dr. Vergara, who accused the doctors of trying to influence the people with baubles and trinkets just as the conquistadores tricked treasure from the Indians. He gave a lengthy analysis of the foreign tricks of psychological warfare and accused Donald Bogue of Chicago of adapting principles of psychology and salesmanship to family planning. Senator Tovar also referred frequently to Bogue, the University of Chicago, and to "those immense academic units of the United States, the great share of whose research departments are in the service of malthusianism for practical ends in the underdeveloped countries." Senator Bayona saved his fire for a nameless malthusian Machiavelli: ". . . then came a conference advised by a Greek charlatan in the service of North American imperialism. . . . the same one who did experiments on a global scale in Puerto Rico and other pseudo colonies with disastrous consequences to their nationality. . . . when the pill and the corkscrew fail, we shall come to total hysterectomy and possibly infanticide."

The Senate debate ended early in 1967 with the appointment of a commission to investigate the matter further.

Consequences of the Public Debate

While we have no measure of effect, it is probable that the generally unfavorable news had a salutary effect on the general climate of opinion on family planning. First of all, it gave the proponents of family planning an unparalleled opportunity to expound their points of view and report on the extensive local research which had been undertaken. They answered the various charges made against them with facts, figures, tables and graphs, etc., which were duly printed in the papers and shown on television. Under normal circumstances, they could never have achieved so extensive a public forum. How well their research had served them was indicated by the rueful comment of an ANAPO councilman who had forcefully attacked the Bogotá Secretary of Health for the city's alleged birth

control program. After a barrage of statistics of several hours duration, the councilman "recognized the brilliant form and high debating
standard of the Secretary and admitted his audacity in fields he did
not dominate."[6]

Second, the debate produced public support from previously reti-
cent and even unknown supporters of family planning. Thus, when
a large number of Antioquian physicians signed a letter condemning
the family planning activities of ASCOFAME, a somewhat smaller
but more distinguished group signed a counterstatement. The latter
fact, in Antioquia, is much more remarkable and significant than
the former.

Even the nation's President felt compelled to speak out, and in
February 1967 he told the conference of bishops that there was no
foreign compulsion in the family planning program and that it is
the inalienable right of parents to decide the number of their children. That the net effect of the verbal storm was in favor of family
planning is also seen from the conclusions of the congressional
inquiry, which were finally made public in October 1969. They
amounted to a resounding vote of confidence in the family planning
program and supported "the conduct which the government has
assumed in this important matter," expressing the hope "that the
respective plans increase as a first procedure to better the conditions
of Colombian society."[7]

Most significant of all is the fact that the nation's beauty queens
have now spoken up on family planning. In June of 1967 five of
the regional queens were queried about their opinions on the subject.
Four were in favor, but the fifth, eighteen-year-old Miss Ibagué, was
the most politic. When asked whether she favored birth control, she
replied: "Let's talk about the Middle East crisis."[8]

§ BRAZIL

Nowhere in Latin America is the emotional relation between
nationalism, population, and land area seen more vividly than in
Brazil. And why not? Brazil has far more people, far more land,
and, indeed, far more nationalism than any other Latin American
nation. Its Gargantuan size, its language, and its relatively successful
racial blend set it apart from, and, to most Brazilians, above, its
neighbors. Even its failure to conquer and exploit the nation's great

riches has been a source of nationalistic fervor and a cause for demographic explanations and programs.

Both as a way of explaining present weakness and as a prescription for their future greatness, Brazilians place a great deal of stress on two demographic variables—the distribution and the size of their population. An integral part of the Brazilian mystique of "size and greatness" is the "march to the West," symbolism which should not be unfamiliar to North Americans. "To the average Brazilian," writes Preston James, "the *sertões*, the backlands, are deeply mysterious. They exert a force of attraction because of the firm belief that in them is to be found the means of achieving great wealth; yet at the same time they repel because they are so empty and have yielded so seldom to the economic efforts of their inhabitants. Few indeed are the political leaders who do not see in Brazil's future a *marcha para oeste*, a vastly profitable movement away from the coast into the empty interior, a final conquest of the lands of mystery." [9]

In earlier periods the West was viewed as a cornucopia, which would momentarily be exploited. The 5 million immigrants who entered Brazil in the last century were hardly noticeable in the vast expanses of Brazil's hinterland and as late as 1910 were optimistically waiting for the "next generation" to settle the interior. As one early migrant put it: "One seldom meets a fellow-countryman who is not enthusiastic over the possibilities of the country. Those from the little-known interior will tell you that in the tropical forests of the north, on the plains of the south, and beneath the rugged surfaces of the mountains, lies an enormous accumulation of wealth awaiting the industry of the coming generation." [10]

It was not long before the failure to empty the cornucopia began to be attributed to lack of manpower. If the country was big and rich and those riches were not being realized, it was perhaps due to the deficit of people necessary to exploit the vast interior:

If one would know the reasons underlying Brazil's population history, he should first remember that the central theme of the nation's social and economic history is *falta de braços*, which can best be translated as "lack of hands." . . . Thousands of books, pamphlets, and articles have been written about . . . the nation's need for more workers. If one travels through Brazil he will hear the same refrain, *falta de braços*, from Amazonas to Rio Grande do Sul, from Rio Grande do Norte to Mato Grosso.[11]

This, then, is the general background accounting for Brazil's long-standing feeling of underpopulation—a feeling deeply linked to national sentiments of frustrated greatness, a feeling little affected by the realization of a population growth rate of 3 percent per year. Prior to the 1960s a Brazilian reader of newspapers or magazines saw little on the "population problem" which was not cast in the light of Brazil's *underpopulation* problem. Against this background, a new demographic era began when the newspapers began to talk of a different kind of population problem, and the United States began to offer certain kinds of assistance to solve it.

Newspaper Coverage on Population

If Brazil's literate population in the early 1960s knew little about the "population explosion" and the birth control issue, by the mid- and late 1960s they could hardly have avoided learning about them. The number of newspaper clippings on population received by the International Population Program tripled between 1965 and 1967, and Brazil's proportion of all clippings from Latin America climbed from 7 to 8 percent. In 1968, 177 clippings on population were received from the Rio de Janeiro daily *Journal do Brasil* and 118 from *Diario de São Paulo*. Thus, a reader of either of these papers was exposed to an article on population every two or three days of the year.

These overall figures conceal a highly significant fact—that population news in general and birth control news in particular became "Brazilianized" over the three-year period. News and features of Brazilian origin accounted for 46 percent of all clippings in 1965, but 61 percent in 1967.[12] With respect to articles on birth control, while the number of foreign articles increased by less than 70 percent over the three-year period, the number of Brazilian news stories mentioning birth control increased by *700 percent.*

In 1967, no less than 72 percent of Brazilian-originated articles mentioned birth control. No other Latin country approaches Brazil and Colombia in the proportion of local origin clippings mentioning birth control. The total for all countries is 55 percent, ranging from 25 percent in Bolivia to 69 and 73 percent in Colombia and Brazil. In terms of the *themes* of the articles, moreover, Brazil is much more likely than any other country to have family planning as a *major theme* of its articles. In 1965 and 1966, no less than 44 percent were so classified, the second-ranking country being Colombia, with a third of its articles having family planning as a major theme. Thus, in both absolute and relative terms Brazil's public attention to this topic has been considerable in the past few years.

Public opinion, moreover, has apparently been crystallizing on the subject. Between 1965 and 1967, the proportion of local origin news stories on birth control classified as "neutral or ambivalent" toward birth control declined from 68 to 57 percent. The form of the crystallization was, however, distinctly unfavorable. As seen in Table 11, while the ratio of favorable to unfavorable (to birth control) articles in items of foreign origin increased over the three-year period, both news and opinion articles of local origin shifted markedly toward the unfavorable pole.[13] Thus there were over eight news articles favorable to birth control for every unfavorable one in 1965; in 1967 there were more unfavorable than favorable ones.

A month-by-month analysis of the data discloses that August 1966 and May 1967 were extraordinary months, which accounts for much of the changes over time. In each of these years, the month in question accounted for one in every five clips for the total year. In August 1966, 92 percent and, in May 1967, 95 percent of the local news items mentioned family planning. Since these months hold the key to the shifts in quantity and quality of locally based articles for the two-year period, we turn our attention to a detailed consideration of the events of August 1966 and May 1967.

TABLE 11

Ratio of Favorable to Unfavorable Articles,
among Those Mentioning Birth Control,
by Year and Origin

Origin	1965	1966	1967
Foreign	0.9	2.7	4.0
Local news	8.5	1.6	0.8
Local opinion	5.7	2.6	1.5

August 1966*

On August 4, 1966, Brazilian newspapers erupted with such unusual headlines as:

THE GOVERNMENT WANTS TO CONTROL BIRTHS. . . .
BRAZIL ASKS FOR AID TO CONTROL PROGENY. . . .
BRAZIL LIMITS BIRTHS WITH YANKEE AID.

The accompanying articles originated in Washington and reported Secretary of State Dean Rusk's announcement to the House Subcommittee on Foreign Operations that the United States had granted financial aid on population to five Latin American countries, including Brazil. In the next few days headlines and articles expressed the shock, disapproval, and anger of numerous Brazilians prominent in the fields of politics, religion, and education. Reactions to what the editor of *La Folha de São Paulo* called "this story of birth control with dollars nobody asked for" [14] continued occupying a considerable amount of space in the papers for the next ten days.

The Politicians: Political figures expressed their views in press and TV interviews and in speeches in the Legislative Assembly. Deputy Gilberto Azevedo, Vice-president of the Foreign Affairs Commission, warned that it looked ". . . like the work of the Planning Ministry, which is planning everything now, even births," and Deputy Alfonso Arinos, Jr., argued that the proponents of birth control are oligarchs who want to keep population growth compatible with the low productivity of the present economic system.[15] Opposition party Deputy Getúlio Moura told the Chamber never to accept a limitation "imposed by a country which, with the same dimensions as ours, has 300 million inhabitants. The impression is that the American people with their land already overpopulated are concerning themselves with our empty spaces and intend to occupy our territory." [16] Deputy Noronha, Jr., suggested that instead of trying to cut down on the population, it would be more constructive to increase the productivity of Brazilian manpower.[17] Deputy Pereira Pinto attributed the announcement to North American manufacturers of birth control pills and offered to defend as often as necessary the right to be born.[18]

At least three Deputies, however, defended the attention to population problems. MDB Deputy Moab Callas chided his fellow parliamentarians for their opposition to the American offer and painted

* Prepared by **Evelyn Hand.**

a dramatic picture of the hunger and even war which would occur if birth rates failed to decline. This view was supported by the remarks of Deputy Larry Faria and by Siegfried Heuser, who declared birth control to be in the thoughts of all those concerned with the future of mankind.[19]

Government Officials: The day after the initial announcements, José Maria Vilar de Queirós of the Planning Ministry denied that Brazil had requested North American aid for birth control. He said that research by the Demographic Center of the Planning Ministry had only been concerned with the economic implications of population change, without reference to the problem of birth control. In the understatement of the year, harassed government Press Secretary Orlando Carbonar declared: "There must have been some confusion in the news transmitted."[20]

In a television interview on August 23, Planning Minister Robert Campos said, "To say that the problem does not exist is absurd. The problem is not to control, but to know if we ought to put at the disposal of the people the means and information necessary for this measure. Therefore the government will create a Demographic Center to study the problem more deeply, awaiting the official word of the Church before making a definitive decision on birth control." He noted that the unprecedented population growth causes great difficulties in economic planning and cited a recent survey disclosing that more than 40 percent of Brazilian married couples use brutal contraceptive practices such as abortion. Campos quoted the Chilean Jesuit Roger Vekemans, who said, "The statistics on abortions in Latin America constitute the best plebiscite in favor of birth control."[21]

Journalists: Editors and feature writers took full advantage of the opportunity to combine a sensational subject with criticism of the government. An editorial in *O Jornal* explained that the nation was only experiencing an urban population concentration, thanks to the government's abandonment of the countryside, and gave its opinion that birth control is a theme advocated only by crazy foreigners.[22] Feature writer Hermano Alves declared that the neo-Malthusianism of certain functionaries in the underdeveloped nations is manipulated by the big laboratories. Brazilian neo-Malthusians preach birth control in order to remove pressures capable of causing important economic and social reforms. Their attitude rather than the church's is reactionary. It is in North America's geopolitical interest to reduce the number of underdeveloped populations, of Asiatic nations, or of United States Communists. Not birth control but drastic structural reforms are the answers to Brazil's problems.[23] In a lively feature in *O Povo* entitled "Depopulators of Deserts," Henrique Pongetti held that the key to Brazil's prosperity lies in her beds and hammocks. Brazil needs 20 or 30 million inhabitants so that her lands will cease to figure as reserves of natural resources or vital space in the schemes of Western or Eastern imperialists. Malthusianism in this wilderness of economic possibilities only makes sense to the fanatical lovers of failure or the psychopaths afflicted with anthropophobia. "Brazilians," he concludes, "let us continue loving and proliferating! God did not give us all this greatness for the installation of an abortion or sterilization industry. Forward! Forward! To the children! To the children!"[24]

At least two major feature articles took issue with the majority of journalists. "The pill is in the order of the day," insisted José Luís Grunewald, writing in *Correio da Manha*. Brazil is suffering from a deficit of housing, education, and food and from poor health. Some argue that Brazil should populate the nearly empty regions. How and with whom? Populating that would increase poverty and misery is not populating in the Christian sense of the word. Colonizing without planning is frivolity. Colonizing without even having anything to plan is not frivolity—it is administrative insanity.[25] A feature writer for *O Povo*, Ademar Tavora, pointed out that the population is growing at a dizzy pace, that there are large expanses of soil unsuitable for agriculture, and that Brazilians have caused such depredations on the choicest land that it will cost future generations dearly. "It would be preferable for Brazil to have a population of a hundred educated, well fed and healthy individuals than to have 200 million semi-illiterate, undernourished, ill people. If in the things we use daily, quality prevails over quantity, how much more reason there is to accept this principle when it is a question of mankind who the sacred Scriptures say was made in the image of God?"[26]

The Doctors: Members of the medical profession showed a marked lack of enthusiasm for the government program except for its value in the prevention of abortions. Dr. Fabio Fonseca, president of the Belo Horizonte Regional Council of Medicine, noted that the yellow race, more than 750 million already, needs space and would not hesitate to seek uninhabited places like the immense Brazilian regions, if settlement of them by Brazilians is not promoted. A minimum population of 150 million is needed instead of the present 80 million. "Perhaps the major need of the country today is for education and health so that we can sustain the rise in population, without recourse to artificial restrictive methods." [27] Deputy Valdir Mozzaquatro, a physician, said that birth control would be a crime against the country, although he was not opposed to its use for medical and economic reasons. Birth control would not help bring about demographic equilibrium: fewer mouths to feed mean fewer hands to produce. [28]

Dr. Miriam Kelner, president of the Gynecology Association of Pernambuco, stated that while birth control was not essential to national salvation in view of the great lands still to be populated, contraceptives should be distributed in order to prevent abortions. [29] Gynecologist Arnaldo de Morais, Jr., revealed that 90 percent of 11,000 married couples studied in the state of Guanabara resorted to induced abortion or contraceptives to limit the number of children. Birth control is a solution for countries of increasing population density, but the people should first be educated in hygiene to aid them in making decisions on family growth. [30]

The Professors: Professor Lidio Machado Bandeira de Melo of the Law School of the Federal University of Minas Gerais declared that "instead of limiting births, we ought to stimulate them. We need more people to populate this country the size of a continent where there are fertile areas entirely uninhabited, and in order to do this, our population must grow." The head of the Minas Gerais Law School, Professor Lourival Vilela Viana, who had recently proposed that birth control be included in the Civil Code as a crime, said there is no reason to fear the future, since the resources of the earth have not been explored sufficiently, much less those of the sea. [31] João Camilo de Oliveira Torres, professor of history and Catholic leader in the state of Minas Gerais, noted Brazil's need for people to settle the vast regions of Central and Northern Brazil. The government should take no action before hearing from experts, and Catholics should wait for word from the Vatican. [32]

The Clergy: Church spokesmen were not uniformly unfavorable to birth control nor to the government's taking an interest in population problems. Indeed, virtually no church spokesman unequivocally condemned birth control, though most condemned a U.S. inspired campaign. On the whole, representatives of the Catholic Church were more favorable to dealing with the population problem than any other major group whose opinions were expressed in the press.

Cardinal Dom Jaime de Barros Camara saw nothing wrong in the government's concern about birth control, pointing out that a committee named by Pope Paul VI was in the final phase of a study of the demographic explosion. The Pope would soon make an announcement that would clarify all aspects of "the momentous question." [33] Friar André Muniz de Rezende, prior of the Dominican Convent in Belo Horizonte, noted that the church must look to the sciences for new discoveries which can easily reconcile better social solutions with the demands of a clear Christian conscience. "The pills, from the merely ethical point of view, seem to meet those demands. It is up to medical science to say if there are counter-indications." When sociology, medicine, anthropology, and other sciences provide new gifts for theology, the latter cannot stagnate but must change in accordance with the evolution of new human experiences.[34] The archbishop of Brasilia, Don José Newton de Almeida Batista, declared that demographic growth does not constitute a problem in Brazil with its riches and vastness; the problem is the discrepancy between demographic and economic growth. "Give us dollars," he said, "and we shall be powerful provided that we also grow in number so that we can take possession of the immense territory God gave us. . . . Without denying the population problems, I think we ought to seek a socio-economic solution." About a week later the archbishop explained that his indignation had not been directed against birth control but against "the campaign." The church itself is making an official study of the question of contraceptive means, thus admitting ipso facto the existence of a demographic problem. Doubt will disappear for Catholics with the long awaited word from the Pope.[35] Dom José Castro Pinto, auxiliary bishop and vicar-general of Rio de Janeiro, declared that birth control would weaken the country in every way, beginning with military defense, since the country is very big and has large uninhabited regions, "which are coveted by other peoples." [36] Dominican Friar Pedro Secondi, of Leme, protested against "American interference in a question both delicate and extremely personal, which needs a solution compatible with the inclinations and beliefs of the Brazilian people." [37]

The smoke settled with surprising speed, and no apparent practical consequence came from the public discussion. It paved the way, however, for the even more sensational events of 1967, which began in March but reached a crescendo in May.

May 1967

In early March 1967, a United Press dispatch datelined Washington stated that Brazil had requested assistance from the Agency for International Development (AID) in order to establish a university population center for the training of demographers and physicians. This item sparked an inquiry in the Brazilian Parliament just as a similar dispatch had touched off the heated debates the previous year.

The news prompted Senator Mário Martins (MDB, Guanabara) to ask the President[38] what was being done about complaints that sterilization and contraceptives were being used in public hospitals. He maintained that a high birth rate is auspicious for both development and national security. "It would be incomprehensible and inconceivable," he said, "for the Brazilian Government to become involved in a policy of restriction of births, to the detriment of the nation and in the interests of a foreign power."[39]

A few weeks later Reverend Bezerra de Melo, Arenist Deputy from São Paulo, charged that in the last session of the Ecumenical Council, "some Brazilian bishops were approached by North Americans who offered them a million dollars if they would support birth control in their dioceses . . . the North Americans were repulsed, almost with violence."[40] The bishops were subsequently identified, and some papers referred to the Americans as "high officials" of AID.[41]

In the same session, Deputy José Maria Magalhães (MDB, Minas Gerais) introduced a debate and investigation which lasted for months. Having heard rumors of experiments with intrauterine devices (IUDs), Magalhães called for a Parliamentary Investigatory Committee (PIC) on birth control. In a vehement speech he declared, "The national conscience is traumatized by the criminal use of contraceptive apparatus applied *en masse* under control of an American organization." Condemning the "interference of the North American Government for the purpose of impeding the development of Brazil," he asserted that "the struggle against underdevelopment cannot serve as a pretext for affronting the dignity and morality of a people. . . . limiting births would be the worst means to use for development since there is still uninhabited territory in Brazil and a frightening level of infant mortality." [42]

Deputy José Richa (MDB, Paraná) and Deputy Julia Steinbruck (MDB, Rio) supported Magalhães's request for a PIC. Steinbruck declared herself "revolted" by the "crime" that was taking place. "It would not surprise me" she said, "if the campaign were aimed at depopulating the region, to allow foreign penetration in the not too distant future." [43] Another MDB Deputy, Carlos Cotta, called "sterilization by the IUD a process of euthanasia or 'mini-aborto,'" [44] MDB Deputy Monsignor Arruda Cámara saw "an attack against the Brazilian nation which has immense areas that are a target for foreign imperialistic greed." [45]

Vague accusations became more specific when, on May 2, Capuchin Friar Gil de Novato, vicar of Estreito, informed the health officials of San Luís of the "unpatriotic and immoral" activities of Presbyterian missionaries. He reported that women had come to his clinic in great pain asking for removal of intrauterine devices prescribed by the missionaries. Friar Gil claimed that the women were "sterilized by agents of the Intrauterine Contraceptive Device Study, a genuinely American organization which is transforming Amazônia into a field of guinea pigs. . . ." According to Friar Gil, the missionaries "subtly and insidiously" gain the confidence of the people by giving them medicines and milk and treating sick children. Then they invite the women to so-called "mother's clubs" where they are brainwashed by propaganda in favor of birth control "until they submit like lambs," and their "castration" is carried on in the utmost secrecy. [46]

On May 3, inch-high headlines in *Jornal do Brazil* proclaimed, "IVO SAW THAT AMERICANS ARE STERILIZING," and *Diario de Minas* stated, "MINISTER CONFIRMS MASS STERILIZATION OF WOMEN IN NORTHEAST." The reports stated that Ivo Arzua, Minister of Agriculture, had first-hand information on the missionary birth control program as a result of a recent trip with the Ministers of Planning and of Transportation. It was said that Arzua and members of his staff had interviewed several of the women involved and would report to the Ministry of Health. [47] These statements were quickly denied by Arzua, who said that he was proposing that a thorough investigation be made by the Ministry of Health. [48] (The committee later excused Arzua from testifying because he had "already made it clear that he did not know the major details about the use or nonuse of the coil, limiting himself to merely transmitting to the Health Minister the rumors prevailing along the Belém-Brazília highway concerning the IUD." [49])

A few days after the charges against the missionaries, U.S. Ambassador John Tuthill declared that the United States government had no birth control program in the nations which they were assisting. He quoted President Johnson's 1966 message to Congress, stating that U.S. aid would be given only if solicited. Tuthill added that no requests for assistance had been received from the Brazilian government, nor had the United States offered any. Some AID money would be devoted to demographic research, however. [50]

The Reverend Boanerges Ribeiro, president of the Supreme Council of the Presbyterian Church of Brazil, denied that his missionaries were sterilizing Brazilian women and denied that the U.S. government had participated in the missionary program along the Belém-Brasília Highway. Reverend Ribeiro explained that after careful study the Presbyterian Council had found that the mission stations, working in cooperation with the Brazilian Association for Family Welfare (BEMFAM), "were furthering the rights of humanity and the family." These include the right of couples to limit the number of their children; the right of children to be born where they are wanted and where they can be properly brought up and educated; and the right of sterile couples to receive medical aid to enable them to have children. To achieve these goals, "the Medical Station of Estreito, in addition to its other welfare services, is conducting family planning by methods that are internationally accepted and in accordance with generally accepted Christian ethics and in conformity with the laws of Brazil." Reverend Ribeiro emphasized that birth control was not prescribed by ministers but by doctors and nurses and that patients entered the clinic voluntarily. [51]

According to *Diario de São Paulo*, "Reverberations of the denunciation (of birth control activities) echoed in the military cupola," and the National Security Council became greatly concerned with "the transformation of women into guinea pigs." This was aggravated by "the fact that all of the 'scientists' were foreigners conducting their 'experiments' without the consent of the Brazilian Government or even any communication with it." [52] The Army queried the Eighth Military District about the wholesale use of contraceptives in Amazônia and its possible effect on national security. General Dirceu de Araújo Nogueira went to Belém to ask the military commanders to assist in the Health Ministry's investigation. It was later reported that the Army would extend its investigation to other parts of Brazil.[53]

On April 25, Congress asked Health Minister Leonel de Miranda to investigate the "irregular experiments" by North American missionaries. In the absence of the Minister, Acting Minister Luis Pires Leal traveled to the Northeast with members of his department. On his return, he outlined the following points from a twenty-three-page report prepared by Dr. Luis Miguel Scaff, head of the National Department of Rural Diseases of Pará: (1) Contraceptive methods, including IUDs, were being prescribed in medical stations of the Presbyterian Mission of the North. (2) Such treatment was done by specially trained Brazilian doctors and nurses. (3) Use of contraceptive devices was not experimental but for the purpose of family planning with the full consent of both husband and wife. (4) The exaggeration and sensationalism of certain newspapers leads to the suspicion that "there is a connection between the occurrences and a previously prepared anti-American plot."

Pires Leal expressed surprise at the sudden publicity on family planning "since use of the coil is not new in Brazil. . . . The Health Ministry does not prescribe its use, since its side effects are still not known, but the matter is so delicate, involving intimate aspects of family life, that we could scarcely take action against its use." The Minister noted that birth control programs were supported by such organizations as the Ford Foundation, the World Neighbors, and BEMFAM and by Father Alfonso Pastore's course on birth control. He added that "the Presbyterian Mission of the North, which together with Catholic organizations is working in the Amazon region, has been in Brazil for 112 years."[54]

Apparently infuriated, members of the MDB party declared that the Acting Minister had released his report "prematurely"; that he had erred in applying the report from Pará to the entire region; and that the accusations of anti-Americanism were "improper and insulting," reflecting on the Parliamentarians of both parties and on the Brazilian journalists. MDB leader Hermano Alves read a party statement in a plenary session of the Chamber, censuring Pires Leal and announcing that Dr. Scaff would be called upon to prove the serious charges he had made.[55]

During the Parliamentary debate various Deputies presented proposals for laws regulating birth control. Deputy Erasmo Martins Pedro (MDB, Guanabara), presented an amendment to the penal code to permit family planning, "a solution which is truly humane and natural and attacks abortion."[56] Deputy Ivete Vargas (MDB, *SP*) proposed a law defining use of intrauterine devices as criminal abortion.[57] Deputy Janduy Carneiro (ARENA, Paraíba) introduced a law to establish disciplinary rules for family planning, according to which "birth control is permitted as long as it occurs by the free will of the couple or of a woman of legal age." Birth control would be carried on by medical professionals or licensed midwives registered at the Ministry of Health; all unlicensed foreign doctors and other unauthorized persons carrying on birth control activity or even seeking patients would be expelled from the country.[58]

In Pernambuco, Dr. Reinaldo Fernandes, professor of gynecology and obstetrics of the Federal Medical School, accepted full responsibility for the IUD campaign in Jaboatão. He defended IUDs among poor people with more than six children, saying that he had chosen Jaboatão as the center of his activities because the average family there has more than ten. The women's health is benefited since the preliminary examination frequently reveals tumors or inflammation. He explained that the Family Planning Center of Brazil, with 20 regional centers, has as its objectives responsible parenthood and the fight against criminal abortions, which surveys show to be 1,500,000 annually. He had received a request from a large trade union to conduct a birth control campaign in Recife.[59] In Rio de Janeiro, Dr. Roosevelt Ribeiro, president of the local medical association, told the Chamber's health committee that the association considers family planning to be exclusively the affair of married couples, but added that the association condemns the IUD because of possible harmful consequences; it should be used under absolute medical control and only with people of at least average intelligence. There is also some question as to whether the method might be microabortive.[60] The IUD had been used with more than 600 women of Praia do Pinto with fully satisfactory results, according to the head of the local outpatient clinic, Dr. Assis Moura. The clinic functions in the Federal Medical School at Rio in cooperation with BEMFAM. Its program includes cancer prevention, antiabortion measures, and treatment of sterility. The IUD is not abortive and does not cause sterility. "Possibly those who wanted to exploit criminal abortion tried to start the campaign against the 'evils of the IUD.'"[61] In São Paulo, Professor José Galucci of the University of São Paulo recommended mass use of the coil, asserting that it is much less dangerous than induced abortions. Birth control is the solution to Brazil's excess population in the nonproductive age groups. "As one cannot get rid of the old people, the way out is to avoid an increase of new births." He mentions that the clinic's free services include the Ogino-Knauss method, pills, and the IUD.[62]

Finally, BEMFAM's president, Dr. Otávio Rodrigues-Lima, professor of clinical obstetrics at the National School of Medicine, told Maria Christina Penna of *Correio da Manha* that the leftists of Brazil are defending a bourgeois custom. He said it is not proper for the leftists, who claim to be champions of the poor, to campaign against birth control, a bourgeois privilege denied to the poor. Dr. Rodrigues-Lima stated that birth control actually is being carried on in Brazil in the form of 713,000 annual abortions and 320,000 infant deaths. Wálter Rodrigues, director of BEMFAM, said, "We are not in favor of the IUD or the pill as such but consider that they are at present the best contraceptive methods. The ideal method would be 100 percent effective and have no side effects."[63]

On May 15 a petition signed by 150 Deputies requested the establishment of a Parliamentary Investigatory Committee. The duties of the committee of eleven (seven from ARENA and four from MDB) were to determine whether Brazil had a birth control plan; to check reports of sterilizations and birth control; to ascertain the degree of interference by local or foreign groups in promoting birth control; and to consider the legal, moral, social, religious, economic, and political aspects of the problem. The committee was charged with reporting in three months and granted a budget of 30 million "old cruzeiros."[64] It started operations on June 6 when several of its members flew to Goiãnia to interview Friar Gil. There, after hearing a two-hour TV speech by Senator Mário Martins on the occupation of Brazil by a foreign power, they declared themselves "ready to get to the bottom of this matter."[65]

A declaration against the coil was soon made in the hearings by the president of the Medical Association of Brasilia, Dr. Fernando Veloso. Deputy José Maria Riberio, also a physician, stated that the medical group of the whole region is almost entirely against use of that device because of the dangers to health. Arenist Deputy Nunes Freite termed the coil "abortive, temporarily or permanently sterilizing, and contraceptive." [66] Dr. Sami Helou, professor in the University of Goiás, testified that the IUD was used by 99 percent of the women in the city of Estreito, basing his statement on interviews with fifteen women, fourteen of whom had used this method. "These women," the doctor said, "are being used as guinea pigs in an uninhabited region which needs to be populated for the security of the nation." He added that this work is part of the five-year biological plan directed by the Pathfinder Foundation of Boston. In his opinion, the combination of birth control and a high mortality rate in Amazônia could completely depopulate the region within ten or fifteen years. [67]

The next day the Reverend Eduardo Lane, physician in charge of the Presbyterian medical stations in Amazônia, maintained that the IUD is not abortive and stated that the device had been used in 80 percent of the 265 indigent patients of BEMFAM in Campinas, São Paulo. [68] Preoccupation with the coil continued as Walter de Freitas, professor and specialist in penal law, called the IUD an instrument of criminal abortion, use of which should lead to a prison sentence. "These devices ought to be seized by the police," he said, "prohibiting once and for all their free and illegal sale and their unwarranted use in clinics."

Dr. Mário Vitor de Assis Pacheco of the Guanabara Medical Association stated that the coil is still too experimental for use on humans and denied that the medical councils of São Paulo and Guanabara had ever authorized its use, directly contradicting testimony given the previous day by Reverend Lane. Dr. de Assis Pacheco, referring to birth control programs in Puerto Rico, Haiti, and Mexico as laboratory experiments with "noble guinea pigs," warned that now the same laboratories are turning to the women of Brazil. [69]

After suspending operations during the July recess, the PIC announced that it would broaden its investigation of the birth control problem, basing its decisions on strictly scientific findings. Committee Chairman Tourinho Dantas said that the affair had gone beyond mere complaints about the IUD and involved the general appropriateness of birth control in a country like Brazil; the question of the abortive nature of the IUD and its effect on health; and, finally, whether advertisement and sale of contraceptives violate Article 20 of the Penal Law, which forbids the advertisement of "any process, substance, or object destined to induce abortion or to avoid pregnancy." [70]

One of the PIC's first witnesses after the winter recess was the archbishop of Goiânia, Dom Fernando Gomes. After declaring that he had nothing against the United States or any nation, the archbishop charged that North American groups "had committed all sorts of crimes and absurdities" in Brazil, but that unfortunately nothing could be said about them "for fear of being labeled a Communist." The archbishop testified that he had learned about the sterilization of Brazilian women at the recent bishops' conference and had seen records proving "the indecent activity of the North American missionaries." [71]

Ex-Secretary of Education of the state of Rio Grande do Norte, Calazans Fernandes, now a journalist for *La Folha de São Paulo,* told the PIC that the U.S. government, through AID, has a world program of birth control, which represents "undue intervention in the affairs of other nations." AID had invited journalists to attend the IPPF Conference in Chile, offering to pay their way. At the conference it became evident that a definite birth control program was required of nations applying for external investments. He surmised that AID investments in the North of Brazil might complicate the demographic situation because the birth rate might rise as living standards improve.

§ CONCLUSIONS

The Brazilian Parliamentary Investigation Committee has not, as of the time of writing, filed a report. Like the Colombian case, the public attack on family planning gave its proponents a chance to counterattack in public. BEMFAM has sponsored a Family Planning Bill which would legalize contraception, has signed a contract with the city of Campinas to develop family planning services for the city, and has sponsored a number of conferences and seminars on family planning in different parts of the nation. It has not yet won its struggle, but the public debate may have shortened the war considerably.

NOTES

1. *El Espectador* (Bogotá), July 13, 1965, and *El Correo* (Medellín), July 10, 1965.
2. Alberto Lleras Camargo, Aug. 11, 1965. See *Three Talks on Population,* The American Assembly, n.d.
3. Since the newspaper files of the Population Division of the Colombian Association of Medical Schools were more complete than our own after July 1965, we have largely utilized this source of data in the present analysis. Articles were read and coded in Colombia by five International Population Program students: Joanne Edelson, Betsy Cohen, Joseph Enright, Jeffry Gibson, and Antonio Marino.
4. "Liberal" refers to the party currently in power, "Conservative" to the other major party.
5. A more complete account of the events of this period, as well as the original sources for the quoted materials, can be found in *Latin American Newspaper Coverage of Population and Family Planning,* no. 2, Cornell International Population Program, May 1967.
6. *El Espectador* (Bogotá), June 9, 1967.
7. Thomas G. Sanders, "Family Planning in Colombia," *American Universities Fieldstaff Reports,* vol. XVII, no. 3, January 1970.
8. *El Cronista* (Ibagué), June 28, 1967.
9. Preston James, "Brazilian Agricultural Development," in S. Kuznets, W. E. Moore, and J. J. Spengler (eds.), *Economic Growth: Brazil, India, Japan,* (Durham, N.C.: Duke University Press, 1955), p. 78.
10. Charles W. Donville-Fife, *The United States of Brazil* (London: Francis Griffiths, 1910), p. 87.
11. T. Lynn Smith, *Brazil: People and Institutions* (Baton Rouge, La.: Louisiana State University Press, 1963), p. 51.
12. During this period local news stories increased at a much more rapid rate than local features and editorials. While the latter doubled, the former increased almost sevenfold.
13. The overall tone of the article was scored. Thus, e.g., if a news item reported a speech judged by the coder to be unfavorable to birth control, the article was scored as unfavorable; if the headline was unfavorable and the statement in the article favorable, the article was scored as ambivalent.
14. *La Folha de São Paulo,* Aug. 6, 1966.
15. *Ultima Hora* (São Paulo), Aug. 6, 1966.
16. *Diario de Noticias* (Porto Alegre), Aug. 17, 1966.
17. *Jornal do Brasil* (Rio de Janeiro), Aug. 5, 1966.
18. *Ibid.,* Aug. 13, 1966.
19. *Diario de Noticias* (Porto Alegre), Aug. 11, 1966; *Correio do Povo* (Porto Alegre), Aug. 10, 1966; *O Jornal* (Rio de Janeiro), Aug. 13, 1966.
20. *Jornal do Brasil* (Rio de Janeiro), Aug. 5, 1966.

21. *Diario do Comercio* (São Paulo), Aug. 26, 1966; *Diario de São Paulo,* Aug. 25, 1966; *Diario de Minas* (Belo Horizonte), Aug. 24, 1966; *O Globo* (Rio de Janeiro), Aug. 24, 1966; *Jornal do Brasil* (Rio de Janeiro), Aug. 24, 1966.

22. *O Jornal* (Rio de Janeiro), Aug. 5, 1966.

23. *Correio da Manha* (Rio de Janeiro), Aug. 10, 1966.

24. *O Povo* (Fortaleza), Aug. 19, 1966.

25. *Correio da Manha* (Rio de Janeiro), Aug. 24, 1966.

26. *O Povo* (Fortaleza), Aug. 9, 1966.

27. *Diario de Minas* (Belo Horizonte), Aug. 5, 1966.

28. *Ultima Hora* (São Paulo), Aug. 6, 1966; *Correio da Manha* (Rio de Janeiro), Aug. 12, 1966.

29. *Jornal do Brasil* (Rio de Janeiro), Aug. 13, 1966.

30. *Diario de São Paulo,* Aug. 7, 1966.

31. *Jornal do Brasil* (Rio de Janeiro), Aug. 5, 1966.

32. *Diario de Minas* (Belo Horizonte), Aug. 5, 1966.

33. *Jornal do Brasil* (Rio de Janeiro), Aug. 25, 1966.

34. *Estado de Minas* (Belo Horizonte), Aug. 18, 1966.

35. *Correio Braziliense* (Brasilia), Aug. 6 and 12, 1966.

36. *Jornal do Brasil* (Rio de Janeiro), Aug. 5, 1966.

37. *Ibid.*

38. *A Tribuna* (Santos), Mar. 1, 1967.

39. *Correio Braziliense* (Brasilia), Mar. 4, 1967; *Correio da Manha* (Rio de Janeiro), Mar. 4, 1967; *A Tribuna* (Santos), Mar. 4, 1967; *Jornal do Brasil* (Rio de Janeiro), Mar. 4, 1967.

40. *O Diario* (Belo Horizonte), Apr. 29, 1967; *Diario de Minas* (Belo Horizonte), Apr. 29, 1967; *Estado de São Paulo,* Apr. 29, 1967.

41. *Correo* (Lima), May 7, 1967.

42. *Jornal do Brasil* (Rio de Janeiro), Apr. 29, 1967; *O Diario* (Belo Horizonte), Apr. 29, 1967; *Diario de Minas* (Belo Horizonte), Apr. 29, 1967; *Estado de São Paulo,* Apr. 29, 1967; *Correio Braziliense* (Brasilia), Apr. 21, 1967.

43. *Ibid.*

44. *Diario da Tarde* (Belo Horizonte), June 6, 1967.

45. *Correio Braziliense* (Brasilia), Apr. 21, 1967.

46. *Jornal do Brasil* (Rio de Janeiro), May 3, 1967; *Correio Braziliense* (Brasilia), May 3, 1967; *Estado de São Paulo,* May 3, 1967.

47. *Jornal do Brasil* (Rio de Janeiro), May 3, 1967; *Diario de Minas* (Belo Horizonte), May 3, 1967.

48. *O Globo* (Rio de Janeiro), May 4, 1967; *La Razón* (Buenos Aires, quoted *Ultima Hora,* Rio), May 6, 1967.

49. *Correio da Manha* (Rio de Janeiro), July 8, 1967.

50. *Estado de Minas* (Belo Horizonte), May 9, 1967; *Estado de São Paulo,* May 10 and 11, 1967.

51. *Diario de São Paulo,* May 12, 1967; *Estado De São Paulo,* May 12, 1967.
52. *Diario de São Paulo,* May 5, 1967.
53. *Diario da Tarde* (Belo Horizonte), May 10, 1967; *Diario de São Paulo,* May 21, 1967.
54. *Estado de Minas* (Belo Horizonte), May 17, 1967; *O Globo* (Rio de Janeiro), May 16, 1967.
55. *Jornal do Brasil* (Rio de Janeiro), May 17, 1967.
56. *Ibid.,* June 6, 1967.
57. *Jornal do Brasil* (Rio de Janeiro), Sept. 1, 1967.
58. *Diario de São Paulo,* May 4, 1967; *O Globo* (Rio de Janeiro), June 19, 1967.
59. *Jornal do Brasil* (Rio de Janeiro), May 10, 1967.
60. *Correio Braziliense* (Brasilia), Apr. 21, 1967; *Jornal do Brasil* (Rio de Janeiro), June 15, 1967.
61. *Ibid.,* July 11, 1967.
62. *Correio da Manha* (Rio de Janeiro), May 24, 1967.
63. *Ibid.,* July 9, 1967.
64. *Diario de Minas* (Belo Horizonte), May 16, 1967.
65. *Jornal do Brasil* (Rio de Janeiro), June 7, 1967.
66. *Diario de São Paulo,* June 23, 1967.
67. *Jornal do Brasil* (Rio de Janeiro), June 28, 1967.
68. *Ibid.,* June 29, 1967.
69. *Correio da Manha* (Rio de Janeiro), June 30, 1967.
70. *O Globo* (Rio de Janeiro), July 15, 1967.
71. *Correio Braziliense* (Brasilia), Aug. 11, 1967.

CHAPTER 9

Parish Priests in Bogotá

Prepared by **S. Betsy Cohen.**

> There are those priests who are very much open in their interpretation of norms, and, in some cases, they permit certain things. But I stick strictly to doctrine. I'm old, educated in the old school, and it is difficult for me to learn the new modern thoughts.

The above statement was made by one of fifteen Bogotá priests, interviewed in the summer of 1967, and reveals the dramatic polarization of orientations within the Catholic Church, an institution commonly regarded as monolithic. The priests were not chosen at random, but largely as a result of their public position for or against family planning. In most cases they were identified through newspaper articles, but in some cases (especially for those opposed to family planning) they were identified by other priests or by authorities in the family planning movement. The interviews were of a semistructured, open-ended nature, lasting between 1½ and 2½ hours each.

In addition to the developments specific to Colombia outlined in Chapter 6, we should bear in mind as background the more general crisis occurring within the Catholic Church as a consequence of the Vatican II Council. As one priest put it:

> The council did not create the crisis—it merely manifested it and clarified the terms of the crisis. . . . It brought about the confrontation of mentalities

between those on the one hand who felt the council had only a peripheral meaning, and those who, on the other hand felt it implied for the church highly fundamental revisions. These two positions are naturally personified—the first among the older ones—the governors of the church—and the second among the younger priests who are capable of a more rapid theological evolution.

For the younger priests the council was calling for revolutionary changes in Catholic doctrine concerning the very nature and role of the church and encompassing, among others, fundamental revisions in attitudes towards the nature of love, the ends of marriage, and the role of sexual relations and procreation. Whereas traditional church structure had stressed absolute authority and resulted in consequent acceptance and passivity of the "flock," modern church teaching emphasizes that the individual is morally responsible to himself before God. Whereas traditional doctrine emphasized procreation over love and companionship in marriage, modern doctrine eliminates the distinction and calls for a responsible parenthood within marriage. Whereas the traditional basis for judging the morality of birth control was essentially the biological nature of the sexual act—condemning as illicit all artificial techniques and accepting as licit only continence and periodic abstinence—modern thought views the sexual act as an expression of love between husband and wife. As such, the question of artificiality disappears; the important considerations are psychological and concern the love between couples.

On a basis of their views on these matters, we classified the fifteen priests into "traditionals" and "progressives." Because of the way in which the sample was chosen, we emerge with a heavy overrepresentation of progressives—ten of the fifteen.

ATTITUDES TOWARD DEVELOPMENT
AND POPULATION

The interviews began with two broad questions: "In your opinion, what are the most important problems confronting Colombia today?" "In your opinion, what are the most important problems confronting the Colombian family today?"

Responses to the first question may be classified into problems of underdevelopment and problems stemming from sociocultural defects. All the progressive priests stressed the former. As a young social scientist put it:

Focusing on the problem in the socioeconomic terrain, the most important problem facing Colombia today is naturally that of underdevelopment. I'm not just referring to it in an economic sense, but as a human problem. It isn't just the economic question of raising production or per capita income; it involves human development in the sense that everyone must have the opportunity to live his life in a human manner. Within this framework there are a multitude of specific problems which include very low productivity and an unfavorable balance of payments. Thirdly, the masses do not enjoy a dignified level of living, for they do not have educational opportunities. There is a shortage of schools, of teachers, of medical services—all these are different aspects of underdevelopment. Then, another aspect is the terrible problem of the type of social stratification we have here. There is a small elite who enjoys all the benefits of modern society, while the majority of the people do not have the opportunity to improve their position and are considered subhuman by the upper classes. A problem which aggravates the situation is a growing atmosphere of dissatisfaction of a revolutionary type. The masses, and also many leaders, have the faith that a profound change in the society will solve the problems of development. This is bad in the sense that with this kind of messianic hope, everyone sits back and waits for magic formulas, rather than working hard to solve our problems of underdevelopment. Sixth, there is the problem of the elites in government and in the economic sectors who have not realized that socioeconomic change is necessary. Spontaneously they will not give up anything, because they wish to protect their interests and their wealth. Only on the threat of losing their privileges will they give anything up.

Almost without exception the progressives located the problem of underdevelopment in a sociopolitical context, seeing the economic goals of development as inextricable from the issues of social change and political reform. They also spoke of cultural ills as manifestations of underdevelopment.

There is an absense of ethical values. One consequence of this is the mediocrity of the leadership class—a class which is very incompetent. Politicians who are solely individualistic with an absence of a sense of the common welfare. Perhaps it is better to term it passivity rather than mediocrity. And this passivity manifests itself also in the peculiar attitude of waiting for the government to solve everything and therefore not taking the responsibility upon themselves and deciding what they can do to solve a problem. . . .

Another priest attributes cultural problems arising from under-development to the

. . . low educational level of the masses and hence a lack of political con-sciousness. The political problem is an urgent one because at this moment there is a need for very important political decisions. We need an effective political system which will serve as the instrument to solve the fundamental problem of development. The two are a little interdependent naturally: little development and education explain why there is little political consciousness, but somewhere the vicious cycle must be broken. Traditionally, in Colombia, national problems always had a political focus—a personalistic politics. But now the parties are looking for a program which will be stimulating for the masses.

Two priests, both of them progressive, brought up the demographic problem when asked about Colombia's most important problems. One of them linked it with problems of the marginality of the poor.

A second problem is the problem of population growth, which means 700,000 new Colombians each year. In ten or fifteen years we will have a yearly increase of about a million people. This is something neither the church nor the state can ignore. And this aggravates the first problem, because they are growing mostly in the marginal sectors. The upper class is limiting its fertility . . . either as a culmination of a cultural process, or from a desire to live more comfortably. . . . On the other hand, the masses are the ones who reproduce most and have the fewest resources. Now, these two problems reinforce each other—the marginality and the population growth.

The second introductory question asked for the major problems confronting the Colombian family. Nine of the ten progressive priests located the basis of Colombian family problems in the area of economic instability and consequent low standards of living. Within this framework they see such socio-cultural ills as *machismo,* female subservience and inferiority, family instability, irresponsible parent-hood, inability to provide a sufficient education, and a crisis of religio-moral values. A typical response:

The most outstanding problem confronting the family is the economic instability. If people can't plan their family budget they can't plan anything. From there arise many other problems such as educating the children, psychological conflicts between husband and wife—a permanent anguish. I always believe, as St. Thomas Aquinas said, that to be able to practice virtue one needs economic stability. It is a luxury to practice virtue which can only be afforded when one has a degree of economic stability.

Whereas most of the progressive priests regarded the economic problems facing the family as the source of the other ills, most of the traditional priests cited isolated cultural or moral problems such as instability, lack of love, or generational conflict as the major problems.

The demographic question was mentioned by half of the progressive priests, who stressed the problem of irresponsible parenthood. One priest expressed it this way:

> One very outstanding problem is the improvised family. . . . Everything is improvised up to love itself. They never have the capacity to view the future and to plan for the future. This is a very Latin characteristic—we are completely improvised! We don't like to plan. With every child that comes along they do not plan how they are going to raise or educate him. . . .

When the traditional priests spoke of the demographic problem, they did so in a different way. One spoke of ways to alleviate the problem by increasing family cohesiveness, and another explained that the problem consisted of the psychological trauma good Catholics were suffering by constantly being told about family planning:

> I think that the gravest problem from the human point of view is the psychological problem that the demographic problem has created within the family. Today, the family that is either just beginning to have children or already has a lot of children hears this discussion about the demographic problem. This latter feels there is no solution for his problems, since he already has ten children, which creates a great psychological trauma. And the others have a psychological problem because the church has yet to pronounce on this question. . . .

After permitting the priests these two opportunities to bring up population problems spontaneously, the third question posed the issue directly. "Do you believe that Colombia has a demographic problem, or has this been exaggerated?" (If yes) "How does the problem manifest itself? In what ways do you see it as a problem?" While all the progressive priests see it as a very important problem and deny that it has been exaggerated, only one of the traditionals views it as such. Further, most of the progressives, but only one of the traditionals, mention its national implications for socioeconomic development.

In summary, the progressive priests have a broad interpretation of Colombia's problems of underdevelopment. They are greatly concerned with social change and economic development and view the demographic problem as an important variable. The traditional priests have a more narrowly focused outlook on the problems facing the nation and the family and fail to see population growth as a national problem or a variable in the development process.

REACTIONS TO NATIONAL EVENTS CONCERNING FAMILY PLANNING

A list of incidents involving family planning was presented to each priest: (1) the Pan-American Assembly on Population held in 1965 in Cali; (2) the January 1967 articles in *El Catolicismo* on family planning; (3) the 1967 Senate debates on the family planning program; (4) the Easter-week pastoral of Cardinal Concha; and (5) the Pope's encyclical, *Populorum Progressio.*

Most of the progressive priests had a generally positive assessment of the Cali conference, but several were highly critical of the participation of Liberal ex-President Lleras Camargo.

• There was a negative factor—Lleras Camargo—who is an individual who is considered to be unconditionally at the service of any North American politician. His presence devalued the conference. If he hadn't participated, it wouldn't have had the political tone it had, and would have been considered more scientific. That was an error—to mix political figures and politics with a scientific conference. People interpreted it as political, not scientific.

• Well, this is what happened. Lleras arrives in Colombia for the first time in a long time, from the U.S., at a point when the political situation was not calling for his arrival, to bring a messianic formula with which he claims we can solve our problems. . . . The meeting began and members began to express their views, and there were no clashes. The clash began with his speech. The impression his participation left destroyed everything that had come beforehand. But this reaction wasn't so much against the campaign itself, but against him. You see, when Lleras was President, there was a great hope among the people. But this hope was frustrated and when he left office the country was bankrupt. So when he came back to Colombia with this program, people thought he was trying to make an a posteriori justification for his failure.

• I had two reactions. The first was a positive one—they were dealing with an important problem in a scientific manner, and so on. The second was of displeasure because I saw it simply as a political campaign. Lleras Camargo shows up—a politician looking for an opportunity to present his politics—political opportunism. It could have been an attempt to achieve acceptance of the idea because a lot of people like him, but it appeared as political opportunism.

Traditionals who gave an opinion regarded the conference as biased. As one of them put it:

. . . I noticed there the unilateral intentions of certain representatives of certain organizations. . . .
Do you know what *"llevar el agua a su molino"* means? Well, it means that you pull out of something only what suits your purposes. I noticed a certain bias in that sense.

Now let us see how they reacted to the articles in *El Catolicismo,* a highly conservative magazine published by members of the Opus Dei, with assistance from some of the clergy.

The magazine's young and progressive editors were replaced by conservatives late in the summer of 1966. What then happened is described by a respondent:

Well, around September when the new government took office, we realized that they were beginning to develop a hidden, subtle, mysterious program which they called family planning, but was really reduced to pure birth control. . . . It was known publicly, because the meetings were all publicized, but with reserved conclusions. Doctors and foreign sociologists attended these meetings—one in Cali, another in La Ceja. So we chatted with sociologists and doctors—both Catholic and non-Catholic, people in agreement with the program and people opposed—to give us their opinions. In this way we determined our position. The government was removing the moral aspect from the question and saying it was purely a socioeconomic one, and that the church has nothing to do with it. . . . So we decided to take the lid off and present it as news. Either the other press didn't know about what was going on, or they weren't interested. . . . The official response the government was giving was that the program was strictly on an educational level, training of doctors, and so on. Our investigations revealed that they were past that stage and that they were handing out contraceptives. The government denied it, but we investigated in official centers, both directly and indirectly, and declared the truth.

Most of the progressives condemned the *Catolicismo* articles, utilizing such adjectives as "reactionary," "emotional," "fanatic," "excessive," "impassioned," "unilateral," "backward," "extreme," and "closeminded." Even among the traditionals, only two had entirely positive reactions, one condemned the articles completely, and two were ambivalent:

Well, in some aspects they were too unilateral and simplistic perhaps. But on the other hand I am glad that everyone has the opportunity to speak because one of the forms of coercion that can and does exist here is to only give publicity to one side of the story. So although I was opposed to their position, I'm glad it was published because the issue requires a lot of discussion from all points of view.

Shortly after the articles were published, heated debates occurred in the Colombian Senate, where Conservative politicians adopted many of the articles' accusations and forced Liberal politicians and government officials to defend the program. The progressive priests thought the debates were "ridiculous" or a "public spectacle," and most of them viewed the whole affair as a political move to embarrass the present Liberal government or to give the impression that the Conservative party is the defender of the church—a tactic central to Colombian politics since independence. One priest became very incensed as he described what he imagined was going on:

Look, in Colombia they still have not comprehended that the church isn't connected with any party. Debates that occur in the parliament on themes like demography, civil marriage, divorce, religious liberty unfortunately will always be oriented more from a political criterion than a human, scientific, and true criterion. They say the Conservatives defend the church, but do you know what the only difference is between the Conservatives and the Liberals? The Conservatives go to the five o'clock mass and the Liberals go at eight!

In March of 1967 the cardinal responded to the controversy in an Easter-week pastoral condemning the government program as immoral and forbidding Catholics to attend the clinics. Whereas all the traditional priests read the letter to their parishioners, *none of the four progressives in a position to read the pastoral in fact did so,* and two others reported that many priests had ignored it. Progressive priests criticized the authoritarian and absolute nature of the document and characterized it as "imprudent" and "inopportune."

• The pastoral letter was very badly received by the majority of the priests. Many of them, or I should say us, did not read it. [I thought it had to be read.] Yes, but today the priests have a certain critical position before the hierarchy. We see it as a need to collaborate. On the one hand we have the people and their needs, and on the other hand we have the hierarchy. And there is the impression of a great distance existing between the hierarchy and the people—that they do not understand the people or their problems, or how to present things to them. A negative pastoral like this one doesn't serve the needs of the people.

• I personally thought that it wasn't appropriate in a magisterial document to make such categorical and definitive affirmations on a theme that the very magistrate is studying. [Was it read?] These letters are supposed to be read, but I don't think many priests read it. I don't think the majority read it. [Did you?] No.

While both progressives and traditionals were critical of the pastoral, they differ in their attitudes towards ecclesiastical discipline. For the progressives, discipline is subordinate to principles, while the traditionals consider it their duty to conform to the hierarchy. The statements below were made by traditional priests:

• Both for reasons of discipline and of personal conviction, I cannot have a different idea than that of the church. . . .

• My views accord with the official norms of the church. . . .

• I believe what the church believes. . . .

• . . . we as members of the church are responsible to the hierarchy. There must be a unity of criteria and discipline—that is imperative. I guess I should be involved with birth control, seeing all those children, but I see above my anxiety that I have to respect the hierarchy.

Two weeks after the pastoral letter, the Pope issued *Populorum Progressio*, an encyclical which lent support to the progressives by affirming the state's right to conduct licit family planning programs. All the priests who responded to this question felt it was a good doctrine. While several of the progressives pointed out that it really contained nothing new, a majority of the traditionals stressed that population was only a minor section of the document.

OPINIONS ON SEX AND CONTRACEPTION

Attitudes towards family planning and contraception were initially elicited by an intentionally vague question, "What about family planning?" Both traditionals and progressives share the following general viewpoint: Family planning falls within the rubric of a responsible parenthood—something Catholics are not only permitted but required to practice and something which is the duty of the state to promulgate. Education and a general uplifting of the cultural level are necessary prerequisites. Inculcation is needed in the values of love, marriage, and the family and for a sense of responsibility towards procreation, so that reproduction is not a biological accident but a planned occurrence, taking into account the financial situation of the family, the health of the mother, the effect of an additional child on the other children, and the ability of the couple to raise and educate their offspring. While this philosophy is common to both categories of priests, the traditionals almost unanimously add that only certain methods are permitted to achieve this end. Because the traditional priests consider mechanical and chemical methods of birth control a violation of Natural and Divine Law, the question of means is as important to them as that of responsible parenthood itself.

They should reduce the number of their children, yes, but only as long as the method is in accord with the dignity of the human being and with Nature. There are some systems of control which are against the dignity of the human being because they are abortives, like the loops. Imagine destroying a little creature the moment it is conceived! Others can be considered as pure masturbation—the ones which impede the semen from reaching the egg. Others are against the integrity of the person—for example the pills might just be harmful—and for the church to allow them might be endangering all of humanity. In this situation the church is defending the woman in spite of herself. Others have no problems at all, like periodic continence and delayed marriage. But this does not exclude the possibility that in the future an acceptable system may be developed.

The reference to masturbation suggests that traditional priests value the sexual act essentially for its reproductive function. Other comments reveal a low esteem for sex:

. . . making responsible parenthood easy by merely handing out drugs and so on doesn't demand anything of the parents in terms of sexual responsibility. It is making the life of a woman nothing but pure sex without the consequences, and this is a demoralization of the woman. Even in a legal family, the man isn't responsible for his children. The only thing that is important to him is sexual relations. He waits for the state to give him everything, or he sends his children out to beg, so he only wants to satisfy his sexual desires. . . . There are other reinforcing factors. For example the worker has no education or diversions, so his home is reduced to his bed. He arrives home drunk and his only family satisfaction is sexual because he is so poor. In the families not established by the church [consensual unions], the woman is even more dependent upon the man. She must satisfy him or he'll walk out on her.

• People criticize the rhythm system—it causes psychological problems they say, or it mechanizes love between two people by setting determined days when they can or cannot make love. But there is a reason for this, and that is that there is a lack of self-discipline, a lack of self-control in the people.

• Love is the end of marriage, but a fertile love. The child is what gives explanation and fullness to the sexual act. [It can't be considered as an expression of love?] No, the sexual act is not dignified in this way.

Rather than attempt our own interpretation of this point of view, we may cite the opinions of two progressive priests speaking of their more traditional colleagues:

• There are a great number in the church who are upset by sex. For them it is a danger zone. They have a tendency to upset the people rather than orient them. The young clergy are moving away from this traditional position that stresses no positive aspect of Christian love. And of course there is such an aspect.

• The state must undertake a sexual education program. . . . The people do not realize, and you can take this down verbatim, that [sex] activity itself is a means of expression of love. There is a great need for a sexual education. But do you know in whose hands this education is entrusted? Hysterical nuns and sterile monks!

For the progressive, the question of artificiality and directness is inapplicable. What concerns them then about the means are their appropriateness for the individuals involved—a decision only the individuals can make.

There is a conflict between two waves of theologians—those who view marital relations in its biological framework, and those who see it in its spiritual sense. For us in the latter group, the question is not the pure biological one of blocking or destroying conception, but the wider concept of the human being. . . . The former interpretation was materialistic really. But now we are accepting that man is a spiritual being who can transform himself. One asks which is more important to preserve in a home—an isolated biological function, or the values of a marriage?

While all the progressive priests feel that the decision on means must be left to the conscience of the individuals involved, four of the five traditionals will permit only church-approved methods, and the fifth can only envision isolated exceptions.

Through their roles as confessors, counselors, and advisers, the progressive priests have become deeply and personally involved with the problems which face the people. Very often these problems have to do with marriage, marital relations, and fear of having another child. At the same time that women find themselves confronting the latter problem, the church tells them they cannot use modern, efficient means to solve it. Many priests believe therefore that the church cannot remain opposed to the needs and desires of the people and that it is its duty to help them rather than aggravate their situation. The progressives are also fearful that in the long run the people will become alienated from the church, and that the institution will lose its moral authority.

• The demographic problem isn't what bothers the clergy too much. The problem which does bother them is the moral one concerning the confessional. They want to keep the faithful from leaving the church. The tendency is to become broader in their advice. They focus on the issue of conjugal love—what is best for the marriage.

• . . . the church cannot deny a solution. . . . There are cases of people who are very poor to whom you cannot say no. More than the biology of the sexual act must be respected. And without a solution the church will go on losing ground. Some people say "It doesn't matter because the church must remain pure." But that is wrong. The church has the responsibility of formation of the people, and they must teach a Christianity, in areas which aren't strictly questions of faith, which doesn't alienate the people from the church. I consider myself more advanced and optimistic than many who are interested only in stopping things. "Don't do this, don't do that!" But this doesn't last. If someone is told not to do something every time he turns around, he is going to stop listening. . . .

The progressive priests are deeply convinced of the need for social change—a change which implies transforming a passive and fatalist mentality into an activist and responsible one. The progressives feel that it is partly the traditional authoritarian structure of the church which has reinforced this mentality. They believe that the priest must stop telling people what to do, must respect their decision-making capacity, and let them take responsibility for their own decisions and actions.

I myself do not give advice to people in this area. I listen, talk, help them to orient themselves, and I tell them to make their own decisions. I don't know if other priests do the same—I doubt it. The majority are inflexible—

"no," "no," "no." Some say "yes," "yes," "yes." But both constitute a lack of respect. Telling people what to do is not letting them mature. They don't take responsibility for themselves. A woman comes to me with an IUD and I ask her why she has one, and she says because Father So-and-so told her she could. What kind of reason is that? [Are contraceptives confessed?] I don't really know, but my own ideas are that communion is a very important thing, and something like that shouldn't come between the people and God—I feel that God understands these things.

While the crisis of conscience for the progressive priest is an inability to assume responsibility because of conflicting forces, for the traditional, a crisis of conscience occurs when forces in the secular society pressure the individual to abandon his moral stance. These forces are not the materialistic ones of survival, which are the competing forces in the minds of progressives, but refer to the intangible, psychological pressures of a small-family norm being imposed on people who have, or want to have, or were taught to have many children.

In summary, while all priests favor "responsible parenthood," traditional priests, with a biological view of the sexual act, firmly oppose artificial means of birth control and tend to deprecate sex and the lack of "self control" especially evidenced by Colombian males. Progressive priests view the sexual act as an expression of love, rendering the question of means irrelevant. They believe in respecting the individual's ability to make his own decisions, thus lessening the risk of his alienation from the church.

THE ROLE OF GOVERNMENT IN FAMILY PLANNING

With only two exceptions, all priests take a dim view of North American participation in Colombian family planning programs. Little distinction is made between the participation of private foundations like Ford and Rockefeller and the national policy of the United States government. U.S. motives are usually characterized as self-interested, simplistic, and ignorant of Colombian cultural norms and values. President Johnson's statement about the value of $5 worth of contraception is often criticized in this context. Finally they are critical of the U.S. for its adoption of a vanguard role rather than one of passive assistance. They see the United States as a powerful protagonist for family planning exerting undue pressure on the Colombian government.

• In Europe there are social, economic, and political currents which I think are far more sophisticated, which appreciate the cultural problem in depth. They have a somewhat philosophical outlook and a more global solution. They are more conscious of religious values. Now on the other hand, there are some North American foundations and politicians who are superficial in their analysis of the problem when they turn to other countries. Their analysis is completely simplistic. I don't know to what point they are convinced that a campaign of this type is going to solve the problems of lack of cultural formation, social integration, and so on. But they have a poor, unilateral focus, and it is causing reactions in various sectors, not just in the church.

• The leftists are in agreement with the church—the M.R.I.,† the Marxists, and the youths. They all say that we cannot follow a North American model which substitutes pills for development. That's like international veterinary medicine. Look, here is an example. What is your country doing about depressed areas like the Appalachians? Large investments, educational programs, health programs, community organization, and a little birth control and family education. But is the solution to give out pills? That is a colonialistic focus whose ends are that the people do not reproduce. . . . Like, for instance, what Johnson said about $5 of birth control instead of $95 [sic] of development. . . . Another thing one notices in the foundations is their ignorance in regard to a profound theological and philosophical analysis. The only thing they do is publish things that prove that one must hand out pills. There are many problems in Latin America that do not depend on the population problem—like foreign trade, international markets, balance of payments. Our problems come in part from these things, yet there is no effort to solve them.

The charge of "unilaterality" was also made with respect to the Colombian government. This term is used in two ways, the first of which refers to excessive emphasis on family planning, with insufficient action in the area of economic development and social change. This is the criticism of several progressives and of two traditionals, who refer to the dangers of distraction from "true developmental" efforts. The second meaning, used only by traditionals, refers to birth control efforts out of proportion to efforts in legal protection of the family, sexual education, and education in the philosophical concept of responsible parenthood.

While all the traditional priests are critical of the government for these reasons, the majority of the progressives react positively towards

† A moderately leftist branch of the Liberal party at the time of the interview. In the summer of 1968, the MRL was welcomed back into the mainstream of the Liberal party.

the actions of the government of Carlos Lleras Restrepo. Even those who spoke against Alberto Lleras Camargo and his participation in the family planning movement express deep respect for and trust in Carlos Lleras. The priest whose long condemnation of Alberto Lleras was quoted on page 179–180 went on to say:

> I reacted favorably to Lleras Restrepo's announcement that the government was interested in family planning for three reasons. First of all, because it is necessary; secondly, because I have the impression that Lleras is a mature and capable man; and thirdly, because it is a campaign that has possibilities of success.

Focusing on the actual course of the campaign as conducted by the ASCOFAME, more concrete criticisms begin to emerge. Even among the progressive priests, only a minority are noncritical of the program, and these view the problem as basically medical, calling for a solution only doctors and technical personnel can provide.

> It is fundamentally a problem of public health. I would say that of all the institutions in Colombia, ASCOFAME is the most competent to undertake the program. [Since the issue deals also with love and the family, don't you think the church has a role?] Well, not really. It is more a problem of public welfare that the people should solve with whatever means are available. It's a problem of techniques of administration, public health, and individual health. The priest does not have these means available to him unless he is also a doctor. The problem is fundamentally medical.

Among the other progressive priests, most are critical of the Colombian Association of Medical Schools because they feel it has deceived the church. All the traditionals who responded to this question were critical, reacting against the "mass nature" of the campaign and the consequent violation of individual conscience.

> • I would be opposed to a massive campaign disseminating pills, although I might approve of it in isolated cases for specific reasons. [How about a massive rhythm campaign?] I'd oppose it less because it isn't so contrary to moral conscience. But I know it is ineffective on a massive level because it requires a high level of education.

> • I'm not opposed to handing out information as long as one leaves it up to the consciences of the individuals and bears in mind his educational level. For example, it is not right to inform a peasant about these other methods because although he is profoundly religious, the morality of these systems has never concerned him, so he is tricked into adopting them because they

are more efficient. This does not respect the liberty and conscience of that person.

• It is one thing to instruct them, and then leave it up to their conscience, and another to pressure them with pamphlets. What effect does the pamphlet have on a woman with seven children when she looks at a picture which supposedly compares a family with seven children—crying, and dirty and miserable and hungry, and on the next page a family with two children and a pretty house, a TV, a car, and so on. This creates a sense of shame, an inferiority complex. They make fun of her because she has many children.

On the one hand the traditional priests might permit exceptions for women who cannot practice rhythm, but at the same time the concept of a mass campaign is repugnant to them. They speak of exceptional cases, but never contemplate the possibility that these exceptions might really be the rule. Although they speak of respect for the liberty and conscience of the individual, they feel that, because of low educational levels, the people are not capable of making a moral decision. And although they acknowledge that a responsible parenthood is necessary, they feel it can be achieved by a program which merely preaches it, without any attempt at implementation.

The progressive priests also believe that a family planning program must have a strong educational orientation, involving both values of responsible parenthood and sexual education. Such instruction should precede the phase of disseminating contraceptives. Thus, they share the reluctance of their more conservative colleagues, with the important difference that they will not deny the necessity of instruction in contraceptive techniques. At the same time they stress that these efforts must be accompanied by programs improving the social and economic conditions of the country. But many are bitter about the misinformation or lack of information they allege they have received about the family planning program. For this reason, they are not entirely willing to support it.

CONCLUSIONS

It is doubtful that a contraceptive program will ever gain the support of traditional priests. Though they embrace the need for responsible parenthood, their orientation makes them view the whole idea of mass dissemination of contraceptive techniques as both unwarrented and repugnant. Since they are firmly committed to ecclesiastic discipline, no amount of rhetoric will persuade them to change unless the Pope issues the "final word." The progressive priests, however, are convinced of the necessity of such a program and are already receptive to it, if it is handled in the proper manner. If emphasis is given to a thorough educational framework, if the nature of the program is presented honestly, laying stress on the themes important to progressive priests (e.g., concentrating on human and moral rather than economic aspects), their support could be won. Thus far, however, the rhetoric aired by family planners to avoid alienating the church has essentially been for the benefit of the traditionals.

It is not unlikely that within a decade or so the traditionals will no longer wield the power or influence they do today. Moreover, in the opinion of the progressive priests, the hierarchy *is* responding, although slowly, to pressures for change from above and below.

The progressive sector of the Catholic Church is more than willing to cooperate with a program that is not purely technical, which constitutes one aspect of a broad program of development and social change and which keeps them informed concerning its ends and means. Perhaps the words of a young priest, terminating a long and moving interview, are the most appropriate:

I think the basic problem is the need for a sincere dialogue between the government and the church—a dialogue which honestly discusses what is going on and what they are really doing. A dialogue is what we need.

CHAPTER 10

University Students

Prepared by **Barent F. Landstreet, Jr.,** *and* **Axel I. Mundigo.***

Among the many factors which shape public opinion on population issues, religiosity and political ideology must certainly be considered of special importance.[1] Our objective is to trace the way in which religiosity and political ideology influence the perception of population issues among two samples of university students in Colombia and Honduras. While the two surveys reported here were separate in time and place, they were sufficiently alike in terms of objectives, general design, and populations studied to be compared with some degree of confidence.

Colombia and Honduras are both experiencing high rates of population growth (3.2 and 3.4 percent annually), which place them among the fastest growing nations in the world. Both countries are also experiencing high birth rates, estimated by the United Nations at 41 to 44 births per thousand for Colombia and 47 to 50 for

* Barent Landstreet is responsible for the Colombian study; Axel Mundigo for the Honduran. The Colombian research was made possible by the combined support of Cornell University's Latin American and International Population Programs. The Honduran research was funded partly by Cornell University's International Population Program and partly by a Public Health Fellowship (5 FO3 HD 36949–02) from the National Institute of Child and Human Development.

Honduras. For a Latin American nation, Colombia has a large population, estimated at 20.5 million people in 1969, while Honduras is a relatively small country with an estimated population of 2.5 million people.[2]

The first survey was conducted at the National University in Bogotá, Colombia, where questionnaires were completed by 650 students during the summer of 1966. The second included 410 students at the Autonomous National University of Honduras in Tegucigalpa (the capital) and was completed in early 1970. In Colombia, only second, third, and fourth year students were included in the sample, while in Honduras, first year students were included as well. Table 12 illustrates the academic composition of the two samples.

While accidental, it is fortunate that in both samples medical students represent about half of the total. On the other hand, law students, an important group in the Colombian sample, are scarcely represented in the Honduran since their law school functions mostly as a night school. In the Honduran sample, an effort was made to exclude part-time students, who tended to be older and were more likely to be married and the parents of several children. In Colombia this problem did not arise, as most university students attend on a daytime basis. In terms of age, sex, and marital status, both groups were quite similar.[3]

TABLE 12

Academic Discipline of Colombian and Honduran
Students, in Percent

Academic Discipline	Colombia	Honduras
Economics	18	15
Engineering		14
Health and biology		11
Law	18	5
Medicine	51	47
Psychology	9	8 *
Sociology	4	
	100	100
Number of cases	(650)	(410)

* Social science includes students of sociology, psychology, and philosophy and a few language and mathematics students.

Both samples were of a "purposive" nature; that is, they were neither random nor representative of the respective universities. Our intention was to secure samples containing large numbers of students, with a broad spectrum of social and attitudinal characteristics. To this end, we first discussed the projects with the appropriate university officials and then obtained course lists for the various schools and departments. We contacted the professors whose classes we wished to include in our samples and requested their cooperation in allowing us to distribute our questionnaires during their class time. Most agreed to cooperate, and the questionnaires were filled out in the classrooms. (In Colombia, the permission of the student governments was also obtained.)

As a result of the procedures used to select students, we will not report percentages referring to the total samples, but rather will identify trends in response among subgroups ("right," "center," "moderate left," etc.) within each sample. In addition, since the indicators of religiosity and political ideology differ somewhat between the two studies (as will be discussed below), comparisons between the findings for the two countries must be made with some caution.

RELIGIOSITY

We are concerned here with the relationship between the religiosity of Catholics and their attitudes on a range of issues concerning population and family planning. The influence of the Catholic Church can be seen as potentially operative in two areas: the moral validity of various methods of birth control, on the one hand, and the broader question of the relation between population growth and social, political, and economic factors on the other. Another way to conceptualize this is to distinguish between the *means* and the *ends* of birth control. The church has had a clear and widely known doctrine opposing certain means of birth control, most notably, contraceptives and abortion. Church doctrine with regard to the ends of birth control, however, has generally been vague. By "ends," we refer to views regarding the probable outcomes of the limitation of births—i.e., the desirability of large or small families, the question of whether reducing population growth would decrease poverty and facilitate economic development, etc.

As late as 1961, Pope John XXIII's encyclical *Mater et Magister* seemed to deny that rapid population growth engendered problems of any pressing nature, at least on a world scale:

Now to tell the truth, the interrelationships on a global scale between the number of births and available resources are such that we can infer grave difficulties in this matter do not arise at present, nor will in the immediate future. The arguments advanced in this connection are so inconclusive and controversial that nothing certain can be drawn from them. . . .

When it comes to questions of this kind, we are not unaware that in certain locales and also in poorer countries, it is often argued that in such an economic and social order, difficulties arise because citizens, each year more numerous, are unable to acquire sufficient food or sustenance where they live. . . .

But whatever be the situation, we clearly affirm these problems should be posed and resolved in such a way that man does not have recourse to methods and means contrary to his dignity. . . .

Now the provident God has bestowed upon humanity sufficient goods wherewith to bear with dignity the burdens associated with procreation of children.[4]

The preceding is an illustration of what we mean by the vagueness of church pronouncements on the ends of birth control. Not until 1967, with the publication of Paul VI's encyclical *Populorum Progressio*, was papal authority clearly given to the view that population problems existed for which some governmental solution might be needed:

It is true that too frequently an accelerated demographic increase adds its own difficulties to the problems of development. The size of the population increases more rapidly than available resources, and things are found to have reached apparently an impasse. From that moment the temptation is great to check the demographic increase by means of radical measures. It is certain that public authorities can intervene, within the limit of their competence, by favoring the availability of appropriate information and by adopting suitable measures, provided that these be in conformity with the moral law and that they respect the rightful freedom of married couples.[5]

Thus, although there has been no doctrinal reason why a devout Catholic could not view population problems as real and favor national policies based on morally permissible means of population control (the rhythm method, delayed marriage, etc.), it can hardly be said that until recently papal authority has supported such a view.

In contrast to church vagueness on the ends of birth control, doctrine relating to the means of birth control has been quite clear, and judging from survey data, it would appear that the doctrine has actually influenced behavior in this area. Stycos, analyzing data from seven major Latin American cities, found that devout Catholic women were considerably less likely to have used church-prohibited methods of birth control than "nominal" Catholic women. The relationship, however, only held strongly among the more-educated women (those having more than primary school education).[6] A similar pattern was discovered for several other items having to do with contraception and preferred family size. This suggests that religiosity might be an especially important influence on birth control and population attitudes in our own Colombian and Honduran studies, given the high educational level of the respondents. Further, due to the greater church clarity on the means rather than the ends of birth control, we might expect stronger relationships on items relating to the former than to the latter.

Since the Protestant and Jewish religions do not have doctrines opposing the use of contraception, we have omitted members of those faiths in all analyses involving religiosity. This leaves 97 percent of the original sample in Colombia and 92 percent in Honduras.

The measures of religiosity were different in the two surveys. The measure used in the Colombian analysis was frequency of church attendance during the preceding year, which varied from "more than once a week" to "never." For convenience, we have labeled the five church-attendance categories as follows: very often (more than once a week), often (once a week), occasionally (once or several times a month), rarely (once or several times a year), and never. In contrast, religiosity among the Honduran students was measured by the question, "Do you consider yourself very, somewhat, little or not at all religious?" (Table 13).

TABLE 13

Religiosity of Colombian and Honduran Students, in Percent

Church Attendance: Colombia		Religiosity: Honduras	
Very often	7	Very	6
Often	28		
Occasionally	13	Somewhat	58
Rarely	27	Little	27
Never	25	Not at all	8
	100		100
Number of cases	(637)	Number of cases	(375)

Turning first to the Colombian data, we see from Table 14 that church attendance is a strong predictor of attitudes toward national birth control programs, except where "personal freedom" is involved. In the latter case a large majority of students at all religiosity levels feel that the government should provide birth control services to increase personal freedom of parents with respect to family size. While the relationship between religiosity and opposition to a national birth control program is a linear one with regard to an active program, it is the "occasional attenders" who give the most support to a program of any kind. The influence of religiosity is strongest where church doctrine is clearest. Almost none of the nonreligious would wish a government birth control program to be limited to church-approved methods, while half of the most religious support that position.

Correspondingly, a weaker and less consistent relation is seen between religiosity and certain ends of birth control—the small family on the one hand and the "population-poverty" equation on the other. Although the data are not included in Table 14, similarly weak associations were found between religiosity and questions on the relation between rapid population growth or economic and social development. This shows that the disapproval of the devout refers primarily to the intensity of the government's approach (i.e., a strong propaganda component) or to the birth control methods it adopts. Both reduce themselves to problems of means rather than ends.

There is a negative relation between religiosity and both the amount of attention paid to population issues and the firmness of opinion on these issues. It should be noted that these questions unfortunately combined the topic of population with that of birth control, and as such crosscut the means-ends division. Perhaps church vagueness on the population question, combined with church aggressiveness on the birth control issue, has led both to lack of attention and to ambivalence of attitude on the part of the more devout.

We turn now to the Honduran data. Table 15 shows that, as in Colombia, the relationships between religiosity and the ends of birth control (the difficulties of a large family and the population-poverty equation) are weak. However, while the most religious are least likely to support a national family planning program, it is the "somewhat religious" who give most program support. Furthermore, it appears that religiosity is a rather less powerful predictor of birth control attitudes in Honduras than in Colombia.[7]

TABLE 14

Colombian Students: Selected Population Attitude Items, by Church Attendance, in Percent

	Church Attendance				
	Very Often	Often	Occasion-ally	Rarely	Never
1. * Attitude towards a national birth control program:					
Percent favoring an "active program"	14	31	44	45	49
Percent supporting "any program"	42	69	80	69	66
2. Birth control program restricted to church-approved methods only:					
Percent who "agree"	52	31	13	5	3
3. Government ought to provide birth control for personal freedom:					
Percent who "agree"	85	83	87	86	82
4. How many children should a working-class mother in Bogotá have?:					
Percent answering "2 or less children"	52	50	64	57	62
5. Rapid population growth increases poverty:					
Percent who "agree"	55	84	86	71	79
6. Attention paid to population and birth control issues:					
Percent paying "much attention"	29	35	38	44	43
7. Firmness of opinion on population and birth control issues:					
Percent "firm"	37	48	53	51	58
Average number of cases in base	(43)	(173)	(80)	(171)	(155)

*Items 1–7 correspond to the following questionnaire items:

1. What would be your position with regard to a government population policy to reduce Colombia's birth rate? Would you (a) support an active campaign to convince parents to use birth control, (b) support a restricted program designed only to make available birth control materials to those who already wish to use them [(a) and (b) combined are shown as support for "any program"], or (c) oppose any government interference in this area?

2. If the government were to adopt a national birth control policy, would you prefer (a) that it be limited to church-approved methods only, or (b) that methods be chosen according to their efficiency and acceptability by users?

3. Totally apart from dealing with birth control as a problem of population growth, the government ought to facilitate birth control information and materials so as to increase the personal freedom of parents with regard to their family size.

4. How many children do you think a working-class Bogotá mother should have?

5. Rapid population growth is an important factor contributing to the poverty of the masses.

6. How much attention, if any, have you paid to population growth and birth control issues during the last year? Much, some, or none?

7. Would you say that your opinions on population growth and birth control issues are firm or tentative?

TABLE 15

Honduran Students: Selected Population Attitude Items, by
Religiosity, in Percent

	Religiosity			
	Very Religious	Somewhat Religious	Little Religious	Not at All
1. * Attitude towards a national family planning program:				
Percent who "favor"	17	36	27	29
Percent who "favor" or "partly favor" combined	61	85	78	68
2. Government should recommend that a family of three is sufficient:				
Percent who "agree"	75	89	86	74
3. A large family is a difficulty for the poor:				
Percent who "agree"	91	95	99	97
4. Rapid population growth increases poverty:				
Percent who "agree"	50	47	49	26
5. Attention paid to population and birth control issues:				
Percent paying "much attention"	25	17	11	26
6. Firmness of opinion on population and birth control issues:				
Percent "firm"	38	42	36	45
Average number of cases in base	(23)	(211)	(100)	(31)

*Items 1–6 correspond to the following questionnaire items:

1. What would be your opinion about a national family planning program to reduce the present population growth rate? Would you agree, partly agree, or disagree?

2. If a family has no more than three children, the government should (a) give economic aid to increase this number, (b) recommend that this number is enough (reported above), or (c) avoid interfering in such family decisions.

3. Would you say that for a poor family, having a lot of children is (a) a help or (b) a difficulty? (The latter is reported here.)

4. Rapid population growth is a cause of the poverty of the masses.

5. How much attention have you paid to population growth and birth control issues during the last year? Much, some, or none?

6. Would you say that your opinions on population growth and birth control issues are firm or tentative?

Further contrasts with Colombia are found in the absence of a consistent relationship between religiosity and firmness of opinion. Similarly, there is a weak and inconsistent relation between religiosity and attention to population and birth control issues.

We should note that the Colombian survey was carried out two years before publication of *Humanae Vitae,* and the Honduran survey was conducted after its publication. For some years, there had been considerable speculation that the church might reverse its traditional birth control stand, but *Humanae Vitae* brought these speculations to an abrupt end. On these grounds, it might have been expected that the postencyclical survey would reflect the reassertion of the church's position by showing stronger religiosity differentials on birth control program support than the preencyclical survey. Since the opposite proved true, the explanation may involve the different institutional strengths of the Catholic Church in the two countries.

Colombia is usually referred to as the prototype of traditional Catholic Latin America. According to Vallier, "the Church has a major grip on the country's educational system. . . . In a very deep sense, Colombia is a clerical country."[8] Martz reinforces this assertion: "The inordinate strength of the Roman Catholic Church, only slightly weakened in the last few years, remains a feature of contemporary society. Religion has long been in the forefront of national politics and has played a fundamental role in the rivalry of Liberals and Conservatives. . . . Colombia remains among the most Catholic nations in the hemisphere."[9]

By contrast, Honduras seems to be at the opposite end of the religious spectrum in Latin America. The ratio of priests to population is low—1 per each 10,000 inhabitants—and only 1 in 5 priests is native born.[10] Colombia's ratio of one priest per 3,400 inhabitants, on the other hand, is one of the highest in Latin America.[11] One authority writes: "The role of organized faith in republican Honduras has been weak. Catholic churches have increased in number, and more Protestant agencies have entered Honduras than any other Central American country. But one cannot speak of a twentieth-century renaissance of religion in this country until more persons have been affected."[12] Thus it is not inconsistent for Colombian students to show a greater influence of religiosity in their attitudes toward the more sharply defined issue—the means of birth control—than the Hondurans, where the overall church influence has been less strongly felt.

Finally, with regard to the ends of birth control, we noted that differences by religiosity were weak. It may be that political ideologies have filled the vacuum left by the church in this area. It is to this matter that we now turn.

POLITICAL IDEOLOGY

In analyzing the Colombian data, two indicators of political ideology were used. The first derives from a seven-point scale of attitudes toward government control over the economy, ranging from complete free enterprise (1), through a private enterprise system under strict governmental regulation (3), through a mixed capitalist-socialist system with government ownership of the basic industries and services (5), to complete government ownership of the means of production (7). Only 23 percent of the responses fell in the first three categories, the remaining four having 12, 31, 8, and 11 percent, respectively. (Since the student government of the psychology department requested that this question be omitted among their students, an overall "no response" percentage of 16 was obtained.) By grouping categories 1, 2, and 3 as well as 5 and 6, the four categories of right, center, moderate left, and radical left shown in Table 16 are produced.

As a second indicator of ideology, Colombian students were asked whether they identified themselves with the socioeconomic thought of any man or school. Only about a third replied to this open-ended question, evenly divided among "Marxists" (including answers indicating identification with various communist parties, nations, or political leaders), "socialists" (whose answers did not specify adherence to Marxian socialism or Communism), and "others" (a catchall category including a wide range of political identifications). In this analysis, however, we have used only two categories, Marxists and non-Marxists, excluding the 10 percent who fell into the "socialist" grouping since it is too vague for categorization. Hence the comparison will be between Marxists and those who did not indicate another socialist response.[13]

Since the Honduran survey did not contain a direct question on political ideology, the "radical left" was identified from free comments at the end of the questionnaire. Undoubtedly the 10 percent who could be identified by this procedure represent an underestimate of the radical left. Three other political groupings were formed among the remaining students on the basis of responses to the item: "A revolution would damage the progress of Honduras and should be avoided at all costs." We classified as "prorevolution" those students disagreeing with the statement, as "centrists" those only partly in agreement, and as "conservative" those in full agreement (Table 16).

While we are fully aware of the limitations of these measures of political ideology, the tendency should be to understate rather than exaggerate the statistical relationships between political attitudes and population attitudes.

Tables 17 and 18 show the distribution of responses on a variety of items. In both countries, the radical left reports having paid most attention to population and birth control issues, and in Colombia, Marxists report having paid more attention to these issues and having firmer opinions than non-Marxists. This may in part be due to the visibility of United States interest in these matters. Moreover, certain prominent persons (such as ex-President Alberto Lleras Camargo in Colombia) who are intensely disliked by the radical left have associated themselves publicly with the movement for population control. In Honduras, the farther left, the firmer the opinions on population and birth control issues.[14]

In addition to attention to issues and firmness of opinion, in Colombia an effort was made to investigate the internal consistency of students' attitudes. At two different points in the questionnaire, students were asked (in slightly different wording) whether or not

TABLE 16

Political Ideology of Colombian and Honduran Students, in Percent

Political Position	Colombia	Honduras
Right	25	14
Center	15	20
Moderate left (Col.) or		
Prorevolution (Hon.)	47	56
Radical left	13	10
	100	100
Number of cases	(544)	(407)

TABLE 17

Colombian Students: Selected Population Attitude Items, by Political Ideology, in Percent

	Political Ideology					
	Right	Center	Moderate Left	Radical Left	Non-Marxist	Marxist
1. * Attention paid to population and birth control issues: Percent paying "much attention"	44	40	35	50	36	49
2. Firmness of opinion on population and birth control issues: Percent "firm"	58	59	48	57	50	60
3. Attitude towards a national birth control program: Percent favoring an "active program"	41	30	40	43	40	44
Percent supporting "any program"	68	75	68	51'	70	55
4. Government ought to provide birth control for personal freedom: Percent who "agree"	82	88	84	76	85	79
5. Rapid population growth hurts economic development: Percent who "agree"	73	71	59	44	64	49
6. Rapid population growth increases poverty: Percent who "agree"	85	85	77	61	80	71
7. Rapid population growth increases political power of lower classes: Percent who "agree"	33	44	42	51	38	39
8. Rapid population growth increases probability of violent revolution: Percent who "agree"	84	71	81	81	75	86
Average number of cases in base	(140)	(80)	(254)	(67)	(445)	(61)

*Items 1–8 correspond to the same questionnaire items as described in the footnotes to Table 14, except for the following:

5. In general, the social and economic development of Colombia would be considerably easier if the population growth rate were lower.

7. Supposing that Colombia's population continues growing at the same rate during the next twenty years and that large political and economic changes do not occur, do you believe that the population growth will increase the power of the lower classes?

8. Supposing that Colombia's population continues growing at the same rate during the next twenty years and that large political and economic changes do not occur, do you believe that the population growth will increase the probability of a violent revolution?

TABLE 18

Honduran Students: Selected Population Attitude Items, by
Political Ideology, in Percent

	Political Ideology			
	Right	Center	Pro-revolution	Radical Left
1. * Attention paid to population and birth control issues: Percent paying "much attention"	12	17	14	31
2. Firmness of opinion on population and birth control issues: Percent "firm"	23	45	41	61
3. Attitude towards a national family planning program: Percent who "favor"	38	38	32	22
Percent who "favor" or "partly favor" combined	85	92	77	61
4. What ought to be the population in year 2000? Percent answering "6 million or more"	36	30	42	52
5. Rapid population growth hurts economic development: Percent who "agree"	40	47	37	33
6. Rapid population growth increases poverty: Percent who "agree"	53	42	49	30
Average number of cases in base	(55)	(80)	(224)	(36)

*Items 1, 2, 3, and 6 correspond to items 5, 6, 1, and 4 in Table 15. Items 4 and 5 were as follows:
    4. What ought to be the population size of Honduras in the year 2000?
    5. Would you say that rapid population growth helps or retards the economic development of a country?

they saw rapid population growth as making Colombia's economic development more difficult. Overall, 15 percent of the respondents contradicted themselves in their answers to these two questions. While the rightists, centrists, and moderate leftists all had similar contradiction rates (12, 10, and 14 percent, respectively), the radical left stands out with 22 percent. The same pattern emerged using the other political indicator: 26 percent of the Marxists contradicted themselves, as compared with only 13 percent of the non-Marxists. These findings seem to be a specific case of a more general ambivalence toward population issues among the radical left. It was not uncommon to find, for example, the same individuals asserting that the limitation of population growth in the underdeveloped countries would solve nothing and that population growth would be instrumental in bringing on a revolutionary situation.

Turning to the question of support for national birth control programs, if we look at overall program support (active plus restricted programs in Colombia, and "favors" plus "partly favors" in Honduras), we find that in both countries the greatest support comes from the centrists, the least from the radicals, with the rightists and moderate left falling in between.[15] In Colombia, however, if we look at support for an *active* program only, the centrists drop to the lowest position, with the other three groups giving higher and almost identical amounts of support. Thus for Colombia, the findings must be qualified as follows: The centrists give the most program support but prefer restricted programs, while the radicals give least program support but give almost all of it to active programs. (The Marxists follow the same pattern as the radical left.)

We shall now examine where the various political groupings stand with respect to the ends of birth control, since it is views concerning these which presumably are a major factor in determining the different levels of program support we have just observed.

Honduran students were asked what size population they would like their country to have by the year 2000. In keeping with the above findings considerably more of the radicals than the centrists chose the largest option presented (6 million). The following quote from a radical Honduran student is not atypical:

> Honduras needs more population. Our masses must grow. This will bring about a greater awareness of our reality, it will cause a revolution much sooner, it will increase the demands on the government, and our people would awaken to the fact that the majority of our resources are in the hands of foreigners who exploit them for their own benefit.

In Colombia, a large majority of students in all political groupings agreed that the government should provide birth control facilities to increase the personal freedom of parents with regard to their family size. The radical left and the Marxists, however, gave slightly less support to this than the others.

Both the Colombian and Honduran students were asked about the relationship between rapid population growth and economic development. While less than half of the Colombian radicals believe it hinders development, close to three-quarters of the rightists and centrists think so. In Honduras, a smaller but similar difference emerges.

Similarly, in both countries, Marxists or radicals were less likely than others to perceive a connection between rapid population growth and poverty of the masses.

One point of ideological discussion on the left has been the effect of different levels of population growth rates on the collective power of the working class. Half of the radical left but only a third of the rightists saw Colombia's present rate of population growth as increasing the power of the workers. Although some students gave complex views on this issue in answers to open-ended questions, the matter was most concisely put by a student who said: "It is the working class which opposes birth control, because they know that someday they will win, even if it has to be by numbers."

Many students evidently did not interpret the question to include the possibility of increasing working-class power by bringing on a revolution. When Colombian students were specifically asked about population and revolution, a strong majority of each political category agreed that the nation's rate of population growth would increase the probability of a violent revolution. A conservative student commented as follows:

> Since it is the lower class which is growing the fastest, and they are the ones who have least to contribute to the country, and who also are the most anxious for political changes, I would say that population growth—that is, the growth of the working class—is dangerous.

Rather than illustrate from the majority opinion among the Marxists, we will quote one who dissented:

> If the lower classes increase, this growth means more hunger and ignorance and therefore greater dependence on the dominant classes. It is also unfavorable to a radical change in the social order because ignorant masses cannot be politicized except over a long period of time, and this is bad for the revolutionary process. If this process has to deal with excessive population as a constant factor, and one which interferes rather than helps, then the change will never come.

RELIGIOSITY AND POLITICAL IDEOLOGY

Since political ideologies are related to some extent with religiosity, in Table 19 we show the political composition of each of the religiosity categories. In both countries the more religious tend to be more rightist or centrist, the "middle levels" of religiosity tend to approximate the political composition of the sample as a whole, and the nonreligious are disproportionately radical. We were interested, therefore, in finding out whether the political and religious differentials we had established with regard to support for a national birth control program would be maintained when each causal variable was controlled by the other. In order to simplify the dependent variable, we deal only with the overall amount of support for any birth control program. It has also been necessary to merge several of the religious categories in order to create cells of sufficient magnitude to permit meaningful comparisons. In the case of Colombia, those who attend church often and very often have been merged, as have those who attend rarely or never. In Honduras, the little and nonreligious categories have been merged. Thus, in each country we have reduced the number of religious categories to three, renaming these categories "most religious," "somewhat religious," and "least religious." The results are presented in Table 20.

With regard to religiosity, we find that the somewhat religious give the most support to birth control programs in both countries. In Colombia this holds in two of the three political categories where

TABLE 19

Political Ideology and Religiosity

Political Ideology	Colombia: Church Attendance					Honduras: Religiosity			
	Very Often	Often	Occasion- ally	Rarely	Never	Very	Some- what	Little	None
Right	43	32	23	27	14	13	15	14	6
Center	14	21	22	11	7	33	24	14	6
Moderate left or prorevolution	40	44	53	47	49	46	55	62	58
Radical left	3	3	2	15	30	8	6	10	30
	100	100	100	100	100	100	100	100	100
Number of cases	(35)	(150)	(74)	(119)	(134)	(24)	(227)	(117)	(31)

TABLE 20

Overall Birth Control Program Support, by Religiosity and
Political Ideology, in Percent

	Religiosity and Political Ideology											
	Most Religious				Somewhat Religious				Least Religious			
Country	Right	Center	Mod. Left*	Rad. Left	Right	Center	Mod. Left	Rad. Left	Right	Center	Mod. Left*	Rad. Left
Colombia	56	75	65	†	70	88	79	†	82	76	68	47
Number of cases	(65)	(36)	(80)	†	(17)	(16)	(38)	†	(54)	(25)	(131)	(57)
Honduras	†	†	80	†	97	98	77	69	72	95	76	58
Number of cases	†	†	(11)	†	(32)	(49)	(117)	(13)	(18)	(16)	(76)	(19)

*"Prorevolution" in Honduras.
†Cases in base less than 10.

comparisons are possible, and in three out of four comparisons in Honduras. The most religious in Colombia oppose programs the most, the relationship holding in all three possible comparisons. In Honduras, where due to small numbers of cases only one comparison is possible, the relationship does not hold, but the relevant cell contains only eleven cases.

With regard to political ideology, we find that the centrists give most program support. In Colombia this holds in two of the three religious categories, while in Honduras, it holds in both possible comparisons. The radical left gives least program support. Due to the relative lack of religious radicals, only three comparisons are possible in the two countries. In all three, however, the relationship holds.

In short, our original findings with regard to the influence of religiosity and political ideology on birth control program support are largely maintained.

Another way of looking at the matter is to ask whether, when we combine those religious and political characteristics most strongly associated with program support or opposition, the original relationships are heightened. In the case of program opposition, we cannot do this, since very few individuals combine intense religiosity with radical leftism. The procedure is possible, though, with regard to program support. Thus in Colombia, while 80 percent of the occasional attenders (Table 14) and 75 percent of the centrists (Table 17) support birth control programs, 88 percent of the centrists who are occasional church attenders support such programs (Table 19). In Honduras, while 85 percent of the somewhat religious (Table 15) and 92 percent of the centrists (Table 18) favor programs, 98 percent of the persons who combine these two characteristics do so. This increases our confidence in the findings.

The only finding which seems incongruous is the fact that the somewhat religious, rather than the nonreligious, give the most overall support to birth control programs. In fact, among all the population and birth control variables analyzed by religiosity, direct relationships have been the exception rather than the rule. (In Table 20, such a pattern occurs within only one political group: the Colombian rightists.) While we have no certain explanation for this, we would suggest that the answer may lie in the extent of exposure to church influence. The determinants of attitudes toward birth control among the least religious groups should not be conceived of as due to a "lack" of church influence, but rather as the result of a combination of other positive political and nonpolitical factors.[16]

CONCLUSION

Returning to our distinction between the means and ends of birth control, we found that the influence of religiosity is more strongly witnessed in issues related to the means, for reasons probably having to do with the clarity of church doctrine in this area. Political ideology, on the other hand, seems to exert a strong causal influence in both areas for the obvious reason that people's views on the ends of birth control will be a major influence on whether they feel that any means should be encouraged.

In a sense it is surprising that the influence of religiosity on ends is as weak as it is. Given the doctrinal prohibition of the most effective means of birth control, it might be all too easy for this "blockage" of means to influence one's very perception of ends.

At the same time we have noted that a substantial minority of respondents had ambivalent feelings toward population issues, as shown in the specific example of self-contradiction on the question having to do with economic development. This is particularly acute among radicals and Marxists, since their views on the connection between population trends and social problems are most at odds with what seems to be becoming the dominant ideology on these matters. This ambivalence is perhaps summarized by the Marxist student who could not quite make up his mind where he stood with respect to the population limitation question. He ended his comments in the following quandary: "It ought to be done, for the well-being of all. On the other hand, it ought not to be done—to see if it encourages the revolution."

NOTES

1. J. Mayone Stycos, *Human Fertility in Latin America* (Ithaca, N.Y.: Cornell University Press, 1968). For specific chapters dealing with these issues, see "Population Problems in Latin America," "The Bishops, Politics and Birth Control," and "Contraception and Catholicism in Latin America."

2. United Nations, *Population and Vital Statistics Report,* Data available as of July 1, 1970, series A, vol. XXII, no. 3, New York, 1970, pp. 12–15.

3. In Colombia 71 percent of the students were below age twenty-three, 77 percent were male, and 93 percent were single. The corresponding figures for Honduras were 80, 72, and 88 percent.

4. "Mater et Magister" (excerpt), in L. B. Young (ed.), *Population in Perspective* (New York: Oxford University Press, 1968), pp. 220–222.

5. "Populorum Progressio" (excerpt), in Young, *op. cit.,* p. 230.

6. Stycos, *op. cit.,* p. 177.

7. This must be taken somewhat tentatively, since in Colombia the church attendance question has five response categories, while the Honduran religiosity question has four. This in itself might have produced somewhat wider differentials on program support in Colombia. However, insofar as the relative range of program support depends on the very low figures for the most religious, it should be noted that these persons form comparable proportions of the total sample in each country: 7 percent in Colombia and 6 percent in Honduras.

8. Ivan Vallier, "Religious Elites," in S. M. Lipset and A. Solari (eds.), *Elites in Latin America* (New York: Oxford University Press, 1967), p. 217.

9. John Martz, "Colombia: Qualified Democracy," in M. C. Needler (ed.), *Political Systems of Latin America* (New York: Van Nostrand, 1965), pp. 209–210.

10. Information collected by Mundigo from local sources during field research.

11. Stycos, *op. cit.,* p. 165.

12. F. D. Parker, *The Central American Republics* (London: Oxford University Press, 1968), p. 216.

13. Marxists and those who identified with point 7 on the ideology scale are not identical. Only 58 percent of the Marxists chose point 7, and only 48 percent of those who chose point 7 identified themselves as Marxists. Therefore the two separate analyses seem justified.

14. This is perhaps understandable in light of the fact that radical groups have on several occasions widely distributed leaflets in the university condemning population control. A short selection from a manifesto issued during the time of the survey follows:

> The 23rd of September Revolutionary Front, a genuine defender of the interests of the Honduran people and representing a large segment of the student body of the School of Medicine, wishes to voice its protest against the irresponsible actions of the Department of Preventive Medicine in participating in the extension of family planning campaigns being sponsored by the Family Planning Association. . . .
> We believe this to . . . [form] part of a general policy of population control which is being imposed upon us by our neighbor to the north.
> We are of the opinion that it is not by avoiding more children that we will solve our problems. It is not they who are responsible for the immense class contradictions in which our society finds itself. Or is it that the pro-family planning neomalthusian gentelmen believe that imposing their policies will stop the flow of our wealth into foreign hands? . . .

15. This is consistent with Stycos's typology showing the greatest degree of support for family planning among Latin American elites coming from the center. See "Public and Private Opinion on Population and Family Planning," in *Studies in Family Planning,* No. 51 (March, 1970), p. 16.

16. As previously suggested, it might have been expected that the least religious group would give most support to a birth control program (that is, to be least opposed) because they are not under the direct influence of church doctrine. This reasoning sees church influence as operating on a continuum. We suggest, however tentatively, that the influence of religiosity may be expected to be a direct one only among those who admit to some substantial degree of church influence—that is, in Table 20, the "very" and "somewhat" religious. The level of program support of the least religious, then, would be determined by other (political or nonpolitical) factors, but would be indeterminate from the point of view of religiosity. In keeping with this reasoning, Tables 14 and 15 show that the strongest differentials on almost all birth control and population items are not between the somewhat religious and the least religious, but between the somewhat religious and the *more* religious. In Table 20, we should find an increase in program support between the most religious and the somewhat religious. This in fact occurs within three of the four political categories where comparisons are possible. Finally, we would expect the influence of political ideology to be strongest among the least religious, and Table 20 demonstrates this clearly.

CHAPTER 11

Colombian Professors

Prepared in Spanish by **Sergio Sismondo** *and*
translated by **Marilyn Johnson Landstreet.**

INTRODUCTION

Prior to the field work in our study of Colombian professors, we
initiated a content analysis of the economic literature of Latin
America. A search of general academic and intellectual periodicals
from Mexico, Argentina, Uruguay, and Brazil for the period 1950–
1964 disclosed an almost total absence of articles referring to population problems. Next, a careful selection of 200 general Latin
American monographs on economics was made, and these books
were scanned for demographic content. One hundred eighty references to population problems were encountered in the two hundred
texts. Two categories of texts differed noticeably in their attention
to and treatment of the problem. On the one hand, monographs with
a Marxist orientation (defined by their adoption of the Marxist labor
theory of value or variations of it) discussed the subject in some detail
in 87 percent of the cases. On the other hand, the monographs with
a classical liberal tendency, defined by their adoption of an exchange
theory of value, mentioned such problems in only 54 percent of the
cases. Ninety-eight specific references to the rate of population
growth were found, with approximately the same distribution ac-

cording to political orientation. The almost complete absence of discussions in depth of the problems of population control and distribution severely limited the possibility of further analysis. For example, only four monographs, all of them of classical liberal orientation, argued for policies of population control.

Despite the absence of attention to the problem in scholarly publications, we were aware of the intense interest in the subject on the part of contemporary Latin American intellectuals, and we decided to interview a small group who could be expected to have influence on a nation's political development. As part of the International Population Program's 1965 summer program in Colombia, I interviewed university professors of social sciences at the National University of Colombia in Bogotá.

The decision to focus the study at the National University stemmed both from its importance among academic institutions and from the great variety of ideological positions we understood existed there. A small group of professors from the University of the Andes were also included, in order to increase the variability, but their opinions proved so similar to those from the National University that we have included them in the analysis without differentiation. This decision also arose from our desire to keep the data completely anonymous, a policy which has also influenced our cross-tabulations. For example, in order to avoid possible identification of individuals, we classify the professors either by department or by political orientation, but in no case do we offer a table cross-classifying the two variables.

Most of the staffs of the departments of sociology, psychology, philosophy and humanities, and economics were included.[1] These four categories, plus the small group selected from the University of the Andes, gave us an interviewing target of sixty-one professors, a group more or less homogeneous in their Colombian citizenship, their interest and competence in the social sciences, and, in almost all cases, their full-time dedication to a university career. Seven of these were in fact not interviewed because of difficulty in obtaining appointments, and an additional three refused to be interviewed. Thus, fifty-one interviews were completed, or 84 percent of the selected sample. Despite difficulties in obtaining appointments, cooperation was outstanding once contact was made; interviews averaged two hours and forty minutes and in several cases lasted more than five hours.

POLITICAL ATTITUDES

We have chosen a simple means of classifying political orientation according to the opinions on ownership and control of the means of production. Despite its obvious limitations, characterization of the individual's position with respect to the central problem of economic policy may be more useful than less exact characterizations of more general ideology.

Three categories are first considered: right, center, and left. Among the subjects of the greatest importance in determining these positions were attitudes toward agrarian reform, the nationalization of industry, governmental protection of industry, the autonomy or the nationalization of the banking system, the ownership of subsoil resources, the ownership and control of urban services, etc. Respondents were presented with a list of arguments on the role to be played by the state in each of these and other sectors of the economy. For example, in the case of subsoil resources, three principal positions were considered to correspond to the three political inclinations. The opinion that subsoil resources should be exploited exclusively by private capital, foreign or national, without governmental control of prices or wages, was considered rightist; the opinion that these resources should be exploited by private capital with strict government control and central planning was considered centrist; and opinions in favor of the nationalization of subsoil resources were considered leftist. Concerning agrarian reform, three main attitudes toward distribution of the land were specified: The opinion that the land should not be distributed to the peasantry was classified as rightist; opinions in favor of the distribution of land in family-sized plots, with governmental remuneration of the owner, were classified as centrist; and opinions proposing the expropriation of the land, collectivization of agriculture, or the organization of cooperatives among the peasantry were considered leftist. Opinions concerning the relationship between state and foreign capital gave us even more marked differences. Favoring the entrance of foreign capital without fiscal restriction was considered a rightist opinion; attitudes favorable to the entrance of private capital with fiscal restrictions, or under previous government planning, were considered centrist; and on the left were positions opposing the entrance of private capital or tolerating the entrance of capital only in the form of loans or government financing. Obviously, each opinion is relative to the rest of the sample, and the divisions are somewhat arbitrary. Nevertheless, each respondent discussed a series of topics, giving his opinions on a great variety of similar themes, which partially nullifies the distortions introduced by the arbitrariness of the classification.

Table 21 groups individuals whose responses were rightist, centrist, or leftist on more than half of the issues. The majority were consistent in their attitudes, grouping themselves into three nuclei corresponding to the three political positions described. The rightist group, formed by twelve individuals, turned out to have the greatest homogeneity in attitudes.

The eighteen respondents in the centrist group differed very clearly from the rightists, but not so clearly from the leftists. The leftist group is the least well defined, with 36 percent of its expressed opinion belonging in the centrist group. For this reason, it was considered necessary to subdivide it according to attitude toward violent change in the economic, political, and social order. The eight respondents in the leftist group who seemed to advocate this type of change were treated as a distinct group. Altogether, then, and recognizing the somewhat arbitrary nature of our classification, we have twelve "rightists," eighteen "centrists," thirteen "leftists," and eight "revolutionaries."

That this classification is of some validity can be seen from the relationships between our categories and the explicit indications of political orientation given by the respondents. Two-thirds of the

TABLE 21

Percentage of Rightist, Centrist, and Leftist Responses, by
Overall Political Leaning, in Percent

Replies by Political Leaning	Individuals with More than 50% Rightist Answers	Individuals with More than 50% Centrist Answers	Individuals with More than 50% Leftist Answers
Rightist	80	11	6
Centrist	16	72	36
Leftist	4	17	58
Number of cases	(12)	(18)	(21)

TABLE 22

Political Classification According to Analyst and Self-identification

Self-identification	Analytic Classification			
	Rightists, %	Centrists, %	Leftists, %	Revolution-aries, %
Conservative party	33			
Liberal party	33	40	8	
Revolutionary liberal movement		5	15	
Leftist groups			54	75
No information	33	45	23	25
Total	99	100	100	100
Number	(12)	(18)	(13)	(8)

sample identified themselves in some way with political parties or movements and ideologies. In Table 22, the almost exact correspondence between the two classifications indicates that we are working with political groups which are basically well defined. We can also demonstrate that other aspects of the intellectual life show a strong relationship with their political positions. There is a strong relationship between religiosity and political attitudes, with more than half of the rightists in the category of practicing Catholics and three-quarters of all the leftists in the "no religion" category. Finally, it is not inconsistent with general knowledge that our data disclose a larger proportion of leftists in the department of sociology and a predominance of centrists in psychology and of rightists and centrists in economics. In philosophy and the humanities the personnel are distributed among all four political positions.

RELATIONSHIPS BETWEEN POPULATION AND ECONOMIC GROWTH

Each interview began with the question, "What, in your opinion, are the causes of the low level of development in Colombia?" More than fifty different problems were mentioned, with an average of seven problems per person. Problems mentioned more than ten times were as follows:

Low level of industrial productivity 21
Low technological level 20
Low educational level of the population 20
Unfavorable terms of trade 17
Lack of capitalist spirit 17
Bad distribution of income 16
Monocrop agriculture 16
Extensive tax evasion 14
Flight of capital abroad 14
External dependence 14
Absence of national culture 13
Rapid population growth 11

Social problems, with the exception of the low educational level of the population, have a decidedly lower priority than economic problems even among the sociologists and psychologists. Of the eleven mentions of population, five referred primarily to the birth rate and six to the excessively rapid rate of urban growth. There was no great difference in political orientation among those who mentioned population, but economists were overrepresented due perhaps to the fundamental role which population size plays in the discussion of subjects related to the national product. A liberal economist indicates this in the first sentence of his interview:

The economic growth of the country is exceedingly slow, especially considering that the growth of the population absorbs almost all the growth of the gross national product, leaving a rate of growth of less than 1 percent annually.

Another economist, more optimistic about the Colombian situation, introduced the subject by saying:

There exists a truly vicious circle of low income in all underdeveloped countries; in some countries, the situation is made worse because the pressure of the population grows in such a way that it creates food shortages.

Another economist explained that the problem of development is poorly focused because of the existence of counterproductive demographic myths:

Another myth of the same kind is that of the so-called population problem . . . . there could be no population problem in Colombia because we have enough land to support 90 million comfortably, and we have only 18 million inhabitants.

A sociologist is more concerned with the relation of population growth to problems of education and housing:

A problem related to development is that of population growth. We have a vicious circle: population growth is both the cause and the consequence of the people's ignorance, and its most frequent expressions are the squatters' settlements, unemployment, and all their by-products.

While there were few spontaneous mentions of the population problem, we obtained further information from the direct question, "What do you think is the relationship between population growth and economic growth?" Twenty-seven respondents replied that population growth has a totally negative effect upon economic growth; nine tended toward this opinion, but expressed some ambivalence; seven felt there was no relationship; six maintained that population growth has a predominantly positive effect in development; and two regarded its effects as totally positive.

It is of considerable interest that in only two cases did pronatalist arguments dominate the thinking of our respondents, and both are in the rightist category (Table 23). The first is an economist:

Population growth presents a very debatable thesis. It is said that population growth is a brake on economic development; that is to say, that if the

TABLE 23

Beliefs Concerning the Effects of Population Growth on
Economic Development, by Political Position, Religiosity,
Age, and Sex, in Percent

	Effect of Population Growth				
	Positive (N = 2)	*Somewhat positive* (N = 6)	*None* (N = 7)	*Somewhat negative* (N = 9)	*Negative* (N = 27)
Political position:					
Right	100	33	57	0	15
Center	0	0	0	33	56
Left	0	33	43	33	18
Revolutionary	0	33	0	33	11
Nonbelievers	50	50	63	56	38
Over age 36	0	50	100	22	42
Females	0	50	0	11	43

birth rate were lowered, income would be better distributed. I have a different view; it seems to me that the error was in trying to force an industrial policy—that industrial policy which had brought us the problem of big cities. The country has a very low density and needs a better distribution of the population; and this distribution could be achieved by means of agricultural development. It is obvious that the industrial policy has brought us an unbalanced development, inasmuch as we are forced to import food. On the other hand, we should be able to obtain international markets for such agricultural products as rubber, corn, etc., because we have a great abundance of labor and arable land. I propose, then, the somewhat physiocratic thesis that the growth of the labor force helps us to arrive at a solution for the problems of food production and the balance of payments.

This view contains purely conservative elements. Few respondents would have disagreed with the importance of achieving self-sufficiency in food production, but this economist would be a member of a small minority in proposing the continuation of the dependence of the Colombian economy on agricultural exports.

While the second pronatalist position was also articulated by a rightist, the argument would meet with considerable sympathy among revolutionary and Marxist sectors:

Population growth plays a positive role since it is a factor which can break the vicious circle. Population growth creates a demand for food which can be satisfied only with the breakdown of the classic institutions. We have seen in the case of ancient Greece that the great technological and intellectual advance took place during a period of great population growth and great scarcity of food. In Colombia we ought to transform the church, methods of production, markets, and transportation systems. Population growth [implies] pressures, which in turn force new ideas, and they lead us to the transformation of the status quo.

Among others who saw some advantage to rapid population growth, it was frequently argued that the country needs a large and cheap labor force in order to encourage industrialization. As expressed by a revolutionary:

If in the policies of development one is concerned with birth control, like those who propose neo-Malthusian theories, we will find ourselves in great difficulties due to a shortage of labor. We have seen this problem in the cases of France, England, etc., countries which have a labor shortage. Besides, we can learn from Machiavelli when he tells us that a vast population means international power.

Among the ambivalent respondents an argument cited in seven instances was that there is no relation between population growth and economic growth, a position based on considerations of territorial extension and population density. Curiously, this position appears only among rightists and leftists, and in the latter group only among individuals of a utopian socialist bent. A socialist philosopher explains his opinion clearly:

The country suffers from grave economic cancers, but we cannot speak of a population problem while 90 percent of the national territory remains unexplored. . . . we cannot translate the Asian problem of overpopulation to the Latin American [sphere]. . . .

The most frequent opinion, however, held that population growth was a brake or obstacle to development and economic growth, a position most heavily identified with centrists or liberals. This view of population growth usually involves two fundamental hypotheses: that economic growth is a direct function of the population's capacity for saving and that there can be no economic growth without a drastic increase in the educational level of the people. The following three illustrations come from representatives of the right, center, and far left, respectively:

· While the population grows so rapidly there can be no accumulation of capital; the gross product remains the same year after year. It has been a long time since it has grown more than 1 percent annually. This continuing lack of capital creates unemployment. The only solution is the reduction of the birth rate.

· Savings, and consequently possible investments, are completely absorbed by the growing population; it is not possible to create an infrastructure of industries, nor is it possible to accumulate human capital in education; the government must continually invest its scarce funds in emergency projects (which are, in turn, results of the growing population), and its hands are tied in its efforts toward national development.

· One cannot speak of development while the population lives in subhuman conditions. What can we hope for from an individual subjected to ignorance and poverty? Development implies a common effort by all Colombians; we cannot hope for the cooperation of the masses while they are subjected to lack of education, of housing, and in general of the fundamentals necessary for human dignity. It is unfortunately the very growth of the population which contributes immensely to these subhuman conditions.

If we keep these assumptions in mind, five recurring themes concerning the unfavorable effects of rapid population growth can be recognized:

1. *Population growth is the principal cause of unemployment* (twelve mentions). This argument was mentioned predominantly by rightists and centrists. It is based principally on the results of migration to the cities. A sociologist states:

Unemployment in Colombia originates in the agricultural zones, where population growth is greatest. When mechanization of agriculture was introduced, the demand for agricultural workers decreased; this caused the massive migration to the cities which we have observed. It happens that in the cities the rhythm of industrialization is insufficient to absorb the laborers who arrive from the country. This is principally due to the flight of capital and luxury spending. This process also implies that industry cannot find qualified help. From this, the importance of reducing population growth in rural areas is deduced. Also to be considered as important is the problem of agricultural unemployment. . . .

As in almost all the mentioned relationships between unemployment and population growth, the conditional "rhythm of industrialization" is invoked, reducing the argument essentially to the problem of savings and investments. The discussion of unemployment, as well as the argument which follows, can be termed variations of the argument as to the rate of investment.

2. *Population growth reduces per capita income* (nineteen mentions). The national product is normally regarded as including the sum of the labor of all members of the society; i.e., the product of a constant (which we can call productivity) times the number of hours worked by all members of the society. If the number of workers in the society increases, all producing at the same technological level and all with the same productivity as the original workers, the national product should increase proportionately, thus leaving the per capita production the same. The fact that this does not happen can be explained by any of or all three reasons: (1) The new population cannot be incorporated into the labor force because of lack of capital with which to supply machinery or other technology; (2) the new workers cannot produce with the same productivity as those before, again because of lack of capital or lack of collective demand; or (3) since the new population is necessarily young, it is consequently

dependent and not productive.[2] The first two possibilities lead us once again to the course between population growth and investment growth, and the third reason is of a temporary character, since this population must necessarily reach working age after a determined number of years. It is necessary for us to imagine that these are implications of the answers received, since none of the respondents expressed them clearly. The sentences which were most often used to express the argument were much simpler and in some cases deceptive:

. . . population growth does not permit a rise in the standard of living. . . .

Or equally inexact:

. . . the per capita product does not grow as it might because of the great increase in population. . . .

In some cases the responses were more precise:

The enormous labor force which is offered to industry each year cannot be incorporated because of lack of capital, thus creating a supply of labor greater than the demand, producing as a consequence unemployment and lower wages.

3. *Population growth does not permit an increase in the educational level of the population* (twelve mentions). This argument appears in two different forms. The first reflects the same concern of the two previous relationships:

There is not enough capital in the country to finance the education of as many children as need it. . . .

And in its other form:

Population growth implies that young people, who could be in school, must work in order to maintain themselves because their families cannot, with so many.

Low educational levels, in turn, impede development and encourage population growth:

• The low level of education of the people causes the low productivity of the workers. . . .

• . . . the lack of an adequate professional education causes the incompetence of the ruling classes. . . .
• . . . the lack of civic education produces the political instability which causes the stagnation of economic structures. . . .
• . . . the lack of sexual education causes the high birth rates, prostitution, and other social evils. . . .

4. *Population growth does not permit satisfaction of the population's necessities of housing and urban services* (ten mentions). This argument is also based on the notion of scarcity of capital. An economist tells us:

We start out with a deficit of more than 100,000 units, and we must think in terms of 50,000 units more per year. Solely in order to finance this aspect, we would need in one year more money than the Alliance of Progress contributes to us in five years.

And a sociologist adds:

The urban population grows so swiftly that any urbanization plan is outdated by the time it is completed. For this reason, we cannot plan urban growth, and all the projects for sewage systems, electrification, and housing turn into emergency solutions.[3]

5. *Population growth contributes to misery and social problems.* Few leftists expressed arguments of the fourth type; they do not distinguish between the problems of unemployment or housing and the problems of the social and economic situation of the country in general. They prefer to lump these concepts together as "misery" and to search for underlying structural causes. This fifth type of relationship between population growth and economic growth, therefore, is much more frequently cited by leftists and revolutionaries, with no representation among the rightist group. A young revolutionary tells us:

The social problems are many—prostitution, delinquency, pathological problems, incest—we could make a dictionary of these words —overcrowding, misery, infant mortality—all are variations on the same theme. . . .

For this reason, many of the leftists will argue, as we shall see later, that population is an effect, not a cause, of the inadequate political and economic structures of underdeveloped countries. Or as a sociologist explains it:

> Population growth is another of the results of the conditions of misery and ignorance of the people; we should not think that it is the cause of these phenomena, but the factor which allows us to see more clearly the urgency of these problems. . . .

An interesting variation on this theme of cause and effect was introduced by a revolutionary economist:

> The Malthusian thesis which insists that population growth increases misery is only a position taken in order to justify existing structures. It is a comfortable position. The principal determinant of misery is the poor exploitation and distribution of resources. The population explosion is not, in itself, a cause of underdevelopment.

The majority of the problems mentioned by the leftists as part of the drama of underdevelopment are rooted in the low income of the population, in the high index of unemployment, and in the lack of capital; that is, they are results of the same problems mentioned by the more conservative groups. The essential difference is that the leftists look for causes of a more general nature and place in doubt the ability of present structures to solve the problem.

We may now draw some conclusions concerning the relationship between population growth and economic development. The "compartmentalized" position, which does not admit any relationship between population growth and economic growth, seems to be the product of a conservative and utopian viewpoint. Its proponents hold that population growth can be limited only by lack of food, that food production is a direct function of existing arable land, and that consequently an impulse toward the growth of farm production can permit much greater population growth without introducing major problems in national development.

The centrist group, however, does see important relationships between development and population. In general it concerns itself with variations on the theme of accumulation of capital and growth of population in relation to the national product. Population grows faster than capital accumulates, preventing the new generation from entering productive employment. The new population further aggravates the situation by imposing great demands on the existing capital in terms of services, education, etc.

Finally, the point of view most characteristic of the younger sociologists and philosophers of leftist orientation sees population growth as a problem parallel to the other social evils of the country— the product, and not the cause, of the inability of existing structures to resolve the problem of development. At most, population growth aggravates the general problem.

BIRTH CONTROL

Birth control refers to the voluntary use of contraceptive techniques in order to space pregnancies or to limit their number. Twenty-five respondents mentioned birth control spontaneously. While sociologists had the largest number of mentions (eight), there was little difference by sex, religiosity, or age. By political position, the greatest number of mentions came from the leftist group, with a notable absence of rightists. Basing our decisions on a combination of spontaneous responses and responses to direct questions, we can classify our fifty-one respondents into three categories: unfavorable to birth control (seven), neutral or ambivalent (ten), and favorable (thirty-four).

§ POSITIONS UNFAVORABLE TO BIRTH CONTROL

Six of the seven unfavorable to birth control represent the political extremes—three conservatives and three revolutionaries, and six of the seven are ambivalent or positive concerning the role of population growth in economic development, suggesting a certain consistency between the two sets of opinions.

However, the attitudes against birth control are hardly homogeneous and reflect differing political considerations. Among the rightists, birth control was usually not seen to be connected with the problem of development:

I do not favor a policy of birth control because I do not believe that this is a serious problem in the nation. It seems to me that the more serious problem, with which we should be concerned, is the problem of the lack of education of the people; it is lack of education which does not permit the people to enter into the process of production. There are some countries with a very high population density; in these countries perhaps there will have to be birth control, and this only because food production is not sufficient for all the population. But in our countries whose characteristic is that of having very low density, I do not see how birth control can help the process of development.

Another rightist offers a curious justification:

A policy of birth control would produce very serious mental problems in the population. It cannot be thought that the people, who have always submitted to the doctrine "increase and multiply," could react in any other way than with great mental maladjustment to the new proposition of limiting their growth.

In both attitudes we find a certain lack of concern with the problems of the people—in the first case, blaming the most dispossessed members of society for its grave situation ("the ignorance of the people is to blame"), and in the second, a certain paternalism toward those uneducated individuals who cannot make a "mental adjustment" to the nation's situation.

The revolutionary group resorts to a dogmatism which seems somewhat remote from the reality of the nation's problems:

• The thesis of Mao, that for every mouth there are two arms, seems to be true under certain conditions. In India there does not seem to be enough food for the population, and for that reason it is a grave problem; but in China there does not seem to be a problem: each individual produces more than he consumes, and the great numbers can also be used as an international weapon.

• The neo-Malthusian thesis of Alberto Lleras [ex-President of Colombia] is absurd in that it considers birth control necessary for the development of the country. It is inconceivable that births could be reduced without educating the people first, and it is impossible to educate the people without development; consequently, birth control will be a result of development, and not its cause.

The latter view is quite characteristic of the revolutionaries who insist that population growth is a result rather than a cause of underdevelopment. Other leftist arguments were mentioned by a revolutionary sociologist:

Birth control is very dangerous for our country; it could become a justification for the bourgeoisie not to accept fiscal reforms in the nation. It could, in other words, facilitate the antisocial conduct of the ruling classes. It could take the place of agrarian reform and turn into a real obstacle to it. Birth control cannot be thought of as a solution for the development of the nation because any nation on the road to development needs a large labor force, and also a young labor force. The countries with large labor forces are those which have industrialized most rapidly.

Thus, there are profound differences between rightists and leftists in their arguments against birth control. The rightists do not see any relationship between population and economic growth, while the leftists see both positive and negative ones, proposing in some cases that population growth is a necessary factor in development.

§ AMBIVALENT POSITIONS TOWARD BIRTH CONTROL

Eight of the ten ambivalent respondents are among the older members of the sample, but there seems to be little relation to political position. One of the causes of ambivalence seems to be inadequate knowledge of how fertility might be reduced. As a sociologist expressed it:

It is necessary to be very careful before taking action on this subject. There is not enough information to make a concrete plan. There is a lack of information on family structure in Colombia. First it is necessary to study these problems attentively. A program based on erroneous information could lead us to tragic consequences.

Another fairly common opinion says that birth control, while necessary, can never succeed because of the power of religious training over the minds of the people. As an economist tells us:

I think that a policy of reducing births would be very useful, but I also think that its failure is imminent. It is impossible that such a policy could lead to resolving the problem of high fertility. Very profound traditional values and religious beliefs exist in Colombian society, which mean insurmountable obstacles for birth control.

Or in the words of a sociologist:

The serious problem is that the people have been taught that they should have all the children God sends them, and if they confess having done anything contrary to this command, the priest punishes them under fear of excommunication.

Another point of view which leads to ambivalence is expressed by a sociologist of leftist orientation:

The problem here, and the reason why I oppose birth control, is that the leaders have misunderstood the concept of birth control. A program of development of the government should include some aspect of family planning, etc., but it is incredible what is heard today, when important leaders propose birth control as a solution for development. Alberto Lleras Camargo, for example, sees birth control as a negative solution; he thinks that the problem of underdevelopment is that there are too many poor people, and consequently the country will develop by eliminating the poor people.

A final reason given by respondents to explain their ambivalence tells us that birth control is only necessary because of the absence of economic programing or of real developmental efforts. Mentioned by five of these respondents and by four of those who support birth control, this reason suggests that birth control is an unhappy consequence of the capitalist system; that a change in the economic system of the nation would render population control unnecessary. A leftist philosopher and a leftist economist put it this way:

• If the nation does not find a way of modernizing our production systems, then it will be necessary to reduce births before everyone dies of hunger . . . but if the country's economy could be modernized, then the desired reduction would occur automatically. The increase in education of the people and an elevation of the dignity of the individual would produce a drop in fertility.

• It seems to be a serious result of the capitalist system; under a socialist regime one would not be able to speak of overpopulation; it is only when production is restricted to increase profits that it becomes necessary to balance population artificially in order to put it on a par with food production.

An interesting current underlying these positions is the assumption that a large population is, in itself, desirable. An exaggerated example is provided by a respondent who, in denying the utility of birth control, explains that:

. . . scientists have demonstrated that it is possible to live perfectly well on a diet of marine algae, and before thinking about controlling the number of human beings it is necessary to see to what point science can bring us in order to inhabit other planets and produce artificial food.

§ POSITIONS FAVORABLE TO BIRTH CONTROL

The thirty-four individuals favorable to limitation of births are primarily centrist (thirteen) and leftist (ten), and most of them believe that rapid population growth is a negative factor in economic development. These favorable opinions are accompanied by five principal rationales: economic (eighteen); humanitarian (fifteen); reduction in the abortion rate (seven); increase in free will (five); and modernization of central norms (four).

The economic and humanitarian reasons are much the same as those related to population growth—the speed of population growth does not permit the accumulation of capital; it imposes insatiable demands on the national budget, it reduces the educational level, and it places great strains on housing, health facilities, etc.

The concern with abortion is frequently voiced in the form of a complaint with respect to the position of the Catholic Church, which is seen as encouraging abortions indirectly by prohibiting the use of birth control. A sociologist, claiming to have studied the problem in depth, affirms:

> Criminal abortion is the primary cause of the high mortality rate in the female population; one-third of the deaths of women of reproductive age are caused by induced abortions and by the complications which occur so often. This is due in part to the prohibition of the use of contraceptive methods and in part to the primitive conditions in which these abortions take place.

A revolutionary economist points out sharply:

> Those who, in order to defend the virginity of a superior caste . . . do not permit the use of birth control in the nation, are guilty of a great criminal act. They should see the hospital rooms in Sur de Bogotá, in San Juan de Dios among others, where women come in with incurable hemorrhages, suffering atrociously, and then observe as they withdraw the corpses at the other end of the room.

It is argued that if Colombian women want to limit births so much that they voluntarily submit to the risks of an abortion performed under primitive conditions, these women would accept contraception. After observing that more than 100,000 induced abortions are estimated to occur in Colombia annually, the sociologist quoted above concludes that:

There exists a double standard of morality in the Colombian woman; she thinks it is immoral to avoid conception, but, once pregnant, she does not seem to consider the immorality of the crime of abortion.

Another revolutionary responds to this observation:

The Colombian woman suffers from the immorality of the ruling classes; [they] insist to her that birth control will send her to hell, and at the same time she is not given the opportunity to live humanly; the frustration which follows leads her to abortion, and frequently to death.

The position adopted by these seven respondents is echoed in medical and professional associations in many countries, and the argument for the limitation of induced abortion seems to have been of conclusive importance in the implementation of contraceptive programs in various Latin American countries.[4]

Five respondents, four of them women, mentioned the increase in free will of the population attendant upon the introduction of a contraceptive program. As one of them put it:

Family planning is an inalienable right of woman. The decision about the number of children desired by a couple is a decision of utmost importance, since the parents are responsible for many aspects of their children's lives, and therefore a decision of such importance should not be left to chance, as the church proposes with the rhythm system.

A more militant educator tells us:

Lack of use of birth control is one of the most important factors in maintaining the inferiority of women in society. The emancipation of woman demands birth control. . . . as a woman, I demand it at the top of my voice.

The final argument has to do with demonstrating that the introduction of contraceptive methods in Europe during the past two centuries was one of the principal contributing factors to its modernization. Birth control was one of the rational methods which permitted European men and women to plan their everyday lives, thereby increasing their freedom of action, their productivity, their savings, and, in short, the accumulation of wealth and of happiness.[5]

Recapitulating, we may characterize the positions favorable to birth control as essentially centrist positions, while the unfavorable ones are more characteristic of the political extremists. Birth control tends to be supported by individuals whose vision of the future is evolutionary, and is opposed by individuals who are both conservative and revolutionary. We have the impression that in most cases, the real reasons underlying the rightist opposition to birth control may be of a religious character. Professors of rightist orientation and of Catholic faith may have looked for economic and social arguments to bolster an essentially moral position. The centrist group generally supported birth control, basing its support on economic and humanitarian grounds. The leftist group, especially members of the classic socialist orientation, showed considerable uncertainty, while the revolutionary group was divided, with half of its members opposed to birth control on tactical and political grounds.

POLITICAL PROBLEMS

The principal socialist theme in our interviews is that population growth accelerates social change and that braking it is a weapon of imperialism to avoid such change:

> The worst thing about the North Americans, whether it is in the armed forces or among sociologists, is that they are disposed to give us preconceived solutions in accord with the models they see as desirable for development. But even worse is the fact that they end up by cooperating with the reactionary forces in our countries, although they do not realize it, or do not believe it to be true. Birth control does not frighten me at all because the only means of reducing the birth rate in our countries is to raise the living conditions of the people to a human level; birth control can have no effect without improving the educational level, without raising the standard of living; this has been the case in Europe and it will be repeated in Colombia . . . but the worst aspect of birth control is that you are cooperating with our reactionary forces, which see in birth control their last possibility, the last solution, to avoid the revolution. And so they live in this illusion that nothing will be able to function. . . .

Or in the words of another revolutionary:

> Birth control cannot be justified under our conditions because it is proposed as a means of avoiding a revolution. . . . it is thought that the solution for chronic unemployment is to reduce the number of people at the same time as increasing production. With these goals nothing can be justified.

Another argument stressed by the revolutionary sector is that an increase in numbers among the proletariat is the primordial force for the revolution. Still another suggests that limiting births is an injustice committed against the poor, since it represents the elimination or limitation of the number of such members of society, thus showing that birth control discriminates against certain sectors of the population.

On the other hand there were respondents who, in spite of a strong rejection of imperialism, expressed the population problem with great sensitivity:

> I talk daily about the subject of birth control to meetings of the medical profession, and I cannot even decide if this is a problem for which we ought to formulate a policy, or if it is an individual problem. . . . can we sacrifice the well-being of one or two generations, only in order to increase the probability of our vision, however doubtful, of the future? We say frequently that it is necessary to allow populations to increase in order to increase the pressure on the status quo, and thus to cause social change. But do we have the right to judge society in this way? Or should we limit ourselves to curing the problems of the family as an institution?

Another revolutionary sociologist, also concerned with the problem of the relationship between population growth and social change, tells us:

> . . . there are, then, two ways of seeing the problem of overpopulation: It is a positive fact in that it increases the possibility of social revolution; and it is a negative fact in that it increases the misery of the people. The first theory, although progressive, is the theory of a fanatic; it is based on the absurdity of creating misery in order to then resolve it. . . . given our political situation it is necessary to opt for the second theory; in our condition there is no great possibility of change; then, the second theory has more urgency. If we had a good revolutionary government, we would be able to favor an increase in population, giving awards to the most fertile mothers, as Stalin had to do in the Soviet Union; but in our conditions we must concern ourselves more with the well-being of the multitudes of poor people, because the possibilities of change are few.

And among economists we see the same ambivalence:

> • . . . I am in favor of a large population for Latin America, but I do not see that it is certain that an increase in population is going to lead us to social change. Social revolutions are the product of the mystique of change, not only of hunger and misery.
> • I do not believe that this argument is of major importance; the revolution occurs when there is misery and class consciousness; it does not matter that

five or ten million people exist in conditions of misery. What is needed in Colombia is class consciousness. In our society, even the labor unions are dominated by the oligarchy. If there were class consciousness, there would be revolution, peaceful or violent, without its mattering how many millions participated in it. I have heard it argued that birth control makes the possibilities for revolution more distant, but I think that this is a lack of understanding of the theories of Karl Marx.

We see, then, that a single dogmatic position with regard to population growth and revolution is not characteristic of the revolutionaries. While four are inclined to accept the positive consequences of population growth, and the others mention it, the latter express a variety of reasons for explaining why they cannot accept it.

It was also interesting to find that the reputed relationship between numbers and revolution is frequently mentioned among the rightists. Thus, in effect, the accusations made by the leftists as to rightist motivations are to some extent justified. A Liberal economist tells us:

The increase in population leads to a rise in unemployment, and unemployment is leading us to the anarchic revolution. For this reason, it is preferable to use birth control to diminish the poverty in the nation.

Another economist, of rightist orientation, is even more explicit:

The proletarian masses are those most susceptible to Communist propaganda, and if we do not do something to avoid their growth, we are going to find ourselves in a situation like that of Cuba.

Thus, both rightists and revolutionaries have brought the discussion of birth control to a political plane, by forming ideas about the relationship between birth control and revolution. In so doing, they have frequently lost sight of some of the most important economic implications of the population problem.[6]

INSTITUTIONAL PROBLEMS

§ THE CHURCH

The significance of the Catholic Church in population problems can be seen in the fact that thirty-two respondents mentioned it spontaneously. The majority of the respondents launched a vigorous criticism of the policies of the church with respect to family and social problems in Colombia, a criticism which came as much from practicers of Catholicism as from those who called themselves nonbelievers. According to these accusations, the attitude of the Catholic Church is fundamentally opposed to sexual relations and is a cause of frustration, the breakdown of marriages, and other social ills which lead large sectors of the population to prostitution, abortions, etc. For example, one respondent mentioned that in some rural communities a young woman who becomes pregnant is expelled from her paternal home for religious reasons and is left with no other alternative than prostitution. One of the most frequent arguments suggests that the opposition of the church to birth control drives mothers to abortion. A sociologist argues:

The rates of abortion in Colombia are among the highest in the world. It is calculated that 100,000 criminal abortions occur annually in the nation; and that between five and ten thousand deaths each year are caused by complications arising from these abortions taking place under unsanitary conditions and by inexpert hands. One asks why there are so many abortions in Colombia. The reason is simple: because the economic conditions of our proletarian masses are such that, day to day, mothers find themselves with more children than they can feed; and doubtless when they see themselves pregnant again they must have recourse to the *curandero,* who can make them abort for 20 pesos!

A leftist philosopher:

Our church considers it an immorality to avoid conception, but it accepts with tranquility the thousands of murders which occur each year in the form of abortions.

Another respondent adds:

They have forgotten the fifth commandment. . . .

A Liberal psychologist:

. . . the Catholic Church has led our society to an enormous duality of values. Chastity, purity, and piety are spoken of, but the facts are very clear: women of all social classes give themselves up to prostitution; there is more prostitution in Colombia than in any other country in the world. The church teaches that hell is the only consequence of birth control, but it does not realize that this position is creating an extreme situation concerning the deaths caused by abortions, as much for the murdered children as for the mothers who die in the act, and that they are many thousands. . . .

Some of the respondents were pessimistic. A Liberal economist put it flatly:

No policy of birth control can be successful in Colombia, because it will be sabotaged from the first by the church.

A Catholic lady of rightist orientation is less sure:

It is true that if the church opposes birth control there is nothing which the government can do. But it is also true that the problem is still being discussed in Rome; the Church of Rome has already pronounced itself to be favorable to some methods of contraception.

A socialist philosopher also sees the situation pessimistically:

It would be necessary to get the cooperation of the church in a birth control program; there are educational and cultural factors in which the church dominates the people.

And another philosopher adds:

The church could do a great service to society if it would change its opinion with respect to birth control. With such a change, the government would be obliged to be silent, or simply to deal with sexual education, without entering into the more important subject.

Other respondents, with fewer concerns of a religious character, think along other lines:

It is necessary to consider that the church does not have as much importance as it is thought. There are contraceptives for sale in all the drugstores in the city. A birth control program would have to place itself in open opposition to the church. This problem is so important that, because of it, the church will fall totally, or be transformed into an institution of service to society.

The Ecumenical Council inspired various respondents who anticipated revolutionary changes in Catholic doctrine on contraceptives. Of course, the revolutionaries (with sóme exceptions) criticized the whole Latin American ecclesiastical structure as a weapon of the oligarchy and a banner of the status quo. Some respondents mentioned Father Camilo Torres as an example of the ideological flexibility of Christianity, pointing out that he favored a change in Catholic doctrine toward a liberalization of the use of contraceptives.

§ THE GOVERNMENT

Fourteen of the professors mentioned the role of government spontaneously, and another twenty-two who were favorable to birth control were questioned directly concerning their notion of the government's role in birth control programs. While all thirty-six respondents favor family planning in general, a few believe that the government should not interfere in any way. These individuals preferred to give the responsibility to the church or the universities. A lady of very conservative orientation tells us:

It would be very advantageous for the church to be in charge of this problem; the relations between church and state are a problem in Colombia. If the government took action on this plane without the agreement of the church, this would bring serious consequences.

Each of those who believed that the government should plan an active role in family planning programs made more specific suggestions about the nature of the role.

§ EDUCATION

Sixteen respondents believe that a reduction of births can most effectively be achieved by direct educational programs, with special emphasis on suburban neighborhoods, squatter settlements, and rural areas. The possibility of including sex education programs in the secondary schools was also mentioned several times. Three individuals mentioned the social security system as a prestigeful potential source of education and services.

§ LEGALIZATION OF CONTRACEPTIVES

Although only a few respondents brought up this topic, it is not likely that others would favor the legalization of contraceptives. Four respondents even suggested the legalization of abortion.

§ CONTRACEPTIVE SUPPLIES

Five professors suggested that the government control the prices of contraceptives, since their present price puts them out of the reach of most of the population. Four others suggested free contraceptive services and materials as the only way of reaching the poor, and several stressed the importance of utilizing radio and television, given the difficulty of reaching the rural population.

Many saw the Ministry of Public Health or the new Ministry of Social Welfare as the logical agent for the formulation and implementation of a population policy. The leftist group pointed out that birth control is only one of the tasks which could be facilitated by a system of socialized medicine. Various centrists and liberals concurred, adding that the socialization of medicine is one of the most important factors in the social progress of some European countries and that it is only through social progress that a satisfactory population policy can be reached.

We may conclude that the group favorable to birth control sees the government as the principal agent of population policies and programs.

§ INTERNATIONAL RELATIONS

Most of the respondents commented on the role which foreign individuals and organizations should play in the population problems of Colombia. Only a few were totally unfavorable to foreign participation. While favoring birth control, a socialist warns:

It is much more urgent that foreign help should be apportioned on the educational plane by means of financing new schools, money to print books, etc. By means of an educational program we can change the class mentality; only then can we dedicate ourselves to superstructural changes. It must be remembered that birth control, however necessary, is not the solution to the problems of the country. There are other more urgent problems.

The revolutionary position is that too much U.S. intervention in national politics and economics already exists, and it must be stopped before it gets to the universities, as a form of cultural imperialism. In the case of rightists, the arguments are different: One regards such foreign aid as immoral intervention (that is, Protestant) and the other rejects the United States' "neo-Malthusian doctrine," explaining that he is "much more optimistic about the future of humanity."

An equal number of respondents adopted the opposite position, proposing that foreign powers and individuals enter totally and freely into the planning and implementation of population policy. The most extreme position comes from a rightist:

... I do not see any objection to the entrance of foreigners since the economic problems of the people are very serious, and because the Communist danger grows with the growth of the population.

The principal argument of the others seems to be that there are no individuals in Colombia with sufficient preparation and capacity to carry out a population policy.

The opinions of most individuals fell between these extremes on the question of foreign assistance, generally favoring some degree of international cooperation in order to deal with the problem, but expressing reservations. One respondent maintained that the only possible solution is to deliver the whole question to the United Nations, and two suggested that foreigners carry out sociological research on the problem:

• We must learn to receive with gratitude all which is knowledge and a product of the culture, all which is science and technology; in short, all which can be useful to us.
• I do not find any objection at all to the foreigners studying our problems ... it seems useful to me that this cooperation of information exists. We can speak of foreign intellectual assistance; unfortunately, this help often produces alienation from the national culture. The knowledge of such U.S. intellectuals as J. Kahl and others will be taken into account in formulating programs for development, but these intellectuals should not try to formulate programs. Either they are intellectuals or they are politicians, but they cannot be both.

Eight of these individuals mentioned the dangers involved in permitting the involvement of foreigners in the formulation and execution of developmental programs. Another eight were unfavorable to the participation of foreigners in certain public activities such as conferences, lectures, communal action, etc.

CONCLUSIONS

We will synthesize our findings by presenting the common characteristics of each of the major political types we have described. In so doing we shall do violence to some individual differences, but the net product should be generally valid.

§ THE RIGHTIST VIEW

This group is composed of twelve individuals who are strongly capitalistic and deeply committed to the principle of free enterprise. They are opposed to governmental intervention, they abhor Communism, they generally favor the continuation of the existing class structure in Colombia, and they tend to be sympathetic to the Catholic Church. A third of them participate in the Conservative party and another third in the Liberal party. More than half of them are practicing Catholics.

This group tends to view the population problem from the point of view of density. They see the nation as underpopulated and thus cannot believe in the existence of a population problem. While they are very concerned with the problem of rapid urbanization, they see as its cause the lack of attention given to agricultural development. At least a third of them maintain a romantic sentiment toward country life and maintain ardently that no relationship exists between population growth and the economic development of the nation. The only two respondents who maintain that population growth is a totally positive factor in development also are found in this group. The attitude that food production is the only limit on population growth, together with a tendency to place the blame for existing problems on the most dispossessed classes in society, brings some of the rightists to view the population problem as a strictly educational problem. In this way, they can blame the dispossessed for being the principal cause of this social ill.

As for birth control, the group is divided in its opinion. Among the unfavorable are found the only moral or religious arguments in the whole sample. Among the favorable there were several mentions of the dangers of the anarchic or socialist revolution and, consequently, the necessity of limiting pressures from the proletariat. Thus, the most characteristic attitudes toward birth control among the rightists are that it is immoral for religious reasons, but necessary to avoid revolution. For the latter reason, there are various rightists disposed to accept foreign assistance in carrying out a family planning program. Foreign financing, however, was more likely to be favorably regarded. An economist explains the difference:

Whatever may be the motives of the U.S. foundations in meddling in these matters, we must take advantage of their money because birth control, like so many other things, will be costly. We must pay attention so that the foundations do not put themselves on the plane of formulation of policies because their motivations remain to be examined. I am sure that their motivations cannot be trusted, but when a tangency is found between our plane and those of the foundations we must always take advantage of it. I have always opposed the participation of foreign institutions in the decisions of the nation; but it is almost inevitable that this occurs because of the incapacity of our leaders, who must go to foreigners for help in carrying out every one of their decisions.

In general, we can say that those individuals who favor programs for reduction of births also favor the reception of foreign assistance in order to carry them out. Foreign involvement should be limited to research, to other intellectual activities, and to financing. But, for the most part, the foreigners should not be involved in the formulation of policy or in the execution of programs. This last point, strongly supported by rightists, revolutionaries, and socialists, is given less emphasis among the centrist group.

§ THE CENTRIST VIEW

The centrists are characterized by an orientation of compromise with respect to problems of economic policy. Presented with a problem, they suggest solutions which they judge to be possible within the existing structures. While they have no desire to change the premises of the society, they seek to modify its structures for the solution of social, political, and economic problems. They see the United States and Western Europe as the models of a desirable society, a society which is essentially capitalist and democratic, where the great social problems are resolved by evolutionary means and without altering the accepted ideological principles. They see the problem of underdevelopment as basically economic, in particular the low level of industrialization. While they are favorable to international cooperation and to the capitalist development of Latin America under U.S. supervision, they do believe in national control of industrial development. Their position is best described as liberal capitalism and democratic evolution.

Close to half of the eighteen centrists are active in the Liberal party or in the revolutionary Liberal Movement, and they are overrepresented in the departments of psychology and economics. Their political opinions are the most heterogeneous of the various groups in our sample, exhibiting as many rightist as leftist opinions mixed in with the centrist.

In contrast with the rightist group, none of the centrists denies the existence of a relationship between development and population growth; most posit a negative relationship, and no one suggests a positive relation. They see rapid population growth reducing the per capita income and aggravating educational and urban problems. In general, this group displays the most intense awareness of the Colombian population problem.

All but one of the centrists favor birth control for essentially economic and humanitarian reasons, especially as regards implementation of free will and rationality. The majority agree with the leftists that there should be no foreign participation in the formulation of national birth control programs, but they differ in their willingness to accept financial and technical assistance in research and information.

In general, the centrist's position is a pragmatic rather than an ideological one. He sees national problems and believes in scientific planning for their solution. The government should plan not only the economic but also the social future of the nation. Toward this end the planning of the size and growth of the population is necessary.

§ THE SOCIALIST VIEW

The socialists were identified by their Marxist orientation, principally by their rejection of capitalism as a system of exploitation and injustice. They do not, however, propose violent change by socialism. In short, they are a group of individuals with evolutionary orientation, but with a vision of radical change in the structures and values of society. The majority participate in leftist activities or groups. None are practicing Catholics, and three-quarters report no religion at all.

Of the thirteen socialists, two see population growth as a somewhat positive factor in the well-being of the nation, while eight view it negatively. Some believe that it is the consequence of inadequate social and economic structures; others see it as a serious independent problem requiring its own kind of solution. While some see birth control as a sad but necessary consequence of capitalism, most give it their general approval. Being of evolutionary and humanitarian persuasion, the socialists tend to support birth control as necessary for the reduction of misery in the Andean nations. One should not underestimate the political importance of a group of individuals who can set aside their deepest convictions about society in order to enunciate concrete solutions to immediate problems.

§ THE REVOLUTIONARY VIEW

All members of the group we have designated as revolutionary have a totally negative attitude toward capitalism. Some of its members go farther in defining their goals in terms of antielitism, anti-imperialism, or anti-Westernism. Some are totally disillusioned with the existing orders at the international, national, and local levels. Others see the evils as the result of religious fetishism, industrial fetishism, or other aspects of Western culture. All see the necessity for changing the power structure of the nation by any, including violent, means; and all see the imperialism of the Western nations, especially of the U.S., as their enemy. They tend toward compact and unswerving ideological positions, answering each question in terms of their fundamental philosophical principles. Three-quarters participate in leftist revolutionary activities, and three-quarters claim to have no religious beliefs.

Two individuals see population growth as a somewhat positive factor, since the greater the number of people participating in the revolution, the greater the probability of its success. Under a socialist system, moreover, rapid population increase is seen as a positive factor in national growth. Six individuals, however, see some negative aspects to population growth. Population policy is viewed largely from the point of view of its possible effect on the probability and form of the revolution. The three individuals opposed to birth control felt it would delay the revolution. Additionally, birth control was viewed as part of the U.S. imperialist plan to subjugate the Latin peoples. Others concede this point but conclude that the nation must take advantage of the foreign intentions in order to achieve a scientific population policy. They view the high rate of abortions as unbearable and the clerical position as antiquated and are therefore inclined to support a scientific population policy. The revolutionary thinkers also tell us that the privation of technology existing among the popular masses is a treason to those masses. Such an argument is supplemented by the argument of free will. Perhaps most important of all is the view of that unusually potent source of social change, the revolutionary woman. Appropriately, we will leave the last word to her:

Family planning is an inalienable right of woman . . . . a decision of such importance that it must not be left to chance. . . .

NOTES

1. All teaching staff of the sociology department were defined as eligible for interview with the exception of foreigners and some professors of social work who taught half time or less. In the psychology department, all teaching staff were included except for some less than full-time psychiatrists. All teaching staff in the department of philosophy and humanities were included except for language teachers and foreign professors. All full-time teaching staff of the economics department were included, along with a few who taught less than full time.

2. One can find discussions on the relationship between economic growth and population growth in almost any U.S. textbook on the economics of development. Special reference may be made to the article by Frank W. Notestein, "Some Economic Aspects of Population Change in the Developing Countries," in J. Mayone Stycos and Jorge Arias (eds.), *Population Dilemma in Latin America* (Washington: Potomac Books, 1966). An opposing view can be found in the work of Irving Louis Horowitz, *Three Worlds of Development* (New York: Oxford University Press, 1966). Professor John W. Mellor, in his recent work, *The Economics of Agricultural Development* (Ithaca, N.Y.: Cornell University Press, 1966), explains the situation using imaginary data in the following way: "Suppose that the capital goods of a nation of low income are equal to three times the national income—that is, the coefficient of capital to production is 3 to 1. Then if the population grows at 3% annually, 9% of the national income must be reinvested simply in order to maintain the same coefficient of productivity. If the population grows at a rate of 1% annually, then only 3% of the national income would be needed in order to maintain the same level of capital to product. If a level of reinvestment of 9% could be maintained with a population growth of 1%, the total of the capital goods of the society per person would be able to double in less than 15 years. With a population growth of 3%, a rate of investment of more than 15% would be necessary in order for the capital goods to double in the same period of time." Interesting discussions of this topic in the particular case of Colombia can be found in the works of Dr. L. Currie.

3. The subject of housing occupies a unique position in these arguments in the Colombian context, because the developmentalist plan of Dr. L. Currie, "Operation Colombia," has generated a great debate among Colombian intellectuals. Dr. Currie presents the housing situation in Colombia both as a grave problem for the country and as a point of departure for the solution of Colombian underdevelopment. Dr. Currie proposes a vast program of housing construction as a means of employing a maximum of workers with a minimum consumption

of capital. By increasing income without freezing industrial capital, he avoids what he has called the "low income equilibrium trap." In the majority of the interviews "Operation Colombia" came up in one way or another. Among the economists, criticisms of Dr. Currie's program were encountered, especially since the program implies an increase in the rural-urban migration as a solution to the irrationality of agricultural production.

4. This argument is frequently complemented by one concerning illegitimacy: Colombian women do not wish to procreate indefinitely if they must then abandon their offspring to the streets and vagrancy; birth control is seen as one of the essential steps in alleviating this problem.

5. For a detailed discussion of this historical problem, see Simon Kuznets, "Underdeveloped Countries and the Pre-industrial Phase in the Advanced Countries," in Otto Feinstein (ed.), *Two Worlds of Change* (New York: Doubleday & Company, Inc., 1964).

6. This is unfortunate, in my opinion, since the fundamental problem for development, whether under capitalism or socialism, is one of productivity. Although the present social conditions in Latin America do not permit efficient development of productivity, it is by no means clear that a socialist revolution could resolve these problems with such efficiency as to eliminate the problem of population growth. It is of interest that the French socialist economist Rene Dumont includes population growth in explaining the low Cuban agricultural productivity in the prerevolutionary period, but in addition notes that high population growth after the revolution presented serious obstacles to the economic development, especially with respect to education. [See his *Cuba: Intento de Crítica Constructiva* (Barcelona: Nova Terra, 1965).] I believe that socialist societies can develop their economies more rapidly and efficiently by making it possible for their citizens to limit the size of their families. This would make possible greater investment in more productive age groups and sectors of the population. This is especially important in the agricultural sector, where difficulties have been experienced in socialist planning where the investment of productive capital in cooperatives and collective farms is an urgent necessity. This argument is further reinforced by the policy of socialist societies to incorporate great numbers of women into the labor force. The facilitation of this important aspect of socialist economic growth by birth control is evident. Finally, the rapid increase of population in rural areas has been a principal cause in the massive urban migrations which have taken place in recent decades in Latin America. One of Cuba's biggest economic problems has been the rapid displacement of rural populations to the cities. This phenomenon, with its tragic consequences for the urban economy, cannot be forgotten in socialist economic planning.

Family planning clinic, Honduras.

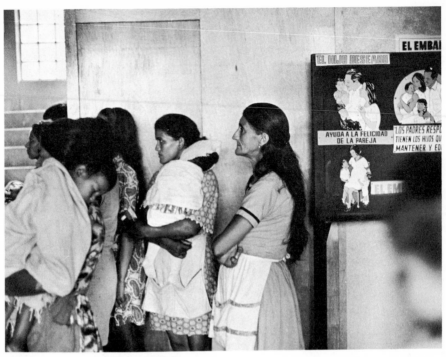

Family planning clinic, Honduras.

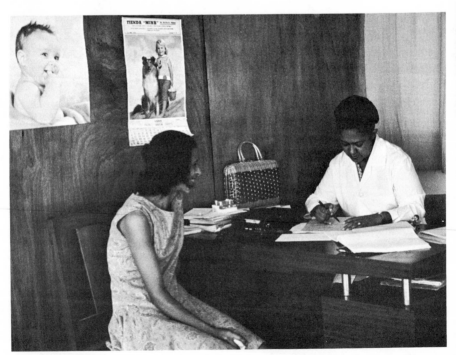

Medical interview at family planning clinic, Honduras.

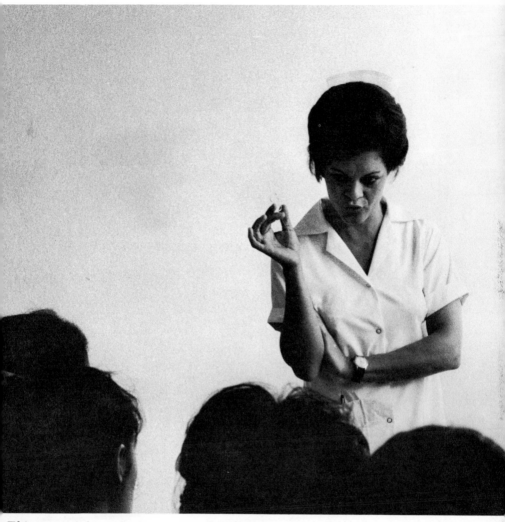

This page and overleaf:
Nurse in family planning clinic lecturing on
contraceptive methods, Dominican Republic.

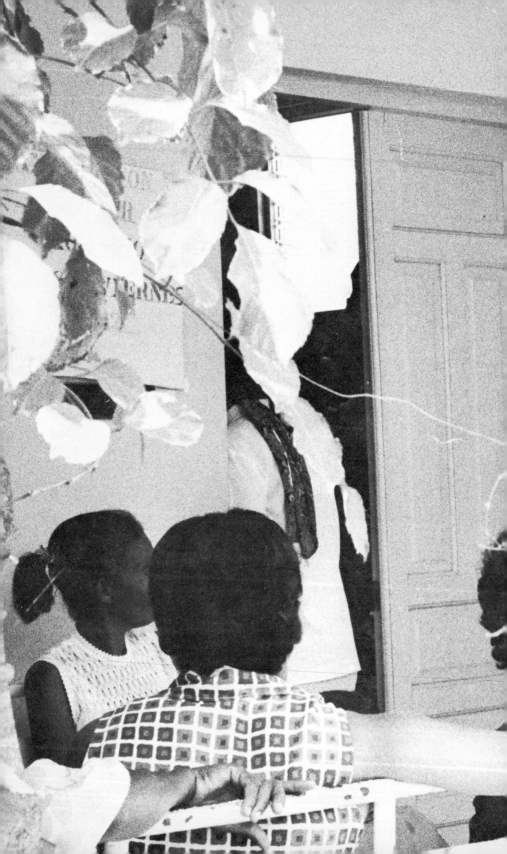

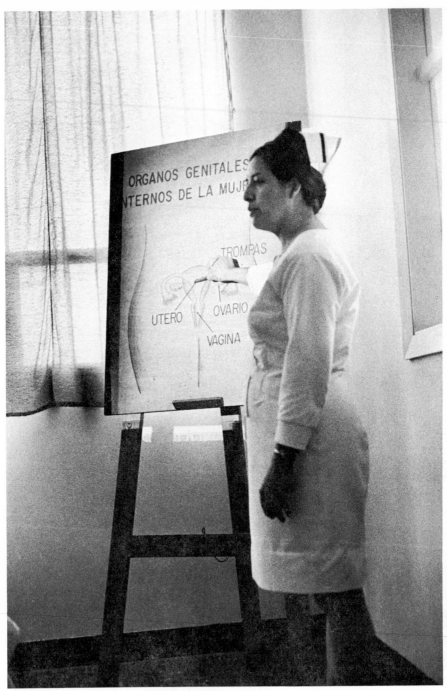

Delivery of lecture on family planning for
maternity ward patients, Honduras.

School-opening ceremonies, San Pedro
Sula, Honduras.

Lower-income neighborhood, Tegucigalpa, Honduras.

PART 3

Private Opinions
of the Public

INTRODUCTION

While the opinions of the elite largely determine whether or not birth control programs will exist, the opinions of the general population largely determine whether or not they will succeed. Since the target of such programs is the lower-income groups of the society, their opinions on the control of their fertility is crucial. Indeed, until recently, the alleged opinions of the masses on the subject constituted one of the principal arguments of elites against family planning programs. Since the masses want large families, the elite argued, programs can only fail if morally correct, and can conceivably succeed only by utilizing unacceptable coercive measures. Two types of arguments have commonly been utilized to support the attribution of pronatalist attitudes to the lower classes—that these classes are highly rational, and that these classes are highly irrational.

The rational school has been eloquently represented by Chile's then Ambassador Radomiro Tomić, who maintains that in rural areas "the numerous family represents an advantage for the family group and each of its members: free labor, possibilities of additional income; help to the mother in her household chores and to the father in his tasks; guarantee against high mortality among children; guarantee for the parent's old age, etc."[1] A more technical source, the Latin American Population and Family Center (CELAP), refers to a "prepaternal drive." While "drives" are not usually regarded as rational in nature, CELAP's explanation shows that both rational and

247

nonrational elements are present, for "apart from the weight that may be assigned to certain traditional features stressed in the literature, such as *machismo,* religion, and the desire to assure the continuity of one's family name, there is the numerical valuation placed on offspring as a potential labor force and a means of augmenting the meager family income."[2]

Somewhere between the rational and nonrational are vague "value systems" and "cultural complexes" attributed to the masses. ". . . procreation and family size," writes Argentine Public Health specialist Dr. Abraam Sonis, "are not the mere result of a routine physiological coupling, but respond to intimate religious beliefs, powerful cultural and psychological motives."[3] One of the most frequently mentioned of these drives is *machismo,* an obsessional complex compelling the male to prove his manhood by means of annual (at a minimum) impregnation. Originally popularized by literati in a perhaps overzealous search for national characteristics, it has become a favorite not only of the Sunday magazine psychologists,[4] but of such psychiatric specialists as Dr. Hernán Vergara. In the following citation, he shows Colombians the programmatic implications of this violent form of neurosis: ". . . it is not enough that the man engage in a formidable sexual activity, but that he produce evidence of it. . . . Even if *machismo* were carried out without deliberately seeking children, the fact that it is accomplished principally through seduction, under violent conditions, makes these unions an improvised matter, without the chance for utilizing the contraceptive services of the nearest health station."[5]

When Professor Sonis discusses the feasibility of family planning programs, he concludes that they are impracticable since their success would require "a complete change in the value system of the community, a system which shapes the community's behavior and ideals."[6] He agrees with an ECLA report which maintains that "the decisive matter is not in changing birth rates, but the attitudes which cause them," but then shows that such a task would be beyond the ability of public health "unless investments in all economic and social sectors be stopped in order to dedicate resources exclusively to birth control campaigns."[7]

Such arguments are believed not only by opponents of family planning, but often by those directly responsible for the success of family planning efforts. If we listen to the public utterances of Chile's

Minister of Health concerning the irrational irresponsibility of the public he is sworn to serve, it is not difficult to explain the absence of dynamism of that nation's family planning program: "Basically, it is in poverty that are to be found the conditions, whether shortage of housing, alcoholism, ignorance which lead to irresponsible procreation. This is one of the real causes of the so-called demographic explosion. In these, social strata family planning programs show enormous weakness. The poorest, who most need them, are least willing to accept them. It is this that has made some say, despairingly, that the effort to reduce the birth-rates among the great populations of the globe . . . have so far had little success."[8]

The plausible and intriguing arguments about lower-class culture cited above suffer from one defect—they are innocent of systematic empirical data on the lower class and stem from a mixture of biased facts and erroneous theories. The "rational" school tends to assume that if the lower classes have big families, they must want them. "Rational" explanations for this desire are then sought. Anecdotal confirmation for such attributions most frequently depend upon domestics and garden boys, types not only unrepresentative of the mass of the population, but notoriously adept at telling the upper classes what they expect to hear. The public opinion surveys analyzed in this section testify to the falsity of such assumptions. Low-income Latin Americans may have big families, but they would prefer to have smaller ones. While the data presented are largely confined to urban dwellers, earlier research by the author in Puerto Rico, Jamaica, and Peru suggests that the discrepancy between fertility ideals and practice is also substantial in rural areas, though both the level of preferred family size and the level of actual family size are higher. People indeed mention assistance in old age and child mortality as reasons for preferring a given number of children, but this number is rarely more than four among classes where actual number of children averages about six.

It is of course much harder to disprove the "irrational" school, which on the one hand posits vague biological drives and on the other such explanations as "laziness," "irresponsibility," and "immorality." With respect to *machismo,* the only direct attempts to measure it have occurred in Puerto Rico, where, according to psychiatrists, social workers, and anthropologists (perhaps even an early sociologist or two), it has always been in full bloom. But when 322 lower-class males were asked, Which of these would be worst for you: to be a henpecked husband, a barren male, or a man of weak character? only 28 percent cited the barren male *as the worst or second worst of the three.*[9] Furthermore, on a battery of items dealing with the desired number of children, *the men wanted fewer than their wives in seven out of the eight questions.*[10] The authors concluded that "machismo exists primarily sociologically, that is, by reputation."[11]

One serious criticism leveled against such findings is that they are invalid, depending as they do on formal interviewing. Thus, one critic of KAP studies feels that stated responses favorable to small family size and to family planning may be less a reflection of a "market for family planning" than ". . . politeness in response to an unmeaningful question in a society in which culture dictates the avoidance of a negative response. . . . It is quite possible that many of the responses in KAP surveys are efforts at politeness to meaningless queries or forced responses to questions to which the respondent really has no answer either before or after the question is put."[12]

My own studies have produced convincing evidence that uneducated women in underdeveloped areas do not in fact give much thought to these matters and that the intensity of their desire for a small to moderate number of children is not great. But I do not regard as tenable the hypothesis that they are merely trying to "please the interviewer" by saying they want few children. One measure of this is provided by data on stated intentions to use birth control. If respondents *really* want to please the interviewer, they should overstate their interest in or intention to use birth control, since this is usually the direct aim of much action research in this field. Of course, a failure to realize one's intentions can be due to many factors other than the intention itself, but there should be some correspondence between the verbal statement and subsequent behavior. Thus, while it should come as no surprise to find that not everyone who says he wants birth control in fact uses it when it is made available, there is nevertheless a strong correlation between the expressed attitude and actual behavior. In Jamaica, for example, while only 6 percent of those who said they had not thought of using birth control in fact reported use six weeks later, 25 percent of those who had thought favorably subsequently reported its use. (In the urban area, where it was easier to obtain contraceptives, the two figures were 6 percent and 35 percent.) The women who were not using birth control were asked about their intention to use it. When responses were followed up two years later, it was found that less than 10 percent of those who did not intend to use birth control were using birth control, 30 percent of those who did intend to use birth control were using it. Finally, of those women who reported that they had attended the family planning clinic, a check of clinic records showed that 97 percent had in fact done so.[13] In short, people's stated intentions and statements of behavior are predictive of their behavior, though the predictability falls short of 100 percent.

To place Latin American opinion of population matters in a comparative context, we turn first to a body of survey data not subject to the usual limitations of the KAP survey. Typically, such fertility surveys are confined to women in the reproductive age groups, and often to women living in relatively stable marital unions. Thus, the opinions of males, older women, and single women are not represented or are underrepresented. Each survey is customarily designed ad hoc, moreover, so that the wording and sequence of questions are rarely the same from survey to survey. Comparisons between surveys conducted ten to fifteen years apart are often made without regard to time, although there have been important shifts of public opinion on population questions over the past decade.

A body of relevant international poll data has recently been made available which is not subject to these limitations. In 1965 the United States Information Agency (USIA) sponsored four questions on population surveys conducted in twenty-two countries.[14] Respondents were not told the sponsorship of the population questions. Local commercial survey organizations and local interviewers were contracted to gather over 17,000 interviews with samples representative of the adult male and female "general population" within each of the places or categories specified in Table 24. (That all the Latin American samples, e.g., are drawn only from the principal city of the nation and that all the European samples are national must of course be borne in mind when making national cross-comparisons.)

The first question involved the respondents' perception of national population growth: "Is it your impression that the number of people in [survey country] is increasing, decreasing, or remaining about the same?" In only five countries do more than 10 percent of the respondents fail to answer this question, and three of these nations are European (West Germany, Italy, and Great Britain). In none of

TABLE 24

Coverage and Sampling in 1965 Surveys on Population

Country	Places	Sample Size	Sample Coverage
Western Europe			
Britain	National	1179	General
France	National	1228	General
West Germany	National	1255	General
Italy	National	1166	General
Latin America			
Mexico	Mexico City	493	Urban
Brazil	Rio de Janeiro	501	Urban
Venezuela	Caracas	500	Urban
Argentina	Buenos Aires	507	Urban
Chile	Santiago	511	Urban
Far East			
Japan	National	1034	General
Thailand	Bangkok	500	Urban
Korea	Seoul	500	Urban
Philippines	Manila	500	Urban
Malaysia	Kuala Lumpur	502	Urban
Singapore	National	509	General
Near East and South Asia			
India	New Delhi	500	Literate, urban
	Bombay	500	Literate, urban
	Calcutta	500	Literate, urban
	Madras	500	Literate, urban
Iran	Tehran	500	Literate, urban
Turkey	Ankara	500	Literate, urban
	Istanbul	500	Literate, urban
Greece	Athens	500	Urban
Africa			
Nigeria	Lagos	500	Literate, urban
	Enugu	400	Literate, urban
Kenya	Nairobi	524	Literate, urban
	Mombasa	336	Literate, urban
	Kisumu	218	Literate, urban
	Nakuru	160	Literate, urban
	Machakos/Kitui	295	Literate, urban
Senegal	Dakar	500	Literate, urban

SOURCE: "Worldwide Opinions about Some Issues of Population Control," United States Information Agency, R-210-65, December 1965.

the underdeveloped nations do less than three-quarters of the respondents believe their population is growing. For all countries, an
average (unweighted) of 86 percent believe their nation is growing.
It is of interest that in the fastest growing region of the world, Latin
America, the mean is only 80. Indeed, in Caracas, in Rio de Janeiro,
and in Mexico City there are over 10 percent who believe their
populations are stationary or decreasing in size. Moreover, as shown
in Table 25, in only one of the five cities do a clear majority feel
their population is increasing "greatly." On the whole, however, there
is a universal awareness of national population growth.

The surveys then shifted to three questions of opinion: "All things
considered, do you think having a larger population would be a good
thing or a bad thing for this country?" "How about the number of
people in the world as a whole? Do you think an increase in the
world population would be a good thing or a bad thing?" "All things
considered, how would you feel about a birth control program to
encourage people in [survey country] to have fewer children—would
you approve or disapprove of such a program?"

TABLE 25

Attitudes toward Population Growth and Family Planning,
Five Latin American Cities, 1965*

	Buenos Aires	Caracas	Mexico	Rio	Santiago
Percent believe population increasing "greatly"	20	50	66	55	49
Percent believe world population increase a "bad thing"	48	41	48	39	48
Percent believe national population growth a "bad thing"	21	18	31	29	30
Percent strongly approving a national birth control program	21	47	41	35	52

*"No answers" and "don't knows" have not been excluded from the bases on all items. Rio
de Janeiro has a considerably higher proportion of these than the other cities.

For this set of questions there is a dramatic increase in the "no opinion" category. In seven of the twenty-two countries the numbers of "no opinions" exceed 20 percent on the first of the three questions. Four of these are developed countries (Japan, Italy, West Germany, and France), but Rio de Janeiro, Kuala Lumpur, and Singapore also fall in this category. On the second question, referring to world population, the "don't know" and "no opinion" categories range from 1 to 41 percent, with eight countries exceeding 20 percent. While cultural differentials may be of some importance, we conclude that there are serious organizational differences among the pollsters in the ways in which "no answers" are accepted and recorded. To improve comparability, we have recomputed the reported USIA figures, excluding the "no opinions" from the bases used for per-centaging.[15] We have grouped the nations sampled by continent and have presented in Table 26 the unweighted averages for the three opinion questions.

The first noteworthy aspect of Table 26 is the predominance of negative opinion concerning world population growth (column 2). In only one of the twenty-two sampled areas (Dakar) do less than half of the people with opinions believe such growth is a "bad thing." There is considerable variation, however, both within and between regions. The greatest variation is among the Asian nations, ranging from 95 and 91 percent in India and Turkey to 55 and 61 percent in Bangkok and Manila. Even within Europe the range is great—from a low of 73 percent in Italy to a high of 92 percent in Great Britain. Nevertheless, and this is the second most important aspect of the table, there is a sharp division between the figures for Africa and Latin America and those for the rest of the world. Only a narrow majority of the inhabitants sampled in the eight major cities surveyed in these continents believed world population growth to be a bad thing. Within the Latin American region there is very little variation.

The first column of Table 26 reveals a substantial difference in opinion when respondents were asked whether they believe having a larger population would be a good or bad thing for *their* country. Far fewer regard it as bad. France drops by 47 percentage points, Tehran by 44, Athens by 37. Among major geographic regions, the proportional decline is greatest in Africa and Latin America. In these regions, whereas a majority of the sampled populations with opinions believe world population increase to be a bad thing, most people

TABLE 26

Attitudes toward Population Growth and Family Planning,
22 Countries, 1965

	Percent Believing National Growth a Bad Thing	Percent Believing World Growth a Bad Thing	Percent Approving a National Birth Control Program
Europe Unweighted mean	67	86	76
Range	(41–86)	(73–92)	(67–83)
Near East Unweighted mean	53	78	74
Range	(22–92)	(61–95)	(62–91)
Far East Unweighted mean	53	71	82
Range	(22–81)	(55–91)	(62–99)
Latin America Unweighted mean	29	56	74
Range	(19–38)	(52–62)	(61–84)
Africa Unweighted mean	33	54	54
Range	(14–47)	(40–61)	(30–71)

SOURCE: "Worldwide Opinions about Some Issues of Population Control," Computed from data in USIA, R-210-65, December 1965.

believe it is a good thing for their own country.[16] There is a universal tendency, most marked in the cases of Africa and Latin America, to believe that *population problems are somebody else's problems*.

When it comes to attitude toward birth control, we note that as early as 1965 a majority of the respondents in every survey other than in Dakar favored family planning. Indeed, in every region there are more people who approve of family planning than who believe that their nation's population increase is a bad thing. This is all the more remarkable when we consider the stringent wording of the question, which refers not merely to the notion of family planning, but to the desirability of "birth control programs to encourage people to have fewer children." In Latin America the range is considerable (Table 25), with half the sample in Caracas and Santiago strongly favoring birth control programs, as opposed to only a fifth in Argentina.

Depending upon their responses to the birth control item we may divide countries into three groups: the Far Eastern countries, three of which have over 85 percent *strongly* approving; Europe, the Near East, and Latin America, where the minimum approval scarcely falls below two-thirds; and Africa, where the level of approval is distinctly lower. (The range in Africa, however, is very large—from 30 percent in Dakar to 71 percent in Nigeria.) Latin America shows the largest discrepancy between attitudes toward population and toward family planning. In the cases of Caracas and Santiago, the percentage-point difference between those disapproving national population growth and those favoring family planning is 60 and 52, respectively.

If we disregard the regional classification and rank the countries from 1 to 22 on each of the three items, we discover an interesting pattern—the Spearman rank-order correlation[17] between the world and national population growth questions is high, .835. Thus, while most countries believe world population growth is a more serious problem than national population growth, how seriously they regard the one is closely related to how seriously they regard the other. The correlation between attitude toward national growth and attitude toward national birth control programs, however, is much smaller, .463, suggesting that national rank on one of these items predicts poorly national rank on the other. If we now divide the countries into two groups on each question, depending on whether they fall in the upper or lower half of the distribution, we emerge with the four types shown in Table 27.

The nations against national growth and in favor of family planning are, with the exception of Great Britain, non-Christian Asian societies, all of which now have active family planning programs. At the opposite pole, the six nations more opposed to family planning and more in favor of national growth include two Latin American, two African, and two Asian states.

The other two categories are especially interesting. The first group of countries are those rather negative to national population growth but also rather negative to family planning. Italy and Manila, with conservative Catholic populations, might be viewed as nations ap-

TABLE 27

Attitudes toward National Population Growth and toward a
National Birth Control Program

Attitude toward National Population Growth	*Attitude toward Birth Control Program*	
	More Positive	*Less Positive*
Less positive	India Turkey Seoul Japan Singapore Great Britain	Italy West Germany Nigeria Manila Athens
More positive	France Kuala Lumpur Santiago Mexico City Caracas	Rio de Janeiro Kenya Buenos Aires Bangkok Tehran Dakar

proving of the ends of population control but not of the contraceptive means. The last group of countries is that in which the Latin American cities are heavily overrepresented, and may correspond to the reverse of the previous group—family planning is approved of, but population control is not—a position explicitly expounded, for example, by Chilean government officials. ("Population control" refers to all those means intended to affect national rates of population growth. "Family planning" refers to those means intended to affect the number and spacing of births within the family. While the technical means are usually the same—e.g., contraceptive methods—the ends are quite different. Espousal of one, therefore, does not imply espousal of the other.)

With respect to private opinions of the general public then, we emerge with several conclusions: (1) There is no relation between a nation's rate of growth and a people's concern about that rate. In 1965 the African and Latin American urban populations sampled were largely unconvinced that their nations were growing at too rapid a rate; and most other nations sampled were more concerned about world growth rates than about the growth rates of their own nations. (2) In most countries the means (birth control) are less controversial than the ends, insofar as we define population control as a major end of birth control. Latin Americans tend to typify the pronatalist, pro-family planning position. (3) Countries most committed both to family planning *and* to the notion of excessive national growth rates were, with the exception of Great Britain, Asiatic nations which have had substantial public family planning programs. Which is cause and which effect is not clear, but it is not unlikely that national public information programs giving attention to both means and ends have had considerable influence in these countries.[18]

In the chapters to follow we further explicate the data derived from KAP surveys. In Chapters 12 and 13 KAP surveys are analyzed, both comparatively (seven cities) and in depth (Medellín, Colombia). In addition, less traditional interviewing approaches are employed. In Chapter 14 an anthropologically trained investigator interviews expectant mothers in a hospital context, and in Chapter 15, a social psychologist utilizes projective techniques for unraveling family size norms among both adult women and young girls. Each technique produces its own special findings, but nowhere do we find evidence of the importance of that irresponsible, irrational, and compulsive lower-class being. If hidden, he hides well.

NOTES

1. Radomiro Tomić, *Family Planning, Economic Development, Respect for the Human Person: Three Inseparable Elements of a Demographic Policy in Latin America,* November 1967. (Mimeographed.)

2. *Sociocultural Factors Affecting Accelerated Population Growth and Unthinking Parenthood,* reference document of the Meeting on Population Policies in Relation to Development in Latin America, Organization of American States, September 1967. (Mimeographed.)

3. Abraam Sonis, *Salud, Medicina y Desarrollo Económico-Social* (Buenos Aires: Editorial Universitaria de Buenos Aires, 1968), p. 71.

4. North American newspapers are no exception. As James Reston explained the *machismo* complex, after a visit to Chile, it refers to the "stubborn vanity and stupidity of the ignorant male in Latin America . . . [who is] worse than the baboon and worships the cult of virility long after he has forgotten the cult of Christianity. . . . The Latin male is not satisfied with love, he must have life—one new life a year, if possible, to prove he is good for something." "The Cult of Virility in Latin America," *New York Times,* Apr. 9, 1967.

5. Hernán Vergara, *El Complejo de Layo* (Bogotá: Tercer Mundo, 1968), p. 61.

6. A. Sonis, *op. cit.,* p. 71.

7. *Ibid.,* p. 76.

8. R. Valdivieso, "Opening Address," *Proceedings of the Eighth International Conference of the International Planned Parenthood Federation* (Hertford, England: Stephen Austin and Sons, 1967), p. 5.

9. R. Hill, J. M. Stycos, and K. W. Bach, *The Family and Population Control* (Chapel Hill, N.C.: University of North Carolina, 1959), p. 101.

10. *Ibid.,* p. 102.

11. *Ibid.,* p. 105.

12. Philip M. Hauser, "Family Planning and Population Programs: A Book Review Article," *Demography,* vol. 4, no. 1, 1967, p. 404.

13. J. M. Stycos and K. W. Bach, *The Control of Human Fertility in Jamaica* (Ithaca, N.Y.: Cornell University Press, 1964), pp. 233–235. (All differences reported are statistically significant at the .05 level.) During the Jamaica project a great deal of resources was invested in assessing reliability and validity of the data, and special attention was paid to evaluating interviewers and the interviewing process. An extensive analysis led us to conclude that interviews on this subject with lower-class people do not demonstrate appreciably more error than standard interviewing—at least if various kinds of safeguards are introduced. See K. W. Bach and J. M. Stycos, *The Survey under Unusual Conditions: The Jamaica Human Fertility Investigation* (Ithaca, N.Y.: Society for Applied Anthropology, 1959).

14. United States Information Agency, "Worldwide Opinions about Some Issues of Population Control," December 1965. See also USIA report R-176-65, "United States Standing in Worldwide Public Opinion—1965," December 1965.

15. Of course statistical "comparability" does nothing about substantive comparability. Excluding the 36 percent "No responses" in Singapore along with the 4 percent in Dakar probably creates or magnifies systematic differences between the two universes which the samples represent.

16. An unfortunate qualification must be made here. Outside the European region, only respondents who said national growth was a good thing were asked their opinion of world growth; the balance were recorded as having a negative opinion on world growth. Therefore the proportion with a negative opinion on world growth could not be less than that observed for national growth. The assumption seems plausible, though by no means certain; more important is the fact that in Europe, where both questions were asked, the shifts were as substantial as in some of the other regions.

17. The degree of similarity or dissimilarity between any pair of rank orders, each with the same number of items, measured on a scale from -1.0 (complete dissimilarity) to $+1.0$ (complete similarity).

18. Reprinted from J. Mayone Stycos, "Public and Private Opinion on Population and Family Planning," *Studies in Family Planning,* no. 51, March 1970. Footnotes 14 to 17 are also reprinted from this article.

CHAPTER 12

Opinion Profiles
of Seven Cities

Prepared by **Edgar H. Elam.**

Education is among those factors associated most closely with human fertility. In general, the average number of children borne is lower for women with greater education, even when other significant factors such as marital status, age, and urban-rural background are controlled.[1] Additionally, a rise in the level of general education in a society is frequently accompanied by a decline in fertility.[2]

For any group of women biologically capable of reproduction, the average number of children borne may be considered to be the result of that group's knowledge, attitudes, and practices (KAP) related to fertility. In this paper, measurements of such variables along with education and age are analyzed to determine whether the generally accepted negative relationship between education and fertility holds true in different cultural settings. Also studied are the effects of age on education-fertility relationships and the degree of consistency among different KAP variables for women grouped according to age and education.

Survey data obtained in 1963 and 1964 for representative samples of women from six major Latin American cities provide the basis for the analysis: Bogotá, Colombia; Buenos Aires, Argentina; Caracas, Venezuela; Mexico City, Mexico; Rio de Janeiro, Brazil; and San José, Costa Rica.[3] The data apply to women aged twenty to fifty years who currently were or previously had been either legally married or consensually mated. The surveys were conducted under the general guidance of the Centro Latinoamericano de Demogafia (CELADE). Personnel of Cornell University's International Population Program collaborated closely in design and preparation of the surveys.[4] Preliminary planning for the surveys took place in Santiago, Chile, at CELADE, and a training seminar was held there in the summer of 1963 for survey directors from the participating countries. Participants received instruction in sampling, interviewer training, and other subjects from the United Nations, CELADE, and Cornell University demographers who had prepared the initial questionnaire design. The questionnaire was field-tested in Chile, and hand tallies were made of pretest results.

The survey was designed to obtain a representative sample of approximately 2,000 women aged 20–50 in each city. Probability cluster samples of about 2,300 were drawn to allow a margin for refusals and other losses. Specific sample designs, training of interviewers, and all survey operations through the punching of IBM cards were performed in the national institutions under the supervision of local directors who had participated in the training seminar at CELADE.

The data used here are taken from IBM cards supplied by CELADE. At Cornell, selected data were drawn from the various cards for each respondent and were combined into a single card in order to facilitate tabulation and analysis. Tapes generated from the analysis cards were used for the computer processing. Control totals for data used in this paper are shown in Table 28. These may differ

TABLE 28

Age, Education, and Birthplace, Six Latin American Cities

Country	Median Age	Percent Completed Elementary School	Percent Born in Rural Area
Bogotá	32.5	49	60
Buenos Aires	37.6	67	15
Caracas	33.0	44	26
Mexico City	33.7	48	28
Rio de Janeiro	35.8	53	3
San José	34.1	52	27

somewhat from results of the same surveys reported elsewhere, due to the discarding of a few cases with incomplete information on age, education, or fertility. The effect on any comparative measure is negligible.

FERTILITY VARIABLES MEASURED

In order to assess the fertility values, sixteen representative KAP variables have been selected from the survey data and grouped into eight categories. Ten of the variables are used for charting rank comparisons and have been assigned item numbers. The numbering order and designation scheme are maintained throughout the paper, in text, figures, and tables. The categories and variables are listed below, with numbers in parentheses designating the ten items used in ranking.

A. Predisposing Factors
    Age at first marital union (1)
    Total number of live births to respondent's mother
B. Knowledge of Child Mortality and Population Growth
    Awareness of declining childhood mortality (2)
    Awareness of rapid population growth in own country
C. Ideal Family Size
    Personal ideal family size (3)
    Normative ideal family size
D. Prior Consideration and Discussion of Ideal Family Size
    Thought of ideal number of children before interview (4)
    Discussed number of children wanted with husband (5)
E. Attitudes toward Birth Control
    Categoric disapproval of family limitation
    Approval of family limitation for economic reasons (6)
    Would use pill to avoid pregnancy
F. Knowledge of Birth Control
    No method of birth control known (7)
G. Use of Birth Control
    Never used any method (8)
    Ever used appliance methods or sterilization (9)
H. Fertility Performance
    Total number of live births (10)
    Total number of living children

The order in which the variables are listed and numbered follows a natural progression from predisposing factors affecting fertility; through knowledge, attitudes, and practices; to actual fertility performance as measured by number of live births and surviving children. Medians and percentages are used in assigning values to these variables. The median is used for quantitative variables such as age at marriage and number of children borne or desired. For more qualitative variables, the *percentages* of women possessing the characteristic or holding the attitude are usually used.

INTERCITY COMPARISONS

We would expect age to bear a negative relation and education to bear a positive one with the kind of knowledge, attitudes, and practices that favor *low* fertility. An examination of Table 28 shows that the samples do vary on both these characteristics. Average age varies by as much as five years between Bogotá and Buenos Aires, and the proportion who have finished elementary school varies from a low of 44 percent in Caracas to a high of 67 percent in Buenos Aires. Variation by place of birth is even more spectacular, ranging from 3 percent born in rural areas in Rio de Janeiro to 60 percent in Bogotá. In short, we should not be surprised to find intercity variations in KAP variables if the cities vary so markedly on important demographic characteristics. Table 29 shows the actual values for sixteen KAP variables. A graphic means of comparison is provided in Figure 3, a rank-comparison profile depicting each city's rank from 1 to 6 on each of the ten variables. Horizontally the chart is divided into ten spaces, with vertical lines extending below the numbers corresponding to the KAP variables. Within the major vertical divisions the relative rank of each city is plotted for each variable, and the positions are connected by a line. Titles of the numbered variables are listed below the chart.[5]

While actual rank is shown by a solid line, a dashed line is used to represent expected rank for each city. The expected ranks were obtained by computing the average rank for each city on all ten variables. This summary measure was then taken as the expected rank of the city on all variables. The procedure is based on the assumption of consistency of intercity rankings on the different KAP variables. The profiles presented in Figure 3 indicate, by deviations

TABLE 29

Comparative Measures on Fertility-related Variables for
Ever-mated Women of Six Cities

Item Measured	Bogotá	Buenos Aires	Caracas	Mexico City	Rio de Janeiro	San José
Median age at first marital union (1)	20.4	23.1	19.7	19.8	21.0	20.9
Median number of live births to respondent's mother	7.2	4.9	6.9	7.2	6.7	7.5
Percentage aware of declining child mortality (2)	31	62	60	64	38	63
Percentage aware of rapid population increase	79	*	80	96	73	90
Median number of living children	3.6	2.1	3.1	3.6	2.6	3.5
Median personal ideal family size (3)	4.2	2.9	4.1	4.6	2.9	4.2
Median normative ideal family size	4.6	3.3	4.5	4.7	3.2	4.5
Percentage who thought previously of ideal family size (4)	44	69	57	54	60	58
Percentage who discussed family size with husband (5)	36	62	38	40	45	45
Percentage expressing categorical disapproval of birth control	12	2	9	16	11	9
Percentage approving family limitation for economic need (6)	42	63	41	39	40	43
Percentage willing to use pill to prevent pregnancy	40	19	32	32	21	34
Percentage not knowing any birth control method (7)	17	7	21	16	14	18
Percentage ever having used birth control (8)	50	79	68	47	61	71
Percentage having used appliance methods or sterilization (9)	15	47	29	17	24	36
Median number of live births to respondent (10)	3.9	2.3	3.4	4.1	2.8	3.8

*Excluded since population growth was moderate rather than rapid.

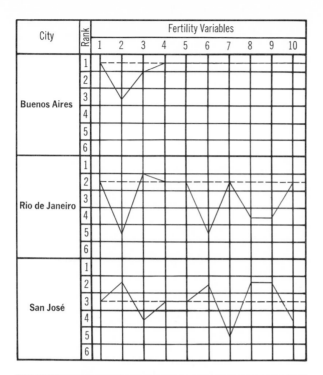
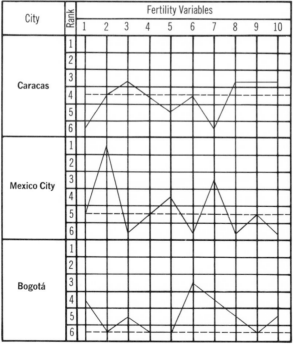

FIGURE 3.
Rank profiles on selected fertility variables for
women of six cities.

from the expected ranks, substantial cultural variation on specific variables as well as on the total ferility value complex.[6]

INDIVIDUAL CITY CHARACTERIZATIONS

§ BUENOS AIRES—RANK 1

Buenos Aires is clearly first among the six cities with respect to knowledge, attitudes, and practices favoring low fertility. Only on one of the ten variables, awareness of declining child mortality (item 2), does this city fall below first rank, though it is tied for first on personal ideal family size (item 3). In both cases the absolute differences between Buenos Aires and the higher-ranking cities are extremely small, as may be seen in Table 29. The high-ranking pattern is what we would expect since Buenos Aires women generally possess the characteristics usually associated with low fertility. In addition to the high level of education, only 15 percent of the women were born in rural areas, and a high proportion were born in European countries. Buenos Aires is the largest city in the sample, the population of the metropolitan agglomeration approximating 7 million in 1960. Finally, it has the smallest proportion of women whose husbands are employed in manual occupations. The combination of many factors has produced a population that is both favorable to low fertility and has achieved it.

§ RIO DE JANEIRO—RANK 2

This city has the second lowest fertility with a median of 2.8 live births and holds second overall rank on variables favoring low fertility. This high rank results from a median personal ideal family size (item 3), equal to the ideal of Buenos Aires and lower than the ideals of the samples from all other cities, plus high percentages who have considered and discussed ideal family size (items 4 and 5) and who have heard of some form of birth control (item 7). Age at marriage (item 1) was second highest among the cities. The women from Rio de Janeiro ranked 4 or below on knowledge of declining childhood mortality (item 2), approval of family limitation for economic reasons (item 6), and use of birth control (items 8 and 9).

Rio de Janeiro ranked second in educational level and had a very low proportion with rural background, even if we allow for the possibility that differences in definition of urban and rural are partially responsible for the low figure of 3 percent with rural birth.[7] These are conditions compatible with the relatively low fertility desired and achieved, in spite of attitudes and practices less favorable to controlled fertility than those of some other cities with a higher level of fertility.

§ SAN JOSÉ—RANK 3

Although it is Costa Rica's capital and major urban center, San José is the smallest of the six sample cities by a substantial margin. In 1964 its metropolitan population was 330,607, while both Caracas and Bogotá, the next larger cities, had populations around 1,600,000. The educational level is very close to that of Rio de Janeiro and is above all other cities except Buenos Aires. The proportion born in rural areas, slightly more than one-fourth, is similar to Mexico City and Caracas.

On most items San José ranks about third, but on knowledge of demographic trends and approval and practice of birth control (items 3, 8, and 9), it ranks higher. Interestingly, it drops to fifth place with respect to percentage of women who had heard of a method of birth control (item 7). This is inconsistent with its high level of education and rankings on other variables related to communication and knowledge. However, the quantitative differences on this item are relatively small, as can be seen in Table 29. Close in overall rank to the sample from Rio de Janeiro on fertility-related variables, the women from San José appear to be favorable to controlled fertility but at a relatively high level.

§ CARACAS—RANK 4

Caracas departs from its overall fourth place in holding lower rankings on age at marriage (item 1), knowledge of birth control (item 7), and discussion of number of children desired (item 5). On the other hand it ranks third on personal ideal family size (item 3), actual number of live births (item 10), and knowledge and use of birth control (items 8 and 9).

Caracas has the lowest percentage of women who completed elementary school, with a quarter born in rural areas and one-fifth in foreign countries. It maintains a middle overall rank consistent with its rank on urban-rural origins and population size.

§ MEXICO CITY—RANK 5

Women of Mexico City desire and have produced larger families than any other city in our samples. Their median personal ideal family size was 4.6 and median number of children borne 4.1. While Mexico City's population of over 3 million is one of the largest in the hemisphere, over 28 percent of the sample women were born in small towns or on farms. Further, as Miró has pointed out, reproduction rates for Mexico City are closer to the rates for Mexico as a whole than are the rates for other sample cities to their national rates.[8]

Mexico City exceeds its overall rank of fifth for only three of the ten variables. The two-thirds aware of the declining trend in infant and childhood mortality (item 2) was more than for any other city, though only the Bogotá and Rio de Janeiro samples were substantially lower on absolute measures of this item. While the 16 percent knowing some method of birth control (item 7) was higher in Mexico City than in three other cities, the 47 percent who had ever used birth control (item 8) was the lowest of all.

§ BOGOTÁ—RANK 6

Of the ten variables Bogotá ranks last among the cities on five items and fifth on three others. While it ranks third on approval of family limitation for economic reasons (item 6), absolute differences between cities on this item are small, other than for Buenos Aires.

The background of the Bogotá women is much more strongly rural than that of any of the other city samples, with 60 percent born in a small town or on a farm. This is more than 30 percentage points higher than any other city. The city ranks somewhat higher on education. It has a higher percentage of women who completed elementary school than either Caracas or Mexico City.

We have already seen that the cities' populations vary widely in place of birth and education. The extent to which their overall rankings on the fertility variables resemble the city ranks by education and rural provenience is seen on page 269.

Rank-order correlation coefficients show a higher degree of association of the overall ranking on fertility-related variables with place of birth ($r_r = .886$) than with education, as measured by percentage having completed elementary school ($r_r = .771$). The magnitude of both coefficients, however, indicates strong relationships. On the

| | Rank | | |
City	Overall	Education	Rural birthplace
Buenos Aires	1	1	2
Rio de Janeiro	2	2	1
San José	3	3	4
Caracas	4	6	3
Mexico City	5	5	5
Bogotá	6	4	6

other hand, the rank-order correlation between education and birthplace is only .543.

AGE AND EDUCATION

Age and education are among the variables of most crucial significance for fertility and for the delineation of target groups for family planning programs. In order to assess their relation to the KAP variables, the ever-married women were divided into four groups of varying age and education, for each of the six cities. The women were classified as "young" if under thirty-five years of age and as "old" if aged thirty-five or more. They were further subdivided according to their degree of education and were classified as "high" or "low" depending upon whether or not they had completed elementary school.[9] The combination of these categories gives us four groups: young-high education, old-high education, young-low education, and old-low education.

Table 30 reveals some differences among the sample cities with respect to the distributions of age and education. In only one instance does an age-education category constitute less than 10 percent of a city sample: the young, less educated women of Buenos Aires, a result of the high level of education in that city. Two-thirds of the Buenos Aires women had completed elementary school, a level achieved by slightly more than half the women from Rio de Janeiro and San José and by less than half from the remaining three cities.

Three hypotheses may be advanced concerning the relation of age and education to the KAP variables: (1) Educational level is positively associated with knowledge, attitudes, and practices favoring low fertility; (2) age is negatively associated with knowledge, atti-

TABLE 30

Age and Education for Ever-mated Women in Six Cities

Age and Education	Bogotá	Buenos Aires	Caracas	Mexico City	Rio de Janeiro	San José
			*Number**			
Total	1,821	1,696	1,744	1,872	2,007	1,597
Young-High ed.	523	507	469	525	530	491
Old-High ed.	378	627	293	369	526	347
Young-Low ed.	573	160	531	535	431	364
Old-Low ed.	347	402	446	443	520	395
			Percentage			
Total	100	100	100	100	100	100
Young-High ed.	29	30	27	28	26	31
Old-High ed.	21	37	17	20	26	22
Young-Low ed.	32	9	30	29	22	23
Old-Low ed.	19	24	26	24	26	25

*The total figures shown are for women classified by both age and education. They exclude a few women for whom information on these topics was not complete. The total numbers of ever-mated women in the city samples were Bogotá, 1,824; Buenos Aires, 1,710; Caracas, 1,744; Mexico City, 1,874; Rio de Janeiro, 2,013; San José, 1,598.

tudes, and practices favoring low fertility; (3) the association between education and fertility-related variables is stronger than that between the latter variables and age.

Tables 31 to 37 give the values for the sixteen KAP variables according to our age-education categories. While some of the differences may be very small and the age-education categories are relatively crude, the comparisons made have a sound underlying statistical basis. For each city sample, measures of chi-square were computed for the frequency distribution of respondents among all categories of each fertility-related variable, with the respondents classified according to the four-way age-education scheme. Almost without exception the differences were significant at the .05 level, suggesting the overall importance of the demographic variables stressed here.[10] Let us now look more closely at the findings.

§ PREDISPOSING FACTORS

A decline in age at marriage can increase total marital fertility as a result of longer exposure to childbirth, if not counteracted by increasing utilization of birth control. Even if average total fertility remains the same, however, a decline in age at marriage and earlier childbearing would reduce the average length of generation and thus result in an increase in the rate of population growth.

Table 31 indicates that in all cities the younger women entered their first marital union (legal or consensual) between one and two years earlier than the older women of comparable education level. While this might suggest a general decline in the age at marriage, a bias is produced by the samples' exclusion of never-mated women, some of whom could be expected to marry at later ages than the women of the same cohort already married at the time of the survey. This would be more important for the younger women since virtually no first marriages were reported after age thirty-five. We have no evidence of the direction and extent of the effect on data for age at marriage resulting from mortality among women who would have been in the sample had they survived to that time.

With age controlled, the better-educated marry from 0.3 to 2.4 years later than women of less education. However, in Bogotá, Buenos Aires, and San José, the age at marriage was lower for the

TABLE 31

Median Age of Respondents at First Marital Union, and
Median Number of Live Births to Respondents' Mothers,
by Age-Education Categories

Age and Education	Bogotá	Buenos Aires	Caracas	Mexico City	Rio de Janeiro	San José
Median Age at First Union (Item 1)						
Total	20.4	23.1	19.7	19.8	21.0	20.9
Young-High ed.	20.5	22.7	20.4	20.7	21.2	20.5
Old-High ed.	21.0	24.1	21.9	21.1	21.6	22.5
Young-Low ed.	19.7	21.5	18.3	18.6	20.2	19.9
Old-Low ed.	20.7	23.0	19.5	19.0	20.7	21.2
Median Live Births to Respondents' Mothers						
Total	7.2	4.9	6.9	7.2	6.7	7.5
Young-High ed.	7.1	3.7	6.5	6.4	5.1	6.7
Old-High ed.	7.0	4.7	6.3	6.1	6.1	7.0
Young-Low ed.	7.6	6.4	7.7	8.0	8.2	9.0
Old-Low ed.	7.2	7.0	6.7	8.0	7.9	8.1

young, more-educated than for the old, less-educated. In these cities, the effect of education is weaker than the generational trend toward younger marriage.

Age at marriage showed greater variation between cities than between age-education groups within the same city, with medians for total samples ranging from 19.7 years for Caracas to 23.1 years for Buenos Aires. In all cities the young, less-educated women had the lowest median age at first union.

Women who were themselves reared in large families might be more likely to accept and repeat the large-family pattern. While most of the women had not yet completed their childbearing, data in Tables 31 and 33 indicate that they were well below the high-parity levels of their mothers. Median number of live births to the mothers of the respondents ranged from 4.9 in Buenos Aires to 7.5 in San José, and only in Buenos Aires was the number below 6. Even among the old, less-educated women, in no city are the women likely to match

TABLE 32

Knowledge of Child Mortality and Population Growth,
by Age-Education Categories

Age and Education	Bogotá	Buenos Aires	Caracas	Mexico City	Rio de Janeiro	San José
	Percentage Aware of Declining Child Mortality (Item 2)					
Total	31	62	60	64	38	63
Young-High ed.	39	74	71	74	44	77
Old-High ed.	41	69	83	85	52	77
Young-Low ed.	22	45	45	47	29	47
Old-Low ed.	20	43	49	54	26	47
	Percentage Aware of Rapid National Population Increase					
Total	79	*	80	96	73	90
Young-High ed.	86		87	98	80	91
Old-High ed.	87		89	99	82	93
Young-Low ed.	71		71	92	61	84
Old-Low ed.	73		78	97	68	91

*Excluded since population growth was moderate rather than rapid.

TABLE 33

Median Number of Live Births, Living Children, and Ideal
Family Size, by Age-Education Categories for Ever-mated
Women of Six Cities, 1963–1964

Age and Education	Bogotá	Buenos Aires	Caracas	Mexico City	Rio de Janeiro	San José
Median Total Live Births (Item 10)						
Total	3.9	2.3	3.4	4.1	2.8	3.8
Young-High ed.	3.3	1.9	2.5	3.2	2.3	2.9
Old-High ed.	5.0	2.4	3.6	4.1	2.9	4.0
Young-Low ed.	3.5	2.1	3.5	4.1	2.9	3.7
Old-Low ed.	5.7	2.5	4.9	6.2	3.8	5.7
Median Total Living Children						
Total	3.6	2.1	3.1	3.6	2.6	3.5
Young-High ed.	3.0	1.8	2.4	2.9	2.2	2.8
Old-High ed.	4.5	2.3	3.2	3.9	2.7	3.8
Young-Low ed.	3.2	1.9	3.2	3.5	2.7	3.4
Old-Low ed.	4.9	2.4	4.3	5.2	3.2	5.0
Median Personal Ideal Family Size (Item 3)						
Total	4.2	2.9	4.1	4.6	2.9	4.2
Young-High ed.	4.1	3.0	3.9	4.2	2.9	4.0
Old-High ed.	4.5	3.0	4.3	4.4	3.1	4.3
Young-Low ed.	4.1	2.8	4.2	4.9	2.8	4.2
Old-Low ed.	4.3	2.8	4.2	5.1	3.0	4.5
Median Normative Ideal Family Size						
Total	4.6	3.3	4.5	4.7	3.2	4.5
Young-High ed.	4.4	3.3	4.2	4.4	3.0	4.2
Old-High ed.	4.7	3.4	4.5	4.5	3.5	4.6
Young-Low ed.	4.7	3.2	4.5	4.9	3.0	4.3
Old-Low ed.	5.0	3.3	5.0	5.1	3.5	4.8

the fertility of their mothers. In all cities except Buenos Aires, however, the old, less-educated women (with median age around forty-
two) have already exceeded their own fertility ideals as measured
by responses to the question: "If you were to start a family now,
how many children would you want?" (Table 33.)

TABLE 34

Prior Consideration and Discussion of Ideal Family Size,
by Age-Education Categories for Ever-mated Women of
Six Cities, 1963–1964

Age and Education	Bogotá	Buenos Aires	Caracas	Mexico City	Rio de Janeiro	San José
	Percentage Who Had Thought of Ideal Number of Children before Interview (Item 4)					
Total	44	69	57	54	60	58
Young-High ed.	62	80	73	70	71	72
Old-High ed.	48	70	68	63	64	66
Young-Low ed.	38	58	53	44	52	51
Old-Low ed.	22	59	38	41	51	43
	Percentage Who Had Discussed Ideal Number of Children with Husband (Item 5)					
Total	36	62	38	40	45	45
Young-High ed.	57	77	62	62	68	63
Old-High ed.	34	60	37	39	45	46
Young-Low ed.	32	58	35	32	42	39
Old-Low ed.	15	47	19	22	23	25

Data on number of live births to respondents and to their mothers indicate that the large family of the previous generation has survived neither as a general ideal nor as a pattern of behavior. They further indicate a long-standing fertility differential associated with education. In all cities, mother's fertility was lower for the better-educated groups.

§ KNOWLEDGE OF CHILD MORTALITY AND POPULATION GROWTH
Close to two-thirds of the ever-mated women in each of Buenos Aires, Caracas, Mexico City, and San José thought that "children are dying less today than 20 years ago," while for Bogotá and Rio de Janeiro only about a third thought so (Table 32). A high of 85 percent is found among the old, more-educated of Mexico City and a low of 20 percent for the old, less-educated of Bogotá. It is interesting that the city most aware of a decline in childhood mortality, Mexico City, is the one which reports the highest losses of children.

The median number of living children is 11 percent below the median number of live births for Mexico City women. The corresponding measure for Buenos Aires is only 6 percent. Mexico City women also evidence the highest fertility, and San José, ranking second in awareness of mortality trends, also averages a high number of live births. These data do not indicate that knowledge of declining childhood mortality has produced a corresponding decline in fertility.

For both groups in all cities, the proportion of better-educated women who were aware of declining infant mortality was at least half again as high as for the poorer-educated women. For similar education levels, older groups showed much higher awareness than younger ones.

With respect to knowledge of population growth, women in Mexico City (96 percent) and San José (90 percent) are again much more aware than are those from all other cities except Buenos Aires. For each of the five cities this item was positively associated with education and, to a lesser degree, age. The lowest percentage for any group was 61 percent for the young, less-educated in Rio de Janeiro; the highest was 99 percent for the old, more-educated in Mexico City.

§ IDEAL FAMILY SIZE AND FERTILITY PERFORMANCE

Both education and age are highly associated with number of children ever borne and number still living. Among young and old groups the less-educated have borne more children, with the differential being a bit smaller for living children than for live births. In Caracas, Rio de Janeiro, and Mexico City, the young, less-educated women had borne approximately the same number of children as the old, more-educated women who had been married some twelve years longer. Variations based on education and city produced wide differences in median number of live births: from 2.4 for old, more-educated women in Buenos Aires to 6.2 for old, less-educated women in Mexico City.

Variations in ideal family size are similar in pattern to those of fertility, though the differentials are not as great. In five cities, the stated ideal number of children for a "family" (here designated as "normative ideal family size") came out slightly higher than the preference for one's own family if one were beginning it anew (designated as "personal ideal family size"). For Mexico City the two measures were virtually identical. The median number of children considered ideal for one's own family ranged from 2.8 for both young groups in Buenos Aires and for young, more-educated women in Rio de Janeiro to 5.1 for the old, less-educated group in Mexico City. Corresponding values for normative ideal family size were 3.0 and 5.1.

In five of the six cities, the old, less-educated have had more births than the number indicated for their personal ideal family size. This also is true for the young, less-educated in Rio de Janeiro and the old, more-educated in Bogotá. In all these cases, however, if the median number of *living* children is taken as the measure of family size, it is seen to be either below or very close to the ideal number of children which would be desired if the respondent were just beginning her family.

The young, better-educated women want the smallest-size family. The young, poorer-educated women also want fewer children than do the old groups in both education levels. In the two cities with the smallest ideal family size, Buenos Aires and Rio de Janeiro, the young, less-educated have chosen smaller ideal sizes for their own family size than has any other of the four age-education groups. Viewed across the age-education classification and intercity comparison, fertility performance is directly associated with ideal family size.

§ PRIOR CONSIDERATION AND DISCUSSION OF IDEAL FAMILY SIZE

The relationship between a woman's personal ideal family size and actual fertility might depend on the degree to which the ideal has seriously been considered and on the kind of action taken to achieve the ideal. For such action to be effective, the cooperation of the husband is helpful or necessary for most contraceptive methods. (Anovulent pills were not available or even known to the great majority of the women interviewed at the time of the surveys.) Accordingly, women were asked whether they had ever thought prior to the interview of how many children they would like to have and whether they had discussed this topic with their husbands. Both age and education are strongly related to these variables, as may be seen in Table 34. More of the young and the better-educated women report having thought about the number of children they want and having discussed this subject with their spouses. Values are similar for the young, less-educated and the old, more-educated, but consistently higher for the latter. Not surprisingly, more women have thought about an ideal number of children than have discussed it with their husbands, but the tendency is especially pronounced among the older women and in the city of Caracas.

The highest percentages of women who had thought about and discussed number of children desired were found among the young, more-educated in Buenos Aires, while minimum measures were recorded for the old, less-educated women of Bogotá. The strength of relationship of these items with age and education is revealed in comparisons of individual age-education groups for the different cities. In considering the possible consequences of thought and discussion about family size on ideals and performance, it is worthy of note that the young, better-educated women of Bogotá had more children and a larger ideal family size than the old, poorer-educated women of Buenos Aires, who reportedly thought about and discussed the topic less. This indicates that the variables considered in this section operate within a strong cultural context of values.

§ ATTITUDES TOWARD BIRTH CONTROL

One of the prerequisites for individual fertility control is acceptance and justification of the process, here measured by three survey items: the percentage of women who condemn family limitation under all circumstances, the percentage who consider limitation justified for economic reasons, and the percentage who state that they would take a pill to prevent pregnancy.

For the first two items, rankings of the four age-education groups are similar to those for previous items, except that among the more-educated groups there is a lower percentage completely opposed to birth control among those age thirty-five and over than among those below thirty-five. For the women with less education the younger women are less opposed to birth control than are the older ones.

The percentage registering categoric disapproval is shown in Table 35. Values ranged from 1 percent for the young, less-educated in Buenos Aires to 23 percent of the old, less-educated in Mexico City. For Buenos Aires, only the old women with little education had more than 2 percent in this disapproving category, while all four groups in both Bogotá and Mexico City had at least 8 percent registering complete disapproval.

Those women who were *not* totally opposed to birth control were asked under what circumstances they would consider it justified.

TABLE 35

Categorical Disapproval of Birth Control, by Age-Education
Categories for Ever-mated Women of Six Cities, 1963–64

Age and Education	Bogotá	Buenos Aires	Caracas	Mexico City	Rio de Janeiro	San José
			Percentage Disapproving Birth Control under All Conditions			
Total	12	2	9	16	11	9
Young-High ed.	10	2	6	10	7	4
Old-High ed.	8	2	5	9	9	10
Young-Low ed.	15	1	10	20	14	12
Old-Low ed.	14	4	12	23	15	13

Among the answers, two indicated a modern attitude favoring low fertility: approval in all cases—which received minimal response— and approval in cases where the family had insufficient money. The latter response is used as the measure of variability on this item.

Those who approved in case of economic need ranged from a low of 30 percent of the old, less-educated group in Caracas to 71 percent of the young, more-educated group for Buenos Aires. The old, less-educated women consistently had lower proportions with "yes" answers to this question, and in all of the cities except Buenos Aires the proportion was only slightly above the minimum reported above for Caracas. Only minor differences were recorded between the two middle groups—old-high education and young-low education. In all cities the group which had the highest proportion approving birth control for economic reasons was the young–high-education group (Table 36).

The approval of family limitation for economic reasons represents a rational approach to reproduction and child rearing that permits a balancing of different values. It could represent a desire for material goods instead of children. Given the phrasing of the question: ". . . if the family has insufficient money," approval of family limitation is more likely to represent a concern for total family welfare which can best be achieved if family size is controlled.[11] Young, better-educated women who rank highest on this item would be personally aware of the advantages of education and would be expected to take the most logical approach to the achievement of family welfare and upward social mobility.

The attitudes toward acceptance and use of a pill to prevent pregnancy generally are inversely related to the other variables favoring low fertility, such as use of birth control methods. Also, the cities with high-fertility attitudes and performance report a higher degree of acceptance of the pill than those cities with low fertility and small-family ideals. Percentages of would-be users of the pill ranged from 13 percent of the old, more-educated in Buenos Aires to 48 percent of the young, less-educated in Mexico City.

It should be noted that only in Mexico City did more than 7 percent of all women report having any previous knowledge of the pill. However, the women who show the highest degree of willingness to use the pill, those under thirty-five with less than an elementary school education, constitute the group whose members have least knowledge of contraception, have an average of more than fifteen fecund years remaining, and are in most cases within one child of

TABLE 36

Economic Motivation for Family Limitation and Attitude
toward the Pill, by Age-Education Categories for
Ever-mated Women of Six Cities, 1963–1964

Age and Education	Bogotá	Buenos Aires	Caracas	Mexico City	Rio de Janeiro	San José
	Percentage Approving Family Limitation in Case of Economic Need (*Item* 6)					
Total	42	63	41	39	40	43
Young-High ed.	52	71	56	48	48	54
Old-High ed.	43	60	42	39	38	39
Young-Low ed.	39	68	38	38	43	43
Old-Low ed.	31	54	30	31	31	34
	Percentage Willing to Use Pill to Prevent Pregnancy					
Total	40	19	32	32	21	34
Young-High ed.	46	18	36	38	23	43
Old-High ed.	27	17	17	24	13	21
Young-Low ed.	48	24	46	41	31	42
Old-Low ed.	34	21	21	22	18	25

attaining their stated ideal family size. We may hypothesize that they viewed the pill as a solution to a pressing problem, while the older and better-educated women had less need for a purported remedy about which they had limited knowledge. Now that information about the pill has been widely circulated, replication of this part of the study would probably show a higher proportion of acceptors among the better-educated women. This item is not used in the rank-comparison charts because of the high percentage of respondents with no knowledge of the pill.

§ KNOWLEDGE OF BIRTH CONTROL

In all cities four-fifths or more of the ever-married women reported that they had heard of some form of birth control when presented a specific list of methods.[12] Education is an important correlate of knowledge. For the women under thirty-five, the percentage with no birth control knowledge was about twice as high among women with less than an elementary education than among women of similar age who had completed elementary school. Among the older women there was less differential with respect to education. With education controlled, the older women in all cities had a larger percentage who reported no knowledge of any method. This was more pronounced among the better-educated. Young, better-educated women of Buenos Aires had the lowest percentage of uninformed (3 percent), while 35 percent of the old, poorer-educated in Caracas and 29 percent in Bogotá reported no knowledge of a method.

Age appears to be a more important correlate of knowledge than education. While the young, more-educated in all cities have the lowest percentage with no birth control knowledge and the old, less-educated have the highest, in five of the six cities the young, less-educated are better informed than the old, more-educated.

§ USE OF BIRTH CONTROL

Use of birth control is positively associated with education and age, education appearing to be the more important in terms of our two-by-two classification scheme (Table 37). In all cities both the better-educated groups have higher proportions of users than either poorer-educated group. The range is from a low of 34 percent of the young, less-educated group in Mexico City to 81 percent of the more-educated groups in Buenos Aires. Within the latter city, the

TABLE 37

Knowledge and Use of Birth Control, by Age-Education
Categories for Ever-mated Women of Six Cities, 1963–1964

Age and Education	Bogotá	Buenos Aires	Caracas	Mexico City	Rio de Janeiro	San José
Percentage Not Knowing Any BC Method (Item 7)						
Total	17	7	21	16	14	18
Young-High ed.	7	3	9	9	5	9
Old-High ed.	21	9	24	18	15	18
Young-Low ed.	15	6	20	14	11	20
Old-Low ed.	29	10	35	23	27	26
Percentage Ever Having Used Any Method (Item 8)						
Total	50	79	68	47	61	71
Young-High ed.	56	81	76	52	68	78
Old-High ed.	62	81	78	64	67	76
Young-Low ed.	35	75	59	34	51	68
Old-Low ed.	49	76	64	44	56	60
Percentage Having Used Appliance Methods or Sterilization (Item 9)						
Total	15	47	29	17	24	36
Young-High ed.	24	55	54	24	35	48
Old-High ed.	22	50	38	25	26	41
Young-Low ed.	7	40	21	9	19	31
Old-Low ed.	9	35	17	11	15	21

young, less-educated women had the lowest proportion of birth control users, 75 percent, but this is more than 5 percentage points higher than for the highest-ranking groups in Mexico City, Bogotá, or Rio de Janeiro.

The types of birth control methods used are also related to education, more of the better educated having used the more effective appliance methods or sterilization.[13] Moreover, women under thirty-five had distinctly higher proportions using the more effective methods than women of similar education who were thirty-five and over. (Methods classified as more effective include sterilization, diaphragm, condom, jelly, and pill, as opposed to rhythm, douche, and withdrawal.[14]) Additionally, we believe that employment of appliance methods or sterilization requires more motivation for initial use than the "natural" methods of rhythm and withdrawal, or of douche, which may be used for cleanliness as well as contraception.

The highest percentage of any group reporting use of more effective methods was 55 percent for the young, better-educated women of Buenos Aires, while the young, poorer-educated of Bogotá, with only 7 percent, were at the other extreme. On a city basis, the ratio of women reporting use of effective methods to women reporting use of any birth control method ranged from a low of 0.3 for Bogotá to 0.6 for Buenos Aires, and is directly correlated with the proportion of women who are users of any method.

§ GRAPHIC RANK COMPARISONS

Graphic comparison of age-education groups on KAP variables is shown in Figures 4 to 10, which are rank profiles on selected fertility variables for women grouped by age and education. These figures are similar to Figure 3, except that vertically they are divided into four divisions for the four age-education groups, each with four subdivisions to represent the four possible ranks. Figure 4 presents combined data for the four age-education groups from all six cities. Values plotted in this chart are average ranks. On five items the young–high-education group ranked first in all six cities. Therefore, this group was assigned first rank overall for those items. Calculated average rank was used when the case was not so clear-cut. In several instances this resulted in ties. For example, on item 6, percent approving family limitation for economic reasons, both the young women with low education and old women with high education had three ranks of second and three ranks of third. In case of ties, the points were plotted at the midpoint between the two rank values. Expected ranks are shown by dashed lines. They represent the overall theoretical ranks on values favorable to low fertility for all groups and are the same for Figures 4 to 10. Theoretical rank order based on our hypotheses is as follows:

1. Young-High education
2. Old-High education
3. Young-Low education
4. Old-Low education

As seen in Figure 4, the two extreme groups are in fact the young, more-educated, with low-fertility values and performance, and the

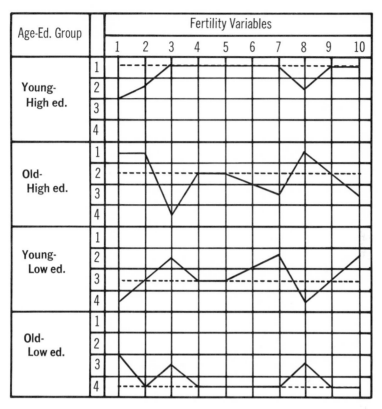

Age-Ed. Group		Fertility Variables									
		1	2	3	4	5	6	7	8	9	10
Young-High ed.	1										
	2										
	3										
	4										
Old-High ed.	1										
	2										
	3										
	4										
Young-Low ed.	1										
	2										
	3										
	4										
Old-Low ed.	1										
	2										
	3										
	4										

FIGURE 4.
Six Latin American cities

old, less-educated, with high-fertility values and performance, as expected. Deviations from theoretical rank for these two groups are less than those of the intermediate groups. The same is true of Figures 5 to 10 for the individual cities. The variation between the rankings of older women with more education and the younger women with less are sensitive to the relative strength of association of age and education with respect to variables related to fertility. For three variables, age and education function in the same direction. This is contrary to the expected negative relationship between age of women and values favorable to low fertility. Graphic evidence is seen in the rank-comparison charts. On item 1, age at first marital union, all young groups are below their theoretical rank. On items 2 and 8, awareness of declining childhood mortality and use of any birth

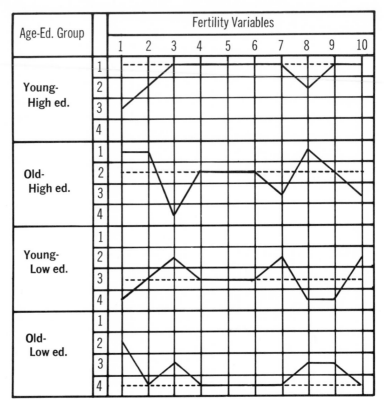

FIGURE 5.
Bogotá

control method, all young groups which do not hold their theoretical rank hold a lower one. Deviations of old groups from the normative ranks on those two items are all upward. But for other variables, age and education are counteracting and ranks are as hypothesized. This is especially true for items 4 and 5, prior consideration and discussion of ideal family size.

Within any one city, differences between the four age-education categories with respect to individual variables could be the result, at least partially, of other factors such as urban-rural background or labor-force status. Comparisons, however, are made between age-education groupings for six cities which differ widely in many cultural characteristics. If a consistent pattern of age-education differentiation is obtained with respect to a fertility-related variable for all or most of the cities, it may reasonably be expected to hold true for Latin American cities in general, whatever the underlying causes may be.

A remarkable degree of consistency exists among the rankings. There is no variable for which ranks both above and below the normative rank are recorded for any age-education group. While the extreme groups—young-high education and old-low education—can vary only in one direction, the intermediate groups can rank either higher or lower than hypothesized. The older women with more education fell below their expected second rank in five out of six cities on item 3—personal ideal family size. They generally perferred larger families than the other groups. On the other hand, this same group ranked first, above even the young–high-education group, in

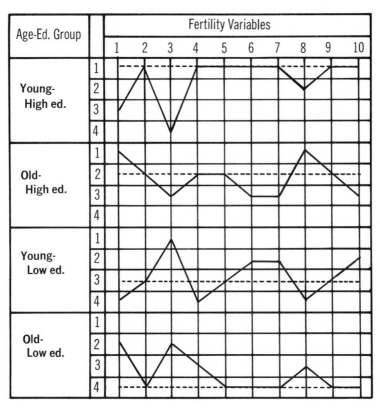

FIGURE 6.
Buenos Aires

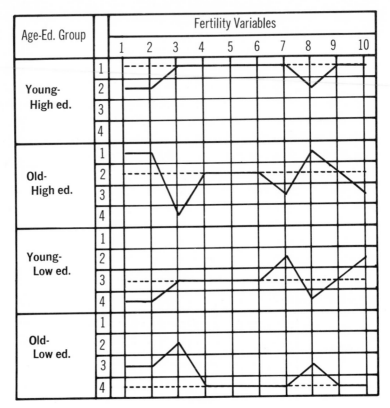

FIGURE 7.
Caracas

five out of six cities on item 2—awareness of declining infant mortality.

A positive relationship between educational level of women and knowledge, attitudes, and practices favoring low fertility exists in the rank-comparison charts. When groups of women of the same age category but different education are compared in Figure 4, only one measure relates in a way not hypothesized. Among the women thirty-five and over, personal ideal family size (item 3) is higher for the high education group than it is for the low, and in Buenos Aires (Figure 6) it is the young women with more education who would like to have the most children of any group, though quantitative variation is low. Except for personal ideal family size, there is no case in which the high education group does not have lower-fertility values when age is controlled.

A simple representation of the basic relationship between age and education and the fertility-related variables may be seen in the relative positions of the two intermediate lines representing the older women with more education and the younger women with less education. When they are in their expected positions, rank 2 for old-high education and rank 3 for young-low education, the hypothesized relationships exist: high education and young age are associated with knowledge, attitudes, and practices favoring low controlled fertility, and the relationship is stronger for education than for age (as defined by our dichotomous measure). This situation holds for items 4, 5, and 9—prior consideration of ideal family size, discussion with husband of number of children wanted, and use of the more effective methods of birth control. The intermediate graph lines move toward each other when the old, more-educated group is below its

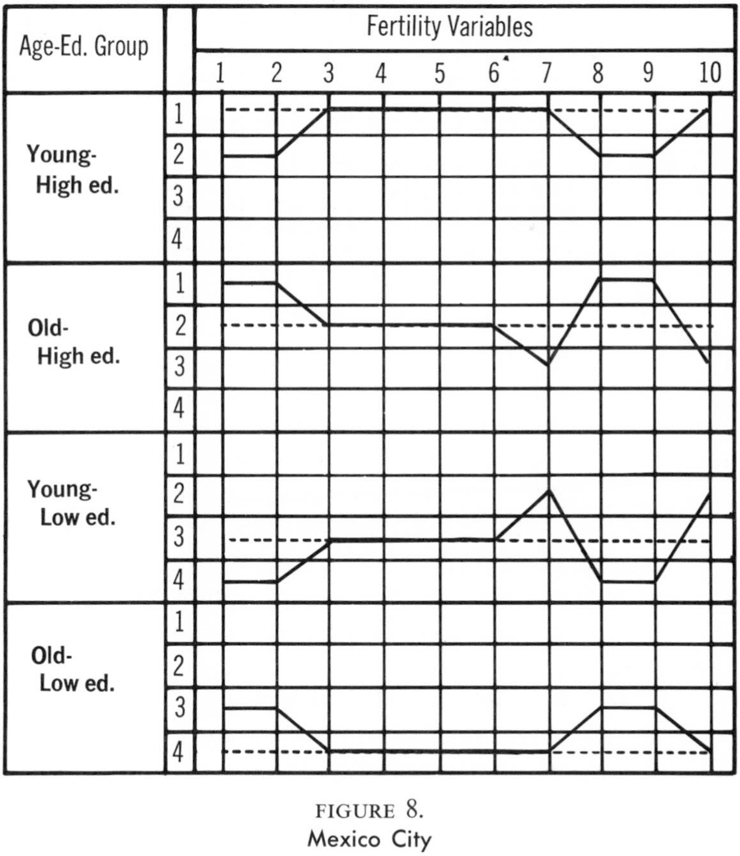

FIGURE 8.
Mexico City

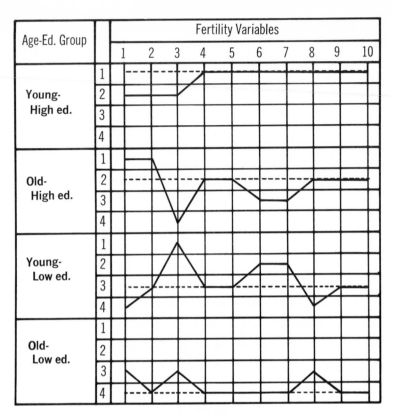

FIGURE 9.
Rio de Janeiro

expected rank and the young, less-educated is higher than expected. This indicates that youthfulness is more strongly associated with low-fertility values on specific variables than is high education; this is the case with items 3, 6, and 10—personal ideal family size, approval of family limitation for economic reasons, and total number of live births (the last for obvious reasons). A divergence of the rank graph lines, with the old, more educated group above expectation and the young, less-educated below, indicates a contradiction of Hypothesis 2, which postulates a negative association between age of women and values associated with low fertility. For items 1, 2, and 8 the lines diverge. These variables are age at marriage, awareness of declining childhood mortality, and use of some form of birth control. The latter two variables are of a type for which the added opportunities and exposure of approximately twelve additional years of age and married life could be expected to produce higher rank. These findings and others are discussed in the following profile descriptions of age-education groups.

SUMMARY PROFILES FOR AGE-EDUCATION GROUPS

§ YOUNG-HIGH EDUCATION

This is the group of women with the knowledge, attitudes, and practices most likely to produce low fertility. Not only have they borne the fewest children, but their chances of achieving their moderate family size ideals are reasonably good. Their lowest rank is on age at marriage, for which they are tied between second and third

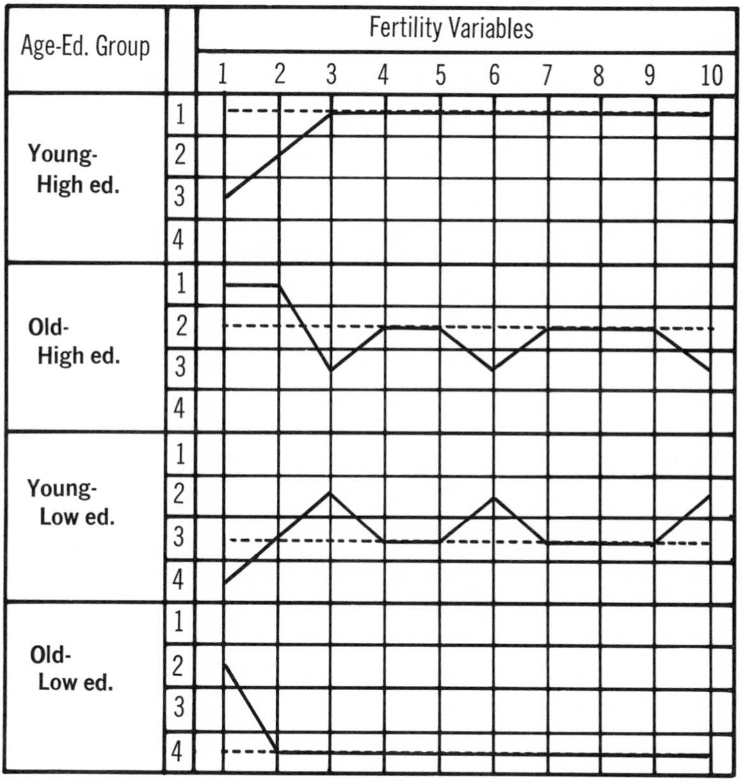

FIGURE 10.
San José

with the old, less-educated women. On attitude toward birth control they have the highest percentage who stated economic need as a situation which would justify family limitation. However, in four out of the six cities this group had higher percentages categorically opposed to family limitation than did the old–high-education group. In every city the young, better-educated women are most likely to know some method of birth control, and in proportions who have ever used birth control they are second only to the older women of high education, who have had more opportunity and reason to practice family limitation. On use of the more effective methods the young, better-educated again rank first.

§ OLD-HIGH EDUCATION

The women over thirty-five who have completed elementary school represent something of an elite since they received more education at a time when education was restricted to a smaller proportion of the female population than it is today. This could indicate a high proportion with urban background which, like education, is associated with low fertility. Nevertheless, the old, better-educated women rank second to the young, better-educated on most items and sometimes fall below the young women with less education, when young age and high education both favor a low-fertility value. This group married later than any other and has the highest percentages both knowing about and having used some form of birth control. They also are most knowledgeable about population growth and mortality trends.

On one item, acceptance of the pill, the old, more-educated group ranks at the bottom. Perhaps they do not need it, since they have a median age of forty-two, and in five of the six cities their average number of living children is less than their stated personal ideal family size. It is likely that ideals regarding family size are conditioned to some extent by past fertility, but this seems an inadequate explanation of the ability of these women to stay within their goals. The goals are not much different from those of the other groups, but number of children borne is substantially lower than for women of similar age and less education.

§ YOUNG-LOW EDUCATION

The young women who have not completed elementary school fall between the better-educated groups and the group of older, poorer-educated women. Starting out in families of orientation larger than any other group, they also married at the earliest ages. At time of interview they had borne more children than women their own age with more education. While their personal size ideal family is smaller than for older women, their chances of *not* exceeding their ideal size are slim. With an average age of twenty-eight, they are in almost all cases within one child of surpassing the number of children they consider ideal for a hypothetical new family.

The young, less-educated are a middle group with respect to attitudes toward family limitation, except for willingness to use a pill to avoid pregnancy. In all cities they rank above all other groups on this item. They rank second of the four groups in knowledge of birth control and ranked lowest in proportion of women who have ever used any method. Among those who have used birth control, however, a higher proportion of these women have used the more effective methods than have the older women with low education. In general, where age is a strong factor and youth favors modern low-fertility values, they score similarly to the old–high-education group. Where age brings knowledge, their rank is generally lower.

§ OLD-LOW EDUCATION

This group of women already has had a greater number of children than any other group, and the women's attitudes and practices are such that they are likely to have more, even though most of them already have exceeded their ideal family size. To a certain extent age has brought knowledge and an attempt to limit fertility. More of the old, less-educated know some form of birth control than do the young, less-educated. This relationship holds also for the practice of birth control in some form. On only one item do the old, less-educated group rank higher than either more-educated group. The proportion willing to use a pill to prevent pregnancy is higher for this group than for women of similar age but with more education.

CONCLUSION

The importance of age and education is amply indicated in the summary profile descriptions of the four age-education categories of women. Young women with high education are most favorable to low fertility, and older women with low education least favorable.

While normally functioning in opposite directions, as noted above, age and education function in combination on certain items related to fertility. In these cases older age has an effect similar to higher education.

Intercity variation was greater than within-city variations by age and education in respect to several measures of fertility. More intercultural studies are needed to discover which elements of the culture are most important as determinants of fertility and to explore the manner in which they function.

A positive relationship between educational level of women in childbearing ages and knowledge, attitudes, and practices favoring low fertility was postulated in Hypothesis 1. Such a relationship was found in all six cities and on all variables investigated, with one minor variation. Older women in the higher-education group stated larger ideal personal family sizes than women of the three other groups, including women of similar age and less education. The expected negative relationship between age of women and values related to low fertility was only partially verified. Younger women were found more likely than older women to know about birth control and to approve of family limitation. However, the older women included higher proportions who had practiced birth control. Younger women did report smaller ideal family sizes and were much more likely than the older group to have used the more effective contraceptive methods to achieve these sizes. Apparently, many who favor family limitation do not begin practicing it until they approach or reach their goals for family size.

According to Hypothesis 3 we expected to find education more strongly related to low fertility values than age. This was true for most variables, notably number of children wanted and discussion of this topic with the spouse. Knowledge and use of the more effective methods of birth control also were more closely associated with higher level of education than with younger age.

The hypothesized relationships between age and education and the fertility-related variables within cities were expected to hold true for intercity comparisons as well. Generally this position was supported, but not in all cases. Thus, cultural influences must be taken into account when generalizations are made concerning the effects of broad variables, such as age and education, on fertility.

Differential fertility with respect to education has existed in the cities studied for more than a generation. Women who have completed elementary school have borne fewer children than women of comparable age and less education, but their mothers also bore fewer children than the mothers of women with less education. In every group fertility ideals and performance substantially lower than the family size of their mother were reported.

Fertility may be declining in Latin America, and it should continue to go down as education increases. While we have not established a cause-and-effect pattern, a strong positive relationship has been found between education and knowledge, attitudes, and practices favorable to low fertility. This is strengthened by the generational trend reflected in the higher degree of favorability of women under thirty-five toward low fertility.

NOTES

1. Ronald Freedman, P. K. Whelpton, and Arthur A. Campbell, *Family Planning, Sterility and Population Growth* (New York: McGraw-Hill Book Company, 1959), pp. 288–295; Robert O. Carleton, "Fertility Trends and Differentials in Latin America," *Components of Population Change in Latin America,* in Clyde V. Kiser (ed.), *Milbank Memorial Fund Quarterly,* vol. XLIII, no. 4, part 2, October 1965, pp. 15–31; Ansley J. Coale, "Factors Associated with the Development of Low Fertility: An Historic Summary," in *Proceedings of the World Population Conference, Belgrade, 1965* (New York: United Nations, 1967), vol. II, pp. 205–209; J. Mayone Stycos, "Education and Fertility in Puerto Rico," in *ibid.,* vol. IV, pp. 177–180.

2. See Refs. 1 and 2 plus A. J. Jaffe, *People, Jobs and Economic Development* (New York: The Free Press of Glencoe, Inc., 1959), pp. 183–184; and Robert O. Carleton, "The Effect of Educational Improvements on Fertility Trends in Latin America," in *Proceedings of the World Population Conference, Belgrade, 1965,* vol. IV, pp. 141–145.

3. Although Panama City was one of the survey cities, Panamanian data were not available in a form comparable to that of the other cities when the tabulations were made. This necessitated the exclusion of Panama City from the present analysis.

4. J. Mayone Stycos, "Survey Research and Population Control in Latin America," *The Public Opinion Quarterly,* vol. XXVIII, no. 3, Fall 1964, pp. 367–372; Carmen Miró and Ferdinand Rath, "Preliminary Findings of Comparative Fertility Surveys in Three Latin American Cities," in Kiser, *op. cit.,* pp. 36–62; and Carmen A. Miró, "Some Misconceptions Disproved: A Program of Comparative Fertility Surveys in Latin America," in Bernard Berelson et al. (eds.), *Family Planning and Population Programs* (Chicago and London: University of Chicago Press, 1966), pp. 615–634.

5. In the one instance of a tie, the rank for each city was plotted halfway between ranks 1 and 2. As we might expect, some cities are constantly high in rank, others low, and others tend toward middle rankings. If a city scored first on all ten variables, it would have a total score (the sum of the ranks) of 10 (values most favorable to low fertility), a score approximated by Buenos Aires with 13.5. A city scoring last (sixth) on all ten variables would have a total rank score of 60, approximated by Bogotá with 51. Thus Buenos Aires is consistently the most and Bogotá the least favorable to low fertility values. The other scores are 25 for San José, 33.5 for Rio, 38 for Caracas, and 49 for Mexico City.

6. A note of caution is given concerning interpretation of the comparative rank graphs shown in the charts. Such an arrangement, by allowing equal space for each variable, implies equal importance. Even if we could assign relative degrees of importance, however, it would be very difficult to depict this graphically in understandable form. The reader should keep in mind that differences shown are differences in rank and that the relative positions of two ranks on the chart are the same whether the difference between them is great or small.

7. See Miró and Rath, *op. cit.,* p. 39.

8. Miró, *op. cit.,* p. 620.

9. Elementary school consists of six grades for all cities except Bogotá, where it consists of five. The public education system of Argentina includes one year of schooling prior to first grade, making a total of seven years of instruction for completion of elementary school. Instituto Interamericano de Estadística, *América en Cifras, 1965. Situación Cultural: Educación y Otros Aspectos Culturales* (Washington: Pan American Union, 1967), pp. 2, 67–68.

10. For several of the variables the distribution used in the tables and charts constitutes only a portion of the distribution for which chi-square values were calculated, and in all cases the actual frequencies have been converted to percentages, or summary measures. For example, medians are used to express age or family size, while specific ages or numbers of children ever borne, or desired, formed the categories in the full distributions. The percentage of women reporting no knowledge of any method of birth control is taken as the most representative single measure in a tabulation of number of methods known. In cases such as these the measures of significance as obtained are not strictly applicable to the data as presented. Nevertheless, the variables used are comparable to the broader distributions from which they were taken and may be considered representative of them.

11. In Puerto Rico both Hatt and Stycos found that there was a desire to provide adequate subsistence and education to all children, which was coupled with a desire for small families. J. M. Stycos, *Family and Fertility in Puerto Rico* (New York: Columbia University Press, 1955), pp. 160–161, 169.

12. Methods listed were douche, sterilization, diaphragm, jelly, rhythm, condom, withdrawal, and pills. Respondents also were asked if they knew any other methods. Abortion was *not* included. The percentages shown in Table 37 for women ever using any method were obtained by subtracting from 100 the percentage who had never used any form of birth control. This procedure, made necessary by lack of more specific tabulations, may include a small "no answer" category in the "users of birth control" category.

13. These data are consistent with interpretations of Requena from a 1962-1963 study in Santiago, Chile. He hypothesizes that education is conducive not only to the use of contraceptives but also to the use of effective measures. Mariano B. Requena, "Studies of Family Planning in the Quinta Normal District of Santiago," in Kiser, *op. cit.*, p. 74.

14. Charles F. Westoff, Robert G. Potter, Jr., Philip C. Sagi, and Elliot G. Mishler, *Family Growth in Metropolitan America* (Princeton, N.J.: Princeton University Press, 1961), p. 362.

CHAPTER 13

Attitudes, Information, and Fertility in Medellín, Colombia

Prepared by **Robert B. Hartford.**

THE CONTROL OF FERTILITY IN MEDELLÍN, COLOMBIA

With more than three-quarters of a million inhabitants, Medellín is Colombia's second largest city, and certainly one of its fastest growing. According to the last two censuses, its average rate of growth in the past decade has been just under 10 percent per year. Throughout Latin America Antioqueños are noted for their pride and vitality. The Department has become the economic heart of Colombia, possessing a thriving light machinery and textile industry, in addition to coffee agriculture; the capitalistic activity of its inhabitants has been favorably compared to that of the best Western businessmen.

Paradoxically, these modern attributes coexist with more traditional values: Antioqueños are also famed for their conservative political leanings and their strong allegiance to the Catholic religion.[1] Large families with numerous children are said to characterize the region, and the city of Medellín has persistently registered a crude birth rate in excess of 40 per 1,000. It was this unusual combination of high fertility and traditional values with a high degree of urban economic development which prompted our selection of Medellín as the site for a survey of human fertility in 1966.

The study was sponsored by the Division of Population Studies of the Colombian Association of Medical Faculties, with financial support from the Population Council of New York, and was directed by the author in collaboration with Dr. Mario Jaramillo Gomez,[2] director of the Centro Piloto de Planificación Familiar. Among other objectives, the project was designed to provide benchmark data on attitudes, practices, and knowledge related to marital fertility and fertility control, in order to plan a public government-sponsored program of family planning in Medellín. The sample was confined to currently mated females between fifteen and forty-nine years of age residing within the municipal boundaries in either legally sanctioned or consensual unions. So that the entire spectrum of the childbearing period for all socioeconomic classes of females would be well represented, a sample of roughly 2,000 cases was stratified into twenty-eight categories of equal size. The categories were generated by the cross-classification of seven 5-year age groups and four education categories.[3]

Although deviating somewhat from the ideal number of sixty-nine cases per cell, Table 38 shows that with few exceptions there are a sufficient number of observations per cell to ensure a reasonable degree of statistical reliability.

The interviewing was conducted in the fall of 1966 by twenty women who had completed a six-week training course and supervised field practice. Their ages ranged from eighteen to fifty, with approximately three-fourths of the group between thirty and forty years of

TABLE 38

Respondents Classified by Age and Education

	Years of Education Completed				
Age	0–2	3–4	5–6	7+	Total
15–19	53	48	36	24	161
20–24	72	110	88	70	340
25–29	81	87	75	80	323
30–34	68	89	83	71	311
35–39	75	89	64	73	301
40–44	73	66	59	71	269
45–49	65	57	46	66	234
Total	487	546	451	455	1,939

age. While predominantly of middle- and upper-middle-class backgrounds, few had completed secondary school.

The interview schedule included a fertility and marital history and a large number of items relevant to the knowledge and use of birth control. In view of the system of sample stratification, our analysis focuses on the independent variables of age and education. In investigating the factors crucial in determining the control of fertility, such as knowledge and use of birth control, we shall stress the role of education; in our analysis of the course of fertility itself, we shall stress the role of age as well.

§ THE DETERMINANTS OF CONTRACEPTIVE USAGE

The practice of birth control is related not only indirectly to one's education, but more directly to the amount of information and degree of concern which one has about limiting family size. But all these factors are mutually interrelated. From Table 39, e.g., we see that whether a woman knows about birth control (or has thought or talked about it or practiced it) is closely related to her educational level. Consequently, we will wish to examine the relation between contraceptive usage and such social-psychological variables as knowledge

TABLE 39

Selected KAP Variables, by Education, Medellín

	Years of Education				
	0–2	3–4	5–6	7+	*Total¶*
Percent know one or more methods*	63	78	84	91	78
Percent have thought about ideal†	58	68	69	74	67
Percent discussed birth control‡	32	45	52	66	47
Percent ever used birth control§	30	40	57	69	47
Number of cases	488	545	451	455	1939

*To "know" a method, the respondent was required either to know how to use a method or to know how one works; simply having heard of a method does not constitute "knowing" a method.

†Those responding positively to the question: "Have you ever thought about how many children you would like to have?"

‡Those responding positively to the question: "Have you and your husband ever talked about the possibility of trying to prevent or space births?"

§Those responding ever-using, without regard to duration or regulation of usage, any one of the following methods: rhythm, the pill, withdrawal, condom, IUD, diaphragm, jellies, creams, suppositories, or folk methods.

¶Standardized for education.

of birth control, the existence of an ideal family size, and husband-wife communication on birth control, holding constant the educational level. The relation of education to usage, moreover, may vary depending upon the status of the social-psychological variables. From Table 39, e.g., we noted a regular increase in the prior existence of an ideal family size with increasing education.[4] Table 40 shows, however, that this is only true for women who know about birth control. For those who do not, not only are they much less likely at every educational level to have thought about an ideal family size, but there is essentially no relation to degree of education.

Controlling knowledge also appears to have a profound effect on the relation between education and discussion of birth control (Figure 11). In the presence of knowledge the proportion having discussed birth control increases steadily from 45 to 72 percent as education rises; in the absence of knowledge not only are the proportions much lower, but there is no longer any relation to education. The values are so low that it seems reasonable to consider knowledge as a necessary condition for discussion, especially since it is difficult—though not impossible—to discuss birth control without specific knowledge of some contraceptive method. Finally, discussion of birth control appears to be more closely related to education and knowledge of a method than does the existence of an ideal family size.

Discussion, however, is much more closely associated with use of

TABLE 40

Percent Who Have Ever Thought about Their Ideal
Number of Children, by Education and Knowledge of
Contraceptive Methods*

	Years of Education				
Knowledge	0–2	3–4	5–6	7+	Total†
One or more	64	71	72	76	70
methods	(315)	(428)	(388)	(421)	(1552)
None	49	61	54	52	55
	(173)	(117)	(63)	(34)	(387)
Total	58	68	69	74	67
	(488)	(545)	(451)	(455)	(1939)

*Denominator n's are given in parentheses.
†Standardized for education.

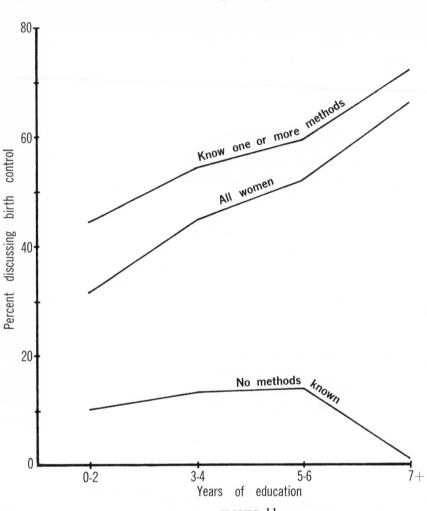

FIGURE 11.
Percent who have discussed birth control with spouse,
by knowledge of contraceptive methods and education.

birth control (Figure 12) than is ideal family size. This close association may in part be due to the size of the ideal and current birth parity. That is, a *small* family ideal may eventually lead to contraception, but only as the ideal number of children is neared or surpassed.[5] On the other hand, while discussion of birth control may not occur until the same conditions are met, once they are met, the

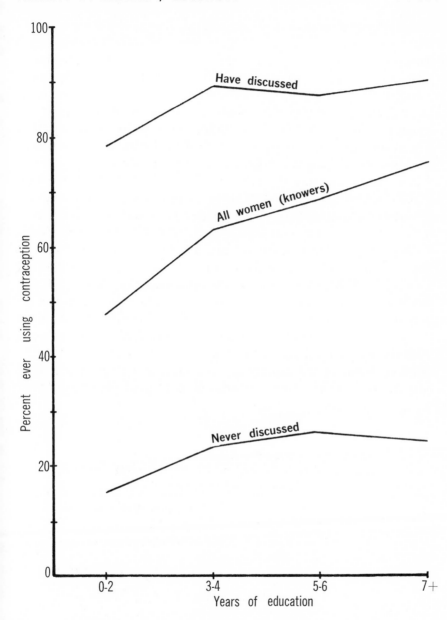

FIGURE 12.
Percent ever using contraception, by education and
discussion with spouse.

probability of discussion increases sharply. In spite of the apparently close association of discussion and usage, 42 to 55 percent of the contraceptors first discussed birth control during the same parity interval grouping in which they initiated contraception. Moreover, considering the high proportion of women who report discussing birth control only after they began to use it, we may suggest that discussion, as a *causal* factor in contraception usage, may be of less significance than the existence of an ideal family size. Discussion, in fact, may be little more than a covariate of usage.

Now let us measure the relation of discussion and the existence of ideal family size to usage of birth control, when the variables are considered simultaneously. We will simplify the analysis by confining it to women who know at least one method of birth control. Table 41 shows again that discussion bears a very close relation to usage, and the existence of an ideal size virtually no relation. Further, the association of education with usage disappears for those who have had more than three years of schooling. Therefore, the relation between usage and education seems to be largely explained by knowledge (proportion knowing a method increases about 50 percent from the lowest to highest educational category) and by the positive relations between the existence of the ideal and discussion to both education and usage. However, over 60 percent of the users of birth

TABLE 41

Ever-usage Rates by Prior Existence of Ideal Family Size,
Discussion of Birth Control, and Education, for Women Who
Know at Least One Method*

Prior Existence of Ideal	Discussed Birth Control	Years of Education			
		0–2	3–4	5–6	7+
Yes	Yes	80	91	88	91
		(111)	(176)	(184)	(236)
No	Yes	78	86	87	89
		(32)	(54)	(53)	(60)
Yes	No	24	34	36	33
		(87)	(129)	(97)	(79)
No	No	19	34	44	39
		(84)	(70)	(54)	(46)

*Denominator *n*'s are given in parentheses.

control have both thought about the ideal size and discussed birth control with their spouses.

In summary, the probability that a woman is a contraceptor is close to unity if she has had at least four years of education, knows of a specific birth control method, has ever thought of how many children she would like to have, and has discussed birth control with her spouse. Although the existence of the ideal may be related to usage, the probability of usage is reduced by less than 5 percent if the other conditions are met. Moreover, if the educational attainment of the woman is at least four years and if she meets the qualifications of knowledge and either the existence of the ideal *or* discussion of birth control, additional education has no effect on usage. In contrast, absence of discussion is associated with a substantial reduction in the probability of usage given the other conditions. Apparently, however, much of the relation between usage and discussion is only associative, since at least one-fourth of the women reported commencing contraception prior to discussion. It seems reasonable to conclude that usage and discussion are reciprocally related: in some cases discussion may precede and lead to usage, while in others the converse may be true. Discussion may play a more important role by increasing regularity and effectiveness of contraceptive practice, once contraception has been initiated.

§ FOUR BIRTH CONTROL METHODS: KNOWLEDGE,
ATTITUDES, AND USAGE

Rhythm, the anovulent pill (called the "pill" hereafter), the condom, and withdrawal constitute over 70 percent of the person-methods known and nearly 90 percent of those reported used. Knowledge of at least one of the four methods increases from about 63 to 91 percent as education rises from the lowest to the highest category (Figure 13). Knowledge of each specific method also increases with education, but the change is more pronounced in the cases of rhythm and the pill. Although withdrawal and the condom are more widely known among the lesser educated, rhythm and the pill are better known by those with seven years or more of education. Only a fifth of those with zero to two years of schooling, but two-thirds of those with seven or more years, know about the pill. Moreover, among the two lower educational groups, rhythm is the method least likely to be known.

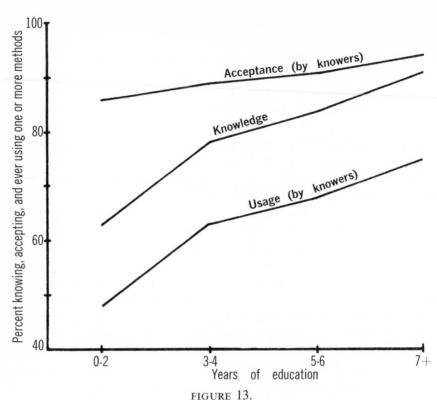

FIGURE 13.

Percent knowing, accepting, and ever using one or more
methods, by education.

The relation of knowledge to age is curvilinear, with a maximum occurring at the twenty-fifth- to twenty-ninth-year age group, suggesting an age-cohort increase in the prevalence of knowledge (Figure 14). A similar pattern prevails for each method. Although we cannot know with certainty, the initial increases are probably due to a combination of exposure and need, while the later decline is due to generational differences.

Ever-use of birth control or a positive response to the question, "Do you consider this method acceptable for your own use in some circumstance?" will be regarded here as indicating the acceptability of a method. While there are limitations to this definition, the assumption that ever-usage constitutes de facto acceptance should not be much in error. Acceptance rates are based only on those persons knowing the method, or, in the case of acceptance of any one method, on those who know at least one.

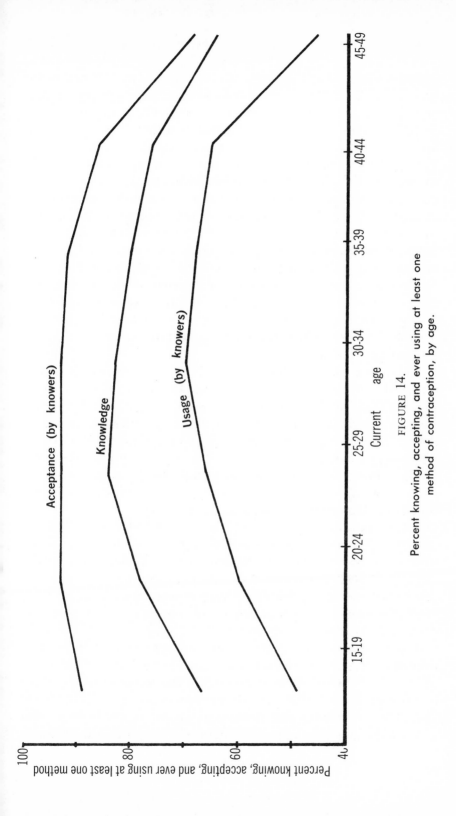

FIGURE 14.

Percent knowing, accepting, and ever using at least one method of contraception, by age.

About nine of every ten women who know a method find one or more methods acceptable. Unlike knowledge, acceptability increases only slightly with education. While acceptability of rhythm and the pill appears little affected by education, acceptance of the condom and withdrawal declines to a minimum among the best educated. The ranking of the methods from most to least approved is rhythm, withdrawal, the pill, and the condom. The only variation occurs at the highest educational level, where withdrawal drops below the pill in acceptance. With the exception of the condom at the extreme educational categories, knowledge of a method is more likely than not to be associated with acceptance. (It is also the case that the *better* the method is known, the more likely it is to be accepted.)

There are only minor variations of acceptance with age until age forty, after which a marked decline may be observed (Figure 14). This pattern is generally true for all four methods, suggesting a possible increase in the legitimization of birth control among the younger generation.[6]

Another way of measuring acceptability is by asking which method is preferred by women who know at least two methods. From Figure 15 we see that rhythm again generally emerges as the most preferred method, especially among the well educated. The pill is usually second choice but exhibits no regular pattern with education. Withdrawal follows a preference which declines with education; preference for the condom, lowest of all, is essentially unaffected by education.

The proportion of knowledgeable women who have ever used birth control doubles from the lowest to highest educational level (Figure 13). Withdrawal is the most widely used method by the three lower educational categories, followed by rhythm. Use of the pill increases with education, but lags far behind rhythm. Condom usage rises initially as well, but declines slightly over the higher educational levels. With the exception of the case of women with two or three years of education, among women who know the method in question, the condom is the method least used.

A curvilinear relation between age and use of birth control by women who know a method is seen in Figure 14 to be similar to the relation between age and knowledge. This might suggest a cohort increase in use as well as "need" conditioned increases at the lower ages. The patterns for individual methods are much the same, but vary somewhat in the apparent extent to which they are subject to

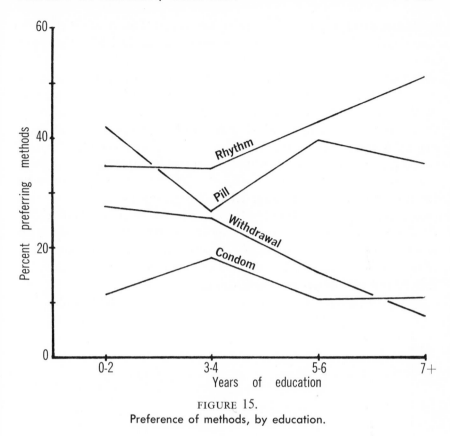

FIGURE 15.
Preference of methods, by education.

cohort increase phenomena (Figure 14). Of special interest is the marked increase in use of the pill among the younger women with seven or more years of education. These data suggest that the time of the interview marked a "take-off" point in the adoption of modern fertility control in Medellín.

Let us try to clarify the effects of need and cohort changes upon usage. If we take birth parity as an index of need and calculate the probability of becoming a contraceptor as a function of this index for each of several cohorts, it should be possible to control separately the two processes of change, need and cohort increases.[7] Since the time at which the methods were learned is not known, it is inadvisable to base the probabilities on the "knowers," for the control would operate inconsistently. Therefore, the probabilities based on all women reflect the effects of learning as well as adoption patterns of birth control (Figure 16). Substantial increases are present at every parity level, but particularly at the lower parities. We see that at the fourth-birth parity, the point at which approximately 75 percent of the women have attained their ideal number of children, only 30 percent of the women forty to forty-nine years of age had started to use contraceptives, while half of the women currently thirty to thirty-nine years of age and 70 percent of the youngest cohort had begun. Apparently cohort change has produced two types of increases in the probabilities: the maximum level has increased (from slightly over 60 percent to about 80 percent), and the rate of response to parity is more rapid. The latter effect may be illustrated more clearly by basing the probabilities only on the contraceptors themselves. Figure 17 shows an accelerated response pattern; the median parity at which contraceptors of the fifteen- to twenty-nine-year cohort first commenced usage was 1.2, about one birth before the second age cohort and two births before the third.

Since contraceptive knowledge and usage are limited among the

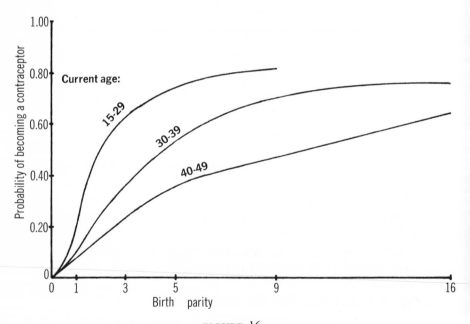

FIGURE 16.
Probability of becoming a contraceptor, by parity for
three age cohorts.

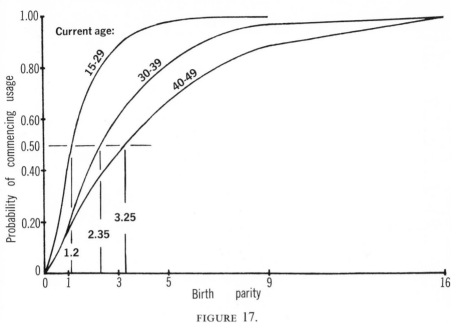

FIGURE 17.
Probability that contraceptors commence usage, by
parity for three age cohorts.

women of the sample, the age at which marital unions are first
formed may be of considerable significance in affecting completed
marital fertility. The median age at first union, determined graphically from the probability of marrying by a given age (Figure 18),
is 20.4 years for the highest educational category, about two years
later than for the lowest educational category. Although these differences probably have little significance for differential fertility, the
absolute levels indicate that there is a substantial reduction of the
risk to childbearing at all educational levels due to the number of
fecund years lost prior to union formation.

§ FERTILITY

In this section fertility will be measured by an estimate of completed live births, the gross completed fertility (GCF), which controls
for marital exposure and is standardized for age at first union. The
GCF is similar to Yaukey's "total fertility rate" in that constituent
rates are specific for five-year intervals subsequent to age at first
union, rather than age intervals.[8]

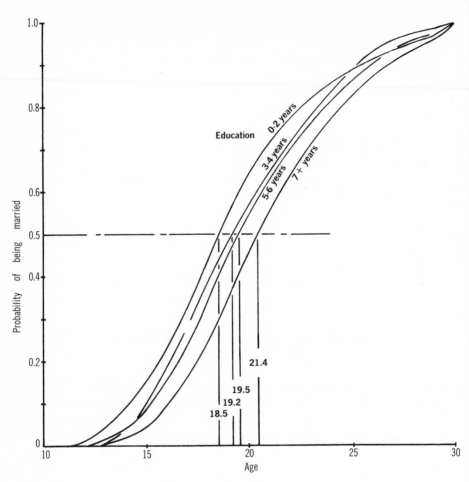

FIGURE 18.
Probability of marrying, by age and education.

The distribution of the constituent exposure interval rates of the GCF examined in another study indicates that there is a close relation between the proportion of total fertility completed and the proportion of total available marital exposure time elapsed.[9] If f_i/f_c is the proportion of total fertility, f_c, completed after i, five-year intervals, and e_i/e_c, the proportion of marital exposure elapsed, a good agreement between f_i/f_c and e_i/e_c is given by $f_i/f_c = e_i/e_c(2 - e_i/e_c)$. e_i is the exposure completed by the interval i and is given by $5.0 \times i$, and e_c is the maximum available exposure—time from age at first union to the terminal age at childbearing, M.[10] For simplicity, $e_i/e_c(2 - e_i/e_c)$ is defined as φ_i, and as Figure 19 indicates, the fit of f_i/f_c and φ_i is quite good. As M is a variable to be determined empirically, the values are chosen to give the best fit of f_i/f_c and φ_i. That best fit values of M, given in Table 42, tend to decline with education probably reflects the increasing use and efficiency of contraception.

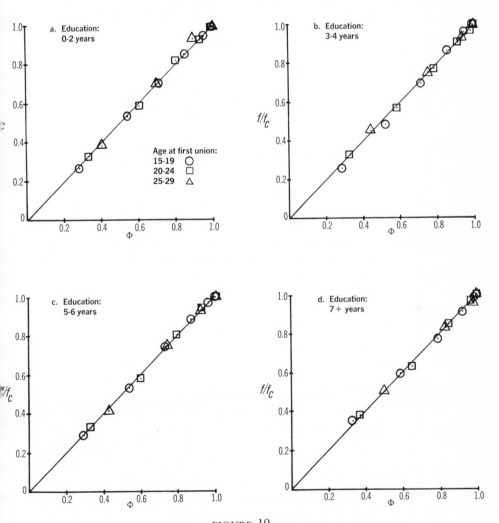

FIGURE 19.
Proportion of total fertility completed by proportion of
exposure completed, by age at first union and education.

TABLE 42

Terminal Age at Childbearing, by Age and
Education

	Years of Education			
Age	2–3	3–4	5–6	7–8
15–19	50.0	50.0	48.5	45.5
	(236)	(254)	(215)	(170)
20–24	49.0	50.0	49.5	46.5
	(127)	(171)	(143)	(179)
25–29	49.0	46.5	47.0	44.0
	(46)	(64)	(50)	(68)

*Denominator n's are shown in parentheses.

There seems to be only a slight tendency for M to decline with age at first union.

Analysis of expected completed fertility by education shows uniformly high figures—approximately eight live births—at the three lower categories.[11] Despite wide differences in contraception, the variation among these educational classes is on the order of only 5 percent. Only at the highest educational level is there a significant reduction (over 20 percent) to 6.3 live births. (See Figure 20.)

Similar expected completed fertility measures by contraceptive experience are also shown in Figure 20. There appears to be a substantial selectivity of usage by fecundity, since the fertility of ever-users is between 8 and 33 percent above the fertility of nonusers. However, this selectivity seems less for the women with seven or more years of education. Apparently, contraception is practiced even by women of reduced fecundity if they are well educated, leaving among the nonusers women of substantially lower average fecundity than at other educational levels. We may partially test this hypothesis by defining as subfecund a union of five or more years duration which has produced no live births or one of ten years or more which has produced only one. As Figure 21 shows, subfecundity is much more prevalent among noncontraceptors, the range being between 0.08 and 0.17, while among contraceptors the values drop to near zero. That the proportions for noncontraceptors do not rise more steadily or sharply with education is probably due to the crudeness of our

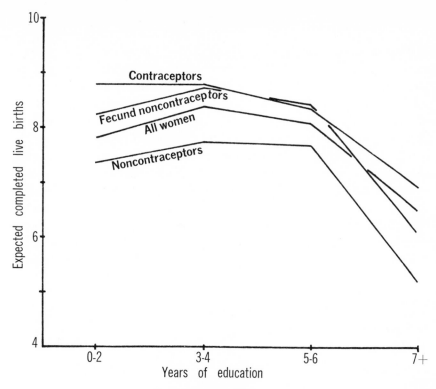

FIGURE 20.
Expected completed live births, by contraceptive usage,
fecundity, and education.

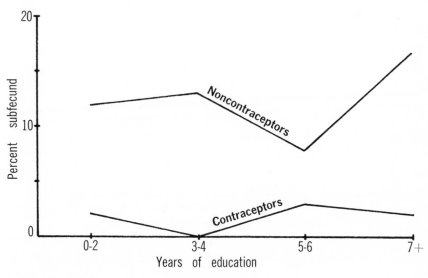

FIGURE 21.
Percent subfecund, by contraceptive usage and education.

definition of subfecundity. Although the definition should cover sterile couples and chronic aborters, it obviously does not include most women affected by secondary sterility or early menopause. The effect of subfecundity may be demonstrated—within limits of the definition—by computing the expected completed fertility of non-contraceptors who are not subfecund. The effect is to "increase" the completed fertility of noncontraceptors by 9 to 17 percent, almost to the level of contraceptors at the three lower educational categories.

To measure the effect of age at first union upon completed fertility, the data for ever-contraceptors and noncontraceptors were combined by standardizing for contraception.[12] The results, presented in Figure 22, show that completed fertility declines almost linearly with increasing age at first union to a zero value at about forty-three years,

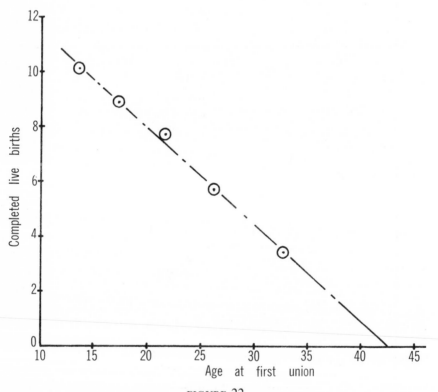

FIGURE 22.
Expected completed live births, by age at first union.

close to the terminal age at childbearing found earlier (between 44.5 and 50.0). By fitting a straight line through the points, we may provide a measure of the effect on completed fertility of the age at first union. Using the median ages,[13] we find that the variation is between 7.9 and 8.5 live births. Although the difference is less than 8 percent, it represents a large portion of the actual fertility differential between the lowest and highest educational categories. The absolute effect of age at first union is, however, much greater at all educational levels. Assuming that 14 years is the average age at menarche and that unions formed past age 44.9 years produce no live births, the reduction in completed fertility would be 15 percent at the lowest educational category and 22 percent at the highest.

SUMMARY

Contraceptive usage is closely associated with education, but primarily through the intervening variable of contraceptive knowledge. Usage is also related to discussion with the spouse about birth control, although discussion appears to be a covariate, rather than a determinant, of usage. Prior existence of an ideal family size, in spite of a weaker association with usage, nonetheless may be an important step eventually leading to attempts to control fertility.

Knowledge, acceptance, and usage of contraceptive methods are already at moderate levels, and the data suggest that the methods are rapidly spreading. However, at the time of the study, the two methods most often used were of the more traditional and less effective type, rhythm and withdrawal.

Estimations of completed fertility show high completed family size levels, a finding consistent with the relative inefficiency of contraception and the use of less effective methods. Contraceptive practice is apparently still so ineffective that the completed fertility of contraceptors is greater than the fertility of those who never attempt to control fertility. Of the variables considered, age at first union is perhaps the most important nonbiological determinant of fertility and accounts for much of the differential among the four educational categories.

In spite of the current state of contraception and its effects, there are concrete indications that significant changes in fertility and in related attitudes, knowledge, and behavior are imminent in Medellín.

NOTES

1. Preston E. James, *Latin America* (New York: The Odyssey Press, 1959), pp. 105–121.

2. See Mario Jaramillo Gomez and Robert B. Hartford, "Encuesta de fecundidad de Medellín. Monografias 1, 2 y 3," in *Regulación de la fecundidad: conocimientos, actitudes y practicas de la población Colombiana* (Bogotá: Ediciones Tercer Mundo, 1968), vol. II.

3. Drawing of the sample was facilitated by a special report prepared by the Municipal Planning Office of Medellín, giving the distribution of persons by household income according to four income classifications in each of Medellín's 155 barrios ("Población de Medellín," Oficina de Planeación Municipal, División de Investigaciones, July 1966). The income groups are upper and upper-middle ($3,500 N/C per month and over), middle-middle ($1,700 to $3,499 per month), lower-middle ($900 to $1,699 per month), and lower (less than $900 per month). At the time of the interviewing, 100 pesos was equal to U.S. $6.25. Barrios with good representation from the various socioeconomic levels were selected, and prelisting for age and marital status was carried out. In order to fill certain extreme cells, quota sampling was required, totaling 17 percent of the total sample.

4. Previous studies have emphasized the variable of ideal family size, in terms of its *magnitude;* i.e., whether the ideal number of children is large or small. Studies by Stycos, however, have shown that large proportions of women have never thought about an ideal family size prior to being interviewed. In the present survey a third of the women reported never having thought of the matter before. Throughout the chapter we could use this measure rather than the reported ideal number. See J. Mayone Stycos, "Family Size Preferences and Social Class in Peru," *American Journal of Sociology*, May 1954; and "Facilitating Mechanisms in Fertility Planning," in Reuben Hill, J. Mayone Stycos, and Kurt W. Back (eds.), *The Family and Population Control* (Chapel Hill, N.C.: University of North Carolina Press, 1959), chap. 5.

5. It is possible to pursue the analysis further by examining the relative time at which the ideal concept was first formed and contraception first initiated. Variables, as well as discussion, were coded by birth parity interval of first occurrence. Of the contraceptors who had previously thought of the ideal, over 60 percent thought of the ideal prior to initiating birth control, 13 percent afterwards, and about one-fourth at more or less the same time. Actually, the proportion thinking of the ideal first are probably underestimated by at least 10 to 15 percent, as the parity intervals used in the coding generally ranged from two to three births. Moreover, these proportions are virtually constant, irrespective of education.

6. We would expect acceptance, like knowledge and usage, to exhibit a curvilinear relation with age. As age increases initially, the need for contraception and the degree of knowledge of specific contraceptive methods should also increase. These changes, in turn, should produce increased acceptance. On the other hand, if acceptance were greater among younger cohorts, but constant by age for any given age cohort, then the pattern of acceptance by age would be one of monotonic decline. As there is other evidence of innovative contraceptive behavior among younger cohorts, we may suggest that increases in acceptance

by cohort have virtually canceled the increases associated with aging and higher birth parity to give the nearly uniform variation of acceptance with age.

7. Actually need is only partially controlled, for we may assume that the need of a woman fifteen to twenty-nine years of age with three children is probably greater than the need of a woman forty to forty-nine years with the same number of children. This is to say that current birth parity is related to fecundity; hence, fecundity is greater in the younger age cohorts than in the older ones at a given parity. Need and usage of contraception will, therefore, almost certainly be higher among younger women (of a given parity), independent of cohort changes in usage patterns. Still, the cohort differences indicated seem so large that we may feel relatively certain that cohort changes are taking place.

8. The similarity of the GCF to Yaukey's measure, as well as comparative analysis of these with other measures of total fertility, may be found in another work by the author: Robert B. Hartford, "Estimation of Completed Fertility with Controls for Age at First Union and Marital Exposure," an unpublished Ph.D. dissertation, Cornell University, Ithaca, N.Y., 1970. The GCF is defined as follows:

Let b_{ij} be the number of live births produced during the ith five-year interval subsequent to age at first union by women marrying in age interval j. The number of births b'_{ij} that would have been produced in interval, had exposure been complete, may be estimated by 5.0 years $\times$ b_{ij} divided by the number of actual marital exposure years in the interval. The estimated number of births completed by the end of interval i is given by

$$f_{ij} = \sum_{m=1}^{i} b'_{mj}$$

Summation over all exposure intervals estimates completed fertility f_{cj} of women marrying in age interval j. GCF is defined as the weighted sum of the f_{cj} over all age at first union intervals; namely, GCF $= \Sigma_j w_j f c_j$, where the w_j are the proportions, calculated by a life-table-like procedure, of women marrying in age interval j.

9. A more complete discussion of the variation of the exposure interval specific rates and the implications for existing notions concerning adolescent subfecundity is to be found in the dissertation mentioned in footnote 7.

10. The derivation of $f_i/f_c = e_i/e_c (2 - e_i/e_c)$ may be found in "Toward the Development of a Method for Estimating Completed Fertility and Controlling for the Effects of Age at First Union and Union Duration," a paper presented by this writer at the 1968 meeting of the Population Association of America in Boston.

11. These results were standardized by weighting the expected completed fertility computed for each age-at-first-union group by a single age-at-first-union schedule. The latter, in turn, was derived by standardizing the probabilities of marrying in each age interval for education. The resulting weight schedule is:

Age at first union	15	15–19	20–24	25–29	30 & over	Total
Weight	0.048	0.420	0.355	0.150	0.025	1.000

12. The weights obtained by standardizing proportions of contraceptors for education are contraceptors, 0.56; noncontraceptors, 0.44.

13. The median ages at first union for the four educational categories are 18.5, 19.5, 19.2, and 20.4 years, respectively.

CHAPTER 14

Lower-income Mothers
in Bogotá

Prepared by **Elizabeth L. Johnson.**

Contemporary Latin America is characterized by two demographic processes of outstanding importance: a very high rate of population growth and a continuing increase in the proportion of the population residing in urban areas. Because the urban population constitutes a significant sector of the population, it is important, in estimating future trends in population growth, to know whether there are factors inherent in the urban environment which might affect fertility-related attitudes and behavior. In an article, "Needed Research on Latin American Fertility: Urbanization and Fertility," J. M. Stycos suggests that migration and marital status may be especially useful in explaining rural-urban fertility differences and that education, female employment, social class, and certain biological factors may provide additional explanations.[1]

Because of the time limits of my study, a rural-urban comparison was not possible. However, in addition to the usual KAP variables, I studied the extent to which social mechanisms for sharing the burdens of the care and the economic costs of children exist in the city. Kingsley Davis has suggested that high fertility is indirectly encouraged in many underdeveloped countries because the individual nuclear family does not bear sole responsibility for the care and expense of children, but instead distributes these responsibilities among members of the extended household or wider kinship group.[2] G. W. Skinner describes the operation of this process in a number of Asian societies in an article entitled "Cultural Values, Social Structure, and Population Growth."[3] Stycos has described how certain institutional mechanisms operate in Puerto Rico to relieve the nuclear family of the pressures of large numbers of children. One such mechanism is the extended family.† Children are often sent to live, either temporarily or permanently, with relatives who are better able to care for them than are their own parents. In addition, the institution of *compadrazgo,* or fellow godparenthood, serves as a mechanism for the redistribution of children. Families with many children or in which one or both parents have died often send their children to be raised by their godparents, who have a sacred obligation to perform this duty. Thus, both the extended family and *compadrazgo* "[serve] to cushion the impact of high fertility on any given family." In this way, pressures on any individual family to limit fertility may be relieved.[4]

I hypothesized, however, that in an urban environment, where living space is limited and the rate of geographical mobility is high, these institutions might not be able to function effectively. In this situation, individual couples, finding themselves faced with the prospect of caring for and supporting large numbers of children, might prefer to have smaller families and be willing to take action to achieve this goal if means for limiting their fertility were available to them.

I was particularly concerned with the following questions: How extensive is the network of social relationships of the lower-class urban woman? Do migrant women differ significantly from women born in the city in this respect? To what extent are children actually distributed among relatives and godparents? What do women perceive the obligations of godparents to be, and what duties do godparents actually perform? To what extent do women rely on persons outside the nuclear family for help with child care in time of need? Does the presence or absence of persons outside the nuclear family

---

† Both *padrino* and *compadre* mean "godparent." However, *padrino* (or *padrina*) is used in the context of the relationship between the godparent and the child while *compadre* (or *comadre*) is used in referring to the relationship between the godparent and the parent.

with whom the burden of child care and support can be shared have any effect on women's attitudes toward family size? What other factors are relevant to women's fertility and attitudes toward family size? What do women actually perceive to be the most important factors in determining whether or not they want to have more children?

THE SETTING

In order to clarify the influence of other factors, I decided to select a sample which would be as homogeneous as possible in social class, number of children, residence, and age—characteristics which have been demonstrated to be relevant to attitudes toward family size. I chose to conduct the study in the Instituto Materno Infantil of the Hospital San Juan de Dios in Bogotá, both because a population of women of the desired characteristics were available there and because the director and staff of the hospital generously allowed me to use their facilities. The I.M.I. is a maternity hospital serving lower-class women, run by the Beneficencia de Cundinamarca. It offers women prenatal care after the seventh month of pregnancy and offers maternity care, as well as treatment of infants up to one year of age, at very low cost. Within the I.M.I., the study was conducted in the Oficina de Asistencia Social, whose principal function is to record social histories of women and children prior to their medical examinations on the first hospital visit. This office offered a structured situation in which interviews (including questions similar to the ones I planned to ask) were being carried out by the two social workers. The social workers obtained such information as the age of the woman, her husband, and her children; her marital status and place of birth; and her husband's occupation and income. With the social workers' assistance, I was able to fit smoothly into the office routine and have my interviews appear to the patients to be part of the normal procedure. Since all the social histories were stored in the office, I was able to draw a sample to determine precisely the characteristics of the patient population. Sufficiently large numbers of women passed through this office to enable me to select a sample of known characteristics for my own interviews. During 1965, 6,654 women, most of them prenatal cases, were interviewed in the Oficina de Asistencia. A study of these records indicated that in the two months available to me I would be able to interview a sample of about 100 women who were currently mated, aged 20–35,[5] presently living in Bogotá, and having at least one living child. Because of the nature of the hospital, all the women were members of the lower class. Furthermore, I restricted the sample to women coming for prenatal care, and hence at least seven months pregnant, in order to control one additional relevant characteristic.

The interviews were conducted as follows. When the social workers had finished interviewing a woman with characteristics which qualified her for inclusion in my sample, they asked her to go to me and answer my questions. Rather than introduce myself, I would simply state that we needed some more information on some of the pregnant women and that the interview would take only fifteen or twenty minutes. In general, no further explanation was necessary, and the women were very cooperative, responsive, and patient, despite the fact that many of them had already been waiting for several hours to see a doctor. In general, they did not volunteer much additional information in answer to the questions, partly, I think, because they had been encouraged by the social workers to give only direct answers to questions and partly because the office was often so crowded and noisy that it was difficult to talk. Furthermore, the interview consisted of a series of direct questions which did not require detailed answers, since I did not understand Spanish well enough to handle unstructured questions.

THE SAMPLE

The ninety-seven women who constituted my sample were all presently living in Bogotá, but only 25 percent were born there. Seven percent were born in other capital cities, and the rest in rural areas, primarily in Cundinamarca and Boyaca. They had an average of about three years of education. A fifth studied one year or less, half had some primary education beyond the first year, only a fifth completed primary school.

Only five women had any remunerative employment at the time of the interview, and of these only one was employed full-time outside her home. Two-thirds of the husbands were employed in manual labor and earned an average of about 19 pesos per day.[6] Some indication of living conditions is given by the fact that twelve women (who had between two and six children) mentioned that they lived in only one room.

Although all were currently mated, only 60 percent were legally married, the remainder living in consensual unions. The average age of married women was twenty-eight years, the unmarried women being about a year younger. Husbands averaged thirty-four years of age. Women in the sample had an average of 3.15 living children (not counting the child soon to be born), the modal number being 2, with a range from 1 to 10. Fifty-seven women had no children die, twenty-nine had one child born alive who later died, and eleven lost two or more children. Adding the deceased children to the living children, the average woman had 3.7 live births. The average age of the women at the birth of their first living child was twenty-one years, the modal age eighteen, and the range from fifteen to thirty-one.

It is possible to compare certain of the characteristics of this sample with those of the universe of women seeking prenatal care. To do this, I drew a 1-in-8 sample of all the cases interviewed by the Oficina de Asistencia between June 1, 1965, and July 1, 1966, yielding a total of 726 prenatal cases. Of this group, 21 percent were not currently mated, and only 40 percent were legally married, as opposed to 60 percent in my sample. Their average age was only twenty-six years, and the average number of children only 2.08. Only 17 percent were born in Bogotá, and 43 percent in rural Cundinamarca. It appears, then, that by restricting my sample to currently mated women, twenty to thirty-five years of age, with one or more living children, I eliminated a rather large group of young, unmarried women, living alone, having their first or second child, and being recent immigrants to the city. It is my impression that most of these women were employed in domestic work.

SOCIAL RELATIONSHIPS

I shall first outline the patterns of the respondents' social relationships and the child-care functions served by these relationships and then relate these to their attitudes about family size. The purpose of this first section is to determine the extent to which the respondents had functioning relationships with people with whom the burden of child care and support could be shared when necessary, thus relieving the pressure of large numbers of children upon the nuclear family.[7]

§ KINSHIP

In order to determine the extent to which persons beyond the nuclear family were members of the respondents' households, the respondents were asked: "Do any other persons live in your household besides yourself, your husband, and your children?" Thirty-four women replied affirmatively. In eight of these cases, the persons were not relatives. Of the remaining twenty-six, fourteen included one or more members of the family of orientation of the respondent (and their spouses in two cases), nine included one or more members of the husband's family of orientation (and their spouses in two cases), and three included other relatives of the respondent or her husband. The number of extra persons ranged from 1 to 7, the average being 2.2. The average household size was 5.5 persons, ranging from 3 to 12.[8]

In order to determine the extent of the respondents' relationships with kin who lived outside their own households, the women were asked: "Do you have any relatives whom you love who live outside your household?" The residence and degree of assistance for each relative mentioned was then queried. Two-thirds named one or more members of their family of orientation, about a fifth named members of their husband's family of orientation, and a fifth named other of their own relatives. A third of the respondents had been helped in some way by one or more members of their family of orientation during the past year, and 10 percent had been helped by their husband's family of orientation.

The kinds of aid given included help in crises, as when the respondent or a child was sick or a child was born; gifts of food, clothing, or money; and help with child care and housework. A number of women mentioned, however, that their relatives could not help them because they were old, sick, or impoverished, or themselves had many children. Ironically, one woman stated that she could not maintain contact with her relatives because she herself had nine children. Dividing the sample into women with one or two children and women with more than two children, I found that the latter were slightly less likely to name members of their family of orientation (66 percent compared to 76 percent) or other relatives (9 percent as opposed to 27 percent). Because a number of women also mentioned that they had lost contact with their relatives because they lived far away, I investigated the relationship between the respondents' place of birth and residence of their relatives. I found the difference between women born in Bogotá and those who had migrated to the city to be striking in this respect (Table 43), although there were no differences between the two groups with respect to help received from relatives during the past year. Particularly interesting is the fact that 16 percent of those women born outside of Bogotá named no relatives at all.

Although this measure does not take the number of relatives into account, it does indicate that the women born in Bogotá were much more likely to have some relatives nearby who could share the problems of child care and support than were the migrant women. This suggests that rural-urban migration might, in accordance with the hypotheses of Davis and Stycos, be an important determinant of family size attitudes.[9]

§ COMPADRAZGO

A second type of social relationship was that between the respondent and her own godparents. In response to the question, "Do you have any godfathers or godmothers?" about two-thirds named

TABLE 43

Residence of Close Relatives, by Place of Birth of Respondent

	Born in Bogotá, %	Born elsewhere, %
Has relatives in same household or barrio	42	23
Has husband's relatives in same household or barrio	23	9
Has relatives in Bogotá outside own barrio	58	37
Has husband's relatives in Bogotá outside own barrio	4	10
Has relatives outside Bogotá	38	69
Has husband's relatives outside Bogotá	8	7
Has no relatives in Bogotá	15	50
Has no own or husband's relatives in Bogotá	12	40
Names no relatives	4	16
Number of cases	(26)	(70)

one or more godparents of baptism, confirmation, presentation, or marriage. Only 2 percent had been helped by their godparents during the past year, however, showing that this relationship is less important than is often supposed.

A third type of relationship studied was that between the respondent and her fellow-godparents. Eighty-five percent named one or more functioning fellow-godparents and a quarter of the respondents had received some form of aid from them within the past year. Over a third of the women who had been born in Bogotá or who had lived there ten years or more had been helped, as compared with a fifth of the other women. Women named as fellow-godparents only the godparents of baptism of their own children and not their children's godparents of other types or the parents of children of whom they themselves were godparents. I suspect that in a less structured situation, in which there was more time to talk and the respondents were less tired, information on these relationships might have been obtained. This does indicate, however, that the women considered only their relationships with the baptismal godparents of their children to be important. Considering the data in terms of the set of *padrinos* of each child (which might be either one or two persons), 11 percent of these *compadres* lived in the same barrio as the respondent, 42 percent lived outside the barrio but in Bogotá, 37 percent lived outside Bogotá, and the residence of 10 percent was unknown. Calculated on this basis, help had been received during the past year from at least one of the *padrinos* of only 20 percent of the children.

§ FRIENDSHIP

A fourth type of social relationship was investigated by means of the question: "Do you have any friends whom you particularly care about?" Only 22 percent named one or more friends, and only 8 percent had been helped in some way by their friends during the past year. The great majority of the friends named were neighbors.

INSTITUTIONS FOR SHARING CHILD CARE

Since my primary interest in studying social relationships was to determine their functions for the care and support of children, I asked a number of questions on child-care arrangements and on the functioning of various institutional mechanisms for the distribution of child-care responsibility.

§ ADOPTION

As noted above, Stycos has suggested that in Puerto Rico children are often adopted, temporarily or permanently, by their godparents or relatives in order to relieve pressures on the nuclear family of large numbers of children or to serve the needs of the adopting family.[10] In the present study, when asked, "Do any of your children live outside your household or do they all live with you?" eighteen women said they had children living with relatives outside their households. In two cases this was clearly a temporary arrangement (in one case because the woman was sick during her pregnancy and in the other because the family had just moved from Cali and had left the children with the respondent's mother). In another case, one child lived permanently with the husband's parents because the respondent had to work, and in a fourth case, two of the respondent's five children lived with their father, the respondent's former husband. For the remaining cases, the reasons were less clear. The social workers hinted that I should not probe too deeply, implying that the children were often the offspring of the respondents' previous unions. Fals-Borda also suggests that it is not uncommon for women in Saucío to leave their illegitimate children for adoption by their parents when they migrate to Bogotá to work.[11] Only one woman of the remaining fourteen explicitly volunteered this kind of explanation, but it was clearly the explanation for another case, in which the respondent was presently living with a man who was not her legal husband. I would suspect that this was true for at least several additional cases, because of the spacing of the children involved and because of the nature of the explanations given. In four cases, the respondent's only child was living permanently with her mother. One stated that this was because "there are problems," another because "she loves her very much," and the third because they were poor and food was cheaper in the country. In one case, the child lived with the respondent's mother to keep her company (the respondent continued to support the child), and in another case the child lived with the respondent's mother because the child was sick. In three cases, the explanation was that the children lived with other relatives so that they could study. Of the remaining three cases, two gave no explanation (the children were living with the respondents' parents), and one stated that two of her children were living with her brothers because she was poor and could not afford a home for four children. In only five of the sixteen cases in which children were living permanently with relatives did the families involved have more than three children, and in only one case did the explanation given suggest that the reason for the arrangement was to relieve pressures on the nuclear family of large numbers of children. I would suggest, then, on the basis of the analysis of these few cases, that for this group of women the redistribution of children was more likely to serve the function of ensuring the care outside the household of children of previous unions than that of sharing responsibility for the children of large families. It is interesting to note that twice as many unmarried as married women had children living with other relatives (28 percent versus 12 percent). In all cases the children were living with relatives rather than with their godparents.

§ IDEAL AND ACTUAL FUNCTIONS OF PADRINOS

Mintz and Wolf have suggested that there are two general types of *compadrazgo* relationships. In the first type, *compadres* are chosen from within the network of the parents' friends and relatives, and their functions are primarily those of mutual aid and responsibility for the godchild, should anything happen to the parents. In the second type, *compadres* are chosen from members of a higher social class, and it is hoped that the relationship will bring material benefit and a possible enhancement of social status.[12] In the group of women studied, two facts suggest that *compadrazgo* relationships were primarily of the first type. First, a third of all the *compadres* named were actually relatives of the respondents or their husbands and therefore probably similar in social status. Second, a cross-tabulation of the respondents' husbands' occupations by the occupations of the *compadres* (Table 44) indicates that despite the choice of a few professional people, in general the *compadres* were of similar social status. (This tabulation does not include all the *compadres* ever chosen by the respondents, of course, but only those cases in which contact had been maintained, in which both the *compadre* and the husband were employed, and in which the respondent knew the occupations of both and gave enough information for the occupation to be classified by type. In 21 percent of the cases the respondents did not know the occupations of the *compadres*.) This rough measure of social class suggests that in general persons were not chosen as *compadres* for the purpose of enhancing the social status of the respondents or their children.

In order to obtain an estimate of the duties which the respondents

TABLE 44

Occupation of Compadres, by Occupation of Husband

	Husband's Occupation	
Compadre's Occupation	Manual, %	Nonmanual, %
Agriculture and manual	60	64
Commercial	18	27
Nonmanual services	13	9
Professional	9	0
Total	100	100
Number of cases	(76)	(11)

believed that *padrinos* should perform, I asked: "What obligations do godparents have to their godchildren?" Twenty-three women replied that *padrinos* had no obligations, and seven replied that they did not know. Of the remaining women, eighteen stated that *padrinos* should take responsibility for the child "if the parents are gone," and five said that *padrinos* should help if the child became ill or died. Eleven said that *padrinos* should help the child with his studies, and seven said that *padrinos* should give gifts of clothing (4) or of money (1) or at special occasions (2). Three said that *padrinos* should help if the family is in trouble, one said that they should help to care for the child, and one that they should set an example for him. The remaining sixteen did not define the type of help that *padrinos* should give. A number of women qualified their statements by saying that their *compadres* had given them no help or were unable to help them. When asked specifically whether they had been helped by their *compadres* during the last year, the women mentioned that their *compadres* had given gifts, meals, and money; that they had helped when the child was sick; that they had helped with the burial when the child had died; and, in one case, that they had taken the child to their home for a few days' vacation. As mentioned above, however, only a quarter of the women had received help from any of their *compadres* during the past year. In answering that their *compadres* had given them no help, some women explained that they themselves were poor or had many children, while a number of women sounded quite bitter or scornful over this fact (stating, for example, "they never come to the house—they baptized the children for me—nothing more"; "they did me the favor of participating in the baptism—nothing more"; "no—it grieves me"). Furthermore, in the sample as a whole, the women had completely lost contact with the *padrinos* of 27 percent of their children. It is my impression that in general the women did not expect their *compadres* to perform anything more than certain limited duties, at best, and commonly did not or could not rely on them to share in the responsibility for the care and support of the child.

CHILD CARE IN SPECIFIC SITUATIONS

In order to determine more precisely the extent to which the respondents actually relied on their *compadres,* friends, and relatives for help with their children, I asked a group of questions concerning the arrangements which the respondents had made for help with child care in situations in which I expected that they would need such help. One question concerned the birth of the last child: "When your last child was born, did you have anyone to help you with him and with the house while you were recovering?" A third responded they had received no help, 13 percent had been helped by their husbands or children ("the oldest little one cares for the youngest"), and 40 percent had been helped by their own or their husbands' relatives. Twice as many of the Bogotá-born women had had help as those born elsewhere. The percentages of married and unmarried women who had received no help were very similar (Table 45).

TABLE 45

Type of Help Received at Last Birth, by Birthplace and
Marital Status

	Total, %	Birthplace		Marital Status	
		Bogotá, %	Other, %	Married, %	Unmarried, %
Type of Help					
None	34	20	38	31	34
Nuclear family	13	10	10	15	8
Other relatives	40	45	39	30	48
Friends and neighbors	13	25	13	24	10
Total	100	100	100	100	100
Number of cases	(86)	(20)	(65)	(34)	(52)

The second question of this type asked was: "Who will care for your other children while you are in the hospital [at the birth of the next child]?" A third did not know or expected help only from their husbands and children. About half expected help from relatives outside the nuclear family, and the balance from nonrelatives. Differences by place of birth were similar to those on the previous question, as were differences according to marital status.

A third question asked was: "Do you have anyone who can help you care for your children during the first weeks after the next child is born?" Half of the women answered that they anticipated no help, and 11 percent only anticipated help from their husbands and children. About a quarter expected help from relatives outside the nuclear family, and 10 percent from neighbors or friends. Again, the differences in the responses according to place of birth and marital status followed the same patterns.

I also asked a subsample of sixty-nine of the ninety-seven women: "Who is caring for your children right now?" Because I did not ask the question of the entire sample, I did not analyze its relationship to attitudes toward family size. The results are interesting, however, in indicating the extent to which respondents could rely on persons outside the nuclear family for help in a situation which was not a real emergency, but in which it was difficult for them to have their children with them. Twenty-three percent stated that they had left their children alone, "locked in the house," giving such explanations as "I have no one to leave them with." Four percent had their children with them, and sixteen percent had left them with their husbands. Twenty-nine percent had left the children with relatives outside the nuclear family, and the remainder had left them with neighbors, with a *compadre* (in one case), or in school.

In order to determine the extent to which arrangements for help with child care might be reciprocal, I asked: "During the past year, have you cared for the children of any other people?" Eighty percent of the women replied negatively, while 5 percent stated that they had cared for the children of relatives and fourteen percent had cared for the children of friends or neighbors.

Thus, in general, respondents do not rely on *compadres* for help with child care in these situations, but do rely to a great extent on members of the nuclear family. In order to find out more precisely the extent to which their husbands helped them, I asked: "Does your husband help you to care for your children?" Seventy-nine percent replied affirmatively to this question, thirteen percent qualifying their answers with "When he can," "When he is out of work," etc. The respondents seemed to accept this as quite normal, describing how their husbands cooked meals for their children, dressed them, and put them to bed. One statement which Fals-Borda makes about Saucio suggests that this type of help may be more common in the city than in the rural areas: "To a certain extent, the father remains aloof and does not concern himself with the child, although he does condescend to caress him and occasionally helps to put him to bed." [13]

Since I suspected that in the city the women might have learned of public or charitable institutions which could help them with child care, I asked: "Are you familiar with any institution which can give you help in caring for your children when you need it?" Of the eighty-seven women who understood the question, only five could name any such institution. Two named the Centro de Higiene, one named the Hospital Infantil, one named the Hermanas de la Asunción, and one named the Guardería of the I.M.I.

Only one woman suggested that neighborhoods sometimes organized themselves to provide mutual aid for their members. She said that she lived in Barrio Florencia, which had organized "acción comunal," meaning that the residents helped each other in time of need.

ATTITUDES TOWARD FAMILY SIZE

Questions were asked in the order in which they are presented in Table 46. While less than half of the women have ever thought about the total number of children they want or discussed it with their husbands, over half did not wish to have the child they were pregnant with, over three-fourths want no more after this child, and two-thirds believe their husbands want no more. The answers of a few women indicated that the problem was of very high salience for them: "We are talking it over now—he says that we have to get treatment so as not to have any more." "He says that I should talk to the doctor about having treatment so as not to have any more."

The last set of questions dealt with the women's knowledge and practice of contraception, and their attitudes toward it. When asked,

TABLE 46

Concern about Family Size

	No, %	Yes, %	Don't know or Other, %	Total, %	Number of Cases
Have you ever thought about how many children you would like to have in all?	40	46	14	100	(92)
Before this pregnancy, did you want another child, or would you have preferred not to have one?	52	35	13	100	(89)
Do you want to have more children than (present number) or not?	78	9	12	99	(96)
Have you spoken with your husband about the number of children you would like to have or not?	52	¹48	0	100	(96)
Do you think that your husband wants to have more children or not?	66	12	21	99	(96)

"Have you ever tried to avoid pregnancies?" 80 percent replied negatively. Of the 14 percent who replied affirmatively, 5 percent did not specify the methods used, 2 percent had used "baths" or "waters," and 4 percent had used something given by a doctor. In addition, one woman stated that her husband had used something, and two women had used pills obtained from friends (one implied that these had been used to attempt to provoke an abortion). Unfortunately, there was not enough privacy in the office to probe further on this question. I next asked the women who had replied negatively: "Are you familiar with any of the methods of avoiding pregnancies?" and asked those who had replied affirmatively: "Are you familiar with any other methods of avoiding pregnancies?" Ninety percent of the women replied negatively, and only 2 percent cited specific methods. Those who knew of no method were asked, "If in the future you were to learn of a method to avoid new pregnancies, would you be inclined to use it?" Half said they would use one if they were to learn of it, a quarter said they would not, and most of the balance were uncertain. Only one of the ninety-six Catholic women expressed any awareness or consideration of the church's position on birth control.

Finally, I analyzed the relationship between number of children and fertility-related attitudes and behavior. The fact that women's desire for more children and willingness to use contraception vary according to the number of living children they have is demonstrated clearly in Table 47. The only variable which appears to be unrelated to number of living children is whether or not the respondent has talked with her husband concerning the number of children they would like to have.

Since fertility-related attitudes were so clearly affected by number

TABLE 47

Mean Number of Living Children, by Fertility-related
Attitudes and Behavior

		Mean
Has thought about desired family size	No	2.9
	Yes	3.3
	Does not know	2.0
	God's will	4.0
Desired this child	No	3.8
	Yes	2.0
	Does not know	2.2
	God's will	5.2
	Other	2.7
Desires more children	No	3.2
	Yes	2.5
	Does not know	1.7
	God's will	4.5
Has spoken with husband about desired family size	No	3.1
	Yes	3.0
Has tried to avoid pregnancies	No	3.0
	Yes	3.9
	Other	3.2
Willingness to use contraception	No	2.4
	Yes	3.4
	Does not know	2.4

of living children, it was necessary to control for number of children before analyzing the effects of other variables upon these attitudes. Because the sample was so small, I split the group as close to the median number of children as possible, so that those women with one or two children formed one group, while those with three or more formed the other. When number of births is controlled in this fashion, little relation between marital status or place of birth and the variables listed in Table 47 is seen. Number of children, however, continues to show a strong relation to the desire for more children and the willingness to use contraceptive methods.

Table 48 indicates that certain of the women's attitudes and actions are quite clearly related to their educational level. The women above the median level of education were more likely to have thought about the number of children they wished to have and to have spoken to their husbands about it. They were also more likely to have tried to avoid pregnancies and were more willing to use some means of contraception than were the less educated women.

TABLE 48

Various Fertility-related Questions, by Number of Living
Children, Years of Education

	1–2 Children		3 or More Children	
	Education		Education	
	0–2 Years	⩾3 Years	0–2 Years	⩾3 Years
Percent who thought about desired family size	32	64	48	60
Percent who did not desire this child	31	47	72	64
Percent desiring no more children	54	86	89	86
Percent spoken to husband about desired family size	44	55	26	62
Percent tried to avoid pregnancies	7	18	11	21
Percent willing to use contraceptives	44	59	53	79
Number of cases	(26)	(22)	(19)	(28)

TABLE 49

Various Fertility-related Questions, by Number of Living
Children and Weekly Church Attendance

	1-2 Children		3 or More Children	
	Church Attendance		Church Attendance	
	⩾1	<1	⩾1	<1
Percent who thought about desired family size	41	45	53	58
Percent who did not desire this child	53	29	81	65
Percent desiring no more children	76	67	82	89
Percent spoken to husband about desired family size	59	47	41	48
Percent tried to avoid pregnancies	18	10	6	23
Percent willing to use contraceptives	65	36	71	67
Number of cases	(17)	(30)	(17)	(26)

The relationships between fertility-related attitudes and behavior and church-attendance frequency are shown in Table 49. The sample was divided into those attending church once a week or more frequently and those attending less frequently. Frequency of church attendance is not related to past use of contraception or present willingness to use it. Those who attend church less frequently were more likely to have desired the child which they were presently expecting, however.

Partial verification for the hypothesis that one determinant of fertility-related attitudes and behavior is the extent to which women can share responsibility for child care with persons outside the nuclear family is shown in Table 50. The three questions used concern the arrangements which the respondents had for help with child care at the birth of their last child, at the birth of the child they were presently expecting, and during the first few weeks after the birth of this child.

The women who had no help, who were helped only by members

TABLE 50

Percent Who Did Not Want Current Pregnancy, by Number
of Living Children and Type of Assistance with Child Care

	1-2 Children	3 or More Children
Type of help at birth of last child:		
Help from persons outside nuclear family	32	54
No help or help only from members of nuclear family	39	71
Type of help at current birth:		
Help from persons outside nuclear family	30	60
No help or help only from members of nuclear family	58	75
Type of help after current birth:		
Help from persons outside nuclear family	33	61
No help or help only from members of nuclear family	41	72

of their nuclear family (i.e., their husbands and children), or who presently did not know who would help them constituted one group, while those who had help from persons outside the nuclear family, either relatives or friends, constituted the other. A clear relationship exists with only one of the fertility-related attitude and behavior questions, but this relationship is consistent for all three child-care questions: that those women who could share responsibility for child care with persons outside the nuclear family were more likely to state that they had desired the child that they were presently expecting than were those who could not.

Because of the small size of the sample, any conclusions must be reached very cautiously, but certain patterns of relationships do seem to exist. Most significant is the striking relationship between level of education and both the salience of family size problems and willingness to use contraception. Equally interesting is the lack of relationship between family-size attitudes and marital status and between frequency of church attendance and willingness to use contraception. Also significant is the strong relation between current number of children and attitudes toward family size and contraception; the women with three or more children are almost unanimous in their desire to have no more children, and most of them express favorable attitudes toward the use of contraception. The fact that women who could rely on persons outside the nuclear family for help with child care were more likely to have desired this child than were those who could not indicates that this relationship merits more intensive investigation as a possible link between urbanization and fertility.

The problem of child care does not seem to have been as salient for the respondents as certain other problems, however. I asked sixty-nine of the women who had stated that they did not want any more children why they felt this way. Interestingly, only two women stated that they did not want any more children because they were not married, and only seven cited their own health or suffering as a reason. Furthermore, only one gave the problems of child care as an explanation. Two women stated that one of their children was sick, and one that it was difficult for a large family to rent a house. However, two-thirds cited their poverty as one reason for not wanting any more children. Thirty-five simply stated this in general terms: "There is great poverty." "Life is very expensive." Four gave as a reason the fact that their husbands did not have regular jobs ("Without full employment I don't want to have any more, because the children are hungry"). Twenty-five women spoke specifically of the economic costs of children, however. Eleven mentioned the cost of supporting a child ("A child costs a lot"), while fourteen specifically stated the cost of education ("We don't want them to be ignorant" and "To send so many children out into the world—they eat well, but how will we educate them?").

These answers suggest that for lower-class urban women the economic burden of children upon the nuclear family, a burden which is apparently not shared to any significant extent, might be a more important determinant of family size attitudes than is the problem of child care. Both problems are closely related, of course, being the result of the relative independence of the nuclear family in the urban environment. It is unfortunate that I did not include a specific investigation of the relevance of the economic problems of child-rearing to attitudes on family size in my study, but this might prove to be a fruitful topic for further research.

NOTES

1. J. Mayone Stycos, "Needed Research on Latin American Fertility: Urbanization and Fertility," *The Milbank Memorial Fund Quarterly,* vol. XLIII, no. 4, October 1965, part 2, p. 303.

2. Kingsley Davis, "Institutional Patterns Favoring High Fertility in Underdeveloped Areas," *Eugenics Quarterly,* vol. 2, no. 1, 1955, pp. 34–35.

3. G. W. Skinner, "Cultural Values, Social Structure, and Population Growth," *Population Bulletin of the United Nations,* vol. 5, July 1956, p. 10.

4. J. Mayone Stycos, "Family and Fertility in Puerto Rico," *American Sociological Review,* vol. XVIII, October 1952, p. 578.

5. I began the study interviewing only women aged twenty-five to thirty-five years, but after one month discovered that this would not yield a large enough sample, and so I had to lower the age range five years.

6. This figure is only approximate for several reasons. First, wages were sometimes given in weekly or monthly figures, which I changed to a daily figure by assuming a 6-day work week and a 24-day work month, which may or may not have been correct. Second, many of the husbands were only irregularly employed, so that these figures probably exaggerate their actual income. Third, the policy of the office was apparently to record a standard figure—usually 21 pesos per day—if the respondent did not know her husband's income, if he was currently unemployed, etc.

7. By functioning relationship, I mean one which the respondent herself considered to be active. Relatives, *compadres,* or friends whom she named but then qualified by saying: "We don't have anything to do with them." "We aren't friends." "It's not possible to visit." or "We don't see them." were not included in the calculations.

8. It is interesting to note that the average household size (5.5) is slightly larger than that found by Fals-Borda in the rural community of Saucio (5 persons) and that the percent of households containing relatives outside the nuclear family in Saucio is exactly the same as that in my sample (27 percent). However, this comparison is not very meaningful, since Saucio includes families at all stages of their life cycles, whereas my sample included only young families. Orlando Fals-Borda, *Campesinos de los Andes,* Monografías Sociológicas, Universidad Nacional, no. 7, Bogotá, 1961, p. 243.

9. This situation, in which a significant proportion of the total sample have no relatives within the city, contrasts with the community of Saucio, which Fals-Borda describes as consisting of a network of kin relationships: ". . . most of the people were mutually bound by family ties." (P. 252.)

10. Stycos, "Family and Fertility in Puerto Rico," pp. 578–579.

11. Fals-Borda, *op. cit.,* pp. 70, 254.

12. Sidney W. Mintz and Eric R. Wolf, "An Analysis of Ritual Co-parenthood," *Southwestern Journal of Anthropology,* vol. 6, 1950, p. 355.

13. Fals-Borda, *op. cit.,* p. 245.

CHAPTER 15

Projective Testing for Ideal Family Size

Prepared by **Alan B. Simmons.**

Survey studies on preferences for family size and attitudes toward family planning have been carried out in many parts of the under-developed regions of the world. The methodology and many of the survey questions are nearly identical in these studies; hence there has been widespread expectation that the data would have unprece-dented utility for cross-cultural comparisons. Proponents of family planning hoped that the data would yield insights into attitudes on family size and into how these attitudes were being modified by changing social circumstances. There is a growing body of criticism, however, suggesting that the studies have failed to meet these ex-pectations, that, at best, the survey data have given us an incomplete picture and, at worst, have given us a false one.[1]

The surveys consistently reveal that a majority of women claim to want "small" families of no more than three to four children. But it has become apparent that often there is considerably less than a perfect correspondence between verbal statements and actual be-havior. Many of the same women who claim to want small families do not take advantage of family planning services when offered, and among those who do, many drop all family planning practices within a year.[2]

When investigators have probed the matter, many respondents have revealed considerable uncertainty and ambivalence regarding the size of an "ideal" family. For example, Jamaican women were asked, early in an interview, whether it was better to have plenty of children, and later in the same interview, whether it was better to have few children. Only 37 percent of the sample showed no inconsistencies.[3] Puerto Rican women who say they want small families also see distinct advantages in large families.[4]

A typical sequence of questions on preferences for family size goes as follows. "Ideally, how many children would you like to have?" "Why do you want 'x' [this number of] children?" Examination of these questions reveals a number of built-in assumptions which the respondent must take into account in answering: (1) that one may have family size preferences, i.e., that it is an issue for discussion; (2) that the respondent *should* have such a preference; (3) that this preference should be expressed as a *single number,* such as "3" or "7," and not as a range, such as "3 to 7"; and (4) that the respondent should have a reasonable explanation for her preference.

These assumptions may be wholly or partially false; hence, in many cases, the answers may reflect the assumptions more than they do reality. In some traditional societies there may be a conceptual void surrounding family size; it is considered to be determined largely by "luck" or "God," so the very thought of a family size preference may seem unreasonable—and the more traditional respondents usually do not hesitate to say so.[5] Family size may be seldom discussed among peers or between couples; a majority of lower-income women in Peru, for example, said that they had never previously thought about the issue.[6] It has also been noted that the stated ideals of the respondent tend to correlate rather well with her actual family size, which in a noncontracepting population may mean not much more than "I like what I have."[7]

These criticisms suggest that cultural definitions related to family size preferences should be explicitly investigated. Rather than assume that women evaluate families in terms of size or that they have size preferences, we should be looking for methods of measuring these tendencies. In this paper we will discuss a projective technique designed to answer the following questions in any social-cultural setting.

1. To what extent is "family size" a conceptual dimension which meaningfully distinguishes families from one another?

2. To what extent will women, consciously or unconsciously, reveal a preference for family size in a situation where there is no stated assumption that they should have such a preference?

3. To what extent will women spontaneously connect differences in family size to social and economic problems in raising and educating the children?

Answers to questions such as these should provide a useful foundation for understanding the meaning of responses to conventional social surveys and for understanding the cognitive-motivational system which influences the outcome of any family planning program.

The projective procedure used in this study is a modification of the approach used by J. M. Stycos in an earlier study of attitudes toward family size in rural Haiti.[8] Stycos presented his respondents (men and women) with large photographs of four Haitian families, asking them to comment on the differences between the families and then to choose the families they liked best, for whatever reason. The families in the photographs differed in size (large and small) and wealth (poor and well-to-do). It was found that only a minority of respondents (45 percent) noticed size differences and considered them to be important. This was taken as evidence that family size is not conceptually or motivationally salient in rural Haiti. Unfortunately, all the subjects in Stycos' sample were equally rural and "backward" (even the mayor of the village worked his land by hand), so we do not know how a better-educated, more urban group would have responded to the projective materials. Greater awareness of and concern with size differences in a control group of this kind would have provided clear support for the rationale underlying the projective method.

Our object in this study is to further elaborate and examine the utility of the projective method. Our approach differs in several important ways from Stycos' pioneering study: Bogotá, Colombia, the site of our investigation, is a rapidly growing metropolis (1966 population over 2 million) in a nation that has experienced substantial social change and industrial growth in the last two decades. As the 1964 CELADE Survey of Bogotá shows, contraceptive knowledge and practice are low among the less educated, but considerably higher among the better educated.[9]

Our study focuses on social-status differences in point of view regarding family size. In analysis, emphasis will be on different status patterns of response, but we have also included a control group of

TABLE 51

Knowledge and Practice of Birth Control by Education,
Bogotá Women, 1964*

	Percent Who Could Name a Method of Birth Control	Percent Who Had Used Birth Control	(n)
Education:			
Less than primary	39	9	(705)
Primary completed	48	16	(596)
Some secondary or more	67	31	(523)
Total	49	18'	(1,824)

*International Population Program, Cornell University, tabulations of 1964 CELADE survey
of eight major Latin American cities. See footnote 9.

young unmarried women to see what influence married life might
have on the responses.

In the CELADE fertility survey of 1964, the majority of Bogotá
women, including a majority of less-educated women with high
fertility, claimed they wanted fewer than four children; yet only 31
percent of those women with less than primary education said they
had thought about the topic before (Table 52). It was this somewhat
contradictory situation of low stated ideals and equally low prior
consideration of ideal family size that initially prompted our interest
in "cultural" definitions of family size. After presenting the projective
materials to the women in our sample, we asked them a typical survey
question on ideal family size, so that a direct comparison between
projective and survey responses would be possible.

The sample is composed of 83 married or consensually mated
women and 127 unmarried high school girls aged 16–19. The high
school girls constitute a control group of females who, while approaching marriage, do not have any direct experience as spouses
and mothers. Such a group allows us to investigate the impact of
married life on perceptions of family size.

Each age group was subdivided into high- and low-social-status
groups, on the basis of father's occupation for the girls and husband's
occupation for the women. An attempt was made to maximize the
status differences among the unmarried girls by selecting the
higher-status girls from an exclusive private school and the lower-

status girls from a rather run-down public school. The fathers of the higher-status girls were generally professionals or well-to-do business men; the fathers of the lower-status girls were generally unskilled or semiskilled. Similarly, to maximize the status differences among the married women, the higher-status group was selected from a women's service organization (husbands were professionals), and the lower-status group was chosen from a line at a free outpatient clinic.

Photographs of twenty-five different conjugal families (mother, father, and their children) were taken by the author in the Bogotá area. The family sizes ranged from one to nine children, with all intermediate sizes represented. Some families were clearly of low status, wearing old or ragged clothing and appearing in front of unpainted wood and tin shanties; others were substantially better dressed and appeared in front of two-floor brick and stucco houses. Other differences, such as age of parents or sex ratio of the children, were kept to a minimum.

At the start, it was not known what range of differences in family size needed to be portrayed. On the one hand, it was expected that the differences between two- and three-child families might be too small to be noticed by anyone. On the other hand, a comparison of two- and nine-child families would almost always be noticed and might produce an invariable preference for the smaller family among all sample groups. What we wanted was an intermediate range of

TABLE 52

Ideal Family Size, Actual Family Size, and Prior
Consideration of Ideal Family Size, Bogotá Women, 1964*

	Median Ideal Family Size	Median Number of Living Children, by Ages 35–39	Percent Who Had Previously		
			Thought about Ideal Family Size	Discussed Ideal Size with Spouse	(n)
Respondent's education:					
Less than primary	4.4	5.1	31	25	(705)
Primary completed	4.0	4.4	53	45	(596)
Some secondary or more	3.9	3.9	71	51	(523)
Total	4.1	4.5	49	40	(1824)

* International Population Program, Cornell University, tabulations of 1964 CELADE survey of eight major Latin American cities. See footnote 9.

A   B

size differences which would most likely elicit perceptual differences between the sample groups.

A pretest was conducted to determine suitable pairs, using all possible combinations of families with one to nine children: a total of thirty-six pairs with size differences. Among half the pairs, social-status differences were introduced, with the relative status of the smaller family in the pair alternating between high and low. These pairs were randomly ordered, then broken into four subsets of nine pairs each. Each subset was presented by slide projection to a group of twelve female high school seniors in a middle-class school. For each pair, the girls were asked to describe the differences and similarities between the two families and to choose the family that they would best like to be mother of.

The pretest disclosed that larger-family size differences were more likely to be noticed and given as a reason for a choice than smaller ones, but that the smaller the two families being compared, the more noticeable the size difference. The difference between six and nine children, for example, was not as salient as the difference between three and six, although the difference is three children in each case.

The introduction of status differences provided another basis for choice, with nearly all preferences weighted toward the higher-status family. When the comparison was between two large lower-status families, many subjects preferred not to make any choice.

Taking these findings into account, the following nine pairs of family photographs were selected for the final sample. (*L* indicates a lower-class family, *M* a middle-class family.)

Order of Presentation	Number of Children in the Family: On the Left	On the Right	Size of Difference
First	7 *L*	8 *M*	1 child
Second	4 *M*	3 *L*	1 child
Third	2 *M*	4 *L*	2 children
Fourth	3 *L*	8 *M*	5 children
Fifth	3 *M*	4 *M*	1 child
Sixth	4 *M*	7 *M*	3 children
Seventh	3 *M*	2 *M*	1 child
Eighth	6 *M*	4 *M*	2 children
Ninth	4 *M*	5 *M*	1 child

The selection and ordering were made with the following considerations in mind: In the first three pairs, size differences move from less salient to more salient, so that the presence of an obvious size difference in the first pair would not make the focus of our study immediately clear to the respondents. Status differences are included in some of the pairs, especially the first ones, so that there would be at least one other salient difference. The last five comparisons try to minimize all differences except size differences, so that all but those least concerned with size factors will tend to take size differences into account. Finally, the pairs mainly cover an "intermediate" range of size differences—only one difference is greater than three children.

When the interview began, the precise nature of the study was not revealed and respondents were told only that the questions were part of a study of "family life." The first questions were accordingly about place of birth, father's occupation, and household possessions. Only after they had responded to all nine pairs of photographs were they asked conventional survey questions about their ideal family size.

In order to present the pictures simultaneously to a number of subjects, the paired photographs were projected onto a large screen.

The girls saw the projections while seated in groups of fifteen to twenty in a school classroom, and the adults while seated in groups of eleven to fifteen in the lecture room of a hospital. Each of the nine pairs was presented for a total of forty seconds. After the first twenty-five seconds, the lights were turned on while the respondents answered the question: "Are there differences or similarities between these two families— if so, what are they?" Then the slide was presented for another fifteen seconds, after which the subjects were asked: "Which of the two families would you prefer to be the mother of?" and "Why do you prefer this family?" Literate subjects completed a questionnaire; nonliterate subjects were personally interviewed.

The responses to the first questions, "Are there differences or similarities between these two families—if so, what are they?" were categorized as "size differences," "status differences," or "extraneous differences" (such as facial expression or age). Typical responses and the code categories which were used to describe them are given below.

Response	Code category for difference noted
1. "The two families are the same; I can see no difference."	1. None
2. "The father in 'A' (family on left) is wearing a hat and the father in 'B' is not."	2. Extraneous
3. "Family 'A' is smaller but wealthier."	3. Size and status.
4. "The family on the right is larger and dirtier—but the children are smiling and look happier."	4. Size, status, and extraneous.

Reasons for preferring one family over the other, if a choice was made, were coded in an identical fashion. The choice itself was also coded. All the data were punched on IBM cards for analysis.

"FAMILY SIZE" AS A CONCEPT

Nearly all the women in our sample have "family size" in their conceptual repertoire (Table 53)—size differences were mentioned at least once by 97 percent of the women. The few women who did

TABLE 53

Percent of Respondents Who Did Not Notice Any Size
Differences

| | Social Status | | | | |
| | Low | | High | | |
	Percent	(n)	Percent	(n)	Total, Percent
Unmarried girls, 16–19	0	(53)	0	(74)	0
Married women, 19–49	13	(48)	0	(35)	7
Total	6		0		3

not mention size even once were all lower-status wives, but even in this group they were a distinct minority of 13 percent.

These women did, however, notice other differences. Everybody in the sample noticed some differences; in fact, everybody noticed status differences at least once.

How do the groups differ in their propensity to apply the "family size" dimension? Each respondent who completed the projective task had nine chances to notice size differences, and the average woman noticed 5.5 differences, or 61 percent of the differences she could have noticed (Table 54). Among the better-educated subgroups (the school girls and the upper-status women), the propensity to notice size differences is at least as high as for the sample as a whole. The lower-status women, however, noticed size differences on only 47 percent of the presentations. In part, this lower propensity to notice size reflects the 13 percent of the lower-status women who did not notice any size differences; but excluding this minority from the analysis does not change the general picture, for the remaining lower-status women noticed size differences on only 53 percent of the presentations.

"COGNITIVE COMPLEXITY"

The lower propensity to notice size differences among the lower-status women appears to be related to a lower propensity to notice any differences (Table 54). The average respondent in the sample as a whole failed to notice any differences on 9 percent of the

TABLE 54

Number of Presentations Where "No Differences," "Size Differences," "Status Differences," and "Extraneous Differences" Were Noticed as Percentages of All Presentations*

| | Unmarried Girls | | Married Women | | |
Percent of Presentations Where:	Low Status	High Status	Low Status	High Status	Total
No differences were noticed	5	4	21	11	9
Size differences were noticed	66	67	47	61	61
Status differences were noticed	47	54	30	46	45
Extraneous differences were noticed	65	51	39	45	51
Number of presentations	(474)	(666)	(432)	(315)	(1,887)

*Percentages total more than 100 because more than one difference was noticed on most presentations.

TABLE 55

Percent of Presentations in Which Size Differences Were Noticed for Each Degree of Family Size Difference

| | Girls, 16–19 | | | | Women, 19–49 | | | | | |
| | Low Status | | High Status | | Low Status | | High Status | | Total | |
Size of Difference of:	Percent	(n)*	Percent	(n)	Percent	(n)	Percent	(n)	Percent	(n)
One child (pairs 1, 2, 5, 7, 9)†	56	(263)	57	(370)	43	(240)	54	(175)	53	(1,048)
Two children (pairs 3, 8)	72	(106)	79	(148)	50	(96)	62	(70)	66	(420)
Three children (pair 6)	69	(53)	79	(73)	56	(48)	91	(36)	73	(210)
Five children (pair 4)	81	(52)	79	(75)	52	(48)	74	(34)	73	(209)
All size differences	66	(474)	67	(666)	47	(452)	61	(315)	61	(1,887)

*(n) = number of presentations.
† Pair number refers to order of presentation. See the text for details on the status and size characteristics of each pair.

presentations, but the average lower-class woman failed to notice any differences on 20 percent of the presentations. In addition to the relatively low propensity to notice "size" differences, the lower-class women were also less likely to notice "status" and "extraneous" differences; that is, the lower-class women are less able to distinguish the families along any dimension.

The lower-class women are also relatively low in sensitivity to increasing size differences. Table 55 shows, for the sample as a whole, that a difference of one child is noticed 53 persent of the time, and a difference of five children 73 percent of the time, for an overall increase of 20 percent in awareness as the size difference increases from one to five. Lower-status women, however, show an increase of only 9 percent in awareness over the same range.

Further study is required to see what relationship, if any, there is between awareness of differences in our projective task and general cognitive competence.

PERSONAL CONCERN WITH SIZE DIFFERENCES

Awareness of size differences does not necessarily imply that these differences are in any way important to the respondent. A woman may notice the size difference between two families, but if it is not important to her, she may ignore it in deciding which family she would prefer to be the mother of. How important were size differences in influencing the family choices made by our sample?

For the sample as a whole, 32 percent of the choices were based at least in part on size differences (Table 56). Married women gave

TABLE 56

Percentage of Choices Which Included Size as a Basis for Choice

	Low Status		High Status		Total	
	Percent	*(n)**	*Percent*	*(n)**	*Percent*	*(n)**
Girls, 16–19	28	(398)	26	(590)	27	(988)
Women, 19–49	41	(327)	38	(248)	40	(575)
Total	34	(725)	30	(830)	32	(1,563)

*(n) = number of presentations where choices were made.

size as a reason more frequently than high school girls; among the married women, the lower-status group most frequently gave size as a reason. These findings are somewhat surprising, for the groups that most frequently noticed size differences (high school girls) were the groups who indicated least concern with them, and the group who least frequently noticed size differences (lower-status women) was the group who indicated most concern with them. Conceptual awareness of size differences and subjective importance of size differences are, then, empirically distinct variables.

Size differences can be offered as a reason for choice only when they have been noticed. Since some groups notice size differences more frequently, the number of choices where "size" was given as a reason is more meaningfully expressed as a proportion of those choices where size differences were noticed. In other words, once a woman has noticed a given size difference, how likely is she to include it as a factor influencing her choice? If the size differences are important to the women, the likelihood should be high.

When we consider only those choices where size was noticed, the overall intergroup pattern of concern does not change, but the magnitude of the intergroup differences is greatly increased. Lower-status women gave size among their reasons on 87 percent of the choices where they noticed size differences, upper-status women gave size among their reasons on 62 percent of these choices, and the girls gave size among their reasons on only about 40 percent of such choices.

The conclusions suggested by this data are somewhat paradoxical. High school girls appear to be cognitively sensitive to, but personally unconcerned with, family size differences. Conversely, lower-status women appear to be cognitively insensitive to, but personally concerned with, these differences. Let us now turn to the relationship between awareness and concern on the one hand and actual family size choices on the other.

CHOICE PATTERNS

If we judge from the overall choice patterns, there would appear to be no general preference for smaller families, for only on about one-half of the choices was the smaller family preferred (Table 57). However, we must remember that in five of the comparisons the

TABLE 57

Percent of Choices That Were for the Smaller Family

Percent Choosing the Smaller Family When:	All Choices		Choices Where Size Difference Was Noticed		Choices Where Size Was Given as a Reason	
	Percent	(n)	Percent	(n)	Percent	(n)
The smaller family had higher status and:						
two fewer children (pair 3)*	80	(193)	81	(157)	94	(86)
The two families had equal status and:						
one child less (5, 7, 9)	51	(466)	57	(281)	72	(118)
two children less (pair 8)	80	(172)	79	(137)	84	(83)
three children less (pair 6)	81	(181)	81	(146)	88	(86)
The smaller family had lower status and:						
one child less (1, 2)	23	(382)	31	(189)	63	(62)
five children less (pair 4)	38	(169)	39	(133)	64	(59)
All pairs	53	(1,563)	59	(1,063)	78	(494)

*Pair number refers to order of presentation. See the text for details on the status and size characteristics of each pair.

families differed by only one child and that in three of them the smaller family was of lower social status. In addition, the size differences were not always noticed or taken into account in the choice. As Table 57 shows, all these factors are important. The preference for the smaller family varies systematically with (1) the relative social status of the smaller family, (2) the magnitude of the size differences between the families, and (3) the respondent's concern with the size differences.

The women have a clear preference for the more well-to-do families. For example, when the smaller family had one child less and was of lower status, it was chosen 23 percent of the time. When the smaller family had one child less and was of equal status, it was chosen 51 percent of the time. Even when the lower-status family had five fewer children (three versus eight children), it was preferred only 38 percent of the time.

When the status of the two families was equal, there was a clear preference for smaller families. For example, when there was a difference of two or three children between two middle-status families, the smaller family was chosen about 70 percent of the time. When this difference was only one child, the smaller family was chosen only about 50 percent of the time.

When we consider only those choices where the respondent noticed the size difference, the previously noted pattern of choices is not substantially altered. However, when we consider only those choices where size was given as a reason, the pattern changes: on each comparison, and especially on those comparisons where the size difference was small or where the smaller family had lower status, there is a large increase in preference for the smaller family. Seventy-eight percent of the choices where size was given as a reason were for the smaller family. In general, then, we can say that personal concern with size differences indicates a desire to have small families.

However, in summarizing Table 57 we must not ignore the sizable minority of choices (22 percent) that were for larger families even when size was given as a reason for the choice. Such responses were given most often when the smaller family had lower status and when the size difference between two equal status families was small. An examination of the full reasons given for these choices reveals that, for these women, a fairly large family of four to eight children is acceptable or even desirable relative to a small family, when it is reasonably well-off financially. Among the one-third of the women who chose a wealthier family with eight children over a poorer one with three (pair 4), the following response was common: "I prefer family B [the wealthier one] because it is on a higher social level, and I want my children to have health and decent clothes. If I can have this, it doesn't matter how many children I have." This may be contrasted with a typical response among the two-thirds majority who chose the smaller, poorer family in the same pair: "I prefer family A [the smaller, poorer family]. . . . While they do not always have enough money, it is easier to look after and educate fewer children." In both examples the burdens of a large family are explicitly recognized, but the effect of economic well-being is appraised differently; for some respondents the moderate wealth of a "middle" status family was sufficient to compensate for the economic and social burdens of eight children, but for others it was not. Yet, in one way or another, nearly all the women indicated that the actual number of children they would be happy with depended in part upon the family's economic circumstances.

RELATIVE PREFERENCE FOR SMALLER FAMILIES

We now turn our attention to group differences in choice patterns. Table 58 shows that married women are more likely than unmarried girls to choose smaller families and that among married women the lower-status respondents are most likely to choose smaller families. This is the same pattern as that for personal concern with size differences shown in Table 56. Given that the choices based partly on size considerations were generally for smaller families, it is not surprising that the lower-status women, who most frequently gave size as a reason, most frequently chose smaller families. Yet, as Table

TABLE 58

Percent of Choices for the Smaller Family, Controlling for Social Status and Age of the Respondent

	All choices		Choices Where:			
			Size Was Given as Reason		Size Was Not Given as Reason	
	Percent	No. of Choices	Percent	No. of Choices	Percent	No. of Choices
Unmarried high school girls:						
Low status	48	(398)	74	(110)	37	(288)
High status	51	(590)	77	(156)	41	(434)
Married women:						
Low status	61	(327)	83	(133)	45	(194)
High status	55	(248)	80	(95)	40	(153)
Total	53	(1,563)	78	(494)	40	(1,069)

58 also shows, lower-status women were more likely to choose smaller families even when we control for concern. In other words, we find that these women were most likely to choose smaller families, whether or not size was given as a reason. This finding suggests that some lower-class women were unconsciously choosing smaller families for size reasons and rationalizing their decision on the basis of other differences which they explicitly noticed.

IDEAL FAMILY SIZE

In contrast to the CELADE survey findings presented earlier in this paper, lower-status women in Bogotá, in response to projective imagery, reveal smaller family size preferences than higher-status women. What, then, is the relationship between responses to survey questions and responses to the projective situation?

After our respondents had completed the projective part of the interview, they were asked: "If you could choose exactly the number of children for your family, ideally, how many children would you like to have?" This is similar to one of the questions on ideal family size used in the CELADE survey. In Table 59 we see that the adults' responses to this question are somewhat lower than those of the Bogotá women in the earlier CELADE survey. However, as in the earlier study, the lower-status women say they want more children than do the higher-status women. This finding helps dispel any doubts that the small 1966 sample was greatly unrepresentative relative to the large sample in the CELADE study.

For the sake of analysis, respondents were arbitrarily divided into

TABLE 59

Median Number of Children Preferred

	Low Status		High Status		Total	
	Median	(n)*	Median	(n)	Median	(n)
Girls, 16–19	3.9	(53)	3.9	(74)	3.9	(127)
Women, 19–49	3.7	(48)	3.1	(35)	3.4	(83)
Total	3.8	(101)	3.7	(109)	3.8	(210)

*(n) = number of respondents.

TABLE 60

Percent Choosing Smaller Family, by Preferred Family Size

Size of Preferred Family Is:		Percent Choosing Smaller Family on All Presentations		Percent Choosing 3-child Family over 4-child Family (pair 5)	
		Percent	(n)*	Percent	(n)
Low-status	Small†	56	(145)	55	(11)
girls	Large‡	43	(253)	40	(22)
High-status	Small	55	(218)	59	(22)
girls	Large	50	(372)	51	(35)
Low-status	Small	58	(185)	67	(18)
adults	Large	65	(142)	67	(15)
High-status	Small	66	(132)	80	(15)
adults	Large	42	(116)	46	(13)
Total (all	Small	58	(680)	65	(66)
respondents)	Large	49	(883)	50	(85)

*(n) is the number of presentations where choices were made by respondents who stated preferred family size.
†Small family is 1–3 children.
‡Large family is 4+ children.

two categories on the basis of their ideal-family-size statements—those desiring a *small* family (three children or less) and those desiring a *large* family (four children or more). Table 60 shows that, for the sample as a whole, respondents with small ideals have a somewhat greater preference for smaller families on the projective materials; 58 percent of the choices by those with small ideals were for smaller families as opposed to 50 percent of the choices by those with large ideals. This relationship between ideals and family size choices is similar for the girls, regardless of status, but is much stronger among the high-status women. For the low-status women, however, the relationship observed for the sample as a whole is somewhat reversed, indicating that the ideal-family-size statements of these women were not at all predictive of their family-size choices in the projective materials.

Table 60 also provides data on the relationship between family-size ideals and preferences for the smaller family in pair 5, the comparison between two middle-status families, one with three children, the

356 : :   IDEOLOGY, FAITH, AND FAMILY PLANNING

other with four. The analysis of this pair is important, for it contains no complicating status differences, and the family sizes (three versus four children) correspond precisely to the division between small and large ideals. Under these circumstances one would expect a stronger relationship between ideals and choices than was found for all pairs combined. Despite the small number of choices on which the percentages are based, this is generally true; however, among the lower-status women there is still no relationship between stated ideals and projective choices, for two-thirds of these women chose the smaller family, regardless of their stated ideals. For the sample as a whole the relationship between stated ideals and actual choices is weak, and for the lower-status women there is no relationship at all.

SUMMARY AND DISCUSSION

The projective results support some findings from direct questions in the earlier CELADE survey. In these instances the mutual validation of findings by quite different approaches gives a firmer base for making empirical generalizations. But the projective results also tell us several things which conventional survey methods cannot. Such additional information allows a better understanding of how attitudes toward family size emerge in the process of social and economic change. Let us consider these points with regard to the aims of the projective study.

In response to our projective stimuli, lower-status women revealed a relative insensitivity to family size differences. They were least likely spontaneously to distinguish families on the basis of size. This finding is congruent with the CELADE finding that ideal family size among these women is not a salient concept—few have thought about how many children they would like to have.

While "family size" is not a salient conceptual dimension among the lower-status women, the concept is not alien to them. Quite to the contrary, 65 percent of the lower-status women commented on at least one size difference on the first two presentations, and nearly 90 percent commented on at least one size difference of the nine presentations. This may be compared with Stycos's finding in Haiti where only 45 percent of his rural respondents (including some with high school education) noticed any size differences on his first two presentations.

On the important issue of family size preferences the projective findings provide some support for the CELADE survey results, but they also go beyond these findings to suggest important qualifications. When women explicitly made their choice on the basis of size, there was a clear preference for smaller families. This would seem to support the stated preference for "small" families (less than four children) generally found in the CELADE survey. However, only a minority (30 percent) of the projective choices were made even partly on the basis of size; and even on those presentations where size differences were noticed, size was given among the reasons for the choice only half of the time. Hence, simply noticing a size difference did not significantly increase the tendency to choose the smaller family. Status differences and extraneous differences, such as sex of children, age of parents, and perceived happiness of parents, were just as important as size differences even when size differences were noticed.

In cases where the larger family was better off financially, size was seldom relevant for the choice; over two-thirds of the choices were directly for the wealthier family. Explicit awareness of size differences did not change this choice pattern. About one-quarter of the respondents went so afar as to say that having many children was an asset, a positive feature of the wealthier family. We may conclude that, for most respondents, the wealth of the "ideal" family was a much more important consideration than size. If the family is relatively well-to-do, more children may be quite acceptable, and for a minority it is a positive feature.

However, there was both implicit and explicit awareness among all those who included size among their reasons for their choices that many children are a burden for a poor family. Awareness of the burdens of many children in a poor family was greatest among the lower-status women and least among the high-school girls. The lower-status women gave size as a reason for their choices most frequently, despite the fact that they were least likely to notice size differences to begin with; high school girls noticed a high proportion of size differences, but these differences were seldom mentioned among the reasons for the girls' choices. Concern with family size differences, once noticed, appears to reflect objective social circumstances of the respondent: married women, especially lower-status married women, have had more experience with the economic burdens that large families can bring.

This stronger tendency to choose small families, and to do so for economic reasons, seems to indicate that lower-status women in Bogotá *want* small families. In fact, the projective choices by the lower-status women who gave size for a reason indicate that they want small families even when their stated ideal family size is for larger families. However, the wider context of our findings warns us that this *want* must be interpreted with caution. In what sense can it be said that these women want fewer children when they have a low propensity to think of families in terms of size? To what extent can we say that they want small families when they view larger ones as acceptable, or even preferable, among the well-to-do?

Combining the projective and survey findings allows us to draw some tentative conclusions about the evolution of attitudes toward family size in the process of social and economic change. In the most traditional situation, such as that described by Stycos in rural Haiti,[10] the conceptual void surrounding family size is almost complete. People do not think of families in terms of size, they are not spontaneously aware of any advantages of smaller families, and the notion of an "ideal family size" is beyond their comprehension. In Bogotá we find a more advanced situation. The dimension "family size" is almost universally recognized; women are aware of the advantages of fewer children, at least for low-income families, and contraceptive knowledge is slowly diffusing down the social ladder. However, even here the lower-status women are still practically in a social and conceptual void with regard to family size. A majority have never previously thought about ideal family sizes, much less discussed these with their husband, and this is reflected in a general insensitivity to differences in family size. The extent to which these conceptual barriers will inhibit the long-term acceptance and use of family planning methods will not be known until family planning services are widely offered and an evaluation of their adoption has been made. Comparative studies combining survey and projective findings with the acceptance of family planning are required before we can use these methods to predict the outcome of family planning programs.

NOTES

1. For a review of many criticisms, see Philip M. Hauser, "Family Planning and Population Programs—A Book Review," *Demography* vol. 4, no. 1, 1967, pp. 397–414.

2. For example, see Freedman, in B. Berelson et al. (eds.), *Family Planning and Population Programs* (Chicago: University of Chicago Press, 1965), p. 818. These points are also discussed by Hauser, *op. cit.*

3. J. Mayone Stycos and Kurt Back, *The Control of Human Fertility in Jamaica* (Ithaca, N.Y.: Cornell University Press, 1964), pp. 23–24.

4. J. Mayone Stycos, *Family Fertility in Puerto Rico* (New York: Columbia University Press, 1955), pp. 169–177.

5. J. Mayone Stycos, "Attitudes toward Family Size in Haiti," *Human Organization,* Spring 1964, pp. 42–47.

6. J. Mayone Stycos, "Social Class and Preferred Family Size in Peru," *American Journal of Sociology,* vol. 70, no. 6, May 1965, pp. 651–658.

7. For discussion of the correlation, see R. Hill, J. M. Stycos, and K. Back, *The Family and Population Control* (Chapel Hill, N.C.: University of North Carolina Press, 1959), chap. 4.

8. Stycos, "Social Class and Preferred Family Size in Peru."

9. In 1964, the United Nations Demographic Center in Santiago, Chile (CELADE), with the cooperation of the International Population Program, Cornell University, carried out an extensive fertility survey in eight major Latin American cities. A summary of the findings may be found in Carmen Miró, "Some Misconceptions Disproved," in Berelson, *op. cit.,* pp. 615–634.

10. Stycos, "Attitudes toward Family Size in Haiti."

PART 4

The Future
of Family Planning

CHAPTER 16

After the Encyclical

On the eve of the encyclical the liberal Latin American clergy slept soundly, confident that the Pope could not fail to respond to public opinion and to the majority report of his Commission for the Study of Population, Family and Births. The report had taken the position that married couples themselves should decide how to plan their families and control their fertility. Subsequent to the report there had been ample evidence that both public sentiment and rank-and-file clerical sentiment were veering in the same direction, if indeed, they had been anywhere else. In 1967 the Catholic International Institutes of Socio-Religious Research (FERES) sponsored a survey of priests and laymen in five Latin American countries (Table 61). A total of 2,500 were interviewed, stratified into various classes: "Bishops, priests of high and low level in the hierarchy, lay directors of religious apostolic organizations, lay militants in these organizations, practicing Catholics, and nominal Catholics."[1] Such a stratification system suggests that the sample contains more upper-rank clericals and more militant Catholics than could be expected by chance—in short, the study is deliberately weighted in the direction of *conservative* Catholic opinion. Nevertheless, when asked, "What do you think the Pope will say about methods of family

TABLE 61

Percent Who Believe Pope Will Permit
Rhythm Only, by Country and Religious
Status

Country	Clerics	Laymen
Brazil	11	13
Chile	9	14
Colombia	11	26
Mexico	20	29
Venezuela	23	13

planning?" the proportion who thought the Pope would allow only the rhythm method totaled only 15 percent among the clergy and 19 percent among the laymen.[2] The balance believed he would leave the matter to the individual conscience. In no country or subgroup did as many as a third expect a rhythm-only pronouncement.

The sample was then asked what their attitude would be if the Pope reaffirmed the current church norms on family planning. Reactions were classified as "satisfaction," "disappointment," and "indifference." While the clerical reaction is not reported, it can perhaps be inferred from that of the directors of Catholic organizations, only 18 percent of whom said they would be pleased by such a pronouncement, while 68 percent said they would be disappointed.

If these were the attitudes and expectations in a conservatively biased sample of Latin Americans, we can only surmise what they were among European and North American Catholics. The editorial position of the *Washington Post* was probably typical: "In 1968, it simply did not seem possible that a great world institution could undertake to review its old stance, receive enlightened advice from a commission of its own appointment, and then turn its face resolutely back to the past."[3] But it did.

The non-Latin world was shocked and indignant. The *New York Times* referred to "the terrible Malthusian nightmare that has prompted thoughtful men around the world to react with astonishment and alarm to the Papal Encyclical"; the *London Evening Standard* called it "the most negative and arguably dangerous doctrine of this century"; the *Washington Star* held it was irrelevant to the "entire Roman Catholic world and to both sexes"; the *New Statesman* regarded it as "the product of a bureaucracy without faith, hope or charity"; *Newsweek* called it "The Pope's Bitter Pill"; the U.S.S.R.'s *Literaturnaya Gazeta* piously opined that "only a wicked and cruel man could forbid effective and inoffensive methods of contraception"; and Italy's *Il Messaggero* concluded that demographic problems "cannot be entrusted to the intelligence of single men."

In West Germany, Belgium, and Austria the bishops told Catholics they had a right to disagree with the encyclical, and the British bishops suggested that their parishioners "pray for light to understand the doctrine" and leave their minds "open to the influence of the Holy Spirit."[4] Briton Thomas Roberts seemed less optimistic. "Even the church," he said, "has not the power to enforce its law in the bedroom."[5] While the North American hierarchy was predictably more conservative, their reactions were surprisingly unenthusiastic. The United States National Conference of Catholic Bishops' official statement asked priests and parishioners "to receive with sincerity what [the Pope] has taught, to study it carefully, and form their consciences in its light." Some of the most important of the American hierarchy made the least enthusiastic sounds. Boston's Cardinal Cushing, while seeming to slam the door, quite clearly left it open: "Rome has spoken," he said, "*and for the time being* the case is closed."[6] [Italics added.]

The eloquent bishop of Rochester, Fulton Sheen, while praising the Pope's courage, did not underestimate his risks: "Paul dared oppose the world," he said, "for which he will be crucified . . . as was Christ on Calvary."[7]

Archbishop Terence J. Cooke of New York seemed to sympathize more with his parishioners than with the Pope: "I pray that God will give them strength to bear their burdens bravely. . . ."[8] he said, while Cardinal O'Boyle made the burden seem even heavier. "Let's pray for the strength we lack," he suggested to the congregation at St. Matthews Cathedral. "Let's accept the cross that Christ is asking us to bear."[9]

CHURCH REACTIONS: THE CONSERVATIVES

By way of contrast, the Latin American hierarchy seemed to be jostling for first place in speedy approbations of a message most had first read in their daily newspapers. The eighty-year-old Mexican

Cardinal Garibi Rivera probably won the race by publicly praising the "precious and magnificently studied encyclical" on July 31.[10] He was enthusiastically followed ten days later by Mexico's other bishops, whose militancy compensated for their tardiness. They scorned "the opinions of theologians against a constant teaching of the Church" and warned the faithful that the encyclical was no "simple opinion."[11] The bishops of Costa Rica made few specific references to the encyclical, but made their fealty to Rome clear by such phrases as "We thank God for having left on this earth an unextinguishable light of truth to guide Humanity with clarity, decision and firmness, on the paths of virtue, which, by the grace of God, enables the human person to live at the height of dignity of his nature, saving and dignifying man redeemed by the blood of the Son of God."[12] The Colombian bishops not only approved the encyclical, but underscored it by equating birth control with "reducing the woman to a simple instrument of pleasure" and "terrible racist aberrations."[13]

The conservative wing of the church did not lose the opportunity to cudgel its enemies. The bishop of Mandonado in Uruguay praised it for "eliminating the doubts of luke-warm theologians who disfigure the *magisterio* of the Church with their opinions."[14] In Argentina some of the bishops used the occasion to urge the Pope to eliminate Communist influences among the clergy. Already disturbed by the progressive working document prepared for the CELAM Conference, a right-wing group known as the Argentine Society for the Defense of Tradition, Family and Property collected the signatures of the cardinal and at least two bishops for their anti-Communist message.[15] Cardinal Jaime de Barros Câmara of Brazil threatened with "ecclesiastical punishments" all who would make public statements "criticising, contradicting, negating or teaching differently ecclesiastical doctrine on the means of birth control."[16] In Costa Rica, journalist-priest José Iglesias condemned the "North American theologians . . . who seem to be trying to improve their country's economy by selling pills . . . afraid that Latin Americans will multiply, progress, become powerful enemies. . . ."[17] In Chile the 1942 statement of Cardinal José Maria Caro was dusted off and proudly republished. The cardinal could not bring himself to mention family planning directly, referring to it only as "A crime against humanity and a sin against God" and "a betrayal of the Creator, abusing his gifts and making a joke of natural law."[18]

Aside from being a political victory for the church's conservative wing, the encyclical was well-received among those who feel a tidal wave of hedonism is sweeping the world. A Costa Rican priest, in congratulating the Papal Nuncio, referred to the "unbraked sensualism and hedonism threatening the family and society" and maintained that the encyclical had "again saved the world from moral ruin." [19] The archbishop of Cuenca in Ecuador believes that it serves to "contain the demoralization of the family and conjugal life," [20] and a cable to the Pope from the Peruvian bishops referred favorably to its defense of "married life against a reigning hedonism." [21] Most explicit of all was Colombia's Monsigneur Valencia Cano, who held that "exhibitionism in all forms is making continence impossible, with the logical sequelae of homosexuality and the most aberrant bestiality. . . . these excesses are most evident in the developed countries. . . . the encyclical is a violent but necessary brake to sexual corruption in the western world." [22]

On the whole, however, it was Catholic lay groups, especially the Christian Family Movements, which stressed the antihedonistic virtues of the encyclical. The Brazilian Confederation of Christian Families noted that "the commercial distribution of contraceptives for an impersonal market, further adds to the degeneration of custom being of the same ilk as economic liberalism and sexual liberty" [23]; the Independent Conservative Directory of Antioquia proclaimed their "unshakable decision to combat the materialism directing all acts of the present government" [24]; the Christian Family Movement of Costa Rica saw "no excess of human beings but an excess of sensuality, irresponsibility, laziness and egoism" [25]; the Peruvian Christian Family Movement declared its opposition to birth control which "offends human dignity and reduces rational beings to the irrational level" [26]; and the General Assembly of the Latin American Christian Family Movement warned against "the danger of self-destruction being provoked by hedonism and eroticism." [27]

A few spokesmen found it necessary to account for the encyclical in supernatural terms. The archbishop of Medellín, Colombia, announced that the decision must have been made "with the special assistance of the Holy Spirit," [28] and the seemingly incredulous secretary of the Colombian hierarchy explained that "this document can only be understood in the light of the supernatural and theological significance of the *magisterio pontifico.* If we don't believe that the Holy Spirit illuminates the Pope, we will never be able to understand it."[29] Whenever directly asked, churchmen noted that the encyclical was not infallible, but it was not usual to make explicit, as did the auxiliary bishop of Montevideo, that it was "consequently reformable."[30] When caught with a direct question on whether the use of contraceptives would henceforth be a venial or mortal sin, an archbishop of Paraguay answered uneasily, "It is hard to say."[31]

The West Indies seemed hardest hit, ranging from Jamaican Bishop McEleney's resigned "Confidence that our good faithful will bear this Cross with dignity in imitation of the loving Savior"[32] to the archbiship of Trinidad's desperate "Continue saying your prayers, earnestly and sincerely, and the all-powerful grace of God will undoubtedly come to your help."[33]

In a number of countries the encyclical was turned against North American financed family planning programs. The archbishop of Tegucigalpa, Monsigneur Hector Enrique Santos, designated the family planning program in Honduras as "totally immoral" and tending to "develop prostitution" in the nation. "A foreign government," he added, which conditions its aid by programs of this kind is not a friend but an enemy which seeks to reduce us to permanent impotence.[34] In Costa Rica the archbishop's office took the opportunity to say, "It would be interesting to find out how many thousands of dollars have been invested in Costa Rica in that campaign of disorientation and disrespect for human dignity. . . . Use of the pill or coil has been used as a condition for medical treatment or family assistance."[35] The apostolic administrator of Colombia, Monsigneur Muñoz Duque, referred to United States aid on family planning as "a flagrant violation of the Rights of Man expressed in the United Nations Charter,"[36] while a Cartagena priest conceived a new form of political masochism. "Any nation accepting such [birth control] conditions," he said, "enslaves in man the freest act of nature."[37]

In some places the arguments produced by the clergy in favor of the Pope brought them quite close to the arguments of their leftist enemies. In the Dominican Republic, the Catholic University rector maintained that "the wombs of Dominican mothers should not be closed in order to maintain the *status quo*," adding that with a proper redistribution of land there would be no danger from increasing population.[38] The auxiliary bishop of Havana announced with pleasure that "the Cuban government has gladly accepted the latest encyclical of His Holiness," [39] and in Guatemala, church authorities publicly thanked leading leftists for sending them supporting materials. The leftist-dominated Medical Association of Guanabara, Brazil, dispatched a letter to the rightist-dominated Cardinal Dom Jaime de Barros Câmara, expressing their pleasure over the encyclical "since it classifies birth control methods as genocide. . . . When President Johnson decided to suspend aid to countries not adopting birth control programs, the Pope proclaimed that the road to development is through education and liberty. . . . doctors are urged to read the encyclical and meditate on its social content." [40]

CHURCH REACTIONS: THE LIBERALS

In their public utterances, church liberals tried gamely to look on the bright side of the encyclical. Cardinal Silva Henriquez of Chile noted that "it is no act of virtue to have more children than one can have. . . . it is an act of virtue to have the number one can bring up well. . . . this is the great value in the encyclical in that the Pope points out the duty and right of couples to determine the number of children they should have. . . ." [41] The bishop of Cuernevaca urged "careful study, in order to understand the precise teaching of the encyclical and the extent to which the faithful are bound by the norms it expresses." [42] The archbishop of Recife, Helder Camara, radical on every issue except birth control, was surprisingly unenthusiastic about the decision. Perhaps uncomfortable at being in too much accord with the establishment, he vowed a reluctant fealty: "I shall strive to preach and obey in a spirit of faith a ruling which will doubtless not be easy to follow, particularly in our underdeveloped areas." Subsequently he cheered up, consoled by the thought that the Pope's message had prevented "the masses of Latin America, Asia, and Africa from being drowned by contraceptive pills." [43] Ivan Illich found himself in a similar dilemma and, struggling valiantly to avoid saying something good about either the Pope or birth control, managed to produce a typical Illichian switch: "the only contact the poor Latin American has with the outside world is via the pulpit . . . contraception has come to Latin America from the pulpit . . . through the official opposition of the Church." [44]

The award for optimism, however, must be given to Venezuela's *El Nacional,* which gave the following large headlines to Monsignor

Henriquez's statement concerning the Pope's "daring, modern vision": THE POPE AUTHORIZES RESPONSIBLE PARENTHOOD.[45]

Statements of outright protest were few, especially from bishops. As one authority puts it: "The bishop does not go around saying he disagrees with the Pope—if he does disagree, he says nothing."[46] However, there were exceptions. While it may create a severe classificatory strain to categorize the Venezuelan bishops as "liberals," their statement is clearly unusual. Not only did they back the general notion of family planning and the legitimacy of the state's role in it, but went one step further. "In a pluralistic society with non-Catholics and non-believers," they wrote, "it is not forbidden to the institutions of the state to give information on other methods to those persons who may decide to use them according to their own consciences."[47]

In Chile the theology professors at the Catholic University wrote a majority and a minority opinion on contraception, helpfully concluding that Catholics might "adhere, after serious study and consideration, to one or other of the theological opinions mentioned."[48]

But it was in Brazil that opposition to the encyclical was most outspoken. In Belo Horizonte the Carmelite fathers stated that the Pope had failed to take into consideration the opinion of the conciliar bishops and his own commission.[49] In Porto Alegre the bishop (who was also secretary general of the National Bishops Conference) flatly disagreed with the encyclical, declaring himself favorable to the contraceptive pill because "if we owe loyalty to the Pope we owe it as well to the people of God."[50] Even more spectacular were *Jornal Do Brazil's* large headlines on August 10 announcing that "DEBATE AMONG PRIESTS APPROVES PILL 4 TO 1." The discussion took place among several priests and physicians at the "Conference of Brazilian Clergy [Religiosos] before an audience of 100 priests, friars and secular Catholics." Father Olinto Pegoraro called the text of *Humanae Vitae* "totally obsolete," and a Benedictine physician, complaining about the encyclical's lack of attention to the fertility problems of the individual, explained that "we cannot expect the Pope to solve (such problems)—he who spent five years finding out whether or not the pill should be swallowed." Dom Tito went on to solve some of these individual problems himself, and recommended to those consciences hurt that they "use the pill and practice periodic abstinence, thus giving each side its due."[51]

In mid-September, the editor of the influential Catholic journal *Vozes* made a number of forthright points in attempting to put the encyclical in a historical framework:

> If we read today the concepts emitted on democracy subscribed to by some Popes of the past, we will be amazed to see the extent to which the monarchial ideal had penetrated, already acquiring a veneer of revelation. The same will take place with contraceptives and family planning. . . . We can categorize "Populorum Pregressio" as on the progressive side, "Humanae Vitae" on the reactionary side, and "Ecclesiam Suam" in the middle.
>
> "Rome has spoken" will not be the authoritative argument that is going to convince or dispense with intelligence. Much less the threats of some bishops that they will suspend priests from the practice of their orders if they do not speak supporting the encyclical, making us utter an angelical *amen*. Such threats were unheard of when "Populorum Progressio" was issued, and no priest that did not talk about it was menaced with suspension. This was because "Populorum Progressio" did not deal directly with sexual morality. Sex and related matters remain tabus in the Church.
>
> Paul VI seemed to be taking a step forward, for his definition of conjugal love is perfect. He retrogressed, though, by taking up again an *obsolete* concept of *nature,* imposing it as a criterion of legality and illegality of contraceptives. . . . In any case, the time has passed when the Church's authority had a monopoly of natural law.[52]

The same spirit was evidenced in a long, scholarly, and reverent article prepared by a group of São Paulo married couples and forwarded to the Pope. Tucked inconspicuously among thirteen amply footnoted paragraphs is the following sentence:

> Having affirmed that the Church is not only the Hierarchy but also the People of God, conscious of representing the thought of a large part of this Church, and having studied not only the Encyclical "Humanae Vitae" but also the different documents of the council, we feel obliged, by irreversible duty of conscience, to manifest to you the impossibility of accepting and practicing your recent determinations.[53]

No one really knows what is happening at the level of the confessional, but one authority's observation strikes us as a reasonably reliable estimate. "I have yet to discuss this matter with a priest in Latin America," he writes, "who did not in counseling leave the contraceptive method up to the individual conscience."[54]

SECULAR REACTIONS: OFFICIAL RESPONSES

As if by improvidential design, *Humanae Vitae* was announced during the first meeting of the newly organized Advisory Committee on Population and Development of the Organization of American States. It vitalized several committee members, who had been leisurely discussing such topics as the improvement of vital statistics; the teaching of demography in Latin American universities; and the need for more research, conferences, and fellowships. Feeling that it would be more embarrassing to ignore the Pope than to comment on him, they chose the latter alternative and issued a ten-point statement which included the following remark:

> . . . the encyclical's message, if it succeeds in interfering with discussions regarding the size of families that people might have been able to adopt otherwise, would be translated into increased sorrow, poverty, despair, and disease for millions.

The declaration went on to challenge the encyclical's "unusual call to heads of state not to sanction practises contrary to Church law" and urged that "governments support family planning programs, provide adequate public information, and encourage dispassionate dialogue on the subject."[55] In consternation the ever antiseptic Pan American Health Organization withdrew its representative to the meeting and the report rapidly leaked to the press. As if the recommendations were not strong enough, the UPI mistranslated the word "*insolita*" (unusual), used in our last citation above, as "insolent" which made even better news. The subsequent publicity caused Brazil and Argentina to file protests with the OAS and gave the newly elected secretary general much to talk about in his tours of Latin American countries. He coolly and courageously backed the committee's right to advise the OAS and maintained that it was his responsibility "to inform governments about the results of studies dealing with Latin American population, and about the implications of population growth for housing, education, and food."[56] Aside from a spasm of editorials from Altamirano in El Salvador and the flurry in Brazil and Argentina, the incident was just one more in the flood of August 1968 news on the encyclical.

As for the reactions of individual nations, flat defiance of the encyclical was encountered at the highest level in the Dominican

Republic, where President Balaguer stated that the government would fulfill the world leaders' statement on birth control which he had signed. He insisted that birth control was a "problem of individual conscience." [57] A day later, Belaguer's Secretary of Health added that it is the right of married couples to choose the contraceptive method most suitable to their needs. [58] A former Secretary of Health, in an apparent reference to the world leaders' statement, went even farther, maintaining that "the Dominican government is obliged to carry out birth control due to an agreement made with the United Nations." [59]

In Nicaragua, Vice Minister of Health, Castillo Quant, announced that the government family planning program would continue, adding that the impact of the encyclical on the "20 Latin American republics with birth control programs" would only be "momentary." [60] (Seven Nicaraguan bishops subsequently asked that the government annul "little by little" its laws favoring family planning, assuring the faithful that in their place "divine blessing will bring work and bounteous supplies of food for the people of Nicaragua. [61]) Chile's President Frei commented that Latin American governments "can carry out family planning in any way, and no one can escape that responsibility." [62]

In most countries, however, the verbal reaction of government officials was hearty approval. In Argentina, the Minister of Foreign Affairs hastened to point out that "Argentina has always assumed a position coincident with the doctrine of the Church . . . and the so called population problem is not in itself one of the great dangers facing the contemporary world." [63] Brazil could hardly contain itself. The Foreign Office relayed a Presidential message expressing the "joy and gratitude of the Brazilian people," adding that the country was underpopulated. [64]

Since Argentina and Brazil have only private family planning organizations, the talk was cheap. In countries with more official programs the public statements of politicians seemed equally enthusiastic but usually contained qualifying phrases. Thus, Costa Rica's Minister of Health announced that the government of Costa Rica "would not adopt any direct means of birth control," [65] going on to talk about "educational programs" to help make couples aware of responsible parenthood. In Peru, having just signed an agreement for a program, the Minister of Health almost outdid himself. He not only claimed the Peruvian government to be in complete accord with the encyclical ("Peru is a Catholic country and has to accept whatever is indicated by the hierarchy"), but went on to say that birth control was unnecessary in Peru, given its low population density.[66] Moreover, he not only talked about the Ministry's concern for responsible paternity education programs, but announced that the church had already agreed to use of the pill "within determined periods, especially post-partum." Somewhat prematurely he announced having reached an agreement with the church on using "not only biological but . . . hormonal treatment."[67] Not surprisingly, on the following day the church issued a vigorous denial maintaining that it had always opposed contraception except under certain limited therapeutic conditions.[68]

In Colombia only the Foreign Minister spoke against the encyclical, but lost his job shortly thereafter. Indeed, smelling blood, Senator Tovar Concha used the occasion to renew his Senate attack on the government program.

On the whole, however, *the bishops have been highly discreet in their avoidance of confrontations with government over family planning programs,* wherever the governments, unlike Nicaragua, have been discreet in handling the encyclical.

SECULAR REACTIONS: THE PRESS

In 1968 the Cornell International Population Program selected fifty-five leading Latin American newspapers for content analysis. With the exception of Brazil and Ecuador, only large newspapers of the capital cities were included.[69] The Burrelle's Press Clipping Bureau provided the clippings, each of which was coded and the codes punched on IBM cards. While the clipping service probably misses up to 50 percent of the actual coverage (due to irregularities of the postal service, newspaper strikes, reader omissions, etc.), there is no reason to believe that the omissions are biased in any relevant direction.[70] In any event, much of our interest centers on a comparison of preencyclical and postencyclical coverage, and the first most striking change was in sheer volume of clippings giving attention to population or family planning.[71]

In August and September of 1968 the number of clippings received from the fifty-five newspapers increased fivefold over the preceding two-month period—from 682 to 3,468. As might be expected, most of the articles in the latter period (70 percent) mentioned the papal encyclical. However, over a thousand articles did not mention it. Thus, even population news not mentioning the encyclical increased by nearly 50 percent, undoubtedly as a result of the heightened public interest in population provoked by the encyclical.

Prior to the encyclical, most articles on population or family planning appearing in Latin American newspapers were of local origin, but in August and September foreign-originated articles on the encyclical inundated the local press and accounted for nearly three-quarters of the stories on the encyclical.

The volume of attention to population matters during this period is truly impressive. Three countries (Colombia, the Dominican Republic, and Venezuela) averaged two articles per day per newspaper in the two months following the encyclical, and six countries (Brazil, Costa Rica, El Salvador, Ecuador, Mexico, and Peru) averaged just over one article per day.

To see where the press was the most "responsive" to the encyclical, we have compared the number of clippings received per month during the months of 1968 prior to the encyclical with the number received in the two months following it (Table 62).

The larger countries, perhaps with the most sensitive and efficient newspapers, showed the greatest increases in utilization of foreign-originated articles. Tenfold or larger increases are noted in Argentina, Brazil, Chile, Mexico, and Venezuela. On the other hand, Costa Rica also falls in this category, while all other Central American countries (plus Bolivia, Ecuador, and the Dominican Republic) show much smaller increases.

Locally originated news should be a more meaningful measure of national concern.[72] Fivefold increases are seen in the cases of El Salvador, Colombia, and Chile, with Peru and Brazil close behind. The smallest increases are seen in several Central American nations, as well as Argentina, Uruguay, Ecuador, the Dominican Republic, Costa Rica, and Mexico. It is of interest that there is no relationship between the increase in local news and the increase in foreign population news (rank-order correlation = .03). Dividing the increases at about the median gives the distribution seen in Table 63.

Since the table shows only increases, it tells us nothing about absolute levels. Thus, the Dominican Republic and Costa Rica start

TABLE 62

Clippings on Population and Family Planning, by Country,
Origin of Clipping, and Period, 1968

Country	Monthly Clippings per Newspaper Prior to Encyclical (1/1 to 7/28)			Increase in Two Months Following Encyclical (Preencyclical Rate = 100)		
	Local Clips	Foreign Clips	Total Clips	Local Clips	Foreign Clips	Total Clips
Argentina	5	7	12	280	1,300	875
Bolivia	2	5	7	350	420	400
Brazil	21	12	33	419	1,133	679
Chile	5	4	9	520	100	733
Colombia	23	12	35	526	925	663
Costa Rica	19	7	26	242	1,086	469
Dominican Republic	15	17	32	287	459	378
Ecuador	14	17	31	157	541	368
El Salvador	8	6	14	512	683	586
Guatemala	8	10	18	288	370	333
Honduras	2	3	5	300	567	460
Mexico	20	8	28	230	1,138	489
Nicaragua	7	3	10	243	700	380
Panama	3	6	9	367	467	433
Paraguay	2	3	5	300	567	460
Peru	10	5	15	430	900	587
Uruguay	2	1	3	100	700	300
Venezuela	11	7	18	373	1,028	628

from a base prior to the encyclical much higher (on a per newspaper basis) than those of Argentina, Peru, Venezuela, Chile, Guatemala, Nicaragua, or Uruguay. The "small" increases in volume in the former countries may be primarily due to their being closer to a saturation point on population news prior to the encyclical.

When we compare, by means of rank-order correlation, the preencyclical volume of population attention with the degree of increase in clippings on population following the encyclical, we find no relation at all (Table 64).

Close to nine out of ten encyclical clippings of local origin could be classified as expressing opinions toward the encyclical, 70 percent of which were favorable toward it.[73] Of the foreign clips, only 42 percent were favorable. Indeed, with the exception of Trinidad, *every*

TABLE 63

Percentage Increase in Foreign-originated Population
Clippings, by Increase in Locally Originated Clippings

	Foreign Increase	
	Small, <800%	Large, ≥800%
Local increase:		
Small, <300%	Dominican Republic	Argentina
	Ecuador	Costa Rica
	Guatemala	Mexico
	Nicaragua	Venezuela
	Uruguay	
Large, ≥300%	Bolivia	Brazil
	El Salvador	Chile
	Honduras	Colombia
	Panama	Peru
	Paraguay	

*nation showed much more favorability in its locally originated clippings
than was expressed in its clippings of foreign origination* (Table 65).
Countries most favorable were El Salvador, Peru, and Ecuador, with
over 80 percent of the local articles taking a favorable position; while
the least favorable were Trinidad, Nicaragua, Dominican Republic,
and Costa Rica, all with less than two-thirds favorable. The rank-
order correlation between local and foreign opinion is zero. (El
Salvador, with the highest proportion of favorable local clippings,
has the lowest proportion favorable among its foreign clippings.)

To what extent did attention to the encyclical affect the newspaper

TABLE 64

Spearman Rank-order Correlations between Preencyclical
Volume and Postencyclical Increases

	Increase in Local Clippings	Increase in All Clippings
Preencyclical local clippings per newspaper	.01	.07
Preencyclical total clippings per newspaper	−.04	−.04

TABLE 65

Percent with Favorable Views toward Encyclical, by
Country and by Origin of Clipping (Clips with
Opinion Only)

Country	Local Clips	Foreign Clips
Argentina*	79	44
Brazil	66	39
Chile	76	38
Colombia	69	47
Costa Rica	63	44
Dominican Republic	61	33
Ecuador*	83	44
El Salvador	90	32
Guatemala*	73	62
Mexico	72	37
Nicaragua*	53	44
Peru	83	43
Trinidad*	40	41
Venezuela	66	35

*Countries with 15 to 20 local clips. Countries with less than this
number have been excluded.

image of family planning? Each article was classified as to whether
or not birth control was mentioned, whether or not an opinion on
birth control can be said to have been expressed, and whether that
opinion was favorable or unfavorable (Table 66). Since stories on
the encyclical all mentioned birth control in one way or another,
there was a dramatic increase in number and percent of all popula-
tion-related articles which *mentioned* birth control—even among
those articles not dealing with the encyclical. However, there was
a dramatic decrease in the proportion of local and foreign articles
favorable to birth control, even among those not dealing with the
encyclical. Nevertheless, because of the huge increase in volume of
articles on birth control, newspaper readers were not only seeing
more negative articles than before, but were also seeing a larger
number of positive ones. In the preencyclical period, articles favorable to birth control were averaging 60 per month, but in August and
September they averaged over 300.

　　Thus, the encyclical caused a spectacular increase in newspaper
attention to birth control both in foreign and locally originated press

materials. While this attention was predominantly unfavorable to
birth control, the amount of information and opinion favorable to
family planning available to newspaper readers was simultaneously
and substantially increased.

For the two-month period following the encyclical, we identified
the source of opinions for 570 locally originated articles which took
a position on the encyclical. These were distributed as follows (in
percent):

Editorials and features	43
Priests	9
Higher-status individual clergy	15
Groups of higher-status clergy	6
Lay religious groups	5
Politicians and government officials	9
Others	13

TABLE 66

Opinion on Birth Control, by Origin of Article, Preencyclical
and Postencyclical, 1968

		July 29–Sept. 30	
	Jan. 1–July 28	Mention Encyclical	No mention Encyclical
Locally originated clips:			
a. Percent mention birth control	46	100	58
b. Percent of "a" with opinion	61	88	63
c. Percent of "b" favorable to birth control	63	20	41
Number of local clippings	(1,325)	(726)	(579)
Foreign-originated clips:			
a. Percent mention birth control	58	100	74
b. Percent of "a" with opinion	56	76	57
c. Percent of "b" favorable to birth control	58	27	39
Number of foreign clippings	(933)	(1,711)	(452)

While the opinion was predominantly in favor of the encyclical, three distinct levels of approval can be distinguished: clerical opinion, almost unanimously in favor; editorials, lay religious groups, and politicians where from 60 to 70 percent are in favor; and "others" where only a third are in favor. (The latter group contains letters to the editor and man-on-the-street interviews.)

Some of the most outspoken criticisms of the encyclical appeared on editorial pages. In Colombia, one of the *Espectador's* three critical editorials opined that "*Humanae Vitae* will last no longer than the human life of the present Pontif" (7/31/68); *Listin Diario* of the Dominican Republic called it "the ethics of the impossible" (8/3/68); Mexico's *Novedades* termed it "legislating against reality" (8/3/68); Nicaragua's *Novedades* regarded it as "demographic catastrophe" (8/17/68); and *Nación* of Costa Rica attributed it to old men who have failed to keep up with modern technology (8/3/68).

Nevertheless, both journalists as a whole and editorials in particular were predominantly favorable to the encyclical, although the editorials were heavily concentrated in a few newspapers. Thus, of thirty-seven non-Brazilian editorials favorable to the encyclical, fourteen were from two newspapers, *La República* of Bogotá (eight) and *El Diario de Hoy* of San Salvador. Four other papers had two favorable editorials each: *Novedades* and *Universal* of Mexico, *Diario de Central America* of Guatemala, and *Estrella de Panamá*.

From the thirty-seven editorials, fifty-two major reasons for support of the encyclical were delineated:

Family planning is imperialism	14
Natural law	12
Obedience to church	12
Antihedonism	9
Demographic reasons	5

SECULAR REACTIONS: THE ELITE WOMAN

A curious pattern of omission has thus far been characteristic of this volume—when the opinions of the lower class are described, they are largely confined to women; when the opinions of the upper classes are described, they are largely confined to men. The omission of lower-class men is due largely to the expense and difficulty of locating them for interviews, as well, perhaps, as to unconscious carry-overs of the birth control movement's traditional hostility to the male and his role in reproduction.[74] The omission of female opinion among the elite is largely because they rarely achieve the kind of position in Latin America which makes their opinion news. Normally then, even if they speak, nobody is listening.

The encyclical, however, provided a unique situation, since journalists *sought out* the opinions of prestigeful women. At last there was a public issue on which the opinions of women seemed relevant. One of the remarkable things brought to light was the willingness of middle- and upper-class women to speak up in public about the issue. They not only freely discussed contraception but freely disagreed with the Pope. Both these facts showed that there had been a revolution among Catholic women, a revolution which the very church, by means of its protracted public debate, had been instrumental in creating.

In Colombia, *El Tiempo* published the names, occupations, and photographs of their interviewees, and the illustrations below give the frank and aggressive flavor of the women's responses.

A public relations expert:

It seems counterproductive. . . . for years the university educated classes have been practicing family planning. In my case in ten years of marriage I have a boy of four and a girl of four months. . : .

A secretary:

Many people will use their own methods and that's what I will do.

An artist:

May the Holy Father, during his visit to an underdeveloped country such as ours, realize the poverty and the demographic problems common to all Latin America.

A singer:

It's the most absurd thing in the world.

A radio announcer:

The necessity not only to plan the family but especially to slow down the demographic explosion is so obvious that it is difficult to explain why the Church made a decision which officializes a latent schism.

Miss Bogotá:

It seems ridiculous that the Church would pronounce against contraception in the way they have. . . . We are in the midst of a terrible population explosion. . . . For people without education it is very difficult to pretend that periodic continence is adequate.

In Brazil, *O Globo* published interviews with five distinguished women and included their names and photographs. Four of them disagreed with the Pope's message.

An actress:

. . . if the Sociologists think that fertility control is necessary, and Medicine approves the pills, there is no reason for the Church to prohibit them.

A model:

I regard it as a real crime for a woman to have a child without the means of rearing and educating it. . . . I am a Catholic, Roman Apostolic, even a Daughter of Maria, but I favor the pills.

Two socialites:

• I am against the Pope's decision. . . . to take or not to take the pills is a problem of the individual conscience. It is more honest to take them than resort to other drastic solutions.

• . . . forty percent of babies born in Brazil suffer hunger before age six through complete lack of aid. The pill is a necessity . . . it prevents low-income people from having many children they absolutely cannot support, much less educate.[75]

The most fascinating interview, however, can best be described as semiprivate. In Costa Rica, *La República's* reporter interviewed six professional women *in a group, published their names and photographs, but did not attribute any particular quotation to any particular woman.* The women were aware of these conditions, their comments seem even less inhibited than those cited above, and the atmosphere is more like a group discussion in a *private* situation. Indeed, the women opposed specific attributions since "that could cause problems with our husbands," and because "most women are against the encyclical, but as we're Catholics and part of a Catholic society, it hurts us to speak publicly against it; and in practice we can't accept what is being asked." The women were united in their alarm over the encyclical, and three of their remarks are given below:

• Rhythm is permitted, but what can assure us a normal cycle? The pills. So we go back to pills to regularize menstruation? That's why the Encyclical is extremely difficult to explain. Too drastic!

• The problem for the priest is tremendous. I'm a good Catholic and go to him when I need advice, but two weeks ago he allowed me to use the pills. Now what? Two weeks ago it wasn't a sin and now it is.

• The Pope speaks of ecumenical Christianity . . . well, the other "Christian" religions permit birth control by the pills and IUDs [*espiral*]. But for Catholic Christians it's forbidden. This is a contradiction!

We do not pretend that these are systematic or scientific surveys, nor have we presented examples of the minority opinions favorable to the encyclical. We only wish to point out that when professional women are willing to speak out publicly and semipublicly with such intensity and frankness, it means that something real and important has happened to professional Latin American women in this decade and that their freedom from certain ancient religious and sexual taboos is becoming a reality. Of the greatest significance for social change is the apparent upper-class progression from private opinion to its public expression—these are the first signs that well-educated Latin American women are beginning to preach what they practice.

SECULAR REACTIONS: THE LOWER-CLASS WOMEN

When the encyclical was announced in late July, a team of Cornell graduate students was working on a population project in Teguci-galpa, Honduras. I cabled them suggesting that they add a number of questions to their various questionnaires. Our first results came from interviews conducted with one hundred randomly chosen women who attended any of the various clinics (other than the birth control clinic) of a health unit serving a low income neighborhood. Two weeks after the encyclical, when asked, "Could you tell me what the Pope said in his last announcement or encyclical?" ninety of the one hundred did not know. The ninety were probed, "Are you sure you haven't heard anything?" Nobody had.

We then took a representative sample of 331 households in the neighborhood served by the clinic. Sixty percent of the neighborhood's seventeen hundred homes have radios. Yet, almost a month after the encyclical, 80 percent of the women said they had heard nothing about the new encyclical. Of the sixty-six cases who had heard about it, two thought the Pope had authorized use of the pills. The remainder were asked the series of questions presented below:

	Responses, in percent			
	Yes	No	Don't know	Total
"Now that the Pope has spoken, have you changed your way of thinking about the number of children a woman should have?"	9	88	3	100

	Yes	No	Don't know	Total
"Do you agree with the position of the Pope on the question of having or preventing more children than desired?"	14	77	9	100

	Yes	No	Doing nothing	Don't know	Total
"Do you think what the Pope said is going to change what you are doing to avoid getting pregnant?"	0	49	38	13	100

In short, either because they did not hear about it or because they seemed to disregard it, most lower-class women of Tegucigalpa felt little affected by the encyclical as of September 1968.

In an attempt to assess effects on attendance at family planning clinics in other countries of Latin America, we were able to assemble relevant data from seven countries (Table 67). These include English-speaking, Portuguese-speaking, and Spanish-speaking nations; very large and very small ones; those in which Catholics form a majority; and those in which they form a minority. In six out of seven nations, caseloads *increased* in the third quarter of 1968, two months of which were in the postencyclical period. The increases between the second and third quarters, moreover, were as large or

TABLE 67

Mean Number of New Patients Admitted to Family
Planning Clinics Per Month, 1968

Country	Jan.–Mar.	Apr.–June	July–Sept.
Brazil	1,289	1,406	1,625
Chile	1,672	1,410	1,729
Colombia	1,368	1,386	1,435
El Salvador	1,027	898	1,126
Jamaica		220	252*
Panama	214	308	253
Trinidad	320	501	842

*Based on data for July and August.
SOURCE: Records of the International Planned Parenthood Federation, Western Hemisphere.

larger than between the first and second. If the encyclical had an impact on caseloads, it certainly was not an appreciable one.

While we have no systematic information on commercial sales, some suggestive evidence is provided from Brazilian sources. About two weeks after the Papal announcement, the Rio de Janeiro daily, *Correio da Manha,* polled nineteen pharmacies. In the Northern zone only one out of eight and in the Southern zone only two out of nine said there had been any change in sales.[76] A month after the encyclical *O Globo* interviewed fifteen other druggists in various parts of the city. Only one reported "a very small decline," and one reported an initial increase "because people were afraid the pills would be prohibited." The others made such comments as follow:[76]

• The people who buy them say "the Pope isn't going to bring up my children."
• Sales stay the same . . . the rich order by telephone.
• We sell about 3000 units a month . . . no change.
• On the contrary, we sell plenty . . . very few by prescription.
• Not the slightest change . . . the well-to-do send their maids to get them.[77]

But let us close our discussion of the lower classes by hearing their own words. In Mexico a family planning clinic interviewed its patients and reported their responses verbatim. We have selected some of them for presentation below. While they are at best representative of a clinic population, the comments are very similar to those reported in Tegucigalpa and give a good indication of the strong feelings lower-class urban women are developing about contraception, as well as providing interesting insights into the opinions of husbands.

• My husband suffers a great deal when we have nothing to give our children in the way of food. If we had some way of supporting them I would not mind having more. For this reason we cannot follow the Pope's wishes. God help me if I am wrong.

• When I went to confession and the priest bawled me out for taking the treatment. I got furious. Since the church won't help me I talked to my husband about it and confessed to him, and he told me, "Do whatever you can to solve this problem, don't you think we have enough troubles as it is?"

• The only thing I have to say is this: How many more does the Pope want me to have? I only want him to tell me the number and I'll gladly have them as long as he will do me the favor to support them.

• Well, like my husband says, "Pray to God and go to Mass, but keep taking the pills because if we have any more children the Pope isn't going to give us a hand to educate them."

• Even though it is bad because the Pope prohibits it, what am I going to do with the children I already have, much less more of them? As you know, my husband is a drunkard and sometimes doesn't give me a cent. I am going to keep taking the pills.

• I would like to use rhythm but don't understand it. My neighbor uses it and she already has two daughters. I confessed and the Father would not forgive me for using the pills. I told him that for me it was much more of a sin to have an abortion or have my children before time so that they die soon after birth. The priests say no to birth control because they don't care when the children die. I think what I am doing is right.

• I respect the opinions of the priests as well as the Pope, but I am going to continue with my treatment. When I read the news in the paper I immediately went to my husband and he told me: "The leaf doesn't flutter by itself but because God moves it. Do you think that if He hadn't inspired the doctors we would have the pill? He thought of something to solve this big problem, so please, don't worry about it." I wish all husbands were like mine.

• I am Catholic but I won't stop my treatment. I have six children now, but if I had only two I wouldn't stop it.

• I hope that He can forgive me. I have so many children that I can't stop using the pills or the device. My husband was afraid but I am sorry, I just hope God can forgive me. I don't know why the Pope made this decision . . . he just doesn't know of our problems.

• I was uncertain about my husband who knew I was coming here and thought that if he found out about the Pope's decision he wouldn't let me come any more. But then the doubts were too much for me and I told him. He said, "why don't we use the rhythm method" and I told him, "you use it if you want to. With all of the children and the things I have to do I can't remember what days I can't be with you." I also told him that I was going to continue with the pills and he said "you know what you have to do. Just don't come to me with your foolishness and tell me you are pregnant and everything will be all right."

• I think that since the Pope was born in silk diapers and he's always been rich, he doesn't understand us poor people. If just one day he would live the hunger we often have he would let us take the pills. But even though he doesn't want it, I am going to keep taking my pills.

• God forgive me if I am committing a sin but I cannot support more children [six] and I do not want to raise any more beggars.[78]

THE FUTURE OF PERIODIC CONTINENCE

When asked about the effect of the encyclical on family planning in Latin America, CELADE's director, Carmen Miró, responded, "It sets us back perhaps 50 years."[79] This is probably a forty-eight-year exaggeration. For within two years the demand for services, stimulated by the private organizations, will be very obvious, the public's indifference to the papal ruling will be manifest, and the failure of alternatives even more striking than is the case today. One of these failures may be attempts on the part of some governments to promote periodic abstinence. Pope Paul, after all, had favored "responsible parenthood" and urged the scientific community to continue to improve "natural methods" of birth control. Moreover, the rhythm method is favored by church conservatives because it involves discipline and a type of "payment in kind" for the necessary evil of sexual pleasure.

Nor is a belief in the "healthy" aspects of periodic continence confined to churchmen. Colonel René Barraza Estrada of El Salvador's Ministry of Defense recently put the Army courageously behind the Pope. "In the army," said Colonel Barraza, "we may teach the young men how to behave when they marry and wish to control the number of children . . . nothing mechanical or chemical. . . . We will only teach rhythm, which means will and discipline, something to which we military men are accustomed."[80]

Even rhythm's celebrated "chanciness" provides a moral advantage for some, who see its very uncertainty as encouraging a greater faith in and dependence on the Almighty than those requiring less super-human efforts. As expressed recently by the bishops of Colombia, "Correct use of the rhythm method does not obviate the healthy practice of a periodic abstinence, and causes its users to place their reliance on the powerful and infallible help of Divine Providence." [81]

We can also anticipate that Christian Family Movements and Catholic Action organizations will be stepping up their pressures on governments for this kind of approach. As optimistically phrased by an Ecuadorean Catholic Action group, "We are convinced that most couples, properly informed and trained on the rhythm method, will be able to adapt their sexual life to the exigencies of morality." [82]

In Peru, in the face of the government's failure to provide services, the Christian Family Movement (MFC) now includes family planning as part of its educational and medical services, but it does so in a most devious manner. The following description shows how:

> The MFC provides its female patients with anovulent pills up to two years after the birth of a child. They argue that the pills have as their principal intention, not the prevention of conception, but the normalization of a process by which nature itself limits births, namely, lactation. According to a document prepared by Father Enrique Bartra, the theological adviser of the MFC, "During lactation ovulation is suspended in a natural manner. If the mother stops lactating, ovulation returns. We assume that the intention of nature is to give a rest to the mother. But, if by medical advice, she stops nursing her child, or even if when nursing, she continues ovulating, it is permitted to suspend the ovulation." Women who participate in the MFC program can obtain pills up to two years after giving birth, even if they do not lactate that long. Thereafter they are expected to adopt rhythm. The MFC claims to have 99 percent effectiveness with rhythm [though family planners in other Lima institutions doubt this], which it argues is enhanced by the previous use of pills and by the participation of the husband in the education program. [83]

We are not told what proportion adopt rhythm after two years on the pill, but even if there are few, the cumbersome nature of such a program, ideologically and operationally, makes it a dangerous model for a national program. Nevertheless, pressured both by the North Americans from without and their own public from within to "do something," and given a legitimate "something" such as rhythm, we should not be surprised to see some governments buying both time and technical assistance for programs of periodic absti-nence. Will they work?

The first problem to be faced with respect to the rhythm method is that most Latin Americans do not know how it works. When Hartford and Jaramillo asked 1,939 women in Medellín, only 853 said they knew the rhythm method. Upon probing the 853 it was found that only 1 in every 4 in fact knew how it worked. One in every five had the fertile and infertile days reversed. In another Medellín survey, of 476 family planning patients who said they knew the rhythm method, close to one in every three "knew it" in reverse.[84]

Among the poorest educated not only is it known by few (less than a third of the Medellín women with less than three years of education said they had heard of it), but it is the *least* known method, as compared with condom, pills, or coitus interruptus. Of these four methods the greatest discrepancy in knowledge between the poorly educated and the women with seven or more years of education occurs in the case of rhythm. *Five times as many* of the latter women have heard of it.[85]

These are, of course, urban women. Pilot studies of about 200 cases each in rural areas of Cartagena and Manizales, Colombia, disclosed that only about 15 percent of the women admitted having heard of rhythm, whereas over half had heard of the pill.[86]

Can the ignorant be taught? One answer is provided by the presidents of the Brazilian Catholic Family Movement, Antonio and Margarida Acauan:

> How can the illiterates of Brazil record numbers, indicate dates, make computations and verify thermometers? . . . Thousands of poor women knock on the door of the family planning clinics. It is Christ they are seeking and to whom they appeal.[87]

Again the experience from Colombia is instructive, since most of the pilot programs of family planning initiated in the Colombian universities in 1965 stressed the rhythm method and kept good records. A pertinent example is provided by two years' experience of the Jesuit University family planning clinic at San Ignacio Hospital. Over a recent two-year period the clinic gave instruction in the rhythm method. While other methods were explained, under "normal" circumstances only rhythm was prescribed. In the words of the research director, "the rhythm method is applied to every woman who has regular menstrual cycles, who has no difference greater than ten days between the shortest and longest cycle, over an eight-month period. For women with menstrual irregularities, we prescribe the anovulatory pills for the time judged necessary by the physician, until her menstrual cycles become normal . . . also patients who have just had a child for the period of lactation."

Over the two-year period a great effort was expended on this service: 2,900 consultations were held and 15 short courses for 1,276 interested women were carried out. The gross consequence was 1,870 patients enrolled and given initial instructions, but at the time of the report *only 133 patients were listed "on rhythm."* Moreover, despite the strong encouragement of rhythm and the restricted conditions for the pill, twice as many were on pills as on rhythm.[88] (It is also of interest that when, as a result of Cardinal Concha's March 1967 pastoral, the Jesuit clinics ceased instruction on other methods, the instructors were faced with "a great number of questions from the audience concerning these methods."[89]

A recent comprehensive review of the experience of ten Colombian clinics initiated in 1965 or 1966 provides further information. In three Cali clinics where only the rhythm method was offered, the percentage of women who decided "no method" was preferable to the rhythm method was 57, 63, and 81.[90]

Other clinics offered methods in addition to rhythm. In this case the procedure was as follows: "By means of short courses, the doctor informs the couples or the women about the physiology of reproduction, responsible parenthood and contraceptive methods, and the priest on the point of view of the hierarchy on the morality of the rhythm method and the immorality of the others."[91]

In these clinics, of the women who selected a method the following percentages chose rhythm:[92]

Quiroga	2.4
Madrid	2.5
Medellín	29.1
Popayan	11.1
Cartagena	.0

An indication of the cost involved in getting a single rhythm patient is provided by the records of El Guabal Clinic in Cali. By the end of 1966 they had had 2,393 medical consultations, 5,642 auxiliary nurse home visits or interviews, 2,324 social worker home visits or interviews, and 188 group meetings. *At the end of 1966 they had 188 couples on the rhythm method,* or "56 contacts per effective couple."[93]

Finally, of that select number of patients who choose the rhythm method, does it work? While the data provided us are not totally satisfactory, some measure of comparative effectiveness is indicated by records on accidental pregnancies in the Medellín clinics. With data on over 3,000 person-months of use of rhythm and 4,000 months of pill usage, *the respective pregnancies per 1,000 woman-years were ten for pills and 47 for rhythm.*[94]

Investigators in many countries may have to repeat such experiences before proving to themselves what they at the least fear but at the most already know—that the rhythm method cannot be relied upon for an effective mass program of fertility control.

In the long run, we simply have to expect better things from the Catholic Church, and we are confident that an institution which is daily increasing its engagement with the realities of the development process in Latin America can only become more realistic. And after all, as phrased by Gilberto Freire, "the role of the Church is not only to give Man a good death, but a good life."[95]

NOTES

1. P. Gustavo Pérez Ramírez, "Expectativa de la Encíclica Humanae Vitae en América Latina durante 1967," Bogotá, October 1968, unpublished manuscript. The remainder of the discussion of the study is drawn from this source.

2. This holds when age, education, type of specialization, or frequency of receiving communion is controlled.

3. *Washington Post,* July 30, 1968.

4. *New York Times,* Sept. 25, 1968.

5. *Daily Gleaner* (Jamaica), Aug. 6, 1968.

6. *New York Post,* July 30, 1968.

7. *New York Post,* Aug. 2, 1968.

8. *New York Times,* Aug. 9, 1968.

9. *New York Times,* Aug. 5, 1968.

10. *Excelsior* (Mexico, D.F.), Aug. 1, 1968.

11. *Novedades* (Mexico, D.F.), Aug. 10, 1968.

12. *La Nación* (San José), Aug. 8, 1968.

13. *El Tiempo* (Bogotá), Oct. 30, 1968.

14. *Presencia* (La Paz), Aug. 1, 1968.

15. *Ibid.,* Aug. 5, 1968.

16. *New York Times,* Aug. 8, 1968.

17. *La Nación* (San José), Aug. 18, 1968.

18. *El Diario Ilustrado* (Santiago), Oct. 10, 1968.
19. Apostolic administrator of Alajuela Diocese, reported in *La República* (San José), Aug. 3, 1968.
20. *El Comercio* (Quito), Aug. 17, 1968.
21. *El Espectador* (Bogotá), Aug. 3, 1968.
22. *El Tiempo* (Bogotá), Aug. 8, 1968.
23. *Estado do São Paulo,* Aug. 10, 1968.
24. *El Siglo* (Bogotá), Aug. 9, 1968.
25. *La Nación* (San José), Aug. 13, 1968.
26. *El Comercio* (Lima), Aug. 4, 1968.
27. *La Crónica* (Lima), Sept. 17, 1968.
28. *El Siglo* (Bogotá), Aug. 3, 1968.
29. *El Espectador* (Bogotá), Aug. 30, 1968.
30. *El Universal* (Caracas), Aug. 3, 1968.
31. *El Espectador* (Bogotá), Aug. 20, 1968.
32. McEleney, *The Daily Gleaner* (Kingston, Jamaica), Aug. 17, 1968.
33. *Trinidad Guardian* (Port of Spain), Aug. 10, 1968.
34. *El Día* (Tegucigalpa), Aug. 19, 1968.
35. *La República* (San José), July 31, 1968.
36. *El Espectador* (Bogotá), Aug. 1, 1968.
37. *Ibid.,* Aug. 8, 1968.
38. *El Caribe* (Santo Domingo), Sept. 23, 1968.
39. *Daily Gleaner* (Kingston, Jamaica), Aug. 21, 1968.
40. *Jornal do Brasil* (Rio de Janeiro), Aug. 17, 1968.
41. *La Nación* (Santiago), Aug. 4, 1968.
42. *New York Times,* Aug. 8, 1968.
43. *Diario el Gráfico* (Guatemala City), Sept. 1, 1968.
44. *El Universo* (Guayaquil), Aug. 26, 1968.
45. *El Nacional* (Caracas), Aug. 3, 1968.
46. Thomas G. Sanders, "The Relationship between Population Planning and Belief Systems; The Catholic Church in Latin America," *American Universities Fieldstaff Reports,* vol. XVII, no. 7, April 1970, p. 3.
47. *Ibid.,* p. 5.
48. *Ibid.,* p. 6.
49. *Ibid.,* p. 7.
50. *Jornal do Brasil* (Rio de Janeiro), Aug. 17, 1968.
51. *Ibid.,* Aug. 19, 1968.
52. *O Globo* (Rio de Janeiro), Sept. 19, 1968.
53. *Estado de São Paulo,* Sept. 1, 1968.
54. Thomas G. Sanders, *op. cit.,* p. 7.

55. *Final Report of the First Meeting of the Advisory Committee on Population and Development,* Organization of American States, n.d. (C. October 1968). (Mimeographed.)

56. *Visión,* Aug. 30, 1968.

57. *Listín Diario* (Santo Domingo), Aug. 1, 1968.

58. *Ibid.,* Aug. 2, 1968.

59. *El Caribe* (Santo Domingo), July 31, 1968.

60. *La Prensa* (Managua), Aug. 1, 1968.

61. *La Prensa* (Managua), Sept. 25, 1968.

62. UPI Teletype 188, September 1968.

63. *Presencia* (La Paz), Aug. 1, 1968.

64. *Jornal do Brasil* (Rio de Janeiro), Aug. 13, 1968. *Correio da Manha* commented that President Costa e Silva's message was hasty, adding that the use of contraceptives should be a personal decision aided by programs of education. *Correio da Manha* (Rio de Janeiro), Aug. 14, 1968.

65. *La República* (San José), Oct. 30, 1968.

66. *El Comercio* (Lima), Aug. 2, 1968.

67. *La Prensa* (Lima), Aug. 2, 1968.

68. *El Comercio* (Lima), Aug. 3, 1968.

69. Newspapers from Rio de Janeiro, São Paulo, and Guayaquil were also included.

70. In 1967 a comparison was made between 6,300 clippings received from the 55 selected newspapers and 8,700 clippings received from all other newspapers covered by the Burrelle's service. In terms of such variables as the proportion of foreign-clippings mentions of birth control and attitude toward birth control, no significant differences are apparent between the two sets. For individual countries, however, there are occasional significant differences.

71. The agency is instructed to clip all articles dealing with population and family planning, excepting the subject of migration.

72. Foreign-originated clips on population were much more likely to mention the encyclical than local clips (79 percent versus 54 percent), and the variation among countries was considerably greater for local clips. Four countries mentioned the encyclical in about two-thirds of their locally originated articles (Brazil, Chile, Dominican Republic, Honduras), while six of them mentioned it in 45 percent or less of the cases (Bolivia, Ecuador, Guatemala, Panama, Peru, and Venezuela). The rank-order correlation between proportion of locally originated clips mentioning the encyclical and the increase in all locally originated clippings on population in August and September was .37.

73. When an article contained any opinion negative to the encyclical, it was classified as negative. Our figures therefore underestimate the degree of favorability toward the encyclical.

74. J. M. Stycos, "A Critique of the Traditional Planned Parenthood Approach in Underdeveloped Areas," in C. V. Kiser (ed.), *Research In Family Planning* (Princeton, N.J.: Princeton University Press, 1962).

75. *O Globo* (Rio de Janeiro), Aug. 5, 1968.

76. *Correio de Manha* (Rio de Janeiro), Aug. 18, 1968.

77. *O Globo* (Rio de Janeiro), Sept. 2, 1968.

78. Asociación Pro-Salud Maternal, A.C., Sept. 13, 1968, no title. (Mimeographed.)

79. *Washington Daily News,* Aug. 3, 1968.

80. *Diario de Hoy* (San Salvador), July 31, 1968.

81. *El Tiempo* (Bogotá), Oct. 30, 1968.

82. *El Telégrafo* (Guayaquil), Aug. 11, 1968.

83. Thomas Sanders, "Family Planning in Peru," *American Universities Fieldstaff Reports,* vol. XVII, no. 6, 1970.

84. Mario Jaramillo, "Informe sobre la Evaluación del Programa Experimental de Medellín," in *Regulación de la Fecundidad,* vol. II.

85. M. Jaramillo and R. Hartford, "Religiosidad y Anticoncepción," in *ibid.*

86. Italo Mirkow, "Algunos Resultados Generales de la Encuesta Piloto de Fecundidad Rural de Cartagena y Manizales," in *ibid.,* p. 102.

87. *Ponto Homen* (Brazil), December 1968. Cited by L. Alting von Geusau in *Studies in Family Planning,* February 1970.

88. Francisco García-Conti, *Third Report on the Development of Family Planning Program and Research in the Physiology of Reproduction,* Colombian Association of Medical Schools, May 1, 1967. (Mimeographed.)

89. Víctor Rodríguez, *Report on Educational Programs in Reproductive Physiology and Family Planning,* Colombian Association of Medical Schools, Apr. 30, 1967. (Mimeographed.)

90. Mario Jaramillo and Juan Lodoño, "Primera Valoración Comparativa de los Servicios Pilotos de Planificacion Familiar," *Regulación de la Fecundidad,* vol. I, p. 43.

91. *Ibid.,* p. 31.

92. *Ibid.* In the case of the Medellín clinic the high proportion may be due to the policy of initially giving pills to regularize the cycle, after which rhythm was supposed to be used. In this connection it is interesting to note that whereas 21 percent began with this method, at the end of a follow-up period only 8.5 percent were using rhythm. By way of contrast, the comparable figures for the IUD are 8 and 27 percent. *Ibid.,* p. 33.

93. *Ibid.,* p. 34.

94. *Ibid.,* p. 35.

95. "Esterilização É Genocidío," *Manchete* (Rio de Janeiro), Sept. 9, 1970.

CHAPTER 17

"Beyond Family Planning"

In 1962 an article was published attacking three biases inherent in the "Traditional Planned Parenthood Approach in Underdeveloped Areas":[1] a medical bias, a feminist bias, and a middle-class bias. Several consequences were seen to follow from these general tendencies within the family planning movement: (1) The primary argument for planned parenthood concerns its salutary effects on maternal health; (2) the distribution of contraceptives should be the responsibility of medically directed clinics; (3) the most desirable methods are female methods; (4) emphasis is placed on spacing pregnancies rather than stopping them altogether; (5) abortions, sterilizations, and coitus interruptus generally meet with disapproval; the condom is accepted grudgingly.

The article was intended to alert poorer countries about to launch family planning programs to the risks of inheriting the biases inherent in European and North American movements, biases which had led to useful hobbies for well-to-do women and a good source of income for private practitioners, but which had produced only the poorest of services for the American poor.

The article was written prior to the widespread utilization of the oral progestins or intrauterine devices. At the time it was written, moreover, only a few Caribbean islands and Mexico had private family planning associations functioning, and only Puerto Rico had a program utilizing public services. Within the next few years, however, voluntary associations were rapidly organized under the aegis of the International Planned Parenthood Federation, Western Hemisphere. By 1967, every country with the exception of Cuba, Nicaragua, and Bolivia had organized a voluntary association, and by 1969, fifteen nations, including Cuba, had government programs. (Colombia, Chile, and Ecuador in South America; Costa Rica, El Salvador, Guatemala, Honduras, Nicaragua, and Panama in Central America; and Barbados, Cuba, Haiti, Jamaica, Dominican Republic, and Trinidad-Tobago in the Caribbean.[2]) How has Latin America fared ideologically in terms of the biases and tendencies described above?

Anyone familiar with the movement today would recognize the same five general tendencies in the Latin American programs. There are at least two important differences: the character of the leadership and the character of the technology.

MALES AND MEDICINE

The most important difference in the Latin American movement has been its domination by males rather than females. The movements assumed a professional character from the beginning and never went through a significant period of leadership by women crusading for female liberation.[3] Thus, in 1969, of eighty-two top positions in seventeen family planning associations, seventy were occupied by males. In no country is the president of the association a female, and only one out of thirteen first vice-presidents is a female.[4] While the predominance of males has had favorable political, financial, and technical consequences for the movement, it has intensified the medical bias and left the middle-class bias intact.

Of the seventeen nations mentioned above, physicians were presidents of the associations in twelve instances and vice-presidents in ten. In addition to the medical directors of each program, at least six major countries have physicians as their executive directors. In the ABC countries and Venezuela, thirty-four out of thirty-eight executive committee members were physicians.[5]

The consequences of medical leadership have been both salutary and unfortunate. There is no doubt that medical leadership has legitimized the movement and given it rapid access to decision makers. Only a rash churchman would challenge a physician's prescribing contraception as a prophylaxis for abortion, and politicians rarely venture where the angels fear to tread. While the emergence of medical leaders equipped with a medico-moral rationale has neutralized a great deal of potential opposition, it has given the movement a loftiness of tone and a narrowness of approach which severely limits the effectiveness of its programs. It is not unlikely that the vaguely spiritual air which pervades the movement is the felicitous product of a conscious adaptation to the church militant and an unconscious vestige of the Catholic conscience.

Perhaps the most important philosophical adaptation has been the aggressive distinction commonly made between birth control and family planning. By denouncing the former and espousing the latter, it is possible to be as spiritual as ever while disseminating pills and IUDs. The medico-moral mystique disassociating birth control from family planning has had several unfortunate consequences. First, it has allowed the programs to evaluate their own effectiveness less in terms of impact on the birth rate or even in terms of number of contraceptives dispersed than in terms of impact on the much vaguer and harder-to-measure concepts of "irresponsible paternity," "maternal health," or "resort to abortion." When queried about the trend in birth rates since the initiation of his program, the director of one of Latin America's programs disclaimed both knowledge and interest, pointing instead to the broader "educational implications" of his program. Closely related is the growing tendency to develop programs of sex education and marital counseling as integral aspects of "family planning services," as opposed to those of birth control. While they are much needed for their own sake and useful for public relations purposes, serious question must be raised about the cost-benefit ratios of such ancillary programs. (While sex education is being given high priority, population education tends to be ignored.)

Indeed, in the scramble to avoid the birth control label, contraceptive programs are typically watered down by such medical impedimenta as Pap smears and lengthy case histories. In at least one Central American program, the patient must be interviewed by a *physician* every time she visits the clinic to pick up her pills. Such questions as "frequency of sexual relations" are often preliminaries to getting pills at all.

Probably the most common way of emphasizing the medico-moral nature of contraception is by burying family planning in a "more comprehensive" program of "maternal and child health." Such a strategem has many advantages for the local Ministry of Health, for along with protecting the program somewhat from political and religious attacks, it allows some diversion of otherwise earmarked AID funds to the broader health problems in which the ministry is much more interested. Unfortunately, the maternal and child health programs are among the weakest in most ministries, and they reach only a small fraction of the public potentially interested in contraception.

Theoretically, the contraceptive innovations of the early 1960s should have vastly increased the number of contraceptors in Latin America. On the other hand, such innovations may have inhibited the potential impact of family planning services, since they have increased the medical monopoly over contraceptive distribution. Should there be an adequate supply of physicians, the establishment of medical channels for contraceptive distribution, though ridiculously expensive, might be feasible. Unfortunately, the average Latin American dies without ever having seen a doctor in his life. Other than in Argentina and Uruguay the number of physicians per 10,000 population ranges between 2 and 6 in the Latin American nations. In 1965 there were more physicians in the state of Tennessee than in all the six Central American nations combined.

Few of these doctors, moreover, are to be seen outside the cities. In Colombia, for example, while less than a third of the population can be found in the provincial capital cities, three-quarters of the nation's physicians and 86 percent of its nurses are there. Less than a tenth of the nation's physicians but nearly two-thirds of the general population live in localities of less than 20,000 population.[6] Other countries are even worse off. In the four nations below (Table 68), the ratio of physicians to population is from six to twenty times as high in the urban as in the rural areas.

In such circumstances, encouraging the participation of paramedical personnel might be expected, but the medical profession has shown little inclination in this direction. The pharmacist in many

TABLE 68

Physicians per 10,000 Population in Capitals and
Large Cities, and in Remainder of These Countries,
around 1962

Country	Capital and Large Cities	Remainder of Country
Brazil	12.8	2.4
El Salvador	7.3	0.9
Guatemala	10.1	0.5
Peru	19.2	1.3

SOURCE: Abraham Horwitz and Mary Burke, "Health, Population, and Development," in J. M. Stycos and J. Arias (eds.), *Population Dilemma in Latin America* (Washington: Potomac Books 1966), p. 180.

Latin American countries, e.g., is the doctor of the poor, especially the urban poor. This is facilitated by the fact that few drugs require a medical prescription. Thus, those women who can afford to, purchase their contraceptive pills directly from the druggist with no medical middleman. Rather than encourage this natural procedure and attempt to facilitate its extension to the poor, a recent meeting of the executive directors of Latin America's voluntary programs clearly put the pharmacist in his place.

The role of the pharmacist is of very great importance in Latin American medicine. Therefore, every training program for this group should create in them a sense of the risks of self-prescription and the need that their clients consult a physician or go to a family planning clinic.[6]

The intrauterine device is even more jealously guarded by physicians, even though evidence from a number of studies has failed to show that doctors possess any measurable advantage over nurses in the fitting of IUDs. (This may, however, be a blessing in disguise, for while the U.S. has two nurses for every doctor, the typical Latin American country has two doctors for every nurse.)

Thus, programs, which in the absence of the new technology might be educating the general population in the use of such cheap, safe, and readily available methods as the condom and coitus interruptus, now bristle with doctors and medical gadgetry. Given the paucity of doctors, it cannot be expected that any large proportion of the population be reached by such an approach. A recent review of the case loads of 310 private and 578 government clinics over the period 1965–1969 shows less than 5 percent of the women in the fertile age groups have been reached.[7]

In 1968, based on figures provided by the Ministries of Health and the private family planning organizations, the percent of eligible women getting oral contraceptives from clinics were only as follows:[8]

Argentina	2.9
Bolivia	0.8
Colombia	3.6
Chile	5.9
Guatemala	1.5
Honduras	5.4
Dominican Republic	2.1

Virtually all these women are confined to cities, and we do not know the extent to which they have merely "switched brands" from a nonclinically obtained contraceptive to a clinical one. Moreover, there is no indication of the extent to which women, once they try the orals, continue to use them. An unknown proportion of the figures represent women who try the method once and never return to the clinic.

On the other hand, such information fails to tell us the extent of commercial distribution of contraceptives. In a nation such as Argentina this can be considerable. Indeed, independent figures for 1968, based on data supplied by pharmaceutical companies, show 420,000 monthly cycles in Argentina,[9] as opposed to the 160,000 reported by CELADE. But Argentina is probably exceptional, with respect both to oral contraceptives and to the other most widely used commercial product, the condom.

In 1968, approximately 47 million condoms were sold in all of Latin America.[10] This number accounted for only about 2 percent of world sales. If the average user utilized between fifty and one hundred condoms during the year, the number of users would roughly be between a half million and a million. As a point of comparison, Mexico alone has about 12 million men aged 15–64.

In the same year, approximately $2\frac{1}{2}$ million cycles of oral contraceptives per month were distributed in Latin America, representing a much higher proportion of world distribution—almost 13 percent.[11] Again, however, it falls far short of requirements, since Mexico alone has almost 10 million women aged 15–44.

Mexico provides a good case in point. One of the largest, most prestigeful and progressive nations of Latin America, it also has one of the highest birth rates. Paradoxically, while it produces 80 percent of the world supply of diosgenin (source of virtually all the progestins used for oral contraceptives), only about a half million of its 10 million women in the reproductive age group were taking the pill in 1968. Further, while Mexico and Argentina are the only Latin American nations producing condoms, only 70,000 dozen were distributed monthly for Mexico's 12 million eligible males.[12] Without doubt, the middle classes form a disproportionate share of the small minorities of condom and pill users. Thus, neither the clinics nor the normal commercial channels are making a serious dent in the potential market for contraceptives—the majority of Latin America's 55 million women of fertile age.

It is also apparent that it does not take long, under the existing system, for clinics to reach a saturation point in the number of new patients. Over the past few years many family planning associations have given an appearance of growth and vitality by demonstrating increasing numbers of new cases. As often as not, however, the increase is more a reflection of an increasing number of clinics than of patients per clinic. It is difficult to secure data by clinic for Latin America, but we have been successful in a few cases. Of three clinics in Santo Domingo, e.g., only one shows as many new cases per month in 1969 as in the latter part of the first year of the clinics' existence. Panama City's two clinics both show declines, as do those of San Salvador. In Bogotá, the Centro Piloto was evidencing fewer new cases per month in the first half of 1970 than during any part of 1967.

One major reason for such declines, as well as for a false sense of security on the part of the associations, may be the huge numbers of *return visits* on the part of patients. Since pill cases must return for supplies and IUD cases for periodic checks, the major share of activity in family planning clinics revolves around old cases rather than new ones. This is demonstrated in Table 69, where we have assembled 1968 information for nine countries. Despite an impressive absolute number of patient visits, only small proportions (from 18 to 40 percent) are represented by new patients. Even these figures

TABLE 69

Control Cases as a Percent of All Cases, 1968

Country	Per-cent	Total Visits*	Sources
Brazil†	82	81,187	BEMFAM no Brazil, "Movimento Clinico," 1966–1968
Chile†	76	60,452	International Planned Parenthood Federation, Western Hemisphere Region
Colombia	75	84,157	Asociacion Pro-Bienestar de la Familia Colombiana, "Estadistica de Servicio Totales Acumulados, 1.965–1.969"
Costa Rica‡	66	10,869	International Planned Parenthood Federation, Western Hemisphere Region
El Salvador‡	68	35,804	Asociacion Demografica Salvadoreña, "Trabajo Realizado en los Consultorios Pro-Salud Materna," 1968
Guatemala	64	33,724	Programa de Planificación Familiar en Guatemala, "Resumen General de Tratamientos Nuevos, Reconsultas y Total de Consultas en el Programa de Planificación Familiar, Guatemala, 1968"
Jamaica§	71	5,497	International. Planned Parenthood Federation, Western Hemisphere Region
Mexico	81	61,201	International Planned Parenthood Federation, Western Hemisphere Region
Panama	58	12,077	Asociacion Panameña para el Planeamiento de la Familia, "Informaciones, Admisiones y Controles Hasta el 31 de diciembre de 1968"

*Data for all private clinics in the nation.
†Nine months in 1968.
‡Eleven months in 1968.
§Six months in 1968.

are inflated by the fact of mixing new clinics, where most of the patients will also be new, with older clinics. Thus in Brazil, Honduras, and Panama, the percentage of new patients in the principal clinic (the "pilot clinic") was only 9, 8, and 19 in 1968; and in 1969 Bogotá's principal clinic showed only 13 percent of its visits to be those of new patients.

Thus, the system may well become clogged with old patients who crowd out the new and lower the per capita quality of treatment, while giving the associations a euphoric sense of bustling and bursting activity. Since most of these return visits are by women seeking renewed supplies of pills, one would expect efforts to divert them to commercial channels of distribution, with appropriate subsidies. In all of Latin America, however, only Costa Rica employs a coupon system whereby the patient may secure supplies at her neighborhood druggist. The rest of the continent prefers to utilize the scarce talents of nurses, nurses' aides, social workers, and even physicians to hand over a few tablets and record information which is rarely utilized.

But this is not the only reason for the slowing down of the new-case intake rate. The passive attitude of the clinics toward case-finding means that the supply of highly motivated women who are willing to seek out the clinic and undergo its mysterious rituals is soon exhausted, leaving a hard core of relatively indifferent women who need a more aggressive educational approach to precipitate contraceptive behavior. Here again we note the instinctive recoil of the medical profession from anything which smacks of "advertising." Several points made by the Palm Beach Manifesto of Latin America's executive directors of family planning programs clearly point the organizations away from either mass distribution of contraceptives or straightforward advertising of them.[13]

• The massive distribution of progesterones would totally undo the work of the family planning centers, where responsible parenthood is facilitated by education and assistance.

• The difference between the two concepts is easily seen by the contrast between publicity and propaganda on the one hand, and education and information on the other.

• The success and prestige of a program consists in increasing the number of rational users of contraceptives—implying an educational process—and not merely augmenting the volume of use, which might be the objective of a commercial campaign.

Such lofty objectives may be expected to have consequences in the family planning area similar to what might be expected from a vaccination campaign which defined basic public health education as its primary aim.

One may well inquire about the roots of such a conservative point of view. Is it merely because we are dealing with a profession which agonizes over the size of shingle it dares to hang out in front of the office? Or with the traditional reserve of the bulk of the medical profession to the techniques and theory of preventive medicine? These are indeed relevant factors, but there is an additional problem of a different nature—it consists of the low priority which the medical profession generally assigns to family planning.

POPULATION AND PRIORITIES

If private programs of family planning are dominated by physicians, public programs are no less so. For both political and administrative simplicity, family planning programs are assigned to Ministries of Health. Thus, Costa Rica's official decree establishing an Office of Population justifies the state's interest exclusively in terms of "protection and promotion of the health and welfare of its citizens" and notes that "changes in the size and structure of the population affect health conditions." In locating the Office within the Ministry of Health, the decree lists as its functions:

1. "Research in fields of health related to population. . . ."
2. "Technical advice and proposals to the Ministry of Public Health. . . ."
3. "To ensure that all operational activities relating to population problems shall be carried out under the supervision of the Ministry of Public Health. . . ."
4. Cooperation with other agencies "on the understanding that the Minister of Public Health shall in all instances have the power of final decisions."
5. "To embody the health projects intended to cope with the population increase in the regular maternal and child health programmes of the Ministry of Public Health, without prejudice to the activities of prevention and care normally carried out under the programs." [14]

The decree leaves little doubt that population problems mean health problems. This situation is viewed by many as a perfectly satisfactory definition of the situation, because it "gets the job done" regardless of "semantics." But if getting the job done refers to lowering birth rates, there are serious problems, for insofar as population problems and family planning are viewed essentially as health problems and health programs, then *they can only be assigned a low priority.* Not only is there poor scientific evidence for a direct relation between high parity and ill health, but it runs counter to experience and common sense to assign a high priority to family planning in a health context. One has only to sit for a few hours in a general outpatient clinic in almost any Latin American country to be convinced that the number and intensity of acute health problems are such that to deploy scarce medical skills and resources to family planning seems both inhumane and unreasonable. To argue that in the long run family planning will alleviate the incidence of some of these health problems is to close one's eyes to the long line of patients standing in the corridors of the clinic. Neither the attending physician in the clinic nor his chief in the Ministry of Health can *afford* to do that, even if convinced of the long-range health gains. Indeed, that the family planning program exists at all is largely due to the fact that foreign financing has made it possible. Few are the national funds, private or public, which have been utilized for family planning in Latin America.[15]

Obviously the foreign donors view the problem in terms much broader than health and see this aid as assisting in the solution of economic problems aggravated by population increase. That the doctors fail to see it in these terms can be inferred not only from their actions, but from their explicit statements. In Chile, for example, where since 1966 the government officially recognized family planning as part of the maternal and child-care services in the National Health Service, the Minister of Health could confess to the delegates of the Eighth IPPF Conference his "doubts as to the advantage . . . of a policy of reduction of population growth . . . and doubts as to the efficacy of family planning to achieve a reduction in the birth rate."[16] Just to make sure, however, a ministerial directive soon established that family planning in the National Health Service would have a "maximum coverage of 15 percent of the fertile female population."[17]

If the typical Latin American intellectual is not convinced that population growth is a serious problem deserving high-priority attention, there is no reason to expect it from physicians; and while the horrors of induced abortion and the promise of foreign aid have been enough to convince them of the desirability of including such programs in their clinics and hospitals, we cannot expect them to give such programs a high priority, given the gravity of other acute health problems. Yet, without a high priority it is doubtful that family planning programs in Latin America can have major impacts on the birth rate. Clearly it should not be the physicians who establish the priorities for family planning; they are doing so only by default. In the next decade, should the economic and social planners become convinced of the significance of population growth in the development process and in turn convince the cabinet or the ruling junta, then we may see an escalation of the population priority, and allocation of resources for its solution stemming not only from Ministries of Health, but from Ministries of Education, Agriculture, Defense, etc. Not only then would more resources be liberated, but new approaches to the problem would be opened up. Unfortunately, as we have seen, intellectuals of Latin America fall far short of the degree of conviction necessary to ensure effective programs.

REFORM AND REVOLUTION

One of the conclusions to be drawn from this book is that the people who use birth control the most—the rich, the intellectuals, the middle class—have the most reservations about it; while those who have the least reservations about it—the poor, the uneducated, the lower class—use it least. The poor are not, of course, accustomed to seeing their wishes realized, a state of mind which often sublimates goal-seeking into daydreaming. It is no more surprising that they do not demand birth control than that they do not demand housing, education, and employment; what is surprising, in the face of myths perpetrated by the rich, is that much of their daydreaming, and even some of their behavior, concerns smaller families than they in fact have. This is hardly enough to guarantee effective action, but it is a long way along. Sellers of toothpaste and breakfast cereals would be more than satisfied if their surveys in Latin America showed comparable degrees of positive motivation. In short, there is potential but not effective demand.

As we have suggested earlier, one school of thought maintains that to activate this demand one must, should, or can wait until the poor become rich. Thus, many planners count on the "automatic" processes of education or urbanization to bring levels of fertility down.

As a leading Puerto Rican planner was reported to have said recently: "The Commonwealth government has no family planning policy, but does not need one. Education [will] automatically serve to decrease the birth rate." [18] Elsewhere we have suggested that "Latin American countries which wait for 'education' to reduce birth rates may wait a long time." [19] Why wait?

The most serious answer to this question is from those who say "*we must.*" Thus, Kingsley Davis writes that ". . . in those [backward countries] with population policies, there is no indication that the government is controlling the rate of reproduction . . . the social structure and economy must be changed before a deliberate reduction in the birth rate can be achieved." [20] Not a few experts would argue with the first part of this statement, though all would admit that conclusive evidence is still lacking. While waiting for the necessary experimental data, let us concern ourselves with the latter, more important generalization, important not only because it is voiced by a leading demographic authority, but because it is consonant with the traditional Marxist position that fertility control should be a consequence and not a cause of economic development. We may approach this question from two angles—is social and economic development sufficient for fertility declines, and is such development necessary for them?

Certainly the experience of the West has been that all countries undergoing development go through a demographic transition which eventuates in low rates of population growth with or without birth control. Even assuming that the same would apply in non-Western and in Latin American cultures, there is the important question of *time.* It is questionable that underdeveloped countries today can afford the luxury of Europe's leisurely closure of the demographic gap. When we look at Mexico's dramatic and early declines in mortality, its substantial education gains, its remarkable economic growth, and its phenomenal urbanization over the past several decades, with no *appreciable consequences on the birth rate,* we can only answer the "sufficiency of development" argument with the position—maybe, but why wait?

Again, it would seem wise to wait only if we must, that is, if development is a *necessary* antecedent to declines in the birth rate. Since proponents of this view do not tell us *how much* development is necessary to effect how much decline in the birth rate, it is difficult to attack the argument with other than experimental data—i.e., the fertility impact of family planning programs in "nondeveloping" societies. Thus the studies in Taiwan, Korea, etc., can be discounted since there is already evidence of "development" as well as evidence of program-independent fertility declines. What I would agree with is the notion that at a family level there is no point talking birth control if the perceived costs of additional increments of children approach zero, and no point in discussing it at a national level if the savings to be invested by government planning are either nonexistent or noninvested.

I believe that most authorities would agree that Haiti is both remarkably undeveloped and remarkably undeveloping. In a situation where poverty is extreme and the chance for change insignificant, the costs of additional children indeed approach zero, for ten children can live wretchedly as cheaply as three (at least until they begin to look for land to cultivate. At this point they begin to look, and often move, eastward.) Indeed, our research disclosed that there was indifference to the question of family size on the part of a sample of rural Haitians, an indifference perfectly well adapted to the psychological and economic realities.[21] Moreover, should any "savings" be miraculously generated by family planning for use by the government, it is doubtful that they would be invested in economic development. Indeed, the most charitable interpretation of Haiti's current interest in a family planning program would be that it is viewed as a way to increase its external aid for the broader purposes of health.

But *how much* economic or social development would Haiti need before family planning would be both feasible and desirable? Very little, I would guess, for how else are we to account for the surprisingly enthusiastic response of Indian males to sterilization, and the modestly encouraging response of Indian females to other methods? The difference between Haiti and India is less in per capita product than in the perception of possible self-improvement—there is more hope for the progress of one's children in India than in Haiti, a hope which has come with only modest economic gains. Whether or not there will be enough response to lower national birth rates significantly is another question, but since a nation will require much experience with family planning organizations before it can expect success, it had better start early, as India did, and undergo much necessary disillusionment, as India has. Thus, to the hypothesis of economic development as a necessary antecedent to fertility declines our anwer is—possibly, but not much development. Moreover, if the family planning programs are at all effective, they should accelerate the economic development itself, and since considerable experience with such programs is probably required, then they should be initiated when there are the first perceptible signs of economic development.

Needless to say, the great preponderance of the necessary investments in development will continue to have to be in other social and economic reforms. As aptly put by a Brazilian expert, "this is because the alleviation of demographic pressure and the relatively small improvement in the socio-economic level of the population resulting from this favors the maintenance of the *status quo* without making it necessary to employ means to really improve the conditions of a significant part of the population. Therefore, birth control should not be the only means designed for solving the problems, but it should be a simple additive to energetic measures of a social and economic nature which act really to raise the level of living of the people."[22]

On the other hand, to the revolutionary who insists that birth control would remove the most effective goad to revolution I can only give my sympathy. For if he has failed to produce revolution, let him not blame his failure on the scarcity of misery in Latin America, any more than the conservative be allowed to blame population growth for the failure of *his* programs. Poverty and misery do not produce revolutions, but modest economic improvements along with disproportionate increases in aspirations do. Indeed, family planning is likely to trip off or accelerate such benefits, rendering revolution more feasible, if the revolutionary knows his job well enough to exploit them.

"BEYOND FAMILY PLANNING"

We may list three ideal steps to the deliberate control of population:

§ 1. POPULATION PLANNING

Following an awareness of the part of the elites of the seriousness of the problem of population growth, population goals are established and rational programing for their achievement is introduced. Ideally, such goals would refer to size, growth rate, and distribution of population and within the growth category include subgoals with reference to fertility, mortality, and migration. With respect to the first, programs should include any legitimate means of reducing fertility, such as measures affecting the age and incidence of marriage, legislation stimulating or discouraging family formations and growth, etc. One of the most important means will be programs to educate the public in family planning.

§ 2. FAMILY PLANNING

It is probably both unnecessary and unfeasible that the general public partake of the same concern for population problems as the national leaders, but inculcation in what is commonly known as "responsible parenthood" would be simpler and more to the point. However, in such an educational program it would be important to go beyond the banalities of "stable family life" by attempting to reduce the average desired family size and raising the average age norm for marriage and cohabitation. Should governments be serious about stabilizing family life, however, they will have to look to stabilizing employment patterns—a matter which would, *et ceteris paribus,* increase marriage, lower the age of marriage, and increase fertility.

Sex education need not be mixed with family planning education, unless it can be shown to sugar-coat the pill. In the light of current ineptitude in sex education teaching methods, it is more likely to make the pill a bitter one. Sex education programs are needed in their own right, but a causal relation between sexual sophistication and fertility control has yet to be demonstrated. The best excuse for the current vogue for including such programs in family planning organizations seems to be that they are more palatable to the church and other conservative groups than either family planning or population education. This remains to be seen; but given the enormous difficulties associated with attempts to change sexual attitudes and behavior, it might be more prudent to *desexualize* contraception (a matter entirely feasible given the trend of modern contraceptive technology).

§ 3. BIRTH CONTROL

One of the consequences of family planning would presumably be the deliberate restriction of pregnancy and birth. While we distinguish between family planning and birth control, we do not make the invidious distinction usual in Latin America. The governments, once they become aware of the larger-than-health implications of birth control, would implement service channels beyond the clinical, including commercial and paramedical. The legalization of abortion would of course greatly accelerate the decline of birth rates. Above all, outreach programs informing the population as to the availability of birth control methods are essential.

These steps would lead, if successful, to *population control*. While Latin America has moved closer to this goal in the past decade than anyone would have anticipated, it still has a long way to go. Birth control facilities reach only a small proportion of the population, and if the general public needs family planning education, the elites need population education even more.[23] If any doubts still linger with the reader, let him ponder these words from *Visión* magazine, at the opening of the decade of the 1970s:

> Both the Organization of American States and the Pan American Health Organization have been compelled this year to reduce their family planning activities, and the U.S. government is being less insistent about aid for such programs. This is due to the public denunciation of birth control by the Argentine President Juan Carlos Ongania, the Mexican Presidential candidate Luis Echeverría, and Brazil's Foreign Minister José da Magalhães Pinto.[24]

To this list should certainly be added the name of Chile's defeated Presidential candidate for the Christian Democrats. Radomiro Tomić curiously chose the occasion of an address to the Association of Women Journalists to characterize birth control as "anti-Chilean" and to make unusual campaign promise: "that his government would guarantee food for every pregnant woman."[25]

Family planning and birth control are recent arrivals in Latin America, but there is no longer any doubt about their presence. Population planning, on the other hand, is nowhere in evidence. Just as family planning was an unexpected product of the 1960s, population planning may be an unanticipated product of the 1970s. Both will be needed for the control of population growth in the 1980s.

NOTES

1. J. M. Stycos, "A Critique of the Traditional Planned Parenthood Approach in Underdeveloped Areas," in C. V. Kiser (ed.), *Research in Family Planning* (Princeton, N.J.: Princeton University Press, 1962).

2. "Evolución de los Programas de Planificacion Familiar en America Latina, Population Reference Bureau, Bogotá, March 1970.

3. To this generalization an important exception must be made: In the establishment of virtually all Latin America's voluntary family planning associations, the prime mover was IPPF's Ofelia Mendoza, a Honduran of extraordinary talents and dedication to the cause of women's rights.

4. Bolivia, Nicaragua, and the English-speaking Caribbean islands are excluded. Positions include executive director, president, vice-presidents, secretary, and treasurer. (Data for 1969 provided by the IPPF Western Hemisphere.)

5. *Ibid.*

6. "Information and Education in Family Planning Programs in the Western Hemisphere," August 1969 meeting of executive directors of IPPF Western Hemisphere Program. Published in BEMFAM (Rio de Janeiro), no. 9, September 1969.

7. Actually, fifteen countries showed an incidence under 3 percent, three between 4 and 6 percent, and four above 10 percent. Of the latter, two are English-speaking islands. See "Evolución de los Programas de Planificacion Familiar en America Latina."

8. *Ibid.,* table 2, p. 3.

9. A. D. Sollins and R. L. Belsky "Commercial Productions and Distribution of Contraceptives," *Reports on Population and Family Planning,* no. 4, June 1970, table 7, p. 11.

10. *Ibid.,* table 6, p. 10.

11. *Ibid.,* table 7, p. 11. These figures were compiled from reports by the principal pharmaceutical companies. In some cases they may not have reported free distribution or cycles sold for national programs of family planning.

12. *Ibid.,* table 9, p. 16. Since Mexico prohibits the importation of condoms, these figures would be complete, other than for contraband supplies.

13. "Information and Education in Family Planning Programs in the Western Hemisphere."

14. Decree No. 3, *La Gaceta* (Costa Rica), Apr. 7, 1967. Cited in *Reports on Population/Family Planning,* Population Council, February 1970.

15. This is not to say that substantial contributions in space and administrative costs have not been made locally. These kinds of "overhead" contributions have made possible the acquisition of foreign direct financial assistance, often for broad programs of maternal health, only one aspect of which is family planning.

16. R. Valdivieso, "Opening Address," *Proceedings of the Eighth International Conference of the International Planned Parenthood Federation* (Hertford, England: Stephen Austin and Sons, 1967), pp. 3–5.

17. "Resumen Normas Basicas sobre Regulacion de la Natalidad en el Servicio Nacional de Salud," Boletin de Informacion Tecnica Santiago, September 1968.

18. Miguel Echenique, cited in *San Juan Star* (Puerto Rico), Nov. 21, 1967.

19. J. Mayone Stycos, *Human Fertility in Latin America* (Ithaca, N.Y.: Cornell University Press, 1968), p. 269.

20. Kingsley Davis, "Population Policy: Will Current Programs Succeed?" *Science,* vol. 158, November 1967.

21. J. Mayone Stycos, *op. cit.*, chap. 8.

22. F. M. Salzano e N. Freire-Maia, *Populacoes Brasileiras* (São Paulo: Editora da Universidade de São Paulo, 1967), p. 53.

23. Population education should be introduced in secondary schools and universities, since it is mainly aimed at the elites. Family-life education could most profitably be introduced in the primary schools, which are attended by the general population.

24. "Planificacion: Mensaje no Atendido," *Visión,* July 19, 1970. For elaboration on the slowdown of the OAS programs, see "La OEA Relega Programmas de Poblacion," *Poblacion,* Population Reference Bureau, May 1970.

25. *El Mercurio* (Santiago), July 1, 1970.

Index